Screening the Royal Shakespeare Company

RELATED TITLES

Broadcast your Shakespeare: Continuity and Change Across Media
Edited by Stephen O'Neill
ISBN 9781474295116

Directing Shakespeare in America: Historical Perspectives
Charles Ney
ISBN 9781474289696

Performing Hamlet: Actors in the Modern Age
Jonathan Croall
ISBN 9781350030756

Queering the Shakespeare Film: Gender Trouble, Gay Spectatorship and Male Homoeroticism
Anthony Guy Patricia
ISBN 9781474237031

Shakespeare and the 'Live' Theatre Broadcast
Edited by Pascale Aebischer, Susanne Greenhalgh and Laurie E. Osborne
ISBN 9781350030466

Shakespeare in the Theatre: Cheek by Jowl
Peter Kirwan
ISBN 9781474223294

Shakespeare in the Theatre: Peter Hall
Stuart Hampton-Reeves
ISBN 9781472587077

Shakespeare in the Theatre: Trevor Nunn
Russell Jackson
ISBN 9781474289580

Screening the Royal Shakespeare Company

A Critical History

John Wyver

THE ARDEN SHAKESPEARE

LONDON • NEW YORK • OXFORD • NEW DELHI • SYDNEY

THE ARDEN SHAKESPEARE
Bloomsbury Publishing Plc
50 Bedford Square, London, WC1B 3DP, UK
1385 Broadway, New York, NY 10018, USA

BLOOMSBURY, THE ARDEN SHAKESPEARE and the Arden Shakespeare
logo are trademarks of Bloomsbury Publishing Plc

First published in Great Britain 2019
This paperback edition published 2020

A catalogue record for this book is available from the British Library.

Library of Congress Cataloging-in-Publication Data
Names: Wyver, John, author.
Title: Screening the Royal Shakespeare Company : a critical history / John Wyver.
Description: London, New York, NY : The Arden Shakespeare, 2019. | Includes
bibliographical references and index.
Identifiers: LCCN 2018056539 (print) | LCCN 2018059261 (ebook) |
ISBN 9781350006591 (epub) | ISBN 9781350006607 (epdf) | ISBN 9781350006584 (hb)
Subjects: LCSH: Royal Shakespeare Company–History. | Theatrical
companies–England–History. | Shakespeare, William, 1564–1616–Film adaptations. |
Shakespeare, William, 1564–1616–Television adaptations. | Film adaptations–History
and criticism. | Television adaptations–History and criticism. | English drama–Film
adaptations. | English drama–Television adaptations.
Classification: LCC PN2596.S8 (ebook) | LCC PN2596.S8 W98 2019 (print) |
DDC 792.0942–dc23 LC record available at https://lccn.loc.gov/2018056539

ISBN: HB: 978-1-3500-0658-4
          PB: 978-1-3501-7407-8
          ePDF: 978-1-3500-0660-7
          eBook: 978-1-3500-0659-1

Typeset by Integra Software Services Pvt. Ltd.

To find out more about our authors and books visit www.bloomsbury.com
and sign up for our newsletters.

For Clare

CONTENTS

FIGURES

ACKNOWLEDGEMENTS

My greatest debt is to Gregory Doran, artistic director of the RSC, who with Antony Sher asked me in 2000 to produce the television version of *Macbeth*, so beginning my most fruitful professional relationship as a producer. Greg initiated the RSC Live from Stratford-upon-Avon project, on which I have worked with him since 2013, and he has been an extraordinarily generous and supportive collaborator on that series, and throughout my research towards this book. Others at the RSC who have been hugely helpful with nuggets of information, thoughts about the company past and present, and ideas about the archive are Erica Whyman, Catherine Mallyon, Liz Thompson, Jacqui O'Hanlon, Geraldine Collinge (to whom particular thanks is due for facilitating access to Executive Council minutes), Philippa Harland, Amy Belson, Jane Ellis, John Benfield, Amanda Carroll and the invaluable Jane Tassell, as well as Michelle Morton and Carolyn Porter for help with images and more. I am also grateful to my RSC Live from Stratford-upon-Avon colleagues, including Sara Aspley, Kevin Wright and Chris Hill at the RSC; Robin Lough, Paul Freeman and Andy Rose, together with their colleagues on the broadcast production teams; Marc Allenby and Alice de Rosa from Trafalgar Releasing; and most especially my professional partners who make it all happen, David Gopsill and Hayley Pepler.

Many thanks to those who contributed interviews during the research, including Bill Alexander, George Anderson, Simon Bowler, Michael Boyd, Peter Brook, Barry Dodd, Terry Hands, Sally Jacobs, Genista McIntosh, Robert Marshall, Adrian Noble and Bill Wilkinson. Two institutions have been absolutely essential to my research: the Shakespeare Birthplace Trust in Stratford-upon-Avon, guardians of the RSC archive, where I owe a particular debt of gratitude to James Ranahan, as well as to all those who work with him; and the BBC Written Archives Centre at Caversham, where I benefited enormously from the assistance of archivist Louise North. Others who have offered access and guidance are Hilary Bishop, Jake Berger and Bill Thompson at the BBC, especially as the game-changing Shakespeare Archive Resource was being drawn together; Kathleen Dickson and those who work with her at the BFI Viewing Service; Robin Bray and Andrew Gavaghan of ITV Viewers Requests; the team at the V&A Theatre and Performance Archives, especially Simon Sladen; and Steve Chibnall and Alissa Clarke, who oversee the Peter

Whitehead Archive at De Montfort University. The too-oft unsung staff of the British Library must also get a shout-out, especially those who run the Listening and Viewing Service, and those on the desks of Humanities 2, which is simply one of the best places in the world in which to research and write. Much of this book was composed in Humanities 2, and some of the rest was scratched out in the London Library, which is glorious in a rather different way.

I am more grateful than I can properly express to my Illuminations colleagues, including Tom Allen, Lucie Conrad, Todd MacDonald, Louise Machin (who has worked so productively on DVD releases of our RSC productions) and Linda Zuck (for a bolt hole in southern Italy, and for so much more). They continue to build with me a stimulating and delightful context in which to develop as a creative producer. And I want especially to thank Sebastian Grant, formerly with Illuminations, who was an invaluable partner in my RSC story. Further thanks are due to those with whom I work at the University of Westminster, including Rosie Thomas, May Adadol Ingawanij, Lucy Reynolds, Pete Goodwin and Neal White. The university offers me a stimulating academic environment as well as essential online access to resources. Academic friends and colleagues who have contributed thoughts and ideas in conversation and at conferences, and from whom I have learned so much, include Pascale Aebischer, Jonathan Bignell, William Boddy, Deborah Cartmell, Catriona Fallow, Dick Fiddy, Susanne Greenhalgh, Maurice Hindle, Peter Holland, Victor Huertas Martin, Jason Jacobs, Ollie Jones, Andy Kesson, Peter Kirwan, Luke McKernan, Irene Morra, Marcus Prince, Paul Prescott, Stephen Purcell, Beth Sharrock, Emma Smith, Erin Sullivan, Olwen Terris, Helen Wheatley and, most particularly, Judith Buchanan, Billy Smart and Amanda Wrigley. Several of them have generously offered comments on and corrections to parts of the manuscript, and I have benefited enormously from their responses. Needless to say, any and all errors are solely my responsibility.

An earlier version of the section in Chapter 2 on *The Wars of the Roses* was given as a keynote presentation for 'Spaces of Television: Production, Site and Style', a conference in September 2013 at the University of Reading organized by the *Spaces of Television* research project. An earlier version of part of Chapter 6 about the production of *Hamlet* was commissioned by Arts Council England. I am grateful to Gill Johnson for the spur to document the production process. This book was begun and developed within the University of Westminster research project *Screen Plays: Theatre Plays on British Television* (2011–15), funded by the Arts and Humanities Research Council. It received a further boost when I worked with Lesley Jones and Barbican Cinema on 'The RSC on Screen' archive presentations in January 2016. At The Arden Shakespeare, it has been a pleasure and a privilege to work with Margaret Bartley, who was a gracious commissioner, and during the production processes with the patient and supremely helpful Mark Dudgeon and Lara Bateman, and with Katherine Bosiacki, Ian Buck and Rebecca Willford. Thanks too to the anonymous reviewer who contributed a number of very helpful suggestions.

Throughout the research and writing, I have been supported and sustained in frequently astonishing and glorious ways by our wonderful children, Kate, Ben and Nicholas, and by their equally wonderful mother, Clare, whom – as I have for the past thirty-eight years – I adore.

NOTE ON THE TEXT

All quotations from Shakespeare's plays refer to *The Arden Shakespeare Complete Works*, edited by Ann Thompson, David Scott Kasten and Richard Proudfoot. London: Bloomsbury, 2011.

Introduction

Among the ghosts of Stratford-upon-Avon are those of the long-gone players who still flicker before us as moving images. The most venerable of such spectres hail from 1910, haunting a silent two-reel version of actor-manager Frank Benson's staging of *Richard III*. Benson had been playing the king regularly since 1886, and although the twenty-two-minute film has lost the closing frames from Bosworth Field his athletic monarch still leaps about the stage of the first Memorial Theatre. Gestural performances by his celebrated company play out before painted back-cloths within a fixed film frame. Looking for Richard elsewhere in the moving-image archives we find almost three decades later Baliol Holloway posed menacingly as the king, just as he played him triumphantly in London and, later, in Shakespeare's home town. As the opening credits of the 1939 documentary *England's Shakespeare* note, Holloway's fleeting appearance on film was 'by courtesy of the Governors of the Memorial Theatre, Stratford-upon-Avon'. From 1964, sanctioned by the governors of what was by then the Royal Shakespeare Company (RSC), we have a television recording of *The Wars of the Roses* with Ian Holm as a charming chameleon-like Richard III. Twenty years after that, Antony Sher's Richard III scuttled about his court on crutches and was captured in fragments for a BBC Two review programme. The performance can also be seen, albeit dimly but at full length, in the company's archival recording made by a fixed camera set far back in the auditorium. From 2007 there is a similarly limited, yet similarly precious, videotape of Jonathan Slinger's Richard III in director Michael Boyd's glorious Histories cycle. From 2012 you can find online, along with other paratextual traces of that year's production, Jonjo O'Neill filmed in cinematic widescreen performing the play's opening on the Stratford stage.[1] And in early 2021 the RSC Live from Stratford-upon-Avon series will broadcast the company's next actor to play the king to cinema screens, schools, mobiles and more around the world.

These Richard riches are just a few fragments of the screen traces of the RSC and of the organization's earlier manifestations. No theatre company in the world has a more extensive and more varied moving-image history, stretching back for over a century. Produced variously for the cinema, for television, for online distribution and for the RSC's own uses, the films, videotapes and digital recordings are preserved only patchily in archives across the world. A handful of titles are frequently lauded; most are screened only rarely. But the ghosts they keep alive have much to tell us, not only about the RSC but also about approaches to Shakespeare, about the theatre, about translations from the stage to screens of many kinds, and about the culture and society that brought them forth. These ghosts and their histories, and to a modest degree also their futures, are the subject of this book.

That first film adaptation with Frank Benson as Richard III was shot thirty-one years after the opening of the theatre in which Shakespeare was celebrated each spring. Newsreels give us glimpses of Stratford, the actors and audiences, in the 1930s and 1940s. Television first presented scenes from a Shakespeare Memorial Theatre staging in 1951, when Anthony Quayle and Richard Burton played highlights, sadly not recorded, of *Henry IV, Part 1* in a Sunday afternoon programme for children. The earliest surviving small-screen broadcast from Stratford is the middle act of *The Merry Wives of Windsor*, transmitted live in October 1955 and preserved as a tele-recording. Television triumphs from later decades include *The Wars of the Roses* (1965), *The Life and Adventures of Nicholas Nickleby* (1982) and *Hamlet* (2009). The earliest RSC production to become a feature film was Henry Livings's play *Eh?*, premiered at London's Aldwych Theatre in 1964, and later adapted as the dismal comedy *Work is a Four Letter Word* (1968). Subsequent feature films that began on the RSC's Stratford stage include Peter Brook's radical *King Lear* (1971) with Paul Scofield, and Adrian Noble's magical *A Midsummer Night's Dream* (1996). And then there are other film and television productions that were originally RSC commissions for the stage, even if they were significantly transformed in adaptation: *Educating Rita* (1983) and *Les Misérables* (2012) on the big screen, and *Our Friends in the North* (1996) on the small. More recently, and following a first outing with *Richard II* in 2013, live broadcasts from the Royal Shakespeare Theatre (RST) have been shown on thousands of cinema screens and in hundreds of schools in Britain and beyond. By the autumn of 2018 two-thirds of the First Folio plays had been screened in this way, with a plan to broadcast each of the thirty-seven titles by 2021.[2]

As a number of these titles witness, this is not a story simply about adaptations of Shakespeare. Even before Henry Livings's *Eh?* was filmed, the RSC had partnered with BBC Television to record Michel Saint-Denis's lucid production of Chekhov's *The Cherry Orchard* (1962). Other writers whose RSC productions have been translated to the screen include Molière, Ibsen, Strindberg, Edmond Rostand, Mikhail Bulgakov, Jean Giraudoux, Harold Pinter, Marguerite Duras and Peter Weiss. In addition, the collectively authored *US*, which in the mid-1960s questioned Britain's complicity in the war being waged by the United States in Vietnam, was adapted twice for the screen, first as film documentation by Peter Whitehead as *Benefit of the*

Doubt (1967), and then far more freely as *Tell Me Lies* (1968), authored by the work's stage director, Peter Brook. The archival researcher can also ferret out screen traces of RSC productions in many other contexts. There are brief appearances in newsreels, including shots of the 1951 Festival of Britain *Richard II*, and later in television news footage. Television documentaries and review shows have frequently featured scenes from productions, and in 1982 the company collaborated with London Weekend Television on the nine-part series of workshop sessions *Playing Shakespeare* (screened in 1984). From recent years there is a plethora of screen paratexts, in the form of trailers and educational videos, produced for dissemination on the company's own website, on YouTube and via other social media channels. Since 1981 the company has preserved single-camera videotapes of many productions, and from 1983 onwards there are more elaborate National Video Archive of Performance recordings of stagings.[3] And closely related to all of these media traces, albeit lacking a visual dimension, are audio tapes and radio broadcasts, the earliest that survives being Peter Brook's 1950 production of *Measure for Measure*.[4] In addition, there are films and television dramas in which the RSC features primarily as an idea – and often an ideal. These include Peter Terson's radio and then television drama *Stratford or Bust* (1973), in which a trio of Derbyshire miners travel to the town by barge, and the feature film *A Bunch of Amateurs* (2008), in which Burt Reynolds is a fading Hollywood star attracted to 'Stratford' to play King Lear. On arrival, he discovers he has been booked to perform in the village hall of the Suffolk hamlet of Stratford St John.

These many and varied RSC adaptations are documents of the achievements of one of the world's leading theatre companies. Reason enough to return to these screen versions are the recorded performances since the 1950s of leading actors including John Gielgud, Anthony Quayle, Peggy Ashcroft, Vanessa Redgrave, Glenda Jackson, Ian McKellen, Patrick Stewart and Hugh Quarshie as well as younger talents such as David Tennant and Paapa Essiedu. The films and television programmes register in mediated form the stage work of Peter Hall, Peter Brook, Trevor Nunn, Gregory Doran and other major directors, as well as the contributions of numerous other creative talents including designers Motley, John Bury, Sally Jacobs and Stephen Brimson Lewis, and composers Guy Woolfenden, Nigel Hess and Paul Englishby. These and many, many other figures are significant in the cultural history of modern Britain as well as being central to the RSC's own sense of its history and traditions.

A significant number of the screen productions are recordings captured in the RSC's theatres in Stratford and London. But even these seemingly straightforward presentations demand to be understood as adaptations, just as do the more elaborate film versions like Peter Brook's *King Lear*. The mediation processes imposed on the original stage productions involve technologies of film cameras, electronic recordings and the like, and each screen version is also determined by a nexus of economic, creative and cultural concerns. The nature of these mediations, as well as their historical and social contexts, offers a second reason for exploring this adaptation history, since the RSC's productions exemplify a strikingly broad range of strategies of adaptation for taking work from the stage to the screen.[5] Productions from the 1950s and 1960s were broadcast and recorded by multiple cameras in theatre auditoria, just as they are for today's RSC Live from Stratford-upon-Avon cinema presentations. Starting in the early 1960s, stagings travelled to studios to be recorded before three or more electronic cameras. Later television films took the casts, the costumes and concepts of particular stagings to a location for interpretation with a single camera. And some feature films – again, the prime example is Peter Brook's *King Lear* – radically reimagined the creative approach of the original staging. In many cases the process involved a negotiation between the original stage director and a specialist television or live cinema director; sometimes, as with the feature films made by Peter Hall and Peter Brook, and with Gregory Doran's trilogy of television adaptations between 2000 and 2012, the shaping figure for the stage version remained the dominant author of the screen version.

More generally, the collectivity of the screen versions can be regarded as a multistranded adaptation of the lives, both public and private, of the RSC as a company. The screen versions of productions are a key strand in what James Steichen calls the 'institutional dramaturgy' of a performance company. In a study of the pioneering live broadcasts by the Metropolitan Opera, Steichen defined the term as 'the techniques by which the Met, or any institution, stages itself for the public'.[6] And interrogating the institutional dramaturgy as a developing adaptation of a company is a third reason for considering all of these traces together. Documentaries like *Sunday Night: How to Stop Worrying and Love the Theatre* (1966) and *Omnibus: Shakespeare's Island* (1971), both made for the BBC, are close-up studies of the company's operations. At the same time consideration of the adaptation history of the RSC as a whole can offer insights into broader social and cultural questions. At each stage this study asks why certain RSC productions were adapted, and others not; what role the company and its creatives had on each occasion in determining what was screened, and how the translation occurred; how the company is presented by a particular adaptation, including in the opening titles and closing credits, and in associated marketing materials; and what meanings or value the RSC is contributing to its partners who, as likely as not, provided production funding and undertook distribution. The BBC, for example, has collaborated on screen versions of RSC productions of Shakespeare at key moments of challenge to the corporation's legitimacy. In the autumn of 1955 *The Merry Wives of Windsor* reminded the nation of the corporation's values just after the launch of the commercial network ITV. Similarly, the 2016 anniversary extravaganza *Shakespeare Live! From the RSC* was commissioned and screened as a new Broadcasting Act was being formulated by a Conservative government looking to limit the BBC's scale and influence. In examining the RSC's film, television and digital media traces as documents, as adaptations and as elements of the company's institutional dramaturgy, questions posed by Barbara Hodgdon about another visual element of theatre's history are pertinent. Writing about the engravings, paintings and photographs that we have of *Hamlet* stagings from 1709 onwards, she has asked:

> Of what, exactly, does an image constitute evidence? What relationships pertain between the image and the facts of performance? In what contexts? What if any ancillary documentation supports such relationships? What power structures lie behind the production and archiving of images used as evidence? What narratives and counter-narratives burr onto the image, make it speak its secrets, connect it to cultural history?[7]

By considering aspects of what might be thought of as 'burred' onto screen versions, my aim is to detail the connections of these adaptations with the history of the RSC and, at times, with that of the nation, over the past century.

Among the critics who have considered the RSC's place in post-war British culture, Alan Sinfield has made the case for the centrality, at least between 1961 and the mid-1980s, of the company's engagement with Shakespeare's plays:

> 'Shakespeare' is not a fixed entity but a concept produced in specific political conditions, a powerful cultural token, a site of struggle and change. The rapid and convincing development of the RSC has been both a cause and an effect of the construction of Shakespeare which has become dominant in modern British society. It intersects fundamentally with our ways of thinking about the plays and about 'the arts' and political change within welfare capitalism.[8]

Arguing more broadly about the nation since the 1953 Coronation, Irene Morra identified the 'alignment of Shakespeare with the writing of national history' during these decades. She stressed the continuing primacy of

> the Shakespearean legacy [that] has also informed some of the most prominent and public assertions of cultural nationalism. It continues to be enforced through some of the most acclaimed theatre, film and television of the New Elizabethan age itself: costume dramas and Shakespearean adaptations proliferate on stage and screen.[9]

Among the significant contributions to this nexus of negotiations are productions by the RSC and especially their adaptations for film and television, not least because many were seen by such large audiences. At the most general level, then, the argument of this book is that the collectivity of RSC screen productions illuminates a complex of relations between the company, the playwright whose work remains central to its activities, the rural location of Stratford-upon-Avon, essentialist notions of Englishness (and Britishness), discourses of national identity and broad conceptions of culture and politics.

There is one other, more pragmatic imperative behind this volume's mapping of the Stratford company's screen archive. Which is, simply, to raise awareness so that the archive can become more available and more useful to practitioners today and tomorrow. As Judith Buchanan has written, 'Working with legacies of interpretation and performance is part of the business of playmaking and filmmaking.'[10] Despite at present being comparatively little-recognized and rarely activated, the moving-image archive of the RSC offers a rich resource for creators to learn from, and for them to reuse and rework, and perhaps especially so as adaptation forms become increasingly complex and hybrid. The archive must not simply be a passive object of study but also needs to be an active contributor to original ways of bringing together stages and screens of all kinds.

Underpinning the discussion of all of the adaptations featured throughout this book is a core belief that they are not simply second-order traces of stage precursors. Nor should they be regarded as inherently inferior to those supposed originals. The contention throughout is that each screen version is a distinctive creative work, whether it features only a few seconds of performance or a full production, and whether it has been recorded from the stage, presented from a studio, or filmed on location. In its screen form it finds audiences beyond the theatre, and viewers derive from it a range of pleasures and construct a multitude of meanings. Among these, on occasion, are those prompted in dialogue with memories of the original stage production. But other dialogues are stimulated too, with the drama's text, with alternative versions of the particular play, with knowledge of the actors or the director, and with other remembered fragments of encounters with the RSC. Yet despite such personal as well as institutional webs of intertextual associations, despite the widely acknowledged achievement of a number of the adaptations and despite the substantial audiences who have seen aspects of the RSC on screen, adaptations have been of marginal interest for previous authors concerned with the history of the company. The most substantial volume about the RSC through to the end of the 1970s is Sally Beauman's invaluable *The Royal Shakespeare Company: A History of Ten Decades*.[11] Only a very few screen adaptations merited even a passing reference here, and there was no acknowledgement of numerous key productions for the screen, including Frank Benson's *Richard III* (despite an extensive discussion of Benson's other achievements) and the BBC recording of *As You Like It* (1963) with Vanessa Redgrave. In a more recent study of the company, Colin Chambers noted that in the 1960s, 'exploitation of RSC productions on television did bring the company's name to a wider audience, especially in the early days when it had the edge on the N[ational] T[heatre] in this regard'. But he was slighting about Peter Hall's features and suggested that Peter Brook's films, including *King Lear*, 'although useful for theatre historians, did not rescue the RSC's awkward relationship to film'.[12] Elsewhere in the literature about Shakespeare adaptations certain productions, most notably *King Lear*, have received extensive scholarly attention. Today, there is a rapidly developing academic interest in live cinema broadcasts.[13] But, in part reflecting the manner in which television has a lower cultural status among both academic and journalistic critics, few of the small-screen adaptations have attracted detailed assessments. The documentaries, performance extracts and archival recordings have been largely ignored

The paucity of critical writing about television adaptations is also a consequence of the difficulties of access to many of the major productions. Circumstances are changing, but rights complexities have restricted viewings of many of the adaptations, rendering them unavailable to all but the most persistent researchers. Negotiations between the BBC and RSC prompted by the 2016 anniversary of Shakespeare's death have meant that more titles can be more easily viewed,[14] yet some productions, including the more obscure feature films could only be sourced for this book from 'grey market' DVD distributors. The RSC's screen history is scattered amongst numerous film libraries and rights holders. The Shakespeare Birthplace Trust in Stratford, which holds the company's physical archives, does an important job in making available viewing copies of many productions, but the fact that there is no comprehensive depository is a reflection of the comparatively low status that the company has historically accorded its screen work.

For all that the RSC's extant adaptations feature numerous riches, it is nonetheless the case that the overwhelming majority of the productions by the company and its Stratford predecessors left no traces for the screen. John Gielgud's Prospero, Richard Burton's Hal, Laurence Olivier's Titus and many, many others live on only in programme notes, photographs, press clippings and the memories of those happy few who were among their audiences. For some associated with the RSC, and indeed for a perhaps diminishing number of those involved with theatre more generally, this is not a cause for regret but rather a consequence of an essential quality of the medium. 'The life of a play', Peter Brook has written, 'begins and ends in the moment of performance. This is where author, actors and directors express all they have to say. If the event has a future, this can only lie in the memories of those who were present and who retained a trace in their hearts.'[15] Yet at different points through his long career and in his essays and interviews, the director has expressed a seemingly contradictory opinion. 'We must even more ... devote ourselves to working on the film document,' Brook said in 1977. 'Whatever the losses involved, it can be very useful for our work.'[16] Moreover, as recording possibilities have developed in recent years, even when there is no full-scale screen adaptation, it is almost inevitable that elements of moving images are created and shared. And for certain notable stage productions we have only fragmentary screen survivals, as is the case with perhaps the most influential of all RSC productions of Shakespeare, Peter Brook's 1970 staging of A *Midsummer Night's Dream*. The story of screen versions of this *Dream* is detailed in Chapter 3, but here it is worth noting that at least three distinct moving-image records of the production exist: thirteen precious minutes of scenes filmed by the BBC; a low-resolution single-camera taping from the Aldwych Theatre circle; and an off-air recording of a Japanese television broadcast. This transmission was professionally shot with multiple cameras before an audience in the theatre, but the master tape appears to have been destroyed on Brook's orders. The archive of NHK, the Japanese public broadcaster, confirms that they can find no trace of a recording.[17] So as well as a celebration and a critical analysis of which elements of the RSC story can be conjured on to screens today, this book is also a study of the contingency, fragility and fragmentary nature of the company's adaptation history. To reflect those qualities, and the dispersal of the extant archive, the discussion of a number of titles includes my own encounters with prints and projections.

To conclude these introductory remarks, it is important to acknowledge I have walk-on roles towards the end of this story. I collaborated with Gregory Doran on his television films, co-producing with Sebastian Grant both *Macbeth* (2001) and *Hamlet,* and producing *Julius Caesar* (2012). My production company Illuminations has released *Macbeth* and *Julius Caesar* on DVD, and in 2016 published *The Wars of the Roses* for the first time for home viewing. Since 2013 I have worked part-time for the RSC as Director, Screen Productions, and I continue to produce the RSC Live from Stratford-upon-Avon cinema broadcasts. I was also the RSC producer on *Shakespeare Live! From the RSC*. My belief is that these engagements have enhanced my understanding of RSC adaptations from the earliest days, and that they continue to do so without compromising my critical judgement of either individual titles or the company's workings more generally. But should you be minded to read on, please do so with a clear-eyed recognition of these entanglements.

1

Beginners, 1910–59

In early April 1910 Frank Benson's celebrated acting company was filmed performing *Richard III* on the stage of Stratford-upon-Avon's Shakespeare Memorial Theatre. The version we marvel at today is disfigured by damage and decay throughout its twenty-two-minute length. Titles and credits are missing, as are what were once its climactic frames. For many years the film was slighted as an example of a 'primitive' cinema in which an unimaginative screen treatment had failed to compensate for theatrical origins. More recently early cinema has been radically reassessed, and audiences as well as scholars have begun to recognize and celebrate the film's pleasures and peculiarities.[1] A precious trace of the Edwardian theatre, Benson's *Richard III* begins the screen adaptation history of the organization that five decades later would be incorporated in 1961 as the Royal Shakespeare Company. During those years, the Memorial Theatre, which reopened in 1932 after the original burned down in 1926, had occasional, opportunistic engagements with film and later with television. Newsreel companies came from time to time, and then in the 1950s first BBC Television and subsequently a small-screen producer from the United States arrived to broadcast a production from the stage. Yet none of these encounters resulted in a sustained engagement with the moving image, and throughout the central decades of the twentieth century it was only radio that returned time and again to Stratford's productions.

The first Memorial Theatre was funded and built as an initiative of local brewer Charles Flower. In 1864, Charles, with his father Edward Fordham Flower, organized a season of six plays in a temporary pavilion to mark the tercentenary of Shakespeare's birth. A decade later, with an awareness of what Richard Wagner was bringing to completion with his opera house in Bayreuth, Charles Flower decided to build a permanent theatre for Stratford for the performance of Shakespeare's plays. His vision was mocked by many, as was the eclectic architecture of the building.[2] But the theatre opened on schedule in 1879, when three plays were given by a company led by the classical actor Barry Sullivan. Short spring seasons in the first years gave little indication of future successes, until in 1885 Charles met the ambitious young actor Frank Benson. Three years earlier at the age of 23, Benson, with his father's financial support, had taken over an ailing touring company. Now he was to lead all but five of the Stratford seasons from 1886 to 1916, as well as making a final appearance in 1919. Benson guaranteed consistency, as Sally Beauman has written: 'Had it continued to present short annual seasons by companies of varying ability, Stratford would undoubtedly have degenerated into little more than a small provincial theatre, fitted in on touring dates, with no aims, no policies, no identity of its own.'[3] The company appears to have done their best work in Stratford during the 1890s, although the productions were resolutely traditional, even as they often took considerable liberties with Shakespeare's texts. At first the seasons lasted for no more than two weeks, with a different play being given each night. During the rest of the year the theatre was dark for long periods. By 1910, Charles's brother Archibald ('Archie') Flower had taken over as chairman of the theatre's governors, and he was to dominate the company until the end of the Second World War.

The cinematograph comes to Stratford

At the end of March 1910, having just enjoyed a week's holiday, Frank Benson's troupe assembled once again in Stratford-upon-Avon. Earlier in the month they had been at the Theatre Royal Bournemouth for six days performing seven different Shakespeare productions along with a version of the medieval Mystery Plays. Now they were to spend a fortnight on the stage of the Memorial Theatre facing not the familiar and forgiving local audience but an unresponsive camera eye. The newly established Co-operative Cinematograph Company had elected to start its production slate with a group of Benson company films. Over two weeks they filmed truncated versions of *Julius Caesar, Macbeth, The Taming of the Shrew* and *Richard III*, and possibly also *Twelfth Night* and *The Merry Wives of Windsor*.[4] In her diary Eleanor Elder recorded her amusement at participating in the filming of *Julius Caesar*:

> Of course, everything had to be changed: business quickened, and a lot of talk left out altogether. Our instructions are to put plenty of movement into it – to keep within certain lines drawn on the stage; to do as we are told, and to obey orders shouted at us without being disturbed, or letting it affect our acting.[5]

Richard III was shot with a single, static camera placed in the centre of the stalls, and each of the fifteen scenes unfolds without camera movement or cuts.[6] As the company's 1910 ledger details, Benson received an initial payment of £200, then at the end of each of the two weeks an additional sum of £250.[7] The total of £700 for a fortnight's work compared very favourably with net receipts of £243 4s. 3d. from the engagement in Bournemouth, which had not quite covered the week's outgoings. All of this was especially welcome since Benson was a poor manager and the company's accumulating debts were becoming an embarrassment to the Memorial Theatre, which eventually had to bail out the operation. Yet his professional reputation as an actor remained high and he was knighted in 1916. That year his son Eric was killed in action, and after the war his fortunes declined. He retired in 1932 and died seven years later.

The Benson films, released in 1911, were among the approximately 300 silent Shakespeare adaptations estimated by Judith Buchanan to have been made by the British, American, French, Italian, German and Danish film industries between 1899 and 1927.[8] In the first years of the century, short films showcasing familiar scenes from Shakespeare's plays often drew on visual conventions from nineteenth-century media including paintings, engravings and lantern slides. But after around 1907 producers were increasingly concerned to develop sustained and self-contained stories.[9] Historian Rachel Low records that at least twenty Shakespeare productions were released in Britain between 1906 and 1914, including versions by London-based producers of *Romeo and Juliet* (1908) and *King Henry VIII* (1911) as well as *Hamlet* (1913) with Sir Johnston Forbes-Robertson.[10] The adaptations made with the Benson company followed the dominant British model in the years before 1914 of memorializing existing stagings, although films made in continental Europe and the USA were increasingly shot on location and had no connection to a theatre production. The decision to shoot *Richard III* on the stage of the Memorial Theatre, rather than in a film studio, where the management of lighting and other logistics would have been easier, is likely to have been motivated by the additional prestige that the older, culturally respectable medium, actualized by the stage itself, was thought to bestow on a cinema struggling to establish its legitimacy.

Richard III opens with a crowded and complex tableau, including a real-life horse, from the aftermath of the Battle of Tewkesbury, with the defeated Henry VI ceding the crown to Edward IV. What follows is a significantly reduced version of the play, with dialogue featured only in a small number of prefatory quotations on title cards before key scenes. The scenes are also only a selection, including Clarence's murder and an invented section of Hastings visiting the Tower to see the princes (played by young women, Kathleen Yorke and Hetty Kenyon). Each sequence is enacted before a detailed painted backcloth, including one of the throne room in front of which Hastings is sent for execution, the Lord Mayor persuades Richard to accept the crown, and the Coronation takes place. Scene 9 realizes the scene described by Tyrrell in the opening lines of 4.3; in the film he is revealed holding a pillow over the faces of figures on a bed, who he then uncovers to show the princes 'girdling one another / Within their alabaster-innocent arms' (4.3.10–11). Buchanan has noted that this murder was not usually part of Benson's production and seems to have been invented for the film. 'When we talk about this film as a compressed record of a stage production', she has warned, 'we need to be aware that there was a little more elasticity in the system and a willingness to adapt than that would imply.'[11] Later, in Richard's dream before the Battle of Bosworth stop-motion effects and dissolves between the figures conjure up the ghosts of those he has killed. On their release in the spring of 1911, Rachel Low notes that the Benson films 'received courteous, if not over-enthusiastic, appreciation'.[12] In a detailed and richly illustrated study of the Memorial Theatre's stage, Benson's scenery and *Richard III*, Russell Jackson reflected that, 'The production also exemplifies the lowly standing of film in its time. First, no mention was made of it or of the other films in the local newspapers, in the minutes of the theatre's governors, or in their published annual reports. This was a non-event as far as Stratford-upon-Avon was concerned.'[13] Writing nearly forty years after the film's release, before early cinema had begun to be reassessed, Rachel Low dismissed the film as 'a mistake'. 'It shows not the slightest appreciation of the possibilities of film making,' she wrote.[14]

Judith Buchanan has proposed that in the later years of the silent cinema 'For cineastes ... Shakespeare came to epitomise the theatrical burden that was inhibiting the cinema from realising its own potential.'[15] But rather than define Benson's film and the other riches of silent Shakespeare in terms of lack, whether of words or of 'the cinematic', she celebrated 'the things that these maverick films delightfully and tellingly *are*, both as film industry products and as performance readings of Shakespeare'.[16] As a relic from the Stratford stage of more than a century ago there is something wondrous about *Richard III*. My most memorable viewing of it was on a late summer evening huddled with my family in a blanket amidst the ruined, spotlit Great Hall of Yorkshire's Middleham Castle, where the historical figure of Richard III lived, both as a boy and later in his married life with Anne Neville. The occasion was a presentation by the University of York project Silents Now, which is dedicated to exploring new ways of bringing audiences to films made before the coming of sound.[17] Accompanying a projection of the film was a live piano accompaniment played by John Sweeney and a group of actors speaking Shakespeare's verse, as well as creating vivid sound effects, in perfect synchronicity with the flickering images. Judith Buchanan realized that during the filming Benson's actors were actually speaking extracts from the play and so by careful study of their lips she was able to construct a script. The Middleham presentation was, like all performance, unique to that moment, and it brought together a hundred-plus witnesses for each presentation in the manner of the best theatre. Yet this was also cinema, as both artefact and social occasion, mysteriously and magically bringing back the past. Here crowding around us were Shakespeare's ghosts, the ghosts of Benson and his company – all of course long dead – and the ghosts of both mythical and real-life Richards, Lady Annes and Tyrells. I remain delighted that 'the remembrance of so fair a dream' (5.3.233) stays with me.

'Words, words, words'

While he will forever remain silent as Richard III, Frank Benson speaks in a 1933 radio broadcast that is one of the earliest recordings of a BBC programme.[18] You can sit in a listening booth at the British Library and hear the critic James Agate introduce him performing speeches by Richard II, by Mark Antony from *Julius Caesar* and by Cardinal Wolsey in *King Henry VIII*. Although we have no recordings that pre-date this, Benson had appeared on radio as early as Christmas Eve in 1923, and his other aural appearances included a broadcast on 23 April 1932 of his toast to 'The Immortal Memory' at the luncheon in honour of the poet's birthday. Throughout the twentieth century and beyond, as is evidenced by the transmission date in 2016 of *Shakespeare Live! From the RSC*, 23 April remained the preeminent moment in the year for newsreels, and then radio and later television, to focus on the town and the theatre. The conjunction of the presumed birthday and 'death day' with the saint's day of St George has been a potent focus for patriotic commemoration in both secular and sacred spheres.[19] Celebrations in the town began with David Garrick's Jubilee in September 1769,[20] but it was only in 1816, in the wake of the Napoleonic Wars that a group of Stratford citizens first put together a programme of locally organized events on the day. Festivities were assembled with mixed fortunes during the remainder of the century.[21] By 1905, however, with the added fillip of a national revival of interest in folklore and dancing, the birthday celebrations included a Ben Jonson masque with music by Ralph Vaughan Williams and a procession, which rapidly became traditional, from the Town Hall to Holy Trinity Church. Association of the observances with the Shakespeare Festival, as the season of plays at the theatre was known, developed gradually after 1879, but as Susan Brock and Sylvia Morris noted, 'In 1907 the Theatre's influence became overt when F.R. Benson ... addressed himself to the birthday celebrations in a campaign to make the festival bigger, better and more prestigious.'[22] The Birthday (as it was by then known) events began to be noticed well beyond Stratford, and in the years after the war they increasingly attracted media attention. But as Brock and Morris have detailed, this was a mixed blessing, since the celebrations started to accrue political significance: 'The Union Jack and the Flag of St George had traditionally been central to the celebrations, providing an obvious opportunity for national and patriotic pride. Politicians found it useful to be seen at the celebrations: as early as 1907 the presence of the local Member of Parliament was noted.'[23] Newsreels and television subsequently extended the patriotic feelings associated with the Birthday, at times embracing the theatre and its companies more closely.

William Bridges-Adams had taken over in 1919 as director of the Stratford Festival. He was committed to developing an ensemble for what by 1926 was a season of twelve weeks of performances, yet he struggled to secure funds and to attract attention. In the early 1920s there was an attempt to convert the theatre into a cinema for the winter months, but when this failed the sophisticated projection equipment was sold to the Stratford-upon-Avon Picture House in which the theatre acquired a significant shareholding. When the Festival was made homeless by the 1926 fire, the cinema became the venue for that year's stage productions, as it continued to be until 1931 while Archie Flower and Bridges-Adams oversaw the construction of the new building. But after the new theatre opened on 23 April 1932 the relationship between its chairman and its director deteriorated, funds were once again constrained, and in April 1934 Bridges-Adams resigned. The next twelve years are seen as a period of decline. Bridges-Adams's replacement, Ben Iden Payne, brought with him a strong interest in Elizabethan methods of staging, but while such ideas had been radical at the turn of the century, they were ill-suited for the new theatre's proscenium stage.[24] In the years remaining before the war it was only the productions of the innovative Russian director Komisarjevsky, including an acclaimed *King Lear* in 1936, that attracted good notices, although tourist audiences ensured that ticket sales remained healthy.

In the following two decades, radio was the main medium by which Stratford disseminated its productions beyond the theatre. Similar concerns to those that later motivated the company's involvement with television, including audience reach and archival preservation, lay behind the interest in radio broadcasting. As a consequence sound deserves a modest place in this volume that is otherwise preoccupied with screens. The first performance from the Shakespeare Memorial Theatre to enjoy a radio broadcast was the town's Choral Society Centenary Concert in June 1936. Then on 12 July 1936 the Festival Company was heard in Iden Payne's production of *Much Ado About Nothing*, transmitted not from the auditorium but from the BBC Midland Region studios in Birmingham. As was, the following year, a live broadcast of Iden Payne's production of *As You Like It*.[25] In a *Radio Times* article linked to the broadcast of the Stratford production, John Bayliss made the argument that Shakespeare was exceptionally well-suited to radio: 'So undeveloped in the devices of scenery was the theatre for which he wrote that wireless is the most perfect medium for his works.'[26] Bayliss's encomium to radio's potential exemplifies Susanne Greenhalgh's characterization of much discussion of radio drama in its first years:

> early attempts at constructing a poetics of radio frequently envisaged it as a mode of performance analogous to the Shakespearean ideal stage evoked by the opening Chorus speech of *Henry V*, in which the 'imaginary forces' of the listener called up an 'inner vision', variously likened to the workings of the mind in dreams, reading, stream of consciousness, or the processes of memory. It was argued that the absence of visual stimuli was compensated for by an experience in which 'the pictures were better.'[27]

The Memorial Theatre did not have a good war, despite continuing to mount an annual Festival under Iden Payne until 1942. Fordham Flower took on the family's responsibilities in 1944 and Barry Jackson was appointed as director the following year. Independently wealthy, Jackson had funded and built Birmingham's Repertory Theatre, which opened in 1913, and in the interwar years he had encouraged bold work and young talent. 'Jackson and Fordham Flower,' Sally Beauman wrote, 'together took over the running of a theatre whose assets, by the end of the war, totalled a remarkable £446,581, but whose prestige was nil.'[28] In 1946 Jackson broke with the past, hiring only actors who had not played the theatre before and bringing in a guest director for each of eight new productions. Among his protégés was the twenty-one-year-old Peter Brook, whose lavish, rococo-inspired *Love's Labour's Lost* was a huge hit. Brook returned the following year to open the season with *Romeo and Juliet*, which looks exquisite in Angus McBean's publicity photographs but was attacked as fiercely as his previous production had been applauded. Jackson's audacious choices of creatives, together with his ability to attract stars of the London stage, increasingly attracted attention and audiences. His relationship with Fordham Flower, however, was difficult, and he stepped down at the end of the 1948 season to be replaced after some fractious months by Anthony Quayle. A brilliant character actor and a director with little interest in experiment, Quayle led the company until 1956, working from 1953 onwards in partnership with Glen Byam Shaw. Throughout these years the presence of John Gielgud, Michael Redgrave and other luminaries burnished the Festival's reputation. And it was in these years that radio developed an important partnership with the theatre, broadcasting at least eleven productions between 1948 and 1958.

The first post-war production to be heard was on 30 October 1948 when the Midland Region only transmitted a studio recording of Anthony Quayle's staging of *Othello*. A year later, John Gielgud's production of *Much Ado About Nothing* was recorded in the studio, and on 20 July 1949 it was similarly broadcast only in the Midland region. A year later, the studio version of Peter Brook's *Measure for Measure*, with Gielgud as Angelo, was honoured with a national broadcast. Brook's much-praised production was his third for Stratford, and a month after the opening the cast recorded their performances for a Birthday broadcast. Remarkably, this was preserved on acetate discs and is now a digital audio file, accessible to anyone with a British Library Reader's Ticket who books an appointment with that institution's estimable Listening and Viewing Service.[29] After two largely fruitless years as director of productions at the Royal Opera House, Brook returned with an austere staging set amongst grey stone pillars. He used no incidental music and the radio version employs only a few trumpets and rowdy street sounds. Gielgud's cold, intelligent performance remains deeply impressive, and the audio overall is strikingly effective, tightly focused on the verse, although with little sense of theatrical effect or space. Occasional lines were added to the radio version for clarity, as when a character says 'My lord, here is the lady Isabel' to indicate Isabel's return in Act 5. The key change was made at the climactic moment, recalled in the stage version by J.C. Trewin:

> At the end Brook used another of his charged and daring pauses, this time before Isabella, at 'Look, if it please you, on this man condemn'd' [5.1.443], knelt to plead for the life of Angelo. He asked Barbara Jefford to pause each night until she felt that the audience could stand it no longer. The silence lasted at first for about thirty-five seconds, On some nights it would extend to two minutes. 'The silence,' Brook said, 'became a voodoo-pole – a silence in which all the inevitable elements of the evening came together, a silence in which the abstract notion of mercy became concrete for that moment to those present.'[30]

Not, however, in the broadcast. Barbara Jefford speaks the line, and there is the briefest of pauses before the narrator says, 'Isabella looks steadfastly at Angelo and then falls to her knees before the Duke.' Almost immediately Isabella picks up her speech. Translation to radio's 'pictures' cannot cope with silence.

The Birthday was marked again the following year with a Home Service broadcast of Michael Redgrave as *Richard II*, the first of Quayle's acclaimed quartet of Histories staged in the Festival of Britain year. In 1953 the Third Programme broadcast a Stratford recording of *As You Like It* with Anthony Quayle (as Jaques) and Barbara Jefford (Rosalind).[31] Later in the year a studio production of Denis Carey's Festival presentation of *The Merchant of Venice*, with Peggy Ashcroft and Michael Redgrave, was feted with the front cover of *Radio Times*.[32] The 1953 productions of *King Lear* and *Antony and Cleopatra* were also broadcast, but in 1955 and 1956 BBC radio felt sufficiently confident to mount its own productions for the Birthday. In 1957 BBC Midland Region renewed its collaboration with Stratford with a recording of Peter Hall's production of *Cymbeline* with Peggy Ashcroft. Stratford's 1957 *King John* and the 1958 *Twelfth Night* directed by Peter Hall were also broadcast. The latter broadcast, however, was to be the last of the collaborations between Stratford and BBC Midland Region, not least because the following year Peter Hall contracted with an American producer to record a full-length version of *A Midsummer Night's Dream* for the upstart medium of television.[33] In addition to radio's numerous broadcasts of Shakespeare's plays, the medium has also carried an extensive commentary on the texts, on productions and on changing critical understandings. Those associated with Stratford have contributed consistently to this dialogue, including Peter Brook who, a week after the broadcast of *Measure for Measure* in 1950, gave a talk on the Third Programme titled *The Contemporary Theatre*.[34] Later contributions that were centred on cast members as well as creatives include the four-part

Radio 4 series in 1990, *Shakespeare at the RSC*, in which Linda Cookson spoke with the teams behind four productions at that time.[35]

Away from BBC radio there are other important audio recordings made by the Stratford company, the earliest of which dates from 1959, the moment of the final BBC Midland Region studio recording. Some years earlier the British Council with the Memorial Theatre, and with The Old Vic, explored the idea of assembling a company to record all of Shakespeare's plays for release on LPs. The prohibitive cost and the impossibility of guaranteeing the same actors throughout the project meant that the idea foundered until George Rylands and Cambridge University's amateur Marlowe Dramatic Society stepped in and, with professional guest stars including many who had played in Stratford, committed thirty-seven plays to disc.[36] At Stratford, the company began its own audio archiving of certain productions, recording performances with a quarter-inch reel-to-reel machine and a single microphone slung above the stage.[37] From 1959 we have both Paul Robeson as Othello in Tony Richardson's production with Mary Ure (Desdemona) and Sam Wanamaker (Iago), and excerpts of Peter Hall's staging of *Coriolanus* with Laurence Olivier. Lacking the professional clarity of the BBC's studio recordings from the 1950s, these audio relics nonetheless have a vivid sense of theatricality and are signally representative of the 'present-tenseness' that Susanne Greenhalgh has identified with radio:

> The sense it gives of an experience still moving towards the future, even when its auditory codes remind us of its historicity, [which] also paradoxically convinces us that its utterances are living and dynamic even when we know the speakers to be long dead.[38]

Views from 'Shakespeare country'

After Frank Benson's *Richard III* released in 1911 we have only the most fleeting of screen performances of Shakespeare from Stratford-upon-Avon until television came to the town in the mid-1950s. Moving images associated with the Memorial Theatre in the interwar years were restricted to newsreel coverage of notable events and travelogues offering virtual pilgrimages to what was hailed by a 1926 title in the *Wonderful Britain* series as 'Shakespeare's Country'.[39] The earliest of the events directly associated with the theatre to be documented on screen was the fire on 6 March 1926 that gutted the auditorium and other parts of the 1879 building. Newsreels showed the aftermath, revealing twisted girders and charred walls no longer topped by a roof.[40] The cameras returned three years later for the laying of the new theatre's foundation stone and the 1928 report 'British and Best' offers glimpses of the architect Elisabeth Scott seated at her drawing board and of her competition-winning model.[41] A more eccentric document is a British Pathé newsreel filmed in New York with mayor James John ('Jimmy') Walker and others being greeted by a man dressed as Shakespeare and signing their names with a quill in a giant donors book for the building fund.[42] The fruits of the fundraising are apparent in a subsequent British Pathé item, 'Sweetest Shakespeare – Fancy's Child' (1932), which features part of the speech by the Prince of Wales at the new theatre's opening on Shakespeare's Birthday.[43] Although on this day attention was focused on the inauguration, in other years the Birthday celebrations themselves were regarded as sufficiently significant to be committed to celluloid. The memorial processions of 1915, 1920 and 1923 were among those immortalized on film. The highlight of each record is the unfurling, with ambassadors in attendance, of national flags on poles erected in the centre of Bridge Street. In 1938, the British Pathé announcer notes that the flag of Austria is absent but that the appearance of the flag of Ethiopia exemplifies the principle that 'Great art knows no political frontiers.'[44] Yet there is a sense in all of these news items shot on St George's Day that Stratford – and the nation – is receiving tributes marking more than a writer's anniversary. If the nations of the world no longer paid obeisance in quite the way they once did to Britain's imperial might, these short films at least celebrated homage to the nation's most famous son.

Among the earliest of filmed visits to Stratford to trace a Shakespearean tourist trail was the Edwardian travelogue *Shakespeare Land* (1910), made by Charles Urban's Kineto company.[45] After shots of other local attractions, the camera looks along the Avon towards Holy Trinity Church before highlighting Anne Hathaway's Cottage. The itinerary continues with Shakespeare's Birthplace, the Grammar School and – in a panoramic shot from the other side of the river – the Memorial Theatre, which is also seen from several other angles. In contrast to later travelogues that excise all signs of modernity, many shots include vivid reminders of the contemporary world, such as motor cars and a tram in Leamington Spa. Yet in other ways, *Shakespeare Land* was the model for later productions such as *Stratford-on-Avon* (1925), made and distributed by film pioneer Cecil Hepworth.[46] The Birthplace, the Grammar School, Anne Hathaway's Cottage and Holy Trinity are all featured, and again exteriors of the 1879 theatre have a supporting role. Each of these films, and many that were to follow, including *Shakespeare's Country* (1926), draw on a construction of 'Shakespeare country' that Nicola J. Watson has argued derives from a 'biographically driven urge to imprint the virtual, readerly experience of Shakespeare onto topographical reality'.[47] The films extend the encoding of Shakespeare's presence within Stratford's buildings that Douglas Lanier has analysed as underpinning

> several interlocking mythic narratives, each celebrating a distinctive set of values: Shakespeare the child of Stratford (Birthplace); Shakespeare the learned man (Grammar School); Shakespeare the bourgeois success story (New Place and Nash's House); Shakespeare the patriarch (Hall's Croft); Shakespeare the lover (Anne Hathaway's Cottage); Shakespeare the rural

villager (Mary Arden's House) ... As a group they work ... to sanctify
the myth of individual authorship and install Shakespeare as its saint.
Implicitly they situate Shakespeare's writings not in the collective labour
of the London theatre industry or in imitative or formulaic compositional
techniques – elements, we might notice, suspiciously allied with modern
mass culture – but locate Shakespeare's authorship firmly within his
individual personal experience.[48]

The travelogues, and indeed more recent films including numerous television
documentaries, developed a print tradition of travel views of Stratford that,
as Watson has identified, began with Samuel Ireland's illustrated publication
Picturesque Views on the Upper, or Warwickshire Avon (1795). Ireland's
publication, as Watson wrote, 'brings together for the first time biography,
pictures, and a first-person account of visiting the place, describing a
visit which readers are effectively urged to repeat for themselves'.[49] Film
travelogues from more than a century later functioned in much the same
way, just as had, in the intervening years, cycles of paintings, photographs
and lantern slides. Moreover, the frontispiece to Ireland's volume includes a
depiction of Shakespeare plucking the strings of a lyre while reclining by the
Avon. A comparable figure of Shakespeare, clothed in loosely Elizabethan
costume, makes walk-on appearances in the cinemagazine 'Around the
Town, no 110' (1922)[50] and in the more substantial *England's Shakespeare*
(1939),[51] although in the latter we see only his disembodied legs and arms,
one of which writes enthusiastically with a quill. In 'Around the Town',
'Shakespeare' woos 'Ann [*sic*] Hathaway' before setting out for London
with a figure identified by a title-card as 'Henslowe'. Roberta Pearson has
argued that such a construction

> of Shakespeare as a country gentleman, divorced from the religious,
> economic and political upheaval of a newly modern London and safely
> ensconced in the heart of a traditional Merrie England related directly to
> the image of the countryside so central to the period's concept of English
> national identity, an image promulgated as well by much British silent
> cinema.[52]

The fullest interwar presentation of the Memorial Theatre in its rebuilt
form is in the eighteen-minute *England's Shakespeare*, produced by the
publicity department of the London, Midland and Scottish Railway. The
film opens on the wheels of a modern steam locomotive, but the sponsor
is otherwise invisible in an extended advertisement encouraging tourists
to visit Stratford and its surroundings. The film is notable for aligning
Shakespeare, Stratford and the nearby countryside, together with the
England of the sixteenth century, in vigorous opposition to modernity,
which is visualized with cropped and angled images of airplanes, electricity
pylons and factories belching smoke. A clipped narration identifies this as

'an age in which poetic imagination is hampered by harsh realism and a too-great weight of knowledge'. Contrasted with this is 'the quiet, peaceful, unhurried England that Shakespeare knew', a world conjured up on screen by bucolic landscapes and sun-dappled rural riverbanks. The script develops a rural fantasy entwined with notions of individual freedom and isolationist nationalism in a manner that at the time would have been familiar from the speeches of Stanley Baldwin, the Conservative prime minister who had resigned in May 1937. Baldwin's ideas about what England meant to him are encapsulated in a passage cherished by many that was published in 1926:

> The sounds of England, the tinkle of hammer on anvil in the country smithy, the corncrake on a dewy morning, the sound of the scythe against the whetstone, and the sight of a plough team coming over the brow of a hill ... These things strike down into the very depths of our nature, and touch chords that go back to the beginning of time and the human race, but they are chords that with every year of our life sound a deeper note in our innermost being. These are things that make England.[53]

From an idyll of this kind *Shakespeare's England* proposes a highly specific idea of sixteenth-century English history and culture with, as the film's narration details, powerful echoes of the contemporary world as Baldwin and his followers wished it to be: 'Under the wise rule of Queen Elizabeth the land is free from civil strife ... Loving craftsmanship is apparent in all the works of men, and the spirit of the age, the spirit of freedom and artistic creation is manifest everywhere.' The early modern past is envisioned as a pre-technological pastoral utopia characterized by the natural rhythms, modest domesticity and time-worn rituals of village life, a distinctively English vision of organic communalism. This, we are encouraged to think, is the true or essential England, the heritage that moulded Shakespeare and of which he is the privileged representative.

Shakespeare's outline biography is recounted by the film, while First Folio title pages feature in a montage, linked by dissolves, with Memorial Theatre Company actors attired as recognizable characters complete with appropriate props. Donald Wolfit appears as Hamlet, seated and staring into the distance; this was a role in which he had attracted high praise during the 1936 season. Wolfit's friend and mentor Randle Ayrton is Shylock, although in the 1936 and 1937 seasons the actor's greatest triumph had been as Lear. As Orlando and Rosalind, Godfrey Kenton and Joyce Bland reprise their roles in Ben Iden Payne's 1937 production. Appearing next is Baliol Holloway, a stalwart of the Festival Company and known (as he appears here) for playing Richard III, although he had not done so by this point in Stratford.[54] The final figure is Clement McCallin, who played Henry V in 1937, and who stands expectantly as the king in full armour. None of the actors speak, and each appears for no more than three seconds, as if they were minimally animated Victorian *cartes de visite*. Every film company that had so far come to Stratford had filmed only exteriors of the theatre, but for its final sequence *England's Shakespeare* ventured inside. We see technicians at work and the empty set for the opening of *King Lear*, before we move outside to watch the audience arriving. The narration continues, 'The players wait their cues and outside the theatre people from the far corners of the earth have come to pay homage to Shakespeare ... His spirit, the spirit of all that is finest in English thought and literature, lives on – and will endure forever.' In *England's Shakespeare*, the writer and his words, Stratford and its rural location, and finally the theatre and its finest actors are corralled in the service of a nostalgic Tory politics that, just over two decades later, the post-war company would come stridently to resist.

As the theatre and the nation recovered from the Second World War, newsreels and travelogues featuring Stratford increasingly featured starring roles for the theatre and its company. Yet pre-war tropes persisted, including seemingly obligatory shots of the major landmarks, as are showcased in the 1950 newsreel item 'Shakespeare's Birthday – A Royal Occasion'. This marked the first visit of a reigning monarch to Stratford, and along with shots of King George VI and Queen Elizabeth, a brief scene is included from *Julius Caesar*.[55] Radio and television also began to adopt the travelogue form, with Richard Dimbleby visiting Stratford with radio's *Down Your Way* in December 1948 and returning for a television Birthday broadcast in 1954.[56] And *BBC Television Newsreel* featured the opening of the theatre's season in the Festival of Britain year.[57] This three-and-a-half-minute item includes shots of auditorium being prepared, a new stage lighting system being tested, the wardrobe department and the cast of *Richard II*, including Michael Redgrave, in their dressing rooms. The short section of the opening of the play that follows, featuring the initial exchange between the king and John of Gaunt, is the first moving-image sequence of a Stratford performance filmed with synchronous sound. Within weeks, the celebrated production of *Henry IV, Part 1* that followed this *Richard II* would be featured on television in a modestly more substantial manner.

Stratford turns to television

Television Shakespeare in Britain began on the afternoon of 5 February 1937 when the BBC service, which had been on air since November, broadcast from Alexandra Palace part of Act 3, Scene 2 from *As You Like It*.[58] Over the next three months there were live transmissions of a further ten Shakespeare excerpts. London-based theatre companies were invited to the studios to present sections of current productions, for example when scenes from Tyrone Guthrie's Old Vic production of *Measure for Measure* were given on 25 October 1937.[59] Stratford-upon-Avon, however, was too distant to make a day trip for rehearsals and a broadcast feasible. Once television had returned after the war in June

1946, television producers at Alexandra Palace, and then later when drama production moved to Lime Grove, increasingly presented original productions of Shakespeare, but theatre companies were still invited to BBC studios, for example on 19 August 1951 distinguished members of the cast of *Henry IV, Part 1* became the first Memorial Theatre players to perform at Alexandra Palace.

By 1951, as Sally Beauman wrote, 'what festival director Anthony Quayle called "this surge of post-war energy and idealism" was felt particularly at the Memorial, not just because of the setbacks of the war years, but because of the stasis which had affected the theatre for years before that'.[60] In the Festival of Britain year, as the country enjoyed a national celebration of its contested past and hoped-for future, the theatre demonstrated its now exceptional strengths by mounting a History plays cycle of *Richard II*, both parts of *Henry IV* and *Henry V*. Frank Benson had played a group of the Histories as 'a week of kings' in 1908, but this was the first time a modern company had brought the quartet together to reveal their developing characters and themes. Quayle, who took the role of Falstaff and directed three of the plays, later noted that 'the practice of presenting the plays singly had only resulted in their distortion ... Their full power and meaning only became apparent when treated as a whole.'[61] Tanya Moiseiwitsch conceived an integrated design for the four plays, and Michael Redgrave played Richard II, Hotspur and Chorus, as well as directing *Henry IV, Part 2*. And more than matching him for charisma and power was Richard Burton as Hal and Henry V. All of this produced the first triumph of what would become a defining grouping for the future Royal Shakespeare Company, evidenced by the quartet together with *The Wars of the Roses* trilogy from 1963 to 1966, Terry Hands's history plays with Alan Howard from 1975 to 1978, Michael Boyd's Histories cycle developed from 2000 to 2008, and Gregory Doran's *King and Country* productions from 2013 to 2016.

Given the significance of the Stratford history plays in 1951 it is perhaps surprising that BBC Television's engagement with them was restricted to the *Television Newsreel* item noted above and the *Henry IV, Part 1* extracts that appeared in a far from prime-time slot on Sunday afternoon aimed at young people. Burton, Quayle, Alan Badel and Robert Hardy, together with three colleagues, travelled to Alexandra Palace on 19 August 1951 to perform live in the *For the Children* strand. We have no recordings of the historic television performance of what seems likely to have been, on the basis of the cast list, Act 2, Scenes 1 and 4, of *Henry IV, Part 1*[62] with in addition to Quayle as Falstaff and Burton's Hal, Badel as Poins and Hardy as a Traveller. Seemingly, there are no reviews, and the only other documentation is a still in *Radio Times*, which was almost certainly provided by the theatre, and a minimal billing.[63] Fortunately, the Stratford company's next appearance on television has left behind more detailed archival traces as well as a recording of the broadcast itself.

By 1955 several of the nation's most prominent theatre companies had been featured on television. Before the war companies from both The Old Vic and the Birmingham Repertory Theatre had broadcast from the television studios at Alexandra Palace.[64] Outside broadcasts had been organized not only from several West End theatres but also from the stage of The Old Vic, beginning in 1952 with a first act of the Bristol Old Vic's production of *The Two Gentlemen of Verona*.[65] The BBC saw a visit to Stratford's Memorial Theatre as similarly desirable, but the television service was constrained in what it could offer by complex and contentious arrangements with both the actors' union Equity and the Theatres' National Committee (TNC), the association that represented commercial managements. Television at the time was presenting two or three plays a week, most of which were dramas written for the theatre but newly produced in BBC studios. Theatrical impresarios saw this as unfair competition and in response were restricting broadcast relays from major TNC-affiliated theatres across the country.[66] In addition, the TNC agreement meant that no more than forty-five minutes of a current play could be transmitted and that under no circumstances could the concluding act of a three act play be shown.[67]

As early as August 1953 the drama executive Cecil Madden was querying internally whether the TNC agreement meant that a Shakespeare play from Stratford could not be broadcast in its entirety.[68] In discussions with the Memorial Theatre, Head of Television Drama Michael Barry had established that it might be possible in March the following year to televise the final dress rehearsal, which was traditionally played to an audience of schoolchildren, of the season's opening play *Othello*. 'We are anxious that Drama should establish one or two annual events or pilgrimages comparable to Glyndebourne,' Barry wrote. 'Stratford is the first and most important in mind.'[69] The reply from Head of Programme Contracts H.L. Streeton, however, was unequivocal: 'I am sorry to say that I see no grounds for approaching the TNC for permission to take *Othello* in full – nor the slightest hope of the TNC agreeing if we were to approach them.'[70] Quayle's 1954 *Othello*, in which he also took the title role, did not reach the television screen.

After the 1951 History Plays cycle Anthony Quayle's company found it difficult to sustain the unalloyed success of the immediately preceding years. Quayle was also preoccupied by the renewed impetus of the project to create a National Theatre in London, which had been focused in July 1951 by the Queen laying a foundation stone on the South Bank.[71] As Sally Beauman has written, Quayle 'felt that if the National Theatre came into being, backed by state subsidy, the Memorial would suffer'.[72] In response he invited Glen Byam Shaw and George Devine to join him in a triumvirate to run Stratford, although Devine soon left to establish the English Stage Company at the Royal Court. The 1955 summer season was a triumph, largely thanks to Laurence Olivier and Vivien Leigh appearing in *Twelfth Night* (directed by John Gielgud), *Macbeth* (Glen Byam Shaw) and *Titus*

Andronicus (Peter Brook). The BBC had not lost interest, and in February 1954 the Memorial Theatre itself approached the TNC to permit *Othello* to be broadcast in full, only to have the request rejected.[73] Then in March 1955 Cecil Madden informed his colleagues that Anthony Quayle had the disappointing news about a possible broadcast that 'the Oliviers have refused for various reasons'. On the other hand, Quayle could offer, either in whole or part, that season's *The Merry Wives of Windsor*. 'He reiterates he is very keen we should come to Stratford,' Madden continued, 'and asks for help from an experienced TV Drama Director to guide what we do from the stage.'[74] Internal discussion continued, with Head of Programme Planning, Television Joanna Spicer detailing why an outside broadcast (OB) from Stratford was important and how it might be possible to persuade the TNC to permit a full play to be shown:

> We feel that the Stratford season occupies a special place in the theatrical output from this country. It is an international season drawing its audiences from all over the world. A visit to Stratford is, we think, a special occasion and we feel that to televise a drama production from Stratford on a Sunday would not endanger the audiences in local theatres in the following week. It seems to us that while the sophisticated part of the audience might compare the Stratford production with other Shakespeare productions in the theatre, viewers will look on it as a separate thing from a visit to their local entertainments.[75]

Streeton tried out the exceptionalist case on the TNC and to his surprise by late May had received a positive answer. But it appears that Quayle was having second thoughts about offering the full play. In July, Joanna Spicer confirmed Stratford's feeling 'that it would be better for us to televise only the second of three acts of *The Merry Wives of Windsor*' on a Sunday night in early October.[76] With an introduction, it was intended that the programme length would run to an hour.

At the point that the BBC and the Memorial Theatre came to an agreement, Glen Byam Shaw's production had just opened to largely positive reviews. 'A thoroughly warm and jolly performance,' enthused Philip Hope-Wallace, commending the design by Motley (Figure 1), Quayle's 'good rich ruby roisterer' of a Falstaff and the Dr Caius–schoolmaster Evans duel (which featured in the second act) as a 'splendidly worked up passage of slapstick'.[77] Almost three months later, a BBC OB unit arrived from Birmingham with much to do to ensure a successful mediation. 'We had to have three special rehearsals', one of the two BBC producers, Barrie Edgar, explained, 'in order to reduce the player's movements to the field of the three cameras.'[78] Additional lighting was installed through Saturday night after a scheduled performance, and as a local reporter noted, 'A special BBC make-up team was in attendance, because normal stage make-up looks coarse and dark before the cameras. There was extra work for the theatre wardrobe

FIGURE 1 *A scene from Glen Byam Shaw's production of* The Merry Wives of Windsor *(1955), designed by Motley; the central act was broadcast live from Stratford-upon-Avon by BBC Television. Photograph by Angus McBean © RSC.*

staff too – attaching pieces of material of contrasting colour to costumes, to prevent them appearing drab in black and white.'[79] A camera was set near the front on either side of the auditorium, with a third positioned centrally in row forty-four of the stalls; a fourth camera was used for the presentation elements.[80] And the invited audience, glimpsed in the broadcast itself and including Stratford's mayor, was addressed from the stage by Barrie Edgar before the curtain rose.

It would be sixty-two years before there was another live television broadcast of a performance from Stratford's theatre, when *Shakespeare Live! From the RSC* was shown on BBC Two for the Birthday in 2016. This first came at an opportune moment both for the Memorial Theatre and for the BBC. In his eight-minute opening presentation, the Scottish critic Alan Dent, who had served as advisor to Olivier on his Shakespeare films, made the case that Stratford and The Old Vic between them fulfilled almost all of the functions of a possible (and for Quayle, threatening) national theatre. And the broadcast as a whole, complemented by a studio production immediately beforehand of Bernard Shaw's *The Dark Lady of the Sonnets* (which is in part concerned with the idea of a national theatre), acted as an implicit riposte by the corporation to an altogether more immediate and significant threat: the arrival in the London area ten days before of Independent Television (ITV). Tainted in the eyes of many by its populism and brash commercialism, ITV was expected to follow the American model of television and to bring over from the United States many of its programmes and formats. A Sunday evening that assembled Bernard Shaw, Elizabeth I and Will Shakespeare (who are characters in *The Dark Lady of the Sonnets*), Falstaff, the Memorial Theatre and the birthplace of the world's greatest playwright was a powerful if high-minded reminder of the BBC's commitment to public service ideals and its centrality to the nation's culture, indeed to its very identity. Writing in a local newspaper, Rosemary Anne Sisson felt that this strategy would have been even more effective if the BBC could have offered *The Merry Wives of Windsor in toto*: 'I should have thought that it was precisely in this sort of full-scale "prestige" production, as they call them in America, that the BBC might prove its superiority over the briefer sorties of the Independent Television Authority (ITA).'[81]

Alan Dent's on-air introduction today appears charmingly inept – tentative, rambling and unable quite to get his eyeline or cues correct. He begins speaking over a rapid tour on film of the familiar sites of Shakespeare country that settles on exterior shots, complete with swans, of the Memorial Theatre and then cuts inside to the audience, drawing the viewer at home into the auditorium. Dent stands at a podium lecturing us on the background to the text, stressing its authorial creativity and, as he maintains, absence of foreign or classical sources. Since the broadcast is about to join the action at the start of Act 2, Scene 3, Dent also has to introduce a dozen characters, each of whom appears in shots filmed earlier against a neutral background. Dent explains the winter settings and the ingenuity of the designs, although Motley, unlike director Glen Byam Shaw, are not name-checked. And he outlines the three main plot strands before, as a music cue is heard, the broadcast dissolves to a shot, seen only this once, of the proscenium framed at full width and height and adorned with a curlicue border. Through the next fifty minutes three cameras alternate long shots, showing groupings of the characters at full length, and mid-shots to the waist, employing only occasional close-ups for emphasis. Director Stephen Harrison deployed the available shots to provide adequate coverage of the stage action, but it is only with the close-ups that he introduced even the most tentative expressive elements. The incongruity of Huw Evans's nervous song 'To shallow rivers' (3.1.16–25), for example, is pointed with two large framings of his face. After two confusing scenes, the broadcast achieves an effective comic quality from Act 3, Scene 2 onwards, with a confident control of farce as Falstaff hides in the laundry basket and as the polished performances of Angela Baddeley (as Mistress Ford) and Joyce Redman (Mistress Page) shine through. The overall sense is of an energetic marital comedy, upmarket perhaps of the Brian Rix slapstick that was beginning to be televised at the time, and authenticated by the audience laughter that is audible throughout.

And this is underlined by both stage blackout and the broadcast close coming as Ford, in his endeavours to find out Falstaff, shoots a musket up the chimney and emerges with a blackened face. Mistress Page tells Mistress Ford that they should confess their tricks to their partners if only 'to scrape the figures out of your husband's brains' (4.2.204–5). At which point, when the theatre enjoyed an interval, the broadcast ends.

A detailed Audience Research Report (ARR) was prepared for internal BBC consumption, and this recorded that the broadcast was watched by 15 per cent of the adult population and that they recorded a Reaction Index (RI) of sixty-four. The figure was felt to be somewhere in the mid-range for studio Shakespeare on television. A 'Civil Servant' said that they 'wished that all who may say they don't care for Shakespeare could have seen this – as amusing as any modern comedy'. But there were caveats also. 'One or two viewers', the ARR noted, 'thought that the cast, understandably, played for a theatre audience too much to be completely effective in the more intimate medium of television.'[82] The *Birmingham Mail* critic, while praising Quayle's Falstaff, was unimpressed overall: 'The players had to get into the usual TV huddles to suit the cameras ... The cameras did their best to bring the actors on the big stage into close-up. We had a taste of the quality of Stratford acting (but without the Oliviers). But we were given little notion of what a unique experience theatre-going is by the Avon.'[83] For *The Listener*, Philip Hope-Wallace preferred *The Dark Lady of the Sonnets*, his description of which summed up succinctly the BBC's sense of its broad mission: 'Shaw's still topical and witty puff for our National Theatre (and where is that, if not the television screen in every home?).'[84]

On the afternoon following the broadcast, Barrie Edgar, whose son David was later to author several plays for the RSC, including the adaptation of *Nicholas Nickleby*, contributed a simple coda. In what had been the old Memorial Theatre's auditorium and was now the Stratford Conference Hall, two cameras showed Edgar talking with the company's head of wardrobe Kegan Smith about his department's work. They held up Olivier's red leather cloak for *Titus Andronicus* and Vivien Leigh's Lady Macbeth dress. Company members Michael Denison and Maxine Audley dropped by to chat, and as the transmission came to an end Rosemary Anne Sisson reflected on the magic of television: 'Over tea and toast, and fires lit against the first chill of autumn, thousands of British housewives all over the country had caught a brief glimpse of the wardrobe of the Shakespeare Memorial Theatre. It was slightly lunatic, but rather gratifying.'[85]

A *Dream* team

The positive but far from overwhelming audience and critical response to the broadcast of *The Merry Wives of Windsor*, combined with the developing recognition among television drama executives that, as Hope-

Wallace had written in his review, 'plays specially prepared for television are more satisfactory',[86] in part accounts for the BBC failing to establish the envisaged annual television pilgrimage to Stratford-upon-Avon. It would be seven years before a new director, Peter Hall, would take the newly established Royal Shakespeare Company into a further collaboration with British television, even though the small screen continued to demonstrate an appetite for Shakespeare. The BBC created its own studio productions of *The Tempest* (1956), *Henry V* and *Twelfth Night* (both 1957) and *A Midsummer Night's Dream* (1958), and then in 1960 an ambitious History plays cycle, *An Age of Kings* (1960).[87] So it was to be an American television company that next brought cameras into the Memorial Theatre to televise a production. And even before that the Memorial Theatre was approached by another company from across the Atlantic with one of the strangest filming proposals that a British theatre company can have received.

American television producers had been occasional suitors of the Memorial Theatre since early 1948, when the recently formed World Video Inc. wrote offering to televise the Festival. Despite World Video boasting the novelist John Steinbeck and photographer Robert Capa amongst its vice presidents, the Executive Council rebuffed the approach.[88] Five years later the council took more seriously, although ultimately to the same end, a proposal from Douglas Fairbanks Jr that the company collaborate on ten films based on its productions.[89] Then in July 1958 Fordham Flower informed the council that he and Anthony Quayle had been approached by representatives of Encyclopaedia Britannica who wished to build a replica of the Globe Theatre in Stratford.[90] At the end of the 1950s Encyclopaedia Britannica Films was the world's largest producer of educational media, and the company wanted to make films 'about Shakespeare's theatre .... to bring to life on film the experience of the theatre-goer of Shakespeare's day'.[91] They had considered reconstructing the Globe in a film studio but had decided that doing so in Stratford was a better idea and that they might complement this with an exhibition, an annual festival for school and university drama societies, publications, conferences organized with the Shakespeare Institute, and a commission to T.S. Eliot or Christopher Fry for a new verse drama. As for the theatre itself, it was being planned by the noted theatre designer Richard Southern and the illustrator C. Walter Hodges, and they were being advised by the scholars Allardyce Nicoll and Richard Hosley. The council considered the idea and sought advice from the local planning authorities, who advised that permission was unlikely to be given for a building on the proposed site of Avonbank Gardens, adjacent to the theatre. On the advice of Glen Byam Shaw, they then decided that the burden of running a second company, as Britannica wished the Memorial Theatre to do, and the threat to the economics of the existing operation constituted too great a risk. At the council meeting on 21 November 1958 the approach was rejected. Had it been built, the history of post-war theatre in Britain might have been very different. Instead, as a quite separate project,

Shakespeare's Globe opened on the south bank of the Thames in London in 1997, following a lengthy campaign led by actor Sam Wanamaker. In 1954 Wanamaker, who had moved to Britain after being blacklisted in the United States, was in the audience for Glen Byam Shaw's Stratford production of *Troilus and Cressida*. The experience prompted him to sketch on the back of his programme a plan to make shortened television versions of productions from Stratford and The Old Vic, but as with the other suitors his approach to the Memorial Theatre was rebuffed.[92] He was back in Stratford in 1959, playing Iago opposite Paul Robeson. Might he then have heard of – and perhaps been inspired by – the Encyclopaedia Britannica plan of the previous year?

In the late 1950s BBC Television may also have stayed away from Stratford in part because of only a modest level of enthusiasm for the productions created under Glen Byam Shaw, who became director on Anthony Quayle's departure in 1956. Among the rare highlights were stagings by Peter Hall, who began his association with Stratford in 1956 at the age of 25 with *Love's Labour's Lost*, following this up with *Cymbeline* in 1957 and, a year later, *Twelfth Night*. In 1958 he was also chosen to succeed Byam Shaw, with effect from the 1960 season. Knowing then that he was to return to Stratford for *A Midsummer Night's Dream*, Hall spent two months in Los Angeles, enjoying in particular the company of Charles Laughton. In the 1930s the actor had left the English stage for Hollywood, but as Hall wrote in his autobiography, 'For twenty-five years up in the hills of Hollywood, [Laughton] had read and dreamed of Shakespeare. This passion had shored up a great deal of his waking life.'[93] As a consequence, the young director was able to tempt the star to Stratford to play both Bottom and, in a Byam Shaw production, King Lear. Despite the decidedly mixed notices for his Lear ('it wanted the ultimate emotional drive', wrote J.C. Trewin),[94] Hall persuaded Laughton to return in the future to play Falstaff, only for the actor to die of cancer before this could be realized. The *Dream* was also received with only moderate enthusiasm from the critics, including Philip Hope-Wallace who grumbled about the verse-speaking. But his *Manchester Guardian* review encapsulated the production's conceit and setting:

> Mr Hall's basic idea has been to present the whole play as though it were amateur theatricals done in the Great Hall of an Elizabethan house. To this end, Lila de Nobili has devised a permanent set of a grand staircase which remains as a stumbling block of a bridge – the woodland merging very prettily from the gauze backdrop.[95] (Figure 2)

Stratford in the summer of 1959 offered not only Charles Laughton but also Paul Robeson as Othello[96] and, in another Peter Hall production, Laurence Olivier as Coriolanus. One of those who travelled to the banks of the Avon was the American television producer Hubbell Robinson, who was soon to mobilize the Memorial Theatre and Shakespeare for a cultural

FIGURE 2 *Bottom, played by Charles Laughton, rehearses with the mechanicals in Peter Hall's staging of* A Midsummer Night's Dream *(1959), recorded for US television but never shown. Photograph by Angus McBean © RSC.*

battle being joined back home. Robinson had started his media career in the early 1930s as an advertising executive. He joined CBS Television in 1947 where he developed popular series including *I Love Lucy* and *Gunsmoke*. He also championed the *Playhouse 90* anthology series of serious dramas, which was perhaps closer to his heart given that CBS Chairman William Paley recorded that 'Culturally, his interests were levels above many of his colleagues ... His special flair was for high-quality programming.'[97] More pithily, Robinson himself claimed that what he was always after was 'mass with class'.[98] When he came to Stratford in 1959 he had just left CBS, and under the banner of Hubbell Robinson Productions he was preparing a series titled *Startime* (1959–60), or alternatively *Ford Startime – TV's Finest Hour*. With sponsorship for the Ford Motor Company, this was an anthology strand of drama and variety for CBS's main rival NBC. The project was also tied up with the Music Corporation of America (MCA), a talent agency headed by Lew Wasserman that 'packaged' the shows in the series with their extensive rosta of stars – which included Charles Laughton.[99] In the late 1950s Robinson was also prominent in a debate within American television about the mediocrity of the medium. As television historian William Boddy noted,

In July 1957, Hubbell Robinson cited heightened public and critical dissatisfaction with network programming and pointed to industry fears that program quality would continue to decline. 'It is obvious to anyone with eyes to see and ears to hear that in television's programming a considerable amount of soft underbelly exists,' Robinson declared, and he scored the industry's 'willingness to settle for drama whose synonym is pap.'[100]

Startime can be seen as a direct response to these concerns, since among the variety shows hosted by Dean Martin and Jack Parr there was Ingrid Bergman (another prominent MCA artist) in a version of Henry James's *The Turn of the Screw* and Rex Harrison (ditto) in a Gore Vidal adaptation of a P.G. Wodehouse story based on a play by Ferenc Molnar, *Dear Arthur*.[101] Since a letter to Peter Hall from director Fletcher Markle refers to 'the Ford people', *A Midsummer Night's Dream* was clearly destined for this series, but the strand was not renewed after its first season ended in May 1960.[102] As a consequence, the production appears never to have been broadcast.

Perhaps surprisingly, network television in the United States had a strong record in producing Shakespeare, although there would be far fewer productions after 1960 as the pressure of ratings feared by Robinson increasingly constrained the medium's cultural aspirations. From 1959 just the one letter already referred to, and the contract between The Shakespeare Memorial Theatre and Hubbell Robinson Productions Inc., signed on 2 November, are all that appear to survive from the negotiations for recording the *Dream*.[103] Markle's letter reveals that the length of the play was a key concern and also that securing agreement on terms for the involvement of the cast was far from straightforward. While the letter stressed that Peter Hall's rights in the production would be respected, as with today's productions, final control followed the money and remained with the television company. Nor at this stage were the plans entirely straightforward, since with less than two months to go before the start of recording the necessary cuts to the 130-minute show remained undetermined. Of the hour and a half of the broadcast twenty minutes would be taken up with commercials, titles and a filmed prologue, a rough cut of which apparently accompanied the letter to England. As for the benefits to the Memorial Theatre, the company, quite separate from fees paid to the cast, was to receive US$25,000 to permit the recording to be shown only once in the United States and in territories in the rest of the world, excluding the United Kingdom.

With terms and script cuts finally agreed, the production moved into the Memorial Theatre after the last night of *King Lear*, initially to remove the first twelve rows of the stalls, to build a camera platform and to set up the equipment. The actual recording began on 30 November, and the next day the *Birmingham Post*'s Keith Gascoigne described the scene:

Three cameras and an enormous microphone boom tracked in front of the stage yesterday on a specially built platform while Theseus and Hippolyta heard the opening arguments of Aegeus and the young lovers … Upwards of a dozen technicians and executives milled around on the platform while the disembodied voice of the producer, Mr Fletcher Markle, who has come from America for the production, boomed from an upstairs eyrie: 'Hold it a moment; that's very good, but there is just one point.'[104]

To record the *Dream*, Hubbell Robinson Productions had hired the first mobile video production unit in Europe equipped to record in the 525-line format used by American television. Based in Paris, Intercontinental Television S.A. had been set up only months before with a team of twenty-one engineers and production personnel who had left NBC. Having already travelled to Moscow and Spoleto in Italy by the time they came to Stratford, they brought with them a scanner that had been built by RCA in Camden, New Jersey, together with a generator.[105] But unlike *The Merry Wives of Windsor*, where the performance was continuous for live transmission, here around fifteen minutes of the production was recorded in short sections throughout each of five sixteen-hour days.

In the 16mm film copy that was presented by Hubbell Robinson Productions to the RSC, and that today is preserved in the Shakespeare Birthplace Trust archives, we see first the nine-minute introduction shot on location around Stratford. The opening image is taken through the windscreen of a car travelling deep into rural England and its villages: 'the heart of England, the county of Warwickshire', as Charles Laughton's off-screen voice informs us. Then we are transported to bustling modern streets, 'the heart of Warwickshire, the town of Stratford-upon-Avon'. With shots of a strikingly diverse range of visitors, the introduction is next at pains to stress that 'All the world comes to Stratford', and that they do so to attend the Shakespeare Memorial Theatre 'to which you are all invited this evening'.[106] Following that, in a sequence in which we first discover our host reclining in a punt on the river, Charles Laughton tours the key locations of 'Shakespeare country', including the birthplace, the schoolroom and Anne Hathaway's Cottage, reprising the concerns of the interwar documentaries discussed above. Finally, Laughton has one other task to perform, which is to reconcile Shakespeare with this new medium:

As proud as we all are of Peter Hall's production of the *Dream* I had some reservations about bringing it to television. After all, Shakespeare surrounded by cowboys, commercials and all that jazz. But then one morning I was walking with my brother-in-law down a Stratford street and I looked up to see the past linked with today – the television antenna on the roof of a Tudor house reminded me that in his day Will was a man of the moment – and I'm sure that if he was a man of this moment he'd be writing for this medium to reach the greatest audience. And if I thought he would resent our cutting one of his plays to meet the demands of the relentless clock, darn it I wouldn't be doing it.

At which point it is clear that the production expected to go to its first commercial break.

We are welcomed back by Peter Hall, with the recording having switched from film to videotape and our location from the Avon riverbank to the auditorium. He is here to show us to our seats. Nearly sixty years on, the adaptation is vivid and consistently enjoyable, with the structure of the play preserved across seventy minutes, although with a good deal of the poetry stripped away. Given Laughton's centrality to the project it is perhaps unsurprising that the scenes with the mechanicals are preserved almost uncut, as is much of the interplay between Oberon and Titania. It is the court scenes that are most heavily truncated, so that in Act 1, Scene 1, out of the first 127 lines through to Egeus' conclusion 'With duty and desire we follow you' (1.1.127) only forty-two are played. Similarly the first thirty-three lines of Act 5, Scene 1 have gone, and the lovers' scenes in the wood are also cut right back.

The stop-start recording process across a full week permitted screen director Fletcher Markle, a veteran of the prestigious CBS drama anthology show *Studio One*, to deploy the three cameras with greater precision and flexibility than had been possible for the BBC's *The Merry Wives of Windsor*. Groupings of characters are precisely framed, and shots combine a foreground figure with another in the background, as when Puck is constantly present behind and within the quarrelling lovers in Act 3, Scene 2. Yet small continuity errors, such as the placing of a hand or the fall of a costume, disrupt the sense of a continuous performance. Markle also underlined key speeches with the use of zooms, as when the camera closes in on Oberon explaining the trick he is to play on his queen, from 'Having once this juice / I'll watch Titania when she is asleep' (2.1.176–77). In this speech too, Robert Hardy's Oberon plays directly down the lens, just as he does when, although 'invisible' he helps Helena to her feet as she says 'Fie, Demetrius' (2.1.239) and then turns to the camera and winks. Others in the cast, including Ian Holm's Puck, also play asides straight to the television audience, although Laughton betrays an uneasiness about this, as when he recounts Bottom's dream (4.1.199–216), speaking as his gaze roams across the empty house and only for brief moments looking directly into the camera. For Laughton's sympathetic biographer, Simon Callow, however, the screen version reveals the actor's Bottom as 'glorious. The predominant impression is of energy – passionate, earthy energy – and appetite, but beside the physical energy is an enormous imaginative turmoil.'[107]

Hubbell Robinson died in 1974 and his production company has not been active for many years. Since *A Midsummer Night's Dream* was never sold to a broadcaster, the 16mm film print in Stratford was until recently the only extant copy.[108] What this rare recording captures is not only Charles

Laughton's performance but also a supporting cast with numerous players who would go on to play key roles in the 1960s with what would soon become the Royal Shakespeare Company. Robert Hardy as Oberon has already been noted, and Lysander is played by Albert Finney, Helena is Vanessa Redgrave, Roy Dotrice is Egeus and one of the unnamed fairies is Diana Rigg. This is a generation of young actors concerned to bring immediacy and naturalism to their verse-speaking, and whose performances contrast in the production with the more classical, refined performances of, for example, Anthony Nicholls as Theseus and, although she presents an alluring sensuality, Mary Ure as Titania. There is also an obvious reticence in the treatment of the relationship between Titania and Bottom transformed into an ass that would soon be blown away, notably in Peter Brook's RSC production of the play in 1970. Here once Bottom has been laid on the fairy queen's bed, she simply rests her head on his ample chest as they fall asleep. In retrospect, the recording marks a transitional moment for Stratford, with the new artistic director Peter Hall about to transform the company and – as his on-screen appearance presages – about to become a media star. What will soon be the RSC is about to become the most challenging and most controversial British theatre troupe of the next decade, and the screen is about to be no longer a side-show to be embraced opportunistically on occasions but, rather, to be at the heart of the new company's operations.

2

Television Times, 1961–68

On 23 April 1964 celebrations around the world commemorated the 400th anniversary of William Shakespeare's birth. Yet Holland Bennett, head of artists' booking for BBC Television, made no mention of the jubilee when he wrote that day to RSC general manager Patrick Russell.[1] Bennett confirmed that the corporation was indeed committed to a television version of *The Wars of the Roses,* the company's triumphant trilogy drawn from Shakespeare's History plays. That the news was communicated on this notable date is pleasingly appropriate. *The Wars of the Roses* was the defining stage production of Peter Hall's years as the RSC's artistic director and one of the company's supreme achievements. The television adaptation, despite being inaccessible for many years, is increasingly recognized as among the finest translations of Shakespeare to the small screen.

At the moment of the quatercentenary, the RSC was unrivalled as a theatre company in Britain. The National Theatre was only months into mounting productions at The Old Vic, no other company was seriously committed to the classical repertoire, and Shakespeare's Globe remained a distant dream. Responding to the internal revolution led by Peter Hall the RSC was presenting controversial contemporary dramas as well as ground-breaking productions of plays by Shakespeare and his contemporaries. And in its experimental work with Peter Brook and others it was challenging the boundaries of theatre. BBC Television, while wary of the more unconventional elements of the company's offerings, was delighted to deliver on its public service responsibilities by taking both full-length versions and selected scenes of mainstream productions to audiences far from the RSC's theatres. Remarkably, since the majority of television drama from before the end of the 1960s has been lost, including several RSC stagings, we are fortunate to have six recordings of exceptional productions from these years (counting *The Wars of the Roses* as three), plus a half of another and some fragments. Archival survivals include a glorious version of *The Cherry Orchard* with John Gielgud, Peggy Ashcroft and Judi Dench, *As You Like It* with a dazzling Vanessa Redgrave, Clifford Williams's hit version of *The Comedy of Errors*, and the opening acts of a richly hued *All's Well That Ends Well*, which was British television's first colour production of Shakespeare. These adaptations, created in a close partnership between the RSC and the BBC, capture much of the energy, originality and brilliance of the company that Peter Hall brought into being.

Early encounters

Within two years of taking over at the start of 1960, Peter Hall had transformed the organization and operations of the Shakespeare Memorial Theatre Company. The Board's chair Fordham Flower had recognized that fundamental change was needed, and in the summer of 1958 he followed Glen Byam Shaw's advice and appointed the *wunderkind* Hall as the next director. Following a November announcement Flower and Hall journeyed with the Stratford company on a triumphant tour to the Soviet Union. During a long night in Leningrad the two men thrashed out a radical plan that, thanks to Flower's stalwart backing, would be achieved by the young director at astonishing speed. Changes included the formation of a true company with three-year contracts for actors, the remodelling of the Stratford theatre to bring the stage closer to the audience, the leasing of the Aldwych Theatre as a London base and the redesign of that stage as well, and then in March 1961 Buckingham Palace approval for the troupe to become the Royal Shakespeare Company.[2] Public subsidy was to be essential for these ambitions, and Hall recognized that the RSC would not achieve that unless Stratford's accumulated reserves were spent, a task that he set about with glee. But he also had to make a strong artistic case for funding, and both the press, which was attracted to this visionary young man with his frenetic energy and glamorous wife Leslie Caron, and the increasingly significant medium of television were tools with which he could work. All of this activity was further complicated by often fraught negotiations with parties, including the treasury, the Arts Council, and principals, amongst whom were Laurence Olivier and Lord Goodman, who were finally taking seriously the founding of the National Theatre.[3] Hall recognized that, whatever form a National Theatre would take, staging contemporary plays and maintaining a high profile in London were essential if the RSC was to compete with, or perhaps become a central component of, this new institution.

Peter Hall's first season for Stratford in 1960 was dedicated to Shakespeare's comedies, and was generally regarded as unremarkable. Interest in the company began to build when, from December that year, new productions opened in succession at the Aldwych. The celebrated radio producer Donald McWhinnie staged a well-received *The Duchess of Malfi* by John Webster, before Peter Hall transferred *Twelfth Night* from Stratford and then mounted Jean Giraudoux's play *Ondine*. As the company took on its new name it presented John Whiting's *The Devils* as its first new play by a British writer.[4] BBC executives were among those to take note, and Whiting's drama was soon the focus of a film for the arts magazine *Monitor*, and then Act 2 of *Ondine* was recorded for transmission in April. At this point news had started to leak out that the RSC and the BBC were discussing an arrangement for two or three full productions to be broadcast annually. In early April the *Daily Mail* splashed a report of 'secret negotiations', with Peter Hall happy to confide that, 'We have not gone into this because of money; we won't get much out of it. But if we can interest the man in the street in the theatre through television then it will be well worthwhile.'[5]

As television's only regular strand devoted to the arts, *Monitor* had since 1958 been hugely influential in shaping cultural conversation in London and beyond. For its edition broadcast on 26 February 1961, less than a week after press night for *The Devils*, producer Nancy Thomas, a film crew and the playwright had travelled to the French town of Loudun, the setting for Whiting's seventeenth-century tale of possession and persecution. Along with brief extracts of Peter Wood's staging, performed in costume in a bare studio by Dorothy Tutin and Richard Johnson, the twenty-five-minute feature explores the playwright's responses to the medieval buildings and characterful faces of the historic location. Thomas choreographs David Prosser's camerawork and Allan Tyrer's editing in a strikingly effective, often expressionistic essay that Whiting himself narrates. At times a subjective camera adopts his point-of-view wandering through the narrow alleys, and this view is elided with that of the play's central character Father Urbain Grandier. Identifying with Grandier's fascination with the devil, the playwright, who two years later was to die of cancer, sits in his sheepskin jacket at a café table to offer a lengthy address about good and evil, love and hate in the modern world.

A month or so after highlighting Whiting's play, BBC outside broadcast cameras visited the Aldwych to record just the second act of *Ondine*, which was broadcast on 11 April. The play is a whimsical fantasy about a German mermaid who is taken from a lake by a passing knight to the court of the King of the Ondines. Opening just before *The Devils*, it was an unlikely choice as the company's first modern play, but Peter Hall wanted a star vehicle for his soon-to-be-former wife, Leslie Caron, as well as what he hoped would be a box office hit. Like other contemporary French dramatists, and most especially Jean Anouilh, Jean Giraudoux was a familiar name to British theatregoers at the time, there having been at least eight post-war productions of his plays in London.[6] When the Aldwych *Ondine* opened in January, however, there was little consistency in the critical responses, although J.W. Lambert enthused about 'a highly delightful evening's diversion: frivolity with a hint of depths below'.[7] The BBC transmission followed a well-established model of screening up to forty-five minutes of a current West End hit, invariably a comedy, that was recorded at a special performance before an invited audience. The duration, and the choice of an excerpt that did not include anything from a concluding act, were as stipulated in an agreement with the Theatres National Committee that had been put in place in 1955. The BBC grudgingly accepted this framework for featuring partial versions of stage shows, and the theatres were content that television assisted them with their marketing. Regular outings had been part of the schedule since 1957, with the three-camera broadcasts usually overseen, as was *Ondine*, by the experienced outside-broadcast producer John Vernon. For certain broadcasts, the writer or stage director offered an introduction, as Peter Hall did for *Ondine*, but neither his welcoming words nor the recorded presentation of the play appear to have survived. Among the few traces left by the transmission is a column by *Yorkshire Post* critic Peter Jackson, who grumbled about the shortcomings of partial broadcasts from theatres, although he was happy to praise *Ondine*: 'I object on principle to these excerpts because they rarely have any intrinsic value, but this Royal Shakespeare Theatre production was pure delight, and we did get threequarters of an hour. This modern satire was sharp enough to transcend the transition from stage to television, even in fragmentation.'[8]

Other BBC appearances by Peter Hall's new company included the Home Service broadcast on 29 December 1960 of *Songs and Sweet Airs*, an anthology that featured scenes from *As You Like It* and other recent Stratford productions. For Shakespeare's Birthday four months later *Monitor* screened extracts from another anthology, *The Hollow Crown*, that would become a touring warhorse for the company and two years later, as is discussed below, would also be filmed more elaborately.[9] Nor was the new Stratford season ignored by the arts strand, since a fortnight later it featured extracts from Peter Wood's new and little-liked production of *Hamlet*, together with comments from the director and from the show's Prince, Ian Bannen.[10] In November *Monitor* included an interview with Michel Saint-Denis about his forthcoming RSC production of *The Cherry Orchard*.[11] Such was the traffic between the Royal Shakespeare Theatre, the Aldwych and the new BBC Television Centre in west London, and such was the alignment of interests, that a more formal relationship must have seemed an obvious next step.

Although Peter Hall leaked the news of talks with the BBC in April 1961, and although *The Cherry Orchard* was recorded in early 1962, a contract was only signed on 5 October 1962. Long-term deals of this kind between a theatre company and a broadcaster were not unknown. ATV had co-produced a series of plays with West End producers H.M. Tennent in the first years of ITV, and both the BBC and other ITV companies had collaborated on groups of shows with stage producers including Henry Sherek and Brian Rix. The nine-page agreement with the RSC envisaged two recordings of company productions to be made in the current year and in the next.[12] The choice of productions was by mutual agreement, and the RSC received a management fee of £2,000 per production. This payment secured the rights of the theatre creative team, including the stage director, as well as the use of RSC costumes. The BBC undertook to pay separately for such copyrights in texts and music as would be necessary for a television broadcast. Artists were paid in accordance with existing arrangements between the BBC and Equity, although it was up to the RSC to secure their involvement.

Under the terms of the agreement the BBC could broadcast each recording twice, with additional fees triggered by repeats. The BBC picked up international television distribution rights, and the RSC received up to two-thirds of net revenues from sales. Since domestic technologies like VHS and DVD had yet to be invented, no provision was made for distribution in other formats, and this has been a significant factor in the recordings not being publicly available. The agreement granted the BBC exclusive television rights to RSC productions during the two years it covered, but the company remained free to develop movies. Creative issues were barely addressed by the document, and the BBC achieved effective control, securing the right, as its Charter required, to make after consultation 'such cuts ... as the Corporation shall deem necessary to conform to the needs of broadcasting'. The choice of television director and other key broadcast creatives was recognized formally as a matter for the BBC alone, as was the choice of whether a production might be recorded in a studio, as *The Cherry Orchard* had been and *As You Like It* soon would be, or in a theatre, as was to be the case with *The Comedy of Errors*.

The financial reward was comparatively modest, but an undated RSC memo preserved in the BBC's Written Archives detailed the company's rationale for the partnership: 'Over the last six months there have been many approaches from commercial companies, both in England and America, to present the Royal Shakespeare Theatre Company on television and we are now convinced that the BBC, while not necessarily providing the most money, will assure us of the best kind of productions.'[13] In addition to what the document recognized would be 'a nominal fee' for the first BBC transmission, it was suggested that 'very considerable' profits could be realized from network screenings in America and elsewhere. Sales to schools and universities were also envisaged as a source of revenue. As a non-profit institution seeking to build a permanent company of actors, the RSC would benefit not only from revenue for itself and its artistes but also from increased awareness at home and abroad, and from having recordings for the archive.[14] The value of the arrangement to the BBC is perhaps less obvious, not least because of the arrival in January 1963 of Sydney Newman as Head of Drama Group, Television. Having produced ABC-TV's *Armchair Theatre* strand from 1958 to 1962, for which he had commissioned original and challenging scripts by contemporary writers, Newman was known to want the corporation to move away from a reliance on theatre plays and classic drama. When the RSC deal was first mooted, however, the previous Head of Television Drama Michael Barry was just starting a leave of absence to oversee the launch of the television service of Irish broadcaster RTE. It may be that the corporation's concern about the supply of high-quality classic drama prompted the RSC deal. Yet in 1964 an extension by a further three years was approved by Newman to encompass *The Wars of the Roses* and other shows. Newman's interests and ambitions were broader than the 'kitchen sink' dramas with which the press had come to associate him, as Asa Briggs has written: 'He wanted to widen his repertoire and to include "old plays", provided that "they should be seen through twentieth-century eyes."'[15] Which was exactly what Peter Hall's RSC promised and what the company would deliver, most spectacularly with *The Wars of the Roses*.

Chekhov and *The Hollow Crown*

Michel Saint-Denis had been an influential presence in British theatre since 1935 when, after working in France alongside Jacques Copeau, he directed a celebrated production of André Obey's religious drama *Noah* with John Gielgud. The following year he opened the London Theatre Studio, and after the war, along with George Devine and Glen Byam Shaw, he ran the Old Vic Theatre School. Although Saint-Denis's work is little known today, Tom Cornford has argued that his 'influence has been found far beyond the schools that he founded, in devised theatre, in new writing, in mask theatre and in classical plays (as well as in places as varied as the École Jaques Lecoq in Paris, The Royal Court Writers' Group, The Royal Shakespeare Company, Joint Stock, The Manchester Royal Exchange and Grotowski's Laboratory), but it has often been unnoticed'.[16] In 1938 Saint-Denis mounted a celebrated staging of *Three Sisters*, about which John Gielgud recalled that the director's preparations were exceptionally detailed but that rehearsals remained open and unpredictable.

Irina in *Three Sisters* was played by Peggy Ashcroft, who later described Saint-Denis as 'the most instructive director' with whom she had worked.[17] The following autumn she began to rehearse Anya in *The Cherry Orchard* for Saint-Denis, but the onset of war meant that the production did not reach the stage. The pair returned to the drama, this time with Ashcroft as Madame Ranevskaya, when in 1961, partly at Ashcroft's urging, Peter Hall invited Saint-Denis to work with the RSC. Concerned to counter the nostalgic *ennui* of a dominant English tradition of staging Chekhov, Saint-Denis intended to moderate 'the romantic and charming qualities which cling to the personalities of [the] household in order to emphasise the frivolity, the ineffectualness, and indeed the immorality of these representatives of a disappearing society'.[18] 'Opinions differ wildly about the quality of Saint-Denis's production,' Michael Billington later wrote. 'Many of the original cast speak of it in tones tinged with disappointment, as if they got less from Saint-Denis than they had hoped: others remember it as one of the best post-war English Chekhov productions.'[19] Following the production's success, Peter Hall invited Saint-Denis to establish a studio in Stratford as a space for learning and experiment. Resources to fully support this were never found, and it wound down in 1965 to 1966 when Saint-Denis's health declined. Yet its legacy has been identified in the *Theatregoround* project, in The Other Place and in the RSC's education work that would become ever more central to the company in the decades to come.[20]

The swirl of differing opinions about *The Cherry Orchard* did nothing to depress sales at the Aldwych where, after a brief appearance in Stratford, the production broke box office records. And the subtleties and complexities of the playing are wonderfully preserved in the recording of the television adaptation screened on 13 April 1962, soon after the close of the London run. The prestigious cast appears to have been the key attraction for the corporation, since the pre-publicity stressed that this was the first BBC television appearance by John Gielgud (who played Gaev and also prepared the English text) and only the second occasion since the war when Peggy Ashcroft had appeared on the small screen.[21] The visual interpretation was entrusted to Michael Elliott, who was known as an innovative television director, and who throughout the 1960s was one of the few figures who successfully maintained simultaneous careers working both for the stage and small screen. The year before *The Cherry Orchard* he had given the RSC another of its early successes with Vanessa Redgrave in *As You Like It*. For the studio transfer, the *Cherry Orchard* set by Abd'Elkader Farrah (known as 'Farrah') was opened out by television designer Norman James, although the settings failed to escape their origins on the proscenium-arch stage. Only in the first part of Act 3, as the dancers at the party whirl, is there a sense of the interconnected spaces of a large house.

Elliott's cameras shaped the exchanges between the characters with sensitivity, enhancing moments of intimacy, as when Trofimov (Ian Holm) outlines his utopian vision to Anya (Judi Dench), and expressing moments of joy, as when Anya rushes into the house in Act 1 and the frame pulls back and climbs rapidly. Shots also visualized the distances between people and their class positions, perhaps most strongly in Act 3 when Lopakhin (George Murcell) announces his purchase of the orchard. A shot foregrounds him with Ranevskaya small and far back in the frame before a reverse cut shows Ranevskaya sobbing close to the camera and Lopakhin deep in the distance. In the next shot the merchant's face fills the frame as he reflects on his ambiguous triumph. Fluid, sometimes restless camera movement also anticipates and follows the frequent movements of the characters, including as they go to doorways and windows to stare out of the space and into both the past and future. Branches seen in shadow under the main titles and in silhouette surrounding the outdoor seat of Act 2 suggest how these people are trapped individually and collectively, just as Firs will be locked in the house alone at the close. For Billy Smart, writing in 2014, the recording 'reveals a tension between theatrical and televisual styles of presentation, with the roaming direction belonging to Television Centre while the acting remains in the Aldwych Theatre'.[22] Many viewers were also unconvinced. The internal Audience Research Report noted a disappointing reaction index of fifty-nine, since although the actors were generally praised, the pacing was felt to be too slow, and there were also complaints about 'the lack of a story'.[23] My own response, watching and re-watching this recording from a DVD, could not be more different. Much of the pleasure is simply that of sharing the greatest play of the twentieth century with such a remarkable cast nearly sixty years after their playing, and overall, I share the assertion of the anonymous reviewer for *The Stage & Television Today*: 'A telerecording should be placed in the archives of the British Theatre Museum without delay.'[24]

With *The Cherry Orchard* recorded and planning underway for the first Shakespeare productions with the BBC, the RSC nonetheless continued to explore other media options. For a brief period in the early 1960s, pay-per-view television delivered to homes by cable appeared to offer an alternative to over-the-air broadcasting. British Home Entertainment (BHE) was the most prominent of the syndicates that planned trials that eventually took place, on a very limited basis, in 1966 and the following year. At BHE's founding in 1960 its chairman, Field Marshal Lord Slim, assured investors that it would focus on creating high-quality productions. 'The aim would be to capture the "lost cinema audience",' *The Times* reported, 'people who want their entertainment in the home and are selective in their viewing.'[25] The company's eminent non-executive directors included Laurence Olivier, and in 1963 the company recorded Olivier's Chichester Festival Theatre production of *Uncle Vanya* in ATV's television studios. BHE then competed with the BBC for rights to film National Theatre performances when they began at The Old Vic in October 1963. Olivier used his influence to secure John Dexter's 1964 production of *Othello* for BHE, with the actor playing the lead role in blackface. BHE also funded recordings with the Royal Ballet and the D'Oyly Carte Opera Company.[26] Exclusivity clauses in the RSC's agreement with the BBC prevented the filming by BHE of most of the company's productions, but the corporation waived its rights in the anthology *The Hollow Crown*. Extracts of this had been shown in *Monitor*, and it had twice been broadcast in its entirety on the Home Service.[27] As things turned out, *The Hollow Crown* was the RSC's only project with BHE, not least because Stratford in the early 1960s was committed to securing the widest possible audience for its screen adaptations.[28] At the National, meanwhile, Olivier's (self-interested) preference for pay-TV was challenged internally by Kenneth Tynan who argued that a deal with the BBC would provide much wider exposure. In the summer of 1966, the National Theatre also began to work on screen versions with the BBC.[29]

Devised by John Barton as, in the words of its subtitle, 'An entertainment by and about the Kings and Queens of England,' *The Hollow Crown* was first tried out at a Stratford poetry festival in 1960 and then mounted at the Aldwych in March 1961. Endlessly revived and toured, including in the United States in 1963 and in Canada as late as 2004, it is an elegant miscellany that combines fragments of medieval chronicles with letters, speeches and diary entries by monarchs and assorted witnesses. The only speech by Shakespeare is the king's lament from *Richard II*, from 'For God's sake let us sit upon the ground' through to 'Bores through his castle wall, and farewell king!' (3.2.155–70), with which the stage version opens. A cast of four actors is joined by three singers and a keyboard player, all in evening dress, and the staging, with curtains, chairs and a lectern, is simple and tour friendly.[30] BHE co-produced the film version of *The Hollow Crown* with the CBS Television network (which would also be central to the company's film production venture later in the decade), and the combined funding paid for a comparatively elaborate, semi-abstract studio set designed by Voytek that references medieval windows, Tudor facades and the outline of a crown. The 35mm monochrome camerawork is by Christopher Challis, who mostly restricts himself to tight, television-style framings, conservatively choreographed by director Charles S. Dubin who had been brought over from the United States.[31] A number of items are addressed by the Readers directly to the camera, while others are spoken as an actor looks reflectively off into space. Fifty years on from its production, when seen on a Steenbeck in a British Film Institute viewing room, *The Hollow Crown* is an engaging soft-edged celebration of the English monarchy, somewhat at odds with Barton and Peter Hall's *The Wars of the Roses*, which was transferred to television at almost exactly the same moment.

Later in the decade the RSC explored on several occasions the production of adaptations to sell to schools and colleges. Plans for distribution either on 16mm or on emerging video cassette formats were initially hazy but on 24 February 1967, Peter Hall enthused to the Executive Council about an intention 'to shoot a series of 13 short documentary-type films on Shakespearean subjects which will be suitable for educational as well as general distribution in the cinema and in television'.[32] Fleshing out the idea was entrusted to associate director David Jones, but by October of that year he had to submit a downbeat report to the Planning Committee. While the market, especially in America, was enthusiastic about the project, the demands on the company would be great and the profits modest.[33] The idea of educational media, however, would be resurrected in later discussions with producer Lew Grade and his ITV company ATV.

Television strategies for Shakespeare

The first adaptations of Shakespeare recorded under the RSC's BBC agreement were two of the company's early defining productions. Peter Hall's second Aldwych season in 1962 featured a transfer from Stratford of Michael Elliott's staging with Vanessa Redgrave of *As You Like it*, and in the same year Stratford audiences adored Clifford Williams's production of *The Comedy of Errors*. This transferred the following year to London and was still in the repertory when its television translation was broadcast in the *Festival* strand on New Year's Day 1964. Both of the BBC adaptations are amongst the most enjoyable of British television's preserved presentations of Shakespeare, although the screen strategies they employ are entirely distinct. *As You Like It* is a recording of the stage production made, like *The Cherry Orchard*, in a multi-camera studio, whereas the recording of *The Comedy of Errors* was achieved in the Aldwych before an invited audience.

According to Sally Beauman, *As You Like It* was 'the only truly successful production' of the 1961 Stratford season.[34] The initial response was far from unreservedly positive, but amongst the almost exclusively male critical establishment there were those whose enthusiasm for Vanessa Redgrave was unbounded (Figure 3). Foremost of these was Bernard Levin, who gushed:

FIGURE 3 *Vanessa Redgrave as Rosalind in Michael Elliott's production of* As You Like It *(1961), which was recorded for BBC Television. Photograph by Angus McBean © RSC.*

Oh wonderful, wonderful, most wonderful and after that out of all whooping – is Miss Vanessa Redgrave's Rosalind … This Rosalind is a creature of fire and light, her voice a golden gate opening on lapiz-lazuli hinges, her body a slender supple reed rippling in the breeze of her love … this is not acting at all, but living, being, loving.[35]

Fifty years later, *The Guardian* critic Michael Billington penned a vivid appreciation of the production, writing that 'I've never seen … a more exciting demonstration of the ecstasy of love … But there was more to Redgrave's Rosalind than striking effects. Her whole performance was about the poleaxing effect of passion.'[36]

Just before Christmas that year, most of the original cast (although Patrick Allen replaced Ian Bannen as Orlando) worked for two days in a studio at the recently opened BBC Television Centre. With them went designer Richard Negri's massive oak tree that was the central element of the setting. Stage director Michael Elliott had, as discussed above, produced the television adaptation of Saint-Denis's *The Cherry Orchard* but the transfer of *As You Like It* was entrusted to Ronald Eyre, who had more than a decade of experience directing studio versions of classic drama for schools television. Writing thoughtfully about the process in *Radio Times,* Eyre recognized the advantages of bringing to the screen an established stage production, in which the cast have played their parts for almost two years: 'performances have grown, new possibilities within the play have been glimpsed and slowly realised … [The actors] have authority. They know how to treat the play. All television has to do is to find out how to treat them: and that is the problem.' Developing an appropriately organic metaphor, he continued:

A thing like this is not a museum piece to be put on a turntable and rotated slowly for the viewers' delight. It is alive. And the only way to respect its aliveness is to let it shed some of the qualities it had in the theatre and find others that belong to television … The show you will see tonight then is not an exact replica of the stage production – something to jog the memory of those who saw it originally. Rather the original cast, on the original set, working within the producer's original conception of the play, have made a new production, right for television and for an audience that has never seen the play before.[37]

The surviving archival print features pin-sharp monochrome images and a clear sound track (complete with added chicken clucks and birdsong), and while the greensward is all too obviously MDF or similar, the recording is a delight. The stage production was cut significantly, with the later scenes involving Phoebe and Silvius, and also Touchstone and Aubrey, substantially reduced. Rosalind's epilogue was also excised and the broadcast version ends with Jacques's exit and an extended wedding dance. Recalibrated for the camera, the performances are almost uniformly exceptional, with Patrick Allen sultry and smitten, Patrick Wymark as an engaging Touchstone and Max Adrian a convincingly cynical Jacques. Also in the cast are Ian Richardson as Le Beau, Russell Hunter as Corin and the future writer and director Peter Gill as Silvius. Rosalind Knight's Celia is prim, proper and a strong foil to Vanessa Redgrave's Rosalind. But where Knight speaks with the voice of mid-century received pronunciation, Redgrave effortlessly brings to the verse the sound of a young woman blossoming in the age of pop and the pill. Celia's body is controlled and constrained, while Rosalind languorously stretches and strains with girlish excitement. Vanessa Redgrave's performance radiates innocent joy, playful confidence and engulfing love, with emotions dancing around her eyes and mouth in the numerous close-ups that the cameras afford her. Robert Shaughnessy has reflected that 'the viewer's gaze is directed by a camera that ... seems unable to tear itself away from her face. The effect is winningly, sometimes almost uncomfortably, intimate.'[38]

What Ronald Eyre described as his 'new production' employs the standard visual lexicon of the multi-camera studio and enhances this with close-ups and reverses, such as the glowing image of Rosalind and Orlando's arrival at the wedding feast. Moments of camera shake and uncertain focus, and the microphone boom caught at the edge of frame, bear witness to the speed at which the recording was made. Yet the confidence and clarity of Eyre's camera script permits the performances to shine through, and he demonstrates a sure touch in many of his framings, his visual juxtapositions of characters, under-stated but always motivated moves, and the use of a crane to rise above the characters and pin them to the forest floor. Viewer response was strikingly positive, with the broadcast achieving a Reaction Index of eighty. As the BBC's internal Audience Research Report noted, this was 'a figure that has only been reached twice before in the history of televised Shakespeare [for *Richard II, Part II* and *Richard III* in the 1960 cycle *An Age of Kings*]'. There was 'a plethora of praise' for the performance, although some among the audience felt that while Redgrave demonstrated '"a wonderful technique" in conveying swift changes of emotion, [this] proved "too prominent" for close-ups'.[39] By and large the critics were similarly enthusiastic, including a carefully attentive response from Mary Crozier: 'beautifully spoken, sure in mood, and so enjoyable that it achieved the rare thing – where usually one sits outside the screen, doubting it, this play dissolved the screen and took the watcher into itself'.[40]

The year in which *As You Like It* played at the Aldwych, and when *The Comedy of Errors* opened in Stratford, was, as Sally Beauman has written, 'the moment when [the company] found the style that was to characterise its best work under Hall's directorship. The triumphs of the next two years ... were forged in the furore, the fights, the overwork, and the sheer excitement of 1962.'[41] In many ways, Clifford Williams's production of *The Comedy of Errors*, which was mounted as a last-minute replacement after the postponement of *King Lear* with Paul Scofield, is symptomatic of that time.

An acolyte of Michel Saint-Denis, Williams focused as much on movement as on text. The production was played on three linked platforms and was presented in costumes that combined rehearsal dress with elaborate baroque fantasies. The playing was fast and furious and funny, and the show quickly proved to be a huge success both commercially and critically. Kenneth Tynan's notice was especially significant:

> The Comedy of Errors is unmistakably an RSC production. The statement is momentous: it means Peter Hall's troupe has developed, uniquely in Britain, a classical style of its own. How is it to be recognised? By solid Brechtian settings that emphasise wood and metal instead of paint and canvas; and by cogent deliberate verse speaking, that discards melodic cadenzas in favour of meaning and motivation.[42]

As with As You Like It, there was an extended period between the Stratford opening of The Comedy of Errors in the summer of 1962, and its broadcast as a recording from the Aldwych theatre some eighteen months later. The television version, directed for the small screen by Peter Duguid, who had been an actor at the Stratford Memorial Theatre in the early 1950s, opens with a sweeping crane shot from the audience to an empty stage. A cut takes the viewer backstage to the actors making final adjustments. The cast, in rehearsal clothes, now parade onto the platforms, with one of their number, Diana Rigg, rushing from backstage towards a camera. Stopping very precisely on a mark, she is framed with a tight shot of her face occupying half of the frame. After title cards over a ritualized greeting by the actors we see the cast backstage again donning more elaborate costumes. By the close of what is effectively a three-minute overture the show has signalled it will be significantly more distinctive than conventional outside broadcast 'coverage' of a stage production.

Much of the glory of the recording that features what by modern standards are indistinct visuals lies in the wondering, and wonderful, performances of Ian Richardson and Alec McCowen as the Antipholus pair, from Ephesus and Syracuse respectively. And the depth of the company at the time is revealed by Diana Rigg playing Adriana, Janet Suzman as Luciana and Donald Sinden commanding the role of the Duke of Ephesus. With cameras in the side aisles, Duguid cross-shoots the deep and narrow staging effectively, also making telling use of close-ups, as when the hand of Antipholus of Syracuse is drawn by Adriana to her breast. Bold compositions, which were probably recorded separately and edited in, deploy the shoulders and arms of foreground figures with distant action unfolding beyond. There are cuts to a camera that is mounted stage right on a higher level, especially to reveal the commedia dell'arte interludes between scenes, and the viewer is offered glimpses of the audience. Frequent laughter and occasional applause underscore the stage's expert deployment of the techniques of farce. John Russell Taylor was impressed by the broadcast, writing that it 'left little or nothing to be desired',[43] but Mary Crozier was far less engaged by the modestly Brechtian flourishes:

> Those points of production which may attract an actual audience on the spot – the actors parading on and off the stage, putting on costumes, and so on – are not those which appeal readily to the television audience, for they lessen the illusion which must be firmly and quickly established. A television production which emphasises two levels – the actual play and the business of acting in the play – is often a weak one.[44]

According to the BBC's internal Audience Research Report, viewers largely disagreed, as it summarized: 'This was, it seemed, pure delight for the great majority of viewers in the sample.' Almost the only caveat was that 'a small minority disliked the unorthodox presentation – the introduction, for instance, showing the various players getting ready for the play proper, the "masque" interludes to denote change of scene and, above all, the bare stage and almost complete lack of props and scenery'.[45]

Made within the framework of the BBC-RSC deal, *The Comedy of Errors* was broadcast on New Year's Day 1964 as the corporation's opening contribution to the celebrations 400 years on from Shakespeare's birth. It was presented as part of the *Festival* strand, which under producer Peter Luke ran for only a single season. *Festival* came to the screen less than a year after the arrival of Sydney Newman as Head of Drama Group, Television, and with a focus on demanding classics that had been written for the stage and produced for a cultured elite, it was out of step with the new regime's concern with original contemporary commissions that at least aspired to reach a broad audience. The launch of BBC Two later in 1964 also presaged a shift of theatrical adaptations to the new minority channel, and this too unsettled how RSC adaptations might be expected to fit with the BBC's plans for television drama.[46] Yet the greatest triumph of the partnership was already in the planning stages and would reach BBC One in the spring of 1965 as the three-part series *The Wars of the Roses*.

The Wars of the Roses: A hybrid production

Apart for the Coronation or the World Cup, BBC drama executive Michael Bakewell believed, the television recording of *The Wars of the Roses* in 1964 was 'one of the most ambitious enterprises undertaken by BBC Television'.[47] Yet surprisingly few photographs appear to exist of the television production in Stratford-upon-Avon. The single behind-the-scenes image that I have uncovered shows, in the middle distance, Susan Engel as Queen Elizabeth standing next to Ian Holm as Richard, duke of Gloucester (Figure 4).

FIGURE 4 *On the stage of the Royal Shakespeare Theatre during the television recording of* The Wars of the Roses *in the autumn of 1964, with Susan Engel (Queen Elizabeth) and Ian Holm (Richard, duke of Gloucester). Photograph © BBC.*

Around them are arrayed the technologies of television and of the theatre of the mid-1960s, while standing watchful guard are screen director Michael Hayes, clutching his script, and, partially hidden by a lamp, BBC producer Michael Barry. Absent are the original creators of *The Wars of the Roses* for the Royal Shakespeare Company, Peter Hall and John Barton, who took co-director credits on the stage production of an adaptation 'by John Barton with Peter Hall'. The photograph may well have been taken on 23 November 1964 during the camera rehearsal for a section of *Richard III*, one of the four Shakespeare History plays – along with the three *Henry VI* plays – that Barton and Hall had plundered, condensed, re-ordered and supplemented with new dialogue. The three plays had opened in Stratford-upon-Avon in the summer of 1963, and had transferred to the Aldwych in London for the winter, playing on three separate evenings and, occasionally, across a single day. Almost from their opening performances they were recognized as defining productions for the RSC and for post-war productions of Shakespeare. '*The Wars of the Roses*', Sally Beauman wrote, 'was a triumph for the RSC, and working on them forged a superb company ... The view was shared almost without dissent, by all the critics.'[48]

Peter Hall and John Barton had met more than a decade before as undergraduates at Cambridge University, and Hall had invited Barton to work alongside him at the RSC in 1961. Shakespeare's *Henry VI* trilogy, written early in the playwright's career, had only rarely been played in Britain in modern times, although the Birmingham Repertory Theatre under director Douglas Seale had demonstrated that the plays could be effectively staged in 1951 to 1953. Hall was convinced, as he later wrote, that 'the plays do not work in unadapted form',[49] while his concern, above all, was to make the plays relevant. As Hall recalled, 'Over the years I became more and more fascinated by the contortions of politicians, and by the corrupting seductions experienced by anybody who wields power ... I was convinced that a presentation of one of the bloodiest and most hypocritical periods in history would teach many lessons about the present.'[50] Immediate echoes, albeit with rather less bloody outcomes, could be recognized in 1963 in the machinations of Conservative MPs as the party chose a leader to replace Harold MacMillan and as the Profumo affair played out in Parliament and the tabloid newspapers.[51]

In 1960 the BBC had mounted, also to considerable acclaim, its own original, and rather more faithful, version of the *Henry VI* plays and *Richard III* as part of *An Age of Kings,* an epic fifteen-episode cycle of all eight Histories.[52] The series was also repeated in the summer of 1963, but despite this Head of Drama Sydney Newman and other BBC drama executives recognized, as Head of Single Plays Michael Bakewell later wrote, 'the new version of the plays themselves [in *The Wars of the Roses*] ... was such a remarkable achievement that the whole work emerged in a totally new light and that we need have no fear of covering the same ground again'.[53] At the same time, Bakewell continued:

From the outset all those concerned were intent on finding a new way of presenting Shakespeare on television. Plays had been transmitted from the theatre frequently before ... but these presentations had been patently a theatre performance, observed in the way that outside-broadcast cameras visit a public event or a football match. What was intended for *The Wars of the Roses* was to re-create a theatre production in television terms – not merely to observe it but to get to the heart of it.[54]

Bakewell's metaphor – 'to get to the heart of it' – combines both a spatial sense and one concerned with expressivity, and is key to understanding the particularities of the production approach that was adopted. It was recognized that the only feasible way of recording all three plays was to do so in Stratford at the end of that year's revival. John Bury's steel-deck monster of a set was essential for the impact of the productions, but transferring this to a London studio was logistically unfeasible. Nor did it make financial sense to bring the huge cast to London for rehearsals and recordings. In interview Michael Barry also highlighted a less pragmatic concern: 'The Stratford company is a close professional community, and by going to them we were able to enter into the very special ambience which they had built up by playing as a group for a long period.'[55]

Former Head of Television Drama Michael Barry, who had developed and produced *An Age of Kings*, was invited by Sydney Newman to return to the BBC as a freelance producer to oversee the project. By early February 1964, just a month after *The Wars of the Roses* opened at London's Aldwych Theatre, the BBC drama department was undertaking detailed costings, and on 23 April Holland Bennett's letter of confirmation to the RSC outlined the terms of a deal.[56] The BBC would take over the Stratford theatre for five weeks in November and December for the recording and pay the RSC £3,250 per week for all costs, excluding cast fees. There would be two further weeks of rehearsals (later extended to three). The BBC would in addition pay a management fee of £2,000 for each of the three plays. In the autumn a BBC team of more than fifty, working to directors Michael Hayes and Robin Midgley, recorded the three plays at a cost of more than £80,000, around half of which was fees to the cast. After just two months of editing in January and February, the plays were first broadcast on BBC One at 8.00 pm (with a ten-minute interval for the News) as *Henry VI*, *Edward IV* and *Richard III* on the Thursday evenings of 8, 15 and 22 April 1965. Early the following year, a version re-edited into eleven episodes (the original proposal had been for ten), each approximately (and sometimes very approximately) fifty minutes long was shown on BBC Two; this was also the version that was sold by BBC Enterprises to overseas territories, including a number of National Educational Television stations in the United States.[57]

The plays were recorded on the Royal Shakespeare Theatre stage after considerable alterations to the auditorium. Half of the seats in the stalls were removed and and replaced by an extensive wooden platform for cameras and sound booms. As with any ambitious drama, the scheduling and production technology were determining factors. It was decided to record each play over three days, with two working days between each session, and that on each recording day the team would aim to achieve up to one hour of screen time. Equity studio regulations at the time mandated that no more than three hours of recording could be undertaken for every hour of broadcast drama, and so the recording was restricted to evening sessions, following camera rehearsals during the day. To have sufficient staff to work on the production and to bring seven cameras plus a spare to Stratford, the recording required two Mobile Control Rooms (or MCRs), of which the BBC owned just fifteen, which had to be prised away from their usual duties for *Grandstand* and ballroom dancing. The corporation also had a rather smaller number of zoom lenses. Given the on-going commitment of the lenses to soccer, jazz and the Whitehall farces, allocation of one to Stratford for five weeks was noted in a production memo as 'out of the question'.[58] As a consequence, zoom shots are rare in the finished programmes. The recording itself was made on site on video tape recorders (VTRs), with back-ups recorded on both 16mm and 35mm made in London across a cabled link via Birmingham. But the only mobile VTRs that were available operated on the BBC One 405-line system, so despite a planned showing via 625-line transmission on BBC Two the inferior system had to be used. Hence, in part, the low-resolution quality of the surviving archival programmes, which are also monochrome since the recording of outside broadcasts in colour was still at least three years in the future. New equipment was manufactured especially for the production, including a 'creeper' camera mounting for floor-level shots, and a tower on wheels for a camera to operate at a height of sixteen feet. Perhaps the most distinctive technical innovation was the occasional use of a hand-held Ikegami camera, which was only very rarely employed in drama at the time. Once the shoot was complete editor Roy Clarke worked with the telerecordings, made by filming a monitor on which the electronic images were playing, to create the final production. This was undertaken during just eight weeks throughout January and February, and was followed in a compact post-production schedule by only seven days of sound dubbing in early March.

The effect of the production preparation was, in Michael Bakewell's development of his spatial metaphor, 'to convert the Royal Shakespeare Theatre into a television studio ... and so to adapt the stage that our cameras could involve themselves as deeply as possible in the action'. Bakewell recognized that the conventional approach to recording a play in a theatre with cameras shooting from the auditorium 'in no way penetrates to the centre of what is going on on the stage or involves the audience vitally in the action'.[59] John Caughie has written in similar terms of the innovations in studio technique adopted by *Armchair Theatre* productions at the end of the 1950s. He described the opening shot of *Lena, Oh My Lena* (ABC-TV, 1960) as a long backward tracking shot opening up the studio into a full three-dimensional space ... The objective was quite explicit: the use of the camera as a way of breaking free from the stasis of theatrical space to the mobility of cinematic space.

    This could be interpreted simply as a liberation of the technology, a move towards the fluidity of narrative cinema. It seems to me, however, to be something more specific to the development of television drama. Crucially for notions of realism in television, what is created in plays like *Lena, Oh My Lena* is a performative space – a space for acting – rather than a narrative space – a space for action. The studio remains a studio, but the actors invest it with meaning.[60]

In *The Wars of the Roses*, the theatre space remains a stage but is at the same time the space of a television studio in which the cameras can move freely across the line of the proscenium and within the set. In addition, through the occasionally uneasy introduction of filmic editing techniques, the recording also gestures towards a cinematic space – in Caughie's words, 'a space for action' – which is constructed, in part, by sequences of shots distinct from those achievable in continuous multi-camera recording. Within a hybrid real world space, the production team developed a hybrid screen language weaving together strands of theatre, television technique and film style, which together create the hybrid screen space of the final recording.

    For the viewer in 1965, the theatrical context of *The Wars of the Roses* was established in advance by the explicit presentation of the drama's stage origins. The front cover of *Radio Times* for the week of the first transmission featured a heraldic illustration by Eric Fraser accompanied only by the programme's title, channel and the words 'The Royal Shakespeare Company.' A short preview film transmitted four days before the first broadcast (and which appears not to have survived) took viewers behind-the-scenes in Stratford-upon-Avon, and on each broadcast day the *Radio Times* listing featured 'The Royal Shakespeare Company' in a larger and more prominent font than either the title of the trilogy or that of each individual play. On screen each play begins with the caption 'The British Broadcasting Corporation presents' below the BBC crest before mixing to the RSC's swan logo and then to a card promising 'The Royal Shakespeare Company in ... '. But unlike other television productions from the time that were derived from RSC stagings there is no visual referencing of the theatrical origin. After the initial cards, each part of *The Wars of the Roses* begins with a filmic crash-zoom to a shot of an abstracted metal setting that, accompanied by ominous sound cues of a rushing wind and a metallic clang, appears to fly out towards the viewer. Onto the end of this shot is superimposed the title of the trilogy. The viewer quickly comes to understand that this is an image of the theatrical set but in this first glimpse it has been abstracted from its usual context and cast into an otherwise featureless 'electronic' space. From these first thirty seconds of each programme theatre and television are contending to present and to contain the drama. In a similar manner the closing roller runs over a still frame featuring the all-important throne around which so much of the drama takes place but which in this closing shot is taken from the stage and set in a black void.

John Bury's set was conceived as a giant metal cage and was built around two huge three-sided towers, or periaktoids, dressed with sheets of metal. Combined with a floor of steel plates, this design contributes an insistent materiality. Swords clang on the metal floors, and doors and walls have a weight and solidity entirely distinct from studio sets of the time. So too does the heavy armour of many of the cast, along with their nearly unmanageably weighty broadswords. Certain sequences, especially those on battlefields, are set in an almost empty space of smoke and darkness, but elsewhere the cameras make great play with the grilles and gratings of the theatre set. Many scenes begin 'outside' a grille, including the opening to the first play, *Henry VI*, when the camera penetrates the mesh, which dissolves away, and a crane shot takes the viewer to the centre of the council chamber. The start of such shots, with the viewer distanced from the scene, suggests the original theatrical space whereas the act of entering as the grille parts or dissolves comes courtesy of the television space. At the end of the trilogy, a version was apparently recorded of the final scene of *Richard III* 'where the victorious Richmond strides towards a great network of bars and hacks it to pieces with his sword'. Michael Bakewell has noted that this was eventually rejected because 'the symbolism was right, but it was the wrong form of reality for television'.[61] Yet the production as a whole betrays an uncertainty about quite what the correct form of reality might be. The theatrical design conjures up a symbolic reality of considerable intensity, but this is exposed at times when a more literal realism is introduced. The duke of Burgundy is seen to dismount from a real horse, for example, and dogs sniff around the field of the dead after the Battle of Tewkesbury.

One of the greatest glories of *The Wars of the Roses* as a television recording is that it captures an ensemble of astonishing actors giving exceptional performances. Watch Janet Suzman as Joan la Pucelle in *Henry VI*, Peggy Ashcroft as Queen Margaret berating Donald Sinden's York,[62] and David Warner's King Henry agonizing during the 'molehill' speech,[63] and you are seeing some of the most glorious, intelligent and moving Shakespearean acting for the screen. The cast are working with a remarkably consistent televisual sense of delivery rather than the heightened effect that would have been necessary in the theatre. Almost all of the main characters also speak direct-to-camera for their soliloquies and asides, achieving an intimacy with their confidences that establishes a disarming complicity irrespective of their villainy. At other moments, stage and screen fuse in a performative space that facilitates lengthy speeches to unfold within a single shot that develops by reframings and camera movement but that eschews cuts to alternative angles. In *Henry VI* the wooing of Margaret by Suffolk (William Squire) is played in a single five-minute shot that includes both characters confiding to the camera before a final soliloquy by Suffolk spoken softly in close-up. In the same play York has several lengthy speeches in which his eyeline holds that of the viewer, as does Ian Holm as the scheming Gloucester in *Richard III*. Perhaps the most notable of Holm's confidences in the compelling four-minute shot towards the end of *Edward IV* just after the new king (Roy Dotrice) has astonished his brothers Clarence (Charles Kay) and Gloucester with the news he is to marry the Lady Grey (Susan Engel).

For much of their length the recordings of the three plays utilize the expected conventions of multi-camera studio recording, or what Jeremy Butler has identified as a kind of style-less 'zero degree style'.[64] As part of this, there are frequent occurrences also of frontal two-shots in which characters speak to each other while both are turned to face the camera. Only rarely does the recording use specifically televisual techniques of superimposition, as it does in *Edward IV* when the king is isolated on the battlefield and he encounters, perhaps in his mind's eye, a father who has killed his son and a son who has slaughtered his father. The face of David Warner as Henry is set in close-up in the front of the frame as, first, the camera pans left to reveal a black space beyond him into which the father is electronically inserted and then, without a change of shot, the camera pans right for the similar insertion of the son. Just before the final battle on Bosworth Field in *Richard III*, King Richard is visited by the ghosts of those he has murdered, and the faces of these appear superimposed over his prone head and staring eyes. In his reflections on the programmes, Michael Bakewell called such shots 'television tricks' and acknowledged their potential for disruption when he wrote, 'One of the basic points of the operation was that the viewer should be conscious neither of the theatrical origin of the works nor of their television interpretation ... The whole aim was to make use of the device [of superimposition] as sparingly as possible. In fact, [with Richard before Bosworth] it palled very quickly and the sequence shortened.'[65] The conventional television screen language is also disrupted at times by cinematic editing, by the use of cameras positioned both at height and close to the ground, and by a number of rapidly cut montages. In the scene in *Henry VI* before the walls of Orleans, for example, a low-set camera looks up to the top of the walls where Joan la Pucelle is seated at a height impossible to achieve in the drama studios of Lime Grove or Television Centre. The scene cuts to a shot looking down on the English from over the shoulder of Joan, which can only have been achieved by editing in post-production. This scene of the siege also features the first of a number of rapidly cut montages of a melee. A comparably filmic montage of cannon shots and fighting men is included in the climactic scene at Bosworth towards the end of *Richard III*, when there is also the most notable employment of the hand-held camera in the urgent physical clash between Richmond and Richard from which the former eventually emerges victorious. The visceral effect is of direct involvement in the fight, with a cinematic sense of action contrasting with the theatrical distance of earlier exchanges of threats.

The unresolved sense of the production's dramatic reality, along with the range of camera and editing techniques that resist cohering into a unified style, together disrupt the unity of the television *The Wars of the Roses*. As a consequence a tension is exposed between the production's theatrical origin and the imperatives of television's presentation. Michael Bakewell's own uncertainty about the status of the final production can be identified in the contradiction between his assertion that 'on the whole what was seen on the screen differed minimally from what was seen at Stratford' and, in the same essay, 'As in so many other moments in the operation it was found that the most successful way of conveying the spirit of the Hall and Barton production was not to imitate what they had done but to achieve the same aim by doing something that would prove more effective in television terms.'[66] After the first broadcast in April 1965, Sydney Newman sent a warm letter of congratulation to Michael Barry in which he wrote, 'Technically the shows were the finest that I have ever seen which have come from a theatre. So beautifully did they work out, I'm sure very few people indeed knew that they weren't studio productions.'[67]

For Newman *The Wars of the Roses* was most definitely television, as he believed that to achieve their aesthetic potential the programmes must be. And yet as the opening titles demonstrated the trilogy retained the prestige and cultural capital of the RSC. Moreover, although this is not unique to *The Wars of the Roses*, by recording the series the BBC acquired some of the cultural capital of Shakespeare and of a theatrical tradition that in a deep way was part of the identity of England and the English. As was the case from the earliest days of television, the BBC wanted and needed the theatre (and far from only as source material), but – and never more so than in this moment in the mid-1960s of increasing (and justified) self-confidence as a medium – television wanted and needed to be *television*.

Endgame at the BBC

After the broadcast of *The Wars of the Roses*, the RSC retained a prominent presence on BBC Television in the mid-1960s. As is discussed below, the next substantial appearance of the RSC was in a curiosity that was part documentary and part performance. *Sunday Night: How to Stop Worrying and Love the Theatre* is focused on the company's *Theatregoround* project, and this and a profile of Peter Hall in *The Impresarios* series exposed the company in new ways.[68] In addition, two post-*Monitor* BBC Two arts magazine programmes produced items about contemporary playwrights working with the RSC. *New Release* profiled David Mercer and featured studio-shot scenes from the Aldwych production of his new drama *Belcher's Luck*, as well as interviews with David Warner and R.D. Laing.[69] Two years later, *Release* included extensive rehearsal scenes from *The Latent Heterosexual* by Paddy Chayefsky that was being staged by the RSC for an American season at the Aldwych.[70] Before the decade was done there was also a short film for *Release* titled *Lear at Stratford*. Eric Porter, by this point acclaimed for his performance as Soames in *The Forsyte Saga*, opened the Stratford season as Lear in Trevor Nunn's production.[71] The programme featured the dialogue between Lear and the Fool in Act 1, Scene 5 being developed in rehearsal and then played in costume on stage. Finally, in 1969, one of the more unconventional appearances of the RSC on television was a contribution to episode 6 of the BBC series *Civilisation*, written and presented by Kenneth Clark. To illustrate Clark's consideration of Shakespeare the company provided the services of three actors for a fragment of *Hamlet*: Ronald Lacey (gravedigger), Patrick Stewart (Horatio) and Ian Richardson (Hamlet).

Most substantially, there were two further adaptations before the company set its sights on the silver screen. *Days in the Trees* (1967), translated from Marguerite Duras's first full-length drama, was screened in *The Wednesday Play* strand; no copy is known to exist. And currently the BBC Archive holds only the first hour of a glowing colour version of John Barton's production of *All's Well That Ends Well* (1968). These recordings, discussed below, reached the screen as the company was increasingly struggling with questions of identity and definition, as well as with severe financial problems. 'From 1965 onwards', Sally Beauman has written, 'the work of the RSC under Hall began to decline, slowly at first, then more rapidly.'[72] There was a feeling shared by many both inside the company and beyond that *The Wars of the Roses* was an artistic peak, and something fundamentally different would be needed for the next stage.

Fledgling director Michael Kustow had set up the RSC Club as a membership organization to bring the company closer to its audiences, and he would go on to work at the National Theatre and in the 1980s be Arts Commissioning Editor at Channel 4. In September 1965 he launched *Theatregoround* as a small touring production of extracts performed by six RSC actors. They played in a number of inner London boroughs, and as Colin Chambers has written, 'the idea was to overcome the socially divisive protocols of theatre-going and take performances to potential audiences in venues of their own milieu'.[73] This would become a commonplace strategy for alternative theatre groups in the near future, but it was sufficiently novel for the idea to be taken up by the BBC for a programme in its *Sunday Night* strand of arts features.

The fifty-minute programme was shot primarily with electronic cameras by a mobile outside broadcast unit at Rutherford School, Paddington, but it begins with a film sequence that discovers reporter René Cutforth outside the Aldwych Theatre where Peter Brook's RSC production of *Marat/Sade* is playing. Cutforth, known as a current affairs broadcaster, reflects on the limited audience that the RSC is reaching and poses this question: 'Shouldn't [the RSC] be reaching out to persuade a very much wider public that this is the place for them, and that plays are for them too?' After interview comments from Peter Hall, the programme shifts to a rehearsal session that the viewer's intermediary Cutforth interrupts by asking Michael Kustow, 'Tell me what it is you're trying to do.' To which the remainder of the programme responds with generous extracts from performance, further thoughts from Kustow and Hall, and and a selection of sceptical vox pop responses. The cast of six – Michelle Dotrice, Gabrielle Hamilton, Paul Hardwick, Davyd Harries, Michael Jayston and Richard Moore – perform in everyday clothes on a raised hexagonal platform with a curtain as backdrop. A scene from *Arden of Faversham* is played as fast, broad comedy with an interpolated narrator on stage explaining the action. Other extracts include Proteus and his dog Crab from *The Two Gentlemen of Verona*, the St Crispin's Day speech from *Henry V*, Hamlet's instructions to the Players, fragments of Molière's *Scapin the Schemer*, the Victorian melodrama *Under the Gaslight* and *The Birthday Party* by Harold Pinter. Together these bear out Michael Kustow's subsequent characterization of *Theatregoround* as a 'misguided, lunatic and yet rather worthwhile attempt to tell the history of the theatre in an hour and half'.[74]

Peter Hall took the starring role in a half-hour documentary in the series *The Impresarios* narrated and directed by Melvyn Bragg that was broadcast eighteen months later. Hall opens the film by speaking about the tension in his professional life between being a creative director and 'an absolute fascination in business, management, executive decisions, organising things' that running the RSC demands. He is observed filming and editing *Work is a Four Letter Word* but most of the documentary is devoted to Stratford. After seeing him at home and driving his sports car to work, the film captures Hall addressing the company, including a glum-looking Paul Scofield, at the start of rehearsals for *Macbeth*. There are scenes in the RSC's administrative offices and the workshops, an introduction to the new associate director Trevor Nunn, and a discussion with designer John Bury about the scenic vision for *Macbeth*. There are no substantial scenes of stage performances, but camera and microphone eavesdrop on David Jones rehearsing Alan Howard and Dorothy Tutin for *As You Like It* and John Barton huddling with Ian Richardson just before the second night of *All's Well That Ends Well*. But there are only passing references to funding problems and the RSC's thorny relationship with the Arts Council of Great Britain.

Earlier in 1967, BBC Television had broadcast a studio production of one of a handful of new European plays that Peter Hall had programmed in London in the summer of the previous year. Maguerite Duras's *Days in the Trees*, dismissed by Sally Beauman as 'a novelist's play that remained obstinately novelistic',[75] was staged by John Schlesinger, who had directed *Timon of Athens* for the RSC the year before. He was already celebrated as a film director, and he was working on *Far From the Madding Crowd* by the time the television version came to be recorded. The production at the Aldwych was greeted by the critics with lukewarm enthusiasm tempered only by rapturous responses to Peggy Ashcroft's central performance. The presence of this stalwart star of the company's first years, together with the need to fulfil the contracted annual pair of adaptations, led the BBC to commit to its recording. We have no archival copy of it, but production correspondence in the BBC Written Archives and a short *Radio Times* preview detail that the television version, directed by Waris Hussein, opened with scenes filmed at Orly airport near Paris. A mother (Ashcroft) returns from a French colony and is greeted coldly by her son, the desolate gigolo Jacques (George Baker).[76] Jacques takes his mother back to the dismal club where he works and introduces her to his mistress, Marcelle (Frances Cuka). The audience was mostly unimpressed, although according to the Audience Research Report, 'a number of viewers ... admired the writing of *Days in the Trees* for its "stripped down" observation of a relationship, at once "sensitive and cruel, warm and blurred", between three well-defined characters ... caught in a process of mutual attrition and debasement'.[77]

Just over a year after this disappointing broadcast, the final BBC-RSC collaboration of the decade was considerably more celebrated. Of the studio production of *All's Well That Ends Well*, directed for the stage by John Barton and for the screen by Claude Whatham, Stanley Reynolds wrote that it was 'the first televised Shakespeare I have seen that looked actually a television play and not like something roughly transplanted from the stage. In fact it is not fullsome [*sic*] to say the production and acting made *All's Well That Ends Well* look as though it were made for television.'[78] First in Stratford (where the production opened in June 1967) and then at the Aldwych (from January 1968) the critical consensus was that this was a modest, elegant production that improved significantly on the transfer to London. The cast had strength in depth and as B.A. Young noted after the London press night, 'The speaking of the verse by the whole company is better than I have heard it for a long time – intelligent, poetic, pointed.'[79] Transferred to the studio in mid-May 1968, *All's Well That Ends Well* was the first British small-screen production of Shakespeare to be recorded in colour (Figure 5). BBC Television's second channel BBC Two had been on air for four years when *All's Well That Ends Well* was broadcast in the *Theatre 625* strand on the spring bank holiday. Regular broadcasts in colour had started on 1 July the previous year, and the output by now was mostly but not entirely in colour. In her book *Spectacular Television*, Helen Wheatley argued that 'a "restrained" and genteel colour palette, as opposed to the "brashness" and "gaudiness" of American colour, was written into television policy in the mid-1960s ... [T]his was interpreted as a search for authentic, realist or "natural" colour by BBC management and programme makers, as opposed to a more "spectacular" version of television colour.'[80] The subdued palette employed by television designer Susan Spence for *All's Well That Ends Well* exemplifies this approach. Following the look established on stage by designer Timothy O'Brien, the interior settings, at least in the surviving half of the production, are silvery-grey and light brown, while the stylized exteriors are shot against a bright cyclorama, with a pale green wash on the floor and ornamental elements of deeper green. The dominant tones

FIGURE 5 *Ian Richardson (Bertram), Clive Swift (Parolles), Daniel Moynihan (Dumaine the Elder) and Phillip Hinton (Dumaine the Younger) during the BBC studio recording of John Barton's production of* All's Well That Ends Well *(1968); the original is in vivid colour. Photograph by Reg Wilson © RSC.*

of the costumes (by O'Brien and Tazeena Firth) are blacks and beiges and dark blues, but Helen's dress, indicative of her social separation from the court world, is pale yellow. The insincere and blustering Captain Parolles (played by Clive Swift), also an interloper, wears red breeches and sports brightly coloured feathers in his extravagant cobalt-coloured hat. As Lafeu (Nicholas Selby) says of him, 'The soul of this man is his clothes' (2.5.43– 44). Following the lead of the theatre, colour is used meaningfully to help define character and delineate relationships. Similarly, while Robert Wright's bright and even studio lighting for the most part adheres to the norms of early colour production, there are nonetheless moments when it too is used more expressively. At the end of Act 2, Scene 5 Bertram and Parolles walk off together to the wars, away from the camera and into silhouette in a darkness offered by the depth of the studio. The effect is echoed when Helen too determines to leave the court at the conclusion of Act 3, Scene 2 (which is also the moment that the extant recording ends).

According to *Radio Times*, stage director John Barton (who also took an 'adapted by' credit) worked very closely with the television director Claude Whatham, and the latter's use of the studio's electronic cameras is highly assured. Especially notable is the way in which Helen, the Countess of Roussillon (Catherine Lacey), the Clown (Ian Hogg) and others use direct address for soliloquies to confide to the camera (and the viewer). The effect enhances the intimacy of the production and is used especially to solicit a sympathetic response to Helen. Direct address, the stylized setting and the use of symmetrical framings all stress the artificiality of the drama, emphasizing the superficiality of the two courts, against which Helen's sincerity is accentuated. Whatham also choreographs his cameras in fluid motions to assemble formal groupings or to isolate individuals. Helen's reflections especially are gracefully accompanied with extended, developing moves, such as for her first lament, 'O, were that all!' (1.1.77–96). As a consequence, the confident visuals underscore Helen's place at the moral centre of this world. All of which contributes to the clarity and beauty of this jewel-like adaptation, and only emphasizes how regrettable it is that the second half of the recording is lost. A similar sense of regret is prompted too by the fact that, despite the successes of the previous decade, after *All's Well That Ends Well* there was to be no further BBC television recording of a full RSC production during the next seventeen years.

By the time that *All's Well That Ends Well* was broadcast, as is discussed in Chapter 3, RSC management, and most especially Peter Hall, were in thrall to Hollywood and focused on significantly larger screens with their associated financial allure. Yet perhaps moving away from television was also something of a relief to some in the company who, during a decade when the medium confirmed its centrality in the social, political and cultural lives of almost every citizen, retained a strain of suspicion towards a contemporary 'upstart crow'. Traces of a wariness about television, combined with a belief in the fundamental superiority of the far more venerable form, can perhaps be identified in the scrappy and sporadically published newsletter *Flourish*, which was sent out to RSC members between the summer of 1964 and early 1974.[81] Several issues of *Flourish* feature cautious, critical engagements with television as a medium, as in the second issue's unsigned editorial, which was almost certainly written by Michael Kustow. A jeremiad about 'mass communications', a catch-all term for 'television, long-play records and swift printing in large quantities', proposes that while this has brought benefits 'this vast apparatus of dissemination has also created new dangers. It seems that beyond a certain size, an apparatus of communication tends to foster uniformity, standardization, simplification; to present life at its lowest common denominator, life with its edges rubbed off.' The theatre, however, is different – and better, since it 'can still go beyond the simple questions, still probe our more disturbing depths, shake our complacent allegiances – and can do so in ways that startle and delight us. The theatre can still express our astonishment at living.'[82] Just over two years later, in an article headlined 'Live theatre dead?', *Flourish* reprised its defensiveness about theatre in face of the threat from television. Terence Hawkes had delivered two radio talks, and in the second, according to an anonymous contributor to *Flourish*, he had 'suggested that television was effuctively [*sic*] the already-existing answer to many of the pleas and aspirations voiced by the apologists of live theatre'. The newsletter printed sections of Hawkes's argument (which had already been published in *The Listener*) and offered rebuttals that managed to be both snide and largely unconvincing. One of Hawkes's arguments ran as follows:

> television offers an almost Elizabethan comprehension of the world; it is the new *theatrum mundi*, the 'Globe', as Shakespeare's own theatre had it. For the television experience will yield not only plays as we traditionally conceive them, but also the larger area of 'drama' covered by news bulletins, comedy shows, music, and other diverse activities, *in the same unit* ... The play written for television gains from the surrounding events *on* screen ... The gain, simply, is the immense, fully dramatic and disturbing dimension of universality and inclusiveness.[83]

Which prompts the squib, 'I think this is wishful assertion, and nothing I have ever experienced in front of my own TV screen makes me believe it.'[84] Yet *The Wars of the Roses*, both on stage and on screen, had drawn for its power not only on Shakespeare's texts, and John Barton and Peter Hall's rewriting and staging but also on exactly the 'drama' of the contemporary world experienced through the television screen. For the next few years, however, the RSC's corporate interest, and the individual imperatives driving Peter Hall and Peter Brook as screen directors, was making movies.

3

Making Movies, 1964–73

Fruitful as the RSC's relationship with BBC Television was in the 1960s, the company also began to develop other media options. The minutes of the RSC's Executive Council suggest that for those leading the organization the cinema was the prize that was especially coveted, in large part because movies were believed to be a solution to the company's persistently precarious finances. In the chase for Hollywood's dollars Peter Hall and the council signed up to a three-picture deal with American production entity Filmways, although by the turn of the decade this proved to be deeply unsatisfactory. In parallel, and with rather different motivations, Peter Brook pursued a characteristically individual path to make films from three of his RSC productions. Central to all of this was film producer and RSC governor Michael Birkett, son of a prominent barrister and inheritor in 1962 of a peerage. The fruits of Lord Birkett and Peter Hall hitching the company to Hollywood included a film adaptation of Hall's venerable production of *A Midsummer Night's Dream* and then a crisis when Paul Scofield's withdrawal caused the abandonment of a contracted version of *Macbeth*. The joint venture also led to *King Lear* (1971), made by Brook, Birkett and Scofield in an arrangement that had only a tangential connection with the theatre company. Yet this powerful film is perhaps the most radical screen version of any RSC stage production. The hoped-for dollars, however, remained frustratingly elusive, and as the company entered the 1970s, the fall-out from the Filmways failure continued. The RSC was forced to recognize that its saviour as a financially challenged theatre company was not to be the cinema.

A future 'bound up with films'

In Peter Hall's first years the relationship with the BBC was welcomed as a way to extend the RSC's audiences, to ensure high-quality recordings for the archives and to earn modest fees. Nonetheless, as early as autumn 1963 there were stirrings of a more expansive vision for the RSC on screen. At the meeting of the Executive Council of the Governors on 25 September, the American journalist and historian Herbert Agar proposed that agents be appointed to promote RSC productions for cinema and television filming. The agreement with the BBC, it was noted, which in any case gave the corporation only 'first refusal' on any stage production, was due to expire at the end of the year (although as noted it was later extended). According to the minutes, Agar said that 'it would be the agent's function to suggest ways of making money whilst maintaining our artistic integrity, and that considerable financial benefit could be realised'.[1] The gathering approved an approach to the agents suggested by Agar, Christopher Mann Ltd.[2] Compared to the £2,000 management fee paid per production by the BBC, the profit from the BHE filming of *The Hollow Crown* was estimated in January 1965 at the rather more meaningful level of £12,000.[3] The following year the Executive Council was informed that the RSC would receive around £7,000 from the filming of Peter Brook's production of *Marat/Sade*.[4] By the summer of 1966, Peter Hall, working with Michael Birkett, who was producing the *Marat/Sade* film, had plans for further film productions to put before the governors. Although nothing significant had to date come from the efforts of Christopher Mann Ltd, Dick Patterson, the individual agent assigned to the RSC, enthused in a letter to Peter Hall that 'people still insist on thrusting money at us'. The producer David Susskind had just called, having had a success on American television with a production of *Death of a Salesman*.[5] Susskind had 'discovered Culture', Patterson wrote, and, 'As there is no one more full of Culture than us, he has been talking to me.'[6] For the right to tape a RSC production for television, Susskind was offering US$50,000, plus a percentage of profits, which was double what Hubbell Robinson Productions had paid seven years before for *A Midsummer Night's Dream*. But Patterson was unconvinced, maintaining in the letter that, 'I still think I am right about *Macbeth* and *Lear* – that we are to go to film and cinemas first.' The company might, however, 'flog' *Twelfth Night*[7] to Susskind, since the BBC appeared not to want it, although Susskind's enthusiasm subsequently waned.

In the mid-1960s Hollywood was thrusting money not only at the RSC but at the British film industry more generally. At the end of the previous decade social realist movies like *Room at the Top* (1959) and *Saturday Night and Sunday Morning* (1960) were the only bright spots in a production slump from which British filmmakers clambered with talent and properties from the theatre. *A Taste of Honey* (1961) and *Billy Liar* (1963) were among the stage hits that became successful films and Tony Richardson and Lindsay Anderson were newly celebrated directors who had come to prominence with their work at the Royal Court. Rising star Albert Finney went from playing Edgar at Stratford to shooting *Saturday Night and Sunday Morning*, and in 1961 the RSC attempted unsuccessfully to hold company member Peter O'Toole to his theatre commitments rather than see him leave to film David Lean's *Lawrence of Arabia* (1962). Having turned down that role, Finney starred in the British production that was commercially so successful that it made American producers look longingly towards London: the Tony Richardson-directed period comedy *Tom Jones* (1963). The film was financed by United Artists, which had also signed up the James Bond franchise (*Dr. No*, 1962; *From Russia with Love*, 1963) and The Beatles, whose first film *A Hard Day's Night* was released in 1964. West Coast producers were increasingly attracted to a production context that not only spawned international hits but also offered lower costs than California plus subsidy monies from the Eady levy. Moreover, London was seen as culturally vibrant, and among its attractions was the RSC led by its youthful, Aston Martin-driving, black T-shirt wearing director, Peter Hall. As Robert Murphy has written,

> London was seen as the centre of a youth-oriented cultural revolution which young Americans found fascinating and appealing. By the mid-60s all the majors and two mini-majors – Filmways and Avco-Embassy – had set up British production subsidiaries. According to the NFFC [National Film Finance Corporation], by 1966 75 per cent of production finance came from American sources. A year later it was 90 per cent.[8]

March 1966 saw the first of the RSC's close encounters with a Hollywood newly committed to producing in Britain. Director Sidney Lumet was in London shooting *A Deadly Affair*, an adaptation of John Le Carré's spy novel *Call for the Dead*. For a ten-minute sequence close to the end of the movie Lumet asked Peter Hall to stage scenes from Christopher Marlowe's *Edward II*. Shot at the Lyric Hammersmith, these feature David Warner as the king and members of the company including Michael Bryant and Timothy West. Short sections of Act 1, Scene 1, and Act 5, Scenes 3 and 5 are played in full costume on a bare set. During the last scene, in parallel with the play's sodomitical killing, an East German espionage chief (Maximilian Schell) silently throttles his erstwhile agent (Simone Signoret) as they sit together in the stalls. 'Broadly speaking', Deborah Willis has argued, 'the film's use of *Edward II* highlights the themes of shifting loyalties, intimate betrayals and state-sanctioned atrocities with which this spy story is also concerned.'[9] The employment of what is featured as the Royal Shakespeare Theatre Company, advertised as such in lights outside the Aldwych theatre, also strengthens the company's association, especially after *The Wars of the Roses*, with the resonances of early modern drama illuminating contemporary *realpolitik*.

Another RSC brush with celluloid in 1966, on a more modest scale, was the filming of part of Hamlet's 'Am I a coward?' soliloquy (2.2.502–37) as performed by David Warner in the celebrated Peter Hall staging. The production had opened in Stratford in August 1965 before transferring triumphantly to the Aldwych. Warner's incarnation of the prince as a truculent teenager was hailed as excitingly contemporary, and a younger-than-usual audience queued through the night for tickets. The idea of a film of the whole production figured at one point in the Filmways negotiations, although this ultimately came to nothing. 'Theatre is ephemeral,' Peter Hall wrote in his autobiography, 'it should burst like a bubble once it has ceased to live before its audience. But there are times when I find myself wishing that I could re-experience performances of the past. David's Hamlet is one of them. It lives for many people as the moment when they realised that Hamlet is always our contemporary.'[10] The only moving-image trace of the production, however, is a 147-second unedited shot preserved in the half-hour documentary *Opus* (1967). A quirky, exuberantly visual montage from the city that *Time* magazine in April 1966 had identified as 'swinging London',[11] *Opus* was produced by the Central Office of Information for screening in the British pavilion at Montreal's international exhibition Expo '67. Bearing witness to the cultural centrality of the RSC at this moment, scenes from two other company productions are also included, although both of these stagings would also be filmed *in toto*. Peter Brook is seen in the studio shooting *Marat/Sade* and there is an exchange between Ian Holm (as Tom) and Vivien Merchant (Ruth) from the first act of Harold Pinter's *The Homecoming*.

Making movies emerged in the summer of 1966 as both a corporate priority for the RSC and a personal one for Peter Hall. In a newspaper interview in June, Hall expressed his belief that 'the future of our company is bound up with films … [although] I can't see us ever calling ourselves the Royal MGM Shakespeare Company or anything like that'.[12] At the July Executive Council meeting, Hall pointed out that he had been working for the RSC for seven years and had only twice taken on an outside directing job. He now wished to make a film (which would eventually become *Work is a Four Letter Word*) early the following year, and he asked the governors for eight weeks' leave of absence annually. Two months later, the Executive Council embraced the more general notion that the RSC itself should produce films. Theatre impresario Emile Littler objected on the grounds of the possible deleterious effect of film on live audiences, but its new chair George Farmer, who as his day job ran the Coventry-based Rover car company, weighed against this the belief that 'the films would reach an audience which would be unobtainable in other ways'.[13] The outline of a plan had been drawn up over the summer and was recorded in two detailed documents: a note, shared with the governors, of a 29 June discussion at which Michael Birkett explained the proposed framework to George Farmer, and a 25 July letter from Birkett to Peter Hall summarizing a recent discussion involving the two of them together with Peter Brook and Dick Patterson. The fundamental principle Farmer was concerned about was that any RSC film venture should be risk-free but with the potential to see significant financial returns. Such a utopian deal, seeking profit without risking pain, is one to which many have aspired, only to see their plans go awry. As was to be the case with the RSC and their chosen partner, Filmways Inc.

The film that Peter Hall took company leave to direct was his debut feature *Work is a Four Letter Word*. Released in 1968, this began life as Henry Livings's comedy *Eh?*, staged by Hall as a RSC production in London from October 1964.[14] A popular success at the Aldwych, *Eh?* wraps a clumsy critique of mechanization inside a farce about a boiler-room operative who has taken his job so as to have a place to cultivate mushrooms. Contemporary reviews suggest that the production's primary attractions included David Warner as the mushroom grower Valentine Brose, and John Bury's spectacular steaming and groaning set. By the time Peter Hall came to shoot the film early in 1967, only Warner remained from the original cast, along with Livings's central characters and just a smattering of his dialogue. To pen the substantially revised screenplay, Hall employed novelist Jeremy Brooks who had joined the RSC as literary manager in 1964. Brooks and Hall filleted the play, opening up its single setting to spread the absurdist action throughout a sprawling factory complex, an associated office block and the homes of Valentine and his *fiancée* Betty Dorrick. Singer Cilla Black made her acting debut as Betty and trilled the title song. In addition to playing up the overall air of wacky 'youthfulness', the film significantly enhanced the hallucinogenic quality of Valentine's mushrooms, signalling this much earlier than in the play and transforming the closing sequence into an extended turned-on love-in. Between the play's premiere and the film's production, LSD and magic mushrooms became far more central to pop culture on both sides of the Atlantic, and the screen adaptation now appears as a monstrously misconceived attempt to respond to this.

The film was financed and produced by the Hollywood studio Universal Pictures. Central to the decade's American take-over of Britain's film industry, Universal under production executive Jay Kanter funded an extensive and eclectic programme of British features. Ultimately without achieving box office success, Kanter backed emerging directors including Karel Reisz, Peter Watkins and Jack Gold as well as Hall, who would also make *Two into Three Won't Go* (1968) for Universal. Like the financing, production of *Work is a Four Letter Word* was organized quite separately from the RSC, although the cast featured company members including Elizabeth Spriggs, Tony Church and Alan Howard.[15] In his overview of British cinema in the 1960s Robert Murphy characterized *Work is a Four Letter Word* as 'messily indulgent'.[16] But such a judgement is too kind for a film that employs racial and sexual stereotypes (Aly is a fussy, flummoxed Asian; Betty, a dim-witted aspirant bride) in ways that have to be excused by their historical moment to be even watchable now. Six years after the film's release, Hall himself recognized the failure of the film: 'Appalling experience tonight. *Work is a Four Letter Word*, my first film, was on BBC 2. I made it in 1968 when I didn't know how to direct films and was anyway going through a very bad patch. Excuses? I suppose so. I watched with glazed horror.'[17]

Hollywood, Stratford

By the summer of 1966 the RSC's film agent Dick Patterson was talking seriously with a suitor. In June, Hall was pleased to let slip to *The Sunday Times* that an American company had approached the RSC with an offer to make five films. Not only would these be seen in cinema and on television but, as the journalist paraphrased Hall, 'they will be turned into long-playing visual records. You buy the tape, just like a gramophone record, then slot it into your TV set and watch when you want.'[18] The far-sighted executive holding out both a cheque and a vision of videotaped Shakespeare was Martin ('Marty') Ransohoff, who at the end of 1965 had set up a London office for his 'mini-major', Filmways Inc. In the mid-1960s Filmways was known for its low-brow 'rural comedies' on the CBS Television network, including *The Beverly Hillbillies* (1962–71), as well as classier feature production, such as the Jules Dassin-directed heist movie *Topkapi* (1964). Now Filmways, backed by a commitment for television sales to CBS, wanted to work with the RSC. With Michael Birkett, Peter Hall and Peter Brook, they conceived an initial group of three feature films for the next two years, with Hall directing *A Midsummer Night's Dream* and *Macbeth*, and Peter Brook making *King Lear* with Paul Scofield. *Dream* and *Lear* were to be based on productions that had been successful in the theatre, while *Macbeth*, also with Scofield, was to be shot after a stage version that would premiere the following year.

The RSC was sufficiently confident of the deal that at the end of July 1966 it announced the project, albeit without mentioning Filmways. The RSC Executive Council, however, remained cautious, as it was deeply concerned about the company's balance sheet. At its September meeting George Farmer revealed that across the years from 1960 to 1966 the company had a cash deficit of £145,000, which had been covered in part by sales of investments. The Filmways offer included the payment during the period 1967–68 of facility fees of £17,500 each for *Dream* and *Macbeth*. Filmways would arrange the funding and, seemingly, there was no financial risk for the RSC. Moreover, additional monies might be earned from a percentage of the profits of the films. Committing to this, however, was a matter of some urgency, as Michael Birkett detailed in a letter sent on 9 August to Peter Hall. The deal was dependent on Paul Scofield agreeing to both *Macbeth* and *King Lear*, and Hall had been expressing some concern about overworking the actor. Birkett outlined the context of the mini-boom in Shakespeare and other classical titles for the cinema, including the successful film he had made with Peter Brook of *Marat/Sade*, the National Theatre *Othello* (premiered as a Royal Command Film Performance on 5 May), Orson Welles's *Henry IV* adaptation *Chimes at Midnight* (recently screened at the Cannes Film Festival), and the forthcoming Royal Ballet film of Kenneth MacMillan's *Romeo and Juliet* with Margot Fonteyn and Rudolph Nureyev.[19] The RSC should not miss this moment, Birkett argued. Among the assurances that

George Farmer on behalf of the RSC looked for was that the £35,000 in fees was non-returnable, that the seven-year option that Filmways expected did not bind the company to making further films (only to offer those it did wish to make to Filmways first) and, once more, that the company had no financial risk. External legal advice stressed to Birkett, Hall and Patterson that the proposed contract was not quite as generous as perhaps the council believed, that the fees were dependent on agreed budgets not being exceeded, and that the company might well be 'liable in damages if it fails to deliver any of the agreed films'.[20]

In November CBS, Filmways and the RSC announced a long-term agreement. Peter Hall was concerned to stress that the RSC would have complete creative control, and also, as he said, 'The productions will not just be a picture of a stage production. The plays will be completely re-thought in film terms.'[21] Speaking to the *Daily Telegraph*, he stressed the importance of the arrangement: 'Before this deal ... [w]e had to cut large-scale productions at the Aldwych, which means no Shakespeare in our London theatre, and we had to do revivals at Stratford. The film money only goes some way towards meeting the situation, but it will make it possible for us to do Shakespeare at the Aldwych.'[22] Negotiations about the details, however, continued into the early months of 1967. A dominant concern for Filmways was securing guarantees that Hall, Brook, Diana Rigg (already slated for the *Dream* and, thanks to *The Avengers* television series, acknowledged as a star by Marty Ransohoff) and especially Paul Scofield, would indeed make the films to which their names were attached. This was eventually resolved to Filmways' satisfaction at the end of July with signatures on Letters of Commitment, although the documents left fees and potential profit participations to be resolved at a later date. Scofield's letter also gave him an effective right of veto over the making of a film of *Macbeth*, with his agent insisting on a clause stipulating that agreement between the RSC, Filmways and Scofield himself would be necessary for *Macbeth* to proceed.

Less than a year later the lack of precision on fees and Scofield's veto were both to prove fundamentally problematic. Moreover, by the spring of 1967 the theatre production of *Macbeth* was already in trouble, as it had not yet opened because Peter Hall's illness had pushed back its press night. The RSC meanwhile was now completely dependent on the fees of £35,000 to make up, along with an Arts Council grant, a significant shortfall of £227,000 in its 1967/8 budget. The Executive Council was also exercised by what they saw as management's failure to secure any real involvement in two other film projects. At the 19 April 1967 meeting Peter Hall had to report that Peter Brook was proceeding with a film of his controversial devised production about Vietnam, *US*, which was to be made independently of the RSC because an oversight meant that film rights had not been reserved by the company. And while Hall's RSC production of Harold Pinter's *The Homecoming* was a success on Broadway, the film rights to this were controlled by the American producer. As the minutes record, 'It was noted that was another example of an unfavourable contract.' The recently appointed company administrator Derek Hornby was charged with ensuring that such mistakes were not repeated.[23]

Principal photography for *A Midsummer Night's Dream* began at the Warwickshire estate of Compton Verney in late September 1967. Journalists invited on location visits during the five-week shoot commented on the inclement weather. 'It is not very mid-summery,' wrote David Nathan. 'The winds ripple the lake surface and the rain occasionally streaks down.'[24] An indication of Peter Hall's approach was given by Michael Birkett a few days before completion: 'I think that when you start something like this film – which is not in any way tricksy or gimmicky, it is a very simple, straightforward, common sense attempt to film Shakespeare – in a way that nobody has tried before, one is naturally apprehensive at the beginning to see if it succeeds.'[25] Speaking earlier in the year, Peter Hall had expressed a related aspiration:

> I want to be very faithful to Shakespeare and to do the text almost complete. But then the play is in many ways a film script made ready. And for me one of the most exciting things about the cinema is … it can bore right into a text, the camera can photograph the inside of actors as well as their outsides.[26]

Just before the end of filming, when the unit had moved inside after shooting for a month in the muddy forest, Peter Hall was interviewed again about his intentions: 'I'm trying to do it completely without illustrative scenes: there are no shots without dialogue. If you're doing Shakespeare it must be Shakespeare – there is no point in "cinematic" purely pictorial scenes. What we're doing is using the camera to make Shakespeare more ambiguous, more subtle – and more human.'[27]

Just before the end of filming the Executive Council were assured that despite the bad weather the shoot had gone well, and that Michael Birkett and Peter Hall were pleased with the results. 'The latest figures', the minutes noted, 'showed that it would not be tremendously over budget.'[28] Just over a month later, however, Birkett was considerably less optimistic in a letter to Derek Hornby; 'it looks as if we shall be badly over the top', he wrote, noting that even the £25,000 contingency would not cover the additional costs.[29] The post-production was far more expensive than envisaged, and an enormous amount of film stock had been used to ensure completion of the film by 7 November. Birkett also complained vociferously about the company's charges for costumes and other elements, and expressed his conviction that the production could have secured these elements more cheaply from other suppliers. Integrating the production schedule with that of the theatre had caused additional problems. Also, 'I had not of course reckoned on making the film ankle-deep in mud.' *Macbeth*, he promised, would be easier and more controllable, not least because it was planned to be shot in the studio. The contracted £17,500 fee, however, was a budget item that remained unaffected, although the excess costs would lower the RSC's share of future profits.

As post-production continued in early 1968, however, the RSC's plans were hit by a further blow when Paul Scofield decided in February that he no longer wished to film *Macbeth*. By April, Filmways was refusing even to make the payment of the fee for the *Dream*, at least until the RSC could guarantee that Scofield would honour the plans for *King Lear*. All of which precipitated a protracted legal tussle. At the 28 June Executive Council meeting the recently knighted Sir George Farmer had to explain (in the 'unfortunate' absence of Michael Birkett) that *Dream* had gone 50 per cent over budget, that fees and the costs of costumes owing to the company might be irrecoverable, and that the commercial entity set up to produce the films, Royal Shakespeare Enterprises Ltd, might well have to declare insolvency. Fortuitously, the anticipated shortfall on the previous financial year's budget could be in part covered by higher than expected returns from the RSC tour to Los Angeles, which meant that the 1967/8 deficit was only £29,477. Moreover, Sir George was pleased to report 'that CBS having seen a rough copy of the film were enthusiastic about it'.

A Midsummer Night's Dream had its cinema premiere in London in late January 1969. Within a fortnight, at 9.00 pm on Sunday 9 February, it was screened nationally on the CBS network. Rank Xerox sponsored the screening and reportedly spent almost US$2 million to promote it, which as London's *Evening Standard* pointed out was 'about three or four times the cost of the film itself'.[30] This corporate support also meant that the film was interrupted only twice for commercial breaks. The press response was exceptionally positive and CBS was sufficiently delighted to continue to discuss further projects with the RSC. The reception from the London critics was significantly more muted, with John Russell Taylor writing in *The Times* that 'this film is frankly terrible on almost every conceivable level'. 'What finally wrecks the film', he continued, 'is not that Mr Hall has a misguided or eccentric conception of the play, but that he seems to have no communicable conception of it at all.'[31] 'Just damn silly,' was Richard Roud's even blunter assessment in *The Guardian*.[32]

Perhaps anticipating the criticisms, Peter Hall contributed a self-justifying essay to *The Sunday Times* just prior to the premiere. Contradicting his earlier assessment that 'the play is in many ways a film script made ready', he now asserted that 'Shakespeare is no screen writer. He is a verbal dramatist, relying on the associative and metaphorical power of words. Action is secondary. What is meant, is said.'[33] In contrast to earlier adaptations like Olivier's *Henry V* (1944), which had made significant cuts to the text, Hall explained that 'I have tried to use the advantages of the cinema not to make a film in the accepted sense, but to communicate [Shakespeare's] words. I have found that film allows the ambiguity of the text to be understood in greater detail than in the theatre.' Certainly the words are distinctly spoken by his distinguished cast: Judi Dench (Titania), Ian Richardson (Oberon) and Ian Holm (Puck), with Diana Rigg, David Warner, Michael Jayston and Helen Mirren as the lovers. But in part because of the use of post-syncing throughout, the words feel dissociated from the action, recorded as they are in the dead space of the studio rather than amongst the living world of the forest.

A Midsummer Night's Dream is, according to Hall, 'a very Elizabethan and very English play'. The mechanicals are agricultural workers of Warwickshire, Theseus 'a country Duke who practises an essentially English brand of pragmatism when things get difficult ... Athens, for Shakespeare, is an English country community suffering, as usual, a very bad summer'. Which permitted him to costume the court in the styles of the late 1960s, with mini-skirts and Nehru jackets, and explained the damp undergrowth and overcast skies. More puzzling, when Hall's words are compared with the finished film, is his assertion that, 'We did long takes, shooting quickly, so the actors could sustain their feelings and preserve continuity. Shakespeare works in paragraphs of emotion rather than sentences.' One of the most irritating aspects of the film's style is the frequent cuts within speeches, often to set-ups that break the visual and spatial continuity. Only rarely does Hall allow a character to unfold a paragraph of emotion in a sustained shot. Moreover, there are very few developing shots – at almost every moment Hall expects his actors to speak within static, frequently close-up frames. Nor is there respite from the relentless pace of the words, as the film offers no space for establishing shots or primarily visual sequences that might contribute shadings of rhythm and tone.

In the years since its release the film has attracted extensive academic attention, much of it arguing that it is a richer and more complex text than the initial reviews (and my own response) might suggest. One of the earliest sympathetic responses was written by Michael Mullin, who asserted that the film offers a distinctive vision in which 'nudity and weird camera effects link the wood demons of Elizabethan folklore with the modern vision of the play as "erotic nightmare"'. He saw the film challenging audiences to set aside notions of conventional adaptations, writing that the play itself 'is of a strange, mixed genre, constantly calling attention to its actors as actors, playing with our suspended disbelief at every turn, and tempting us to dismiss it'.[34] Subsequently, both Jack Jorgens and Frank Ochiogrosso have celebrated the manner in which the film achieves what Theseus identifies as a 'concord of this discord' (5.1.60). Jorgens suggested that in the opening images of rural landscapes in sunshine, rain, wind and snow, 'We glimpse the dislocations of space and time we will experience later in the forest ... In the sounds accompanying this collage of images is posited Shakespeare's sense of the underlying harmony in man and nature.[35]'

Another of the film's academic fans, Graham Holderness, endorsing what he judges 'one of the most inventive and valuable of all the Shakespeare films', linked the idea of discord within concord with strategic self-reflexivity.[36]

For Holderness the film's disruptive montage, spatial and temporal discontinuities, the manner in which characters from time to time address the camera, and the celluloid 'conjuring tricks' that cause the fairies to appear and then disappear from shot, all contributed to a foregrounding of the film's construction and operation. As a consequence, the film offers to 'the spectator an open awareness of the medium as a conjuring and stimulating power which makes "reality", yet renders itself visible in the act of making'.[37] However, Holderness recognized that with the nuptial theatricals the film ultimately resolves into a reinforcement of a harmonious community. Peter Donaldson has similarly argued that the film proclaims, along with Orson Welles's *Macbeth* (1948), *Othello* (1952) and *Chimes at Midnight*, as well as Brook's *King Lear*, 'a recognisably modernist aesthetic ... linked by a shared cinematic practice, ultimately Brechtian in inspiration, which calls into question the status of the represented image by foregrounding the process of representation'. In a manner comparable to Holderness, however, Donaldson concluded that 'Both in its style and in its treatment of gender relations, the radicalism of Hall's *Dream* does not merely fade away but modulates, carefully, toward the cultural and political mainstream.'[38]

After the *Dream* was over

The endgame of the RSC's relationship with Filmways had begun even before Peter Hall took his *Dream* cast before the cameras in September 1967. On 16 August the director's long-planned production of *Macbeth* with Paul Scofield was presented to the press in Stratford-upon-Avon. The occasion had been delayed for just over a month, with the loss of twenty performances, because early in rehearsals Peter Hall was taken ill with shingles, which was sufficiently serious to threaten the sight in his left eye. Even without this the rehearsals had been strained, as understudy Ian Hogg documented in a rehearsal diary: 'It seemed ... as if Hall was trying to impose an idea of Macbeth on [Scofield] – cruel, murderous – while Paul searched for a rationale – something fundamentally good in Macbeth ... He [also] hated the costumes and set ... [but] Scofield never broke down, showed heroic, amazing stoicism.'[39] When the critics did finally see the much-anticipated show, their response was mixed. The visual splendour of John Bury's design was admired and the insistently Christian interpretation noted, but Vivien Merchant's Lady Macbeth failed to impress. Of Scofield's performance, D.A.N. Jones wrote, 'His physical presence is admirable ... But he sounds like a cow in labour. Off-beat and off-key, he chops his speeches into apparently random passages of four or five syllables, punctuated with gulps.'[40] Despite the critical response, there appears to have been no indication that the film was in jeopardy until after a successful tour to Helsinki, Moscow and Leningrad and the Aldwych opening of the production in early January 1968.

A month later, however, Paul Scofield had called off the film and resigned from the Royal Shakespeare Company. 'For artistic reasons', Kenneth Pearson reported in *The Sunday Times*, 'Scofield has declined to play the part [that is, Macbeth] in films. He was not too happy with critical reaction when the production was first launched at Stratford, and obviously would not want to see his discomfort enshrined forever.' The sequence of events remains opaque but it appears that Peter Hall cancelled, perhaps simply for reasons of scheduling, the entry of *Macbeth* into the prestigious Théâtre des Nations festival in Paris, replacing it with *All's Well That Ends Well*. Scofield then announced his resignation from the company. As Michael Birkett wrote to Marty Ransohoff later in the month, 'relations are, to put it mildly, strained'. At the same time he attempted to reassure the Filmways executive that because of his regard for Peter Brook, Scofield would still do the film of *King Lear*. Moreover, Birkett said, Brook was adamant that the film must be made under the RSC-Filmways deal.[41]

One further destabilising factor at just this moment was Peter Hall's decision to step down from running the RSC. The months following Hall handing over the reins saw attempts to keep the *Macbeth* film alive, as well as increasingly fractious exchanges between the RSC and Filmways. Not only was the film company refusing to pay over the all-important production fee for the *Dream* but it was also failing to honour what the RSC believed to be Filmways' debts to creditors. The theatre company had a letter of agreement signed by Scofield in the summer of 1967 that appeared to commit him to the Scottish play on screen. But the last-minute inclusion by his agent of a clause that Scofield had to agree to the film offered him a legal way out. As did the framing of the letter, as another external lawyer explained to Sir George Farmer:

> I am bound to say that I do not think the Agreement [with Scofield] could be enforced against him because the terms relating to remuneration are to be the subject of some future agreement. I am afraid that remuneration is so basic to a contract like this that there is, in effect, no contract. In any case, even if there were a binding contract, such obligations are notoriously difficult to enforce.[42]

In the copy of this communication preserved in the Shakespeare Birthplace Trust archive, two vertical lines have been drawn in the left-hand column, witnessing perhaps Farmer's recognition that the cause was hopeless. The financial loss, nonetheless, was considerable, and it was exacerbated by the collapse of the film financing guarantor for the *Dream* film. The projections were sufficiently serious in early September 1968 for Derek Hornby to write to George Farmer urging him not to embrace either of two possible ways forward. One was to give up the Aldwych and the plans for the Barbican and to retreat to Stratford, while the other was to pursue further the idea of amalgamating with the National Theatre.[43] Two months later, negotiations with Filmways, described to the council as 'difficult', had resolved that most of the outstanding financial commitments to the RSC would be honoured. 'As regards the film of *King Lear*,' Executive Council minutes noted, 'Royal Shakespeare Enterprises Ltd would not now participate in the production but the Theatre would receive a fee of £10,000' (although this was later to be revealed as a fee of £6,000 and profit participation of £4,000).[44] Council meetings during the following three years continued to worry away at Filmways-related issues, as the company sought to deal with its deficit. There was excitement at the prospect of a new CBS deal and enthusiasm about the possibilities of generating revenue from recordings for video cassettes. Both, however, were complicated by the unresolved issue of the extent of Filmways' exclusive rights.

The problems of the partnership, however, were insignificant in the context of the financial difficulties that the whole of Hollywood, at home as well as abroad, faced at the end of the decade. The investments in Britain of the major studios had for the most part failed to pay off, but domestic profligacy was far more serious. 'In 1969–70,' Alexander Walker wrote, 'it really looked as if Hollywood would go corporately bust, so vast was the debt that the "majors" had piled up … in an orgy of over-production and over-spending'.[45] As a consequence, the production boom financed from across the Atlantic came to a sudden end. The opportunities spotted earlier in the decade by United Artists had led other companies, including Filmways, to look for similar profits. Which led to increased competition for projects and people, and an unsustainable cost spiral. Hollywood, Walker reflected, 'had exported its own inflationary drives to Britain, and now found itself horrifyingly deep in debt at home and abroad'.[46] Filmways and their fellow Americans fled to their west coast homes.

Despite the difficulties of securing Filmways' signature on a termination agreement, by the autumn of 1971 the RSC was exploring the production of recordings with other parties for video distribution. In the discussions towards this goal, as well as in the Filmways negotiations more generally, the council was benefiting from the advice of Sir Lew Grade, managing director of ATV, the local ITV franchise. Two years earlier, Peter Hall had enthused in an interview about video:

> I think the future is more exciting for all because of television – films will become more flexible, more varied because of it, let alone the possibilities that lie ahead in the cassette film and the EVR [electronic video recording] system. Soon we shall be involved in creating visual long-playing records; we shall be filming opera, Shakespeare, the classics of the theatre. And it will certainly not be enough to record a good stage performance direct on film. The films must be new productions in their own right.[47]

Lew Grade flirted with the idea of recording the RSC for the new medium, but as is discussed in Chapter 4, in early 1973 it was primarily for regulatory concerns that he committed to a first broadcast collaboration with the company. By this point Peter Brook's film of *King Lear* had been released and the RSC's flirtation with Hollywood had run its course. In the council minutes for 30 November 1969 there is a rueful note that might serve as the epitaph for the whole adventure: 'Sir George Farmer thought that our future activities should be exploited through the employment of experts and that we should not again attempt such activities ourselves.'[48]

In 1973, in a move that dismayed some of his former colleagues in Stratford, the RSC's founder Peter Hall took up the artistic director role at the National Theatre. But before this he continued to direct for the RSC both on stage and on screen. Turning away from the mainstream industry, Hall made a little-seen thirty-five-minute film of Harold Pinter's *Landscape*, eventually released in 1976, and also a screen adaptation of Pinter's *The Homecoming* (1973), drawn from his 1965 Aldwych staging. *Landscape* had been written for the stage in 1967 but refused a licence by the Lord Chamberlain's office because of the 'ornamental indecencies' of its language.[49] A production was broadcast by BBC Radio 3 in April 1968[50] and the following year, after the abolition of stage censorship, it was mounted by Hall for the RSC with David Waller and Peggy Ashcroft.[51] The two actors were reunited for the film at Pinewood, together with designer John Bury, who supplied an austere kitchen set that was lit starkly but in rich colours by cinematographer Alan Hume. Pinter's characters, Duff and Beth, speak independent monologues, seemingly without hearing the other. The film is notable not only for recording the two richly textured performances but because it was one of the few British films shot with the Multivista process. This employed multiple 35mm Arriflex cameras and attached video feeds, allowing the director to mix shots 'live' in the manner of an electronic studio.[52] What it appears to have facilitated for *Landscape* was continuity of performance, which with precise framing, finely judged pacing and a severe style that eschews music, achieves estimable intensity.

When *The Homecoming* opened at the Aldwych in June 1965, in the words of the playwright's biographer Michael Billington, 'Pinter advanced his claim to be seen as Britain's foremost living dramatist ... in its image of the naked violence of family life and of the primal, atavistic power of the female, it shocked, disturbed and seemed to establish a direct line to the collective subconscious.'[53] After the opening, the ABC-TV arts series *Tempo* filmed a half-hour profile of the writer that included two substantial scenes from the production totalling almost eleven minutes.[54] These were shot with electronic cameras in a television studio, with fluid screen direction by James Goddard.[55] The first scene begins with the ritual pouring of coffee that for more than two minutes is sustained entirely without dialogue. Strangely, the broadcast, which features the full Aldwych cast, carries no credit to Peter Hall or to the Royal Shakespeare Company. The *Tempo* scenes were recorded in black and white, whereas a further short scene was filmed in colour in the summer of 1966. Featuring just Vivien Merchant and Ian

Holm in the exchange during which Ruth taunts Lenny to get him to drink from her glass, this was shot for *Opus*, Don Levy's documentary portrait of 'swinging' London. The opportunity to make a full-length film adaptation of the production came some six years later courtesy of American Film Theatre (AFT), an initiative of producers Ely and Edie Landau to produce film versions of classic plays for limited cinema release. For two seasons between October 1973 and May 1975, with support from American Express, AFT screened twelve modestly budgeted films (plus one acquisition) on a monthly basis in around 500 cinemas to subscribers who had only four showtimes to attend each production.[56]

The series began with John Frankenheimer's film of Eugene O'Neill's *The Iceman Cometh*, and the second offering in November 1973 was Hall's icily taut adaptation of *The Homecoming,* which he had shot in England at the start of the year.[57] Paul Rogers, Ian Holm, Terence Rigby and Vivien Merchant reprised their roles from the Aldwych, while Cyril Cusack and Michael Jayston took over the parts originally played by John Normington and Michael Bryant. Each characterization is etched in anger and menace, with Vivien Merchant's Ruth emerging, even if uncertainly and ambivalently, as the victor in the sexual power games. Production designer John Bury developed his Aldwych set into a disconcertingly large suburban front room, with almost bare walls and sparse furniture. The colour palette is restricted to browns and beiges and greys. The cinematographer was David Watkin, who had worked with Peter Brook on *Marat/Sade*, and he flooded the set with bright light that offered the camera considerable depth of field and allowed Hall to keep each element in sharp focus. At the centre of the space, anchoring many of the frames, including those that utilize the mirror above the fireplace, is an astonishingly bright standard lamp (which apparently gave off intense heat on set). This motivates the bleak and shadowless visuals of a camera that probes the room from every angle. The film leaves this space briefly to visit the adjacent kitchen and Lenny's bedroom, neither of which features in the stage play, and on a few occasions it ventures outside the claustrophobic house. There is no music, not even for the opening and closing titles. 'I would regard this *Homecoming* neither as a play nor a film,' Peter Hall later reflected. 'The way it's shot is … slightly stylised but not very much – and not as much as the theatre was.'[58] Hall also noted that the film was edited by Rex Pyke 'on the rhythm of the text, on the pauses, on the silences, on the actual shape of the words … that did pay off I think, and that gives the film a very hard edge'.[59]

Peter Brook and the madhouse: *Marat/Sade*

As the Filmways saga unfolded, three other RSC productions were translated to the screen by the boldest contributor to the company's adaptation history. In a remarkable five-year period Peter Brook directed three major films from his theatre productions, each of which explores a distinct stage to screen strategy: *Marat/Sade* (1967), *Tell Me Lies,* developed from *US* (1968), and *King Lear* (1971). As a schoolboy Brook had been at least as interested in making movies as directing in the theatre, and as an undergraduate he used the resources of Oxford University's film society to make an adaptation of Laurence Sterne's *A Sentimental Journey.* His small-scale staging in 1944 of *Doctor Faustus* caught the eye of Barry Jackson, who invited him to direct for his Birmingham Repertory Company, where Brook first worked with Paul Scofield, and then at Stratford. His production of *Love's Labour's Lost* in the summer of 1946 launched a glittering professional career, which would interweave theatre, television and cinema.[60] His first feature film was *The Beggar's Opera*, released as a contribution to the 1953 Coronation celebrations. Starring a singing Laurence Olivier as the highwayman MacHeath, this John Gay adaptation features a charming Dorothy Tutin as Polly Peachum, and draws on the paintings and prints of William Hogarth for its intermittently impressive Technicolor visuals. The film was a prestigious failure at the box office, and the director was not able to make another feature film in English for a decade.[61] But while he was in New York in 1953 Brook staged a version for television of *King Lear* with Orson Welles,[62] and when he returned to London BBC Television screened an extract of his West End production of the comedy *Both Ends Meet* by Arthur Macrae.[63]

In 1955 Peter Brook's groundbreaking production of *Titus Andronicus* also featured Olivier, along with his then wife Vivien Leigh, and was hailed by the critic Kenneth Tynan as 'tragedy naked, godless and unredeemed, a carnival of carnage in which pity is the first man down'.[64] Many years later Brook recalled that the Hollywood producer Sam Spiegel was moved by the production and offered to finance a recording if it could be shot in ten days. 'This excited me,' Brook wrote, 'as I saw within his budget the possibility to use the widescreen Cinemascope that was just coming into fashion to make a version that instead of copying the stage would be like an epic fresco.'[65] Olivier, however, refused to countenance the idea because he and Leigh were planning a film of *Macbeth*. As Brook continued, 'He wanted to do this as a real film with a long shooting time and a heavy budget ... "If you show that it's possible to make a Shakespeare film in three weeks and cheaply, I won't have a chance!"' The *Titus* project was abandoned and Brook professed to have few regrets. Much as he would also say about *A Midsummer Night's Dream,* he concluded that, 'I feel that our *Titus* belonged to its time and must only remain a memory. The play must be brought to life again with the eyes of today.'[66] Olivier's *Macbeth* was destined also to be one of the unmade films of a Memorial Theatre production. An examination of the screenplay drafts and other archival materials held by the British Library led the scholar Jennifer Barnes to conclude that the film was intended to 'effectively reproduce and cinematize [Glen] Byam Shaw's 1955 Stratford production'.[67] 'This probability is further supported', Barnes wrote, 'by the fact that the proposed *Macbeth* follows the Stratford production closely in terms of its overall design: while Roger Furse's cinematic set designs resemble the Elsinore of [Olivier's film of] *Hamlet* (1948) they also reimagine Furse's 1955 set for Byam Shaw's *Macbeth*.[68] But the modest box office returns in the United States for Olivier's *Richard III* (1955) led to the Rank Organisation backing away and the Scottish film never entered production.

After the triumph of *Titus Andronicus*, Brook directed *Hamlet* with Paul Scofield at the Phoenix Theatre, although the austere staging travelled first to Moscow, where it was received triumphantly and seemingly broadcast on television.[69] Nothing has survived of the ninety-minute condensation of the production that was broadcast to ITV audiences in London and the Midlands in February 1956.[70] Early in 1957 ITV showed the film *Heaven and Earth*, which had been intended for the cinema, and which brought Brook and Scofield together again.[71] Subsequent broadcasts by Brook, at least prior to the full-length BBC interview shown alongside *A Midsummer Night's Dream* in 1971, were restricted to discussions about cultural matters, including a filmed essay about *musique concrète* in the first edition of the BBC arts magazine *Monitor*.[72] Brook had exploited the techniques of *musique concrète* in his own soundscapes for *Titus Andronicus* three years earlier, for *Heaven and Earth*, and for his 1957 Stratford staging of *The Tempest* with John Gielgud. The item, which is lost, was illustrated with a scene from the production re-presented in the studio. At the end of the 1950s Peter Brook spent much of his time in France directing *Moderato Cantabile* (1960) for the screen, but of the films made before his three with the RSC, it is the low-budget, raw *Lord of the Flies* (1963) drawn from William Golding's study of lost innocence that is the most celebrated.[73]

When he accepted an invitation in 1962 to join the RSC as associate director, Peter Brook was sceptical about Peter Hall's relentless expansionism. According to Sally Beauman, Brook 'was pushing for the company to become smaller, to continue to work in both Shakespeare and modern plays, but to try to find, with a small nucleus of actors, a new dynamic'.[74] That year he directed his landmark production of *King Lear* with Paul Scofield, which is considered below, and in 1963 he mounted an exceptional RSC production of Friedrich Dürrenmatt's study of the ethics of science, *The Physicists*.[75] Brook followed this with a programme of research, developed with Charles Marowitz, embracing the approaches to theatre of Genet and Antonin Artaud. The project, and the five-week work-in-progress presentation at the London Academy of Music and Dramatic Art (LAMDA) in January 1964, took the name Theatre of Cruelty, after Artaud's definition in a 1932 letter: 'Essentially, cruelty means strictness, diligence and implacable resolution, irreversible and absolute determination.'[76] As Albert Hunt and Geoffrey Reeves have written, 'Brook was looking for a form of theatre that would not depend on anecdote or character, or on verbal messages, but which would communicate directly to an audience through a combination of all its elements – sound, gesture, the visual relationship between actors and objects.'[77] The controversial LAMDA season featured extracts and sketches by Artaud, Genet and John Arden among others, as well as a cut-up collage by Marowitz after *Hamlet*, a later version of which was filmed for television.[78] Following this, Brook took ideas developed with his collaborators into a staging of Genet's *The Screens* and then rehearsals of a new play by Peter Weiss, *The Persecution and Assassination of Marat as Performed by the Inmates of the Asylum of Charenton under the Direction of the Marquis de Sade*, a title that is invariably shortened to *Marat/Sade*.[79] The company's preparations, one day of which was filmed for a *Monitor* programme broadcast later in the year, included visiting an asylum and studying Goya's art before the Aldwych opening on 20 August 1964.[80]

Weiss's play, translated in vigorous verse by Adrian Mitchell, employs the conceit of a 1808 performance in real time by the inmates of Charenton recreating the assassination of Marat (played in New York and for the film by Ian Richardson) by Charlotte Corday (Glenda Jackson). The action is orchestrated for a group of visitors, and for the modern audience, by Sade (Patrick Magee). Hunt and Reeves described the ending of the stage production:

> The madmen got out of control, attacked the guards, raped the nuns, trampled the fallen and murdered the helpless, until a stage manager, in her everyday twentieth-century clothes, walked on to the stage and blew a whistle, at which point all the actors stopped acting and turned and looked at the audience. They moved down stage and as the audience began to applaud, the actors started clapping back at them, sometimes in rhythm, in a hostile manner.[81]

Peter Brook understood the drama as bringing together the intensity, subjectivity and violence of Artaudian theatre with Brechtian techniques of alienation. 'Alienation', Brook wrote in the Introduction to the published play text, 'is the art of placing an action at a distance so that it can be judged objectively and so that it can be seen in relation to the world.'[82] Approaches drawn from Artaud and Brecht were often seen as opposed, but not for Brook: 'I believe that theatre, like life, is made up of the unbroken conflict between impressions and judgements – illusion and disillusion cohabit painfully and are inseparable.'[83] While the London critics were undecided about the text, Brook's staging was widely praised, with Bernard Levin writing, 'It is without doubt one of the half-dozen most amazing achievements in *mise-en-scène* that the English theatre has seen in my lifetime.'[84] The response in New York was even more enthusiastic, because, or so Brook believed, it resonated for critics and audiences facing up to the war in Vietnam and the emerging counter-cultural reaction. The American enthusiasm ensured that a screen adaptation could be financed.[85]

Peter Brook and Peter Weiss discussed a full-scale costume drama film of *Marat/Sade* before recognizing that such an ambitious project would never attract the necessary funding. Instead, as Brook has recalled, 'One day the head of United Artists [in London], David Picker, offered a very imaginative English producer, Michael Birkett, and me a low budget – $250,000 – to make a film of *Marat/Sade* in complete freedom, any way we chose, provided it came in on time.'[86] In late 1964 Picker and UA were building on the London office's success in establishing the James Bond franchise and backing Tony Richardson's hugely profitable *Tom Jones*, released the previous year. As a company UA also had a reputation for supporting emerging talent, and a cheap, controversial, 'sexy' heritage drama with the added prestige of a RSC connection was an attractive idea. Despite the theatre company's developing interest in film projects, *Marat/Sade* was financed and produced with only minimal involvement by the RSC.

After their New York run, the *Marat/Sade* cast returned to England in spring 1965 for a shoot on a Pinewood Studios sound stage. A tight eighteen-day schedule meant that the film had to draw extensively on the stage production and the cast's familiarity with their roles. 'At the same time', Brook has written, 'I wanted to see if a purely cinematic language could be found that would take us away from the deadliness of the filmed play and capture another, purely cinematic excitement.'[87] In a letter to the cast, Michael Birkett echoed these ambitions: 'We hope ... not to make just a record of this production ... but something which uses every device the cinema has to offer, something of stunning visual (and aural) impact – in fact something new.'[88] Birkett and Brook brought on board director of photography David Watkin, who had recently completed his first two major films, both directed by Richard Lester, *The Knack ...* and *Help!* (both 1965). Rather than set up each shot individually, Watkin bathed Sally Jacobs's largely white set in an even light, which allowed the team to shoot continuously, often with two and occasionally more cameras.[89] As a journalist reported from the set, 'Watkin himself was free to operate the second camera. He and Brook know each others' minds and with a minimum of consultation Watkin, using a long-focus lens with a very shallow depth of field, could pick up a detail while Brook concentrated on the main action.'[90] In certain ways the innovative technique paralleled television's multi-camera shooting of a stage play or a sports event. 'We covered the production like a boxing match,' Brook recalled. 'The cameras advanced and retreated, twisted and whirled, trying to behave like what goes on in a spectator's head and simulate his experience; attempting to follow the contradictory flashes of thought and stomach blows with which Peter Weiss had filled his madhouse.'[91] Throughout, Brook was clear about his intentions, as he said, 'The theatre or the cinema fulfil one precise social function, which is to disturb the spectator ... to disturb a man into a state in which he is uncomfortable with his own ideas and beliefs, in which he is forced to re-open questions that he had long since thought closed.'[92]

The film begins with the camera entering the bathhouse stage amidst the inmates who are to perform. Bars fill the fourth wall of the space, beyond which there is darkness. The aristocratic Coulmier family arrive to watch, and are greeted from within the madhouse, where the camera remains for almost all of the drama. Only occasionally is there a cut to a distanced shot behind a secondary audience, visible in silhouette, watching from outside the bars. Close-ups of characters, often employing direct address to the camera, are counterpointed with panoramic frames shot with wide-angle lenses. Profile framings and out of focus shots contribute to a developing sense of unease, and as the undertones of violence build, sequences increasingly employ hand-held cameras and rapid cutting. Played by a band within the drama, Richard Peaslee's score, and the lusty songs, contribute significantly to the hallucinatory dislocation and eventual breakdown of this world.

Critical response to the film was divided, with several writers, including Dilys Powell for *The Sunday Times*, preferring it to the stage version.[93] Expressing some surprise that Brook's 'theatricality' appeared to work so well on film, Ernest Callenbach contributed one of the most considered contemporary responses:

> the camera throws itself so intently into the situation that we have no time or inclination to cavil ... What is curious and remarkable is that this highly abstract work retains its power on film; its ideas are compelling, the doubts and anguish of its characters are moving, and its vision of the human condition is a large and tragic one.[94]

Writing more than forty years later, however, Evan M. Torner detailed a persuasive critique of the film by returning to the central conflict of the play:

> Weiss intended the dialogue between Sade and Marat, which has been 'written' by Sade, to delineate the opposing political, aesthetic and philosophical arguments of Artaud and Brecht respectively. He pitted the theater of the mind against that of the body, Brechtian idealism against Artaudian nihilism, fighting for a cause against causeless-ness. Moreover, Weiss incorporates Brechtian alienation effects, as well as Artaudian shock tactics, into his script, matching form to content in a skilful dialectic of aesthetics.[95]

While recognizing Brook's acute awareness of the Brecht – Artaud debate, Torner argued that in the film the director turned away from techniques of Brechtian cinema developed by Jean-Luc Godard, Alexander Kluge and Jean-Marie Straub, among others. Their works aimed to expose the artifice of film production and its implication within capitalism. But instead of the film of *Marat/Sade* attempting to apply a Brechtian approach, Torner asserted that it worked 'by cinematically immersing the viewer in the theatrical action, unnecessarily conferring a kind of omniscience onto him/her ... Brook's film betrays a bias for Sade in its primary elements of filmic expression – montage, *mise-en-scène* and cinematography – in addition to its version of the script.'[96] Artaud, for Torner, won out over Brecht. Yet a counter-argument can be mounted, noting that the spare, typographical opening title-card and closing card betray a strong Godardian influence. Working against Artaudian immersion, the film constantly shifts the viewer between watching, as it were, through the eyes of the Coulmier family, observing from beyond the fourth wall of the bars, and being hailed and harangued directly down the lens. Artifice is exposed and a sense of alienation achieved, perhaps, through the interplay of these spectator positions. In any case, Brook's next film adaptation of a RSC production would explore a radically different strategy for translating the theatrical to the cinematic. *Tell Me Lies* (1968) would adopt a different name from the originating play, *US*, and it would embrace far more fully what can be characterized as a Brechtian approach to the screen.

Tell Me Lies: about Vietnam

Peter Brook described his next RSC production as 'a show about Vietnam called *US*, spell and pronounce it as you will … It is an attempt to make the theatre a meeting place of contradictions, to make the *raison d'être* for everything the relation between what happens on stage and the people sitting out front.'[97] A collaborative work that was developed during nearly a year of of research and fifteen weeks of rehearsal, *US* opened at the Aldwych on 13 October 1966 and played in repertory for five months.[98] A fortnight before previews the RSC resisted considerable pressure from the Lord Chamberlain, Lord Cobbold, who still had to license every public performance, to cancel a production that he characterized as 'bestial, anti-American, and communist'.[99] But instead of pro- or anti-anything views, what *US* offered above all were provocations, contradictions and questions about the possible relationships between the war in Vietnam and the audience in a London theatre. In the published play text, which combined fragments of the text with photographs, press clippings and two rehearsal diaries, Brook wrote, 'if everyone could hold in his mind through one single day both the horror of Vietnam and the normal life he is leading, the tension between the two would be intolerable … We wanted actors to explore every aspect of this contradiction.'[100]

The show comprised sketches and songs, which were set to Richard Peaslee's catchy score; descriptions of the self-immolation of a Buddhist monk in Saigon and of a Quaker, Norman Morrison, on the steps of the Pentagon; an extraordinary speech by Glenda Jackson imagining – and glorying in – the coming of napalm to an English garden; and a (staged) ritual burning of a white butterfly.[101] Techniques of agit-prop and activist drama were combined with popular forms exemplified by Joan Littlewood's Theatre Workshop, the techniques of Meyerhold, Artaud and Grotowski, and physical theatre and verbatim theatre. That it was theatrically effective and intellectually provocative was agreed by almost all, but the extensive public debate focused on the question of whether it was or could be *politically* effective. Brook vociferously defended *US* on television and in the press, and he expressed his sense of the strategy of the show in a written statement: 'If democracy means respect for the individual[,] true political theatre means trusting each individual in the audience to reach his or her own conclusions, once the act of theatre has performed its legitimate function of bringing the hidden complexities of a situation into light.'[102]

Uniquely for a RSC staging, two screen adaptations were drawn from *US*. The first, *Benefit of the Doubt*, is a documentary response to the Aldwych production made by Peter Whitehead in January and February 1967. According to Whitehead writing at the end of 1967, during the rehearsals of *US* Peter Brook screened for his cast and collaborators two of the filmmaker's earlier documentaries of the counter-culture, *Wholly Communion* (1965) and *Charlie is My Darling* (1966). Towards the end of the Aldwych run of *US*, Whitehead shot scenes from the play, without an audience, during a specially arranged run-through on a Sunday. This material remains fascinating, not least because it echoes techniques that Brook had used in *Marat/Sade*. Images from two hand-held cameras, one of which was operated by Whitehead, immerse the spectator in the stage action, and – as in the earlier film – respond to and emphasize Artaudian aspects of the production. The 'History of Vietnam' tableaux are featured, as is the scene titled 'The True Story of Barry Bondhus' along with the musical number 'Zapping the Cong'. Some forty minutes of the production, shot in colour, feature in the complete sixty-seven-minute film, the remainder being participant interviews that were filmed in black and white. Geoffrey Reeves, Ian Hogg and Glenda Jackson reflect on the politics of the performance, and there are shots from a packed public discussion about the show. Speaking directly to camera, in what appears to be Whitehead's cutting room, Brook also ruminates on the production. The penultimate sequence presents Glenda Jackson's powerful monologue about wanting the English at home to experience the horrors of contemporary warfare: 'I would like to see an English dog playing on an English lawn with part of a burned hand. I would like to see a gas grenade at an English flower show and nice English ladies crawling in each others' sick.'[103] At the close, Whitehead incorporates footage from an anti-war demonstration outside the United States Embassy in Grosvenor Square and includes the notorious scene of a cast member appearing to burn a live butterfly on stage, whilst Brook speaks about the legal concept of the benefit of the doubt on the soundtrack.

Benefit of the Doubt was received respectfully at festivals from late 1967 onwards and enjoyed a theatrical run in a Paris cinema in the tumultuous spring of 1968. In a *New York Times* review Bosley Crowther described the film as 'a stirring comprehension of the thought and emotion that went into the doing of this play'.[104] Writing in May the following year, Nicole Zand in *Nouvelles Littéraires* suggested that, 'As a description of the English reality of Vietnam, the film aims to denounce the easy conscience, to "destabilize" the audience, and also to require them to question themselves, even to the point of taking action.'[105] Although not typical, one later response was Robert Chilcott's in *Vertigo*, where, while parenthetically asserting that 'Filmed theatre never looks right', he described *US* as it is revealed in the film as 'a ghastly, absurdist, pop-art satire, borrowing from Godard and Brecht but ultimately looking ridiculous'.[106] My response, viewing the film from the British Film Institute's DVD release, could not be more different, and although just over fifty years later the specifics of the Vietnam conflict no longer resonate so strongly, the engagement with American militarism, imperial ambition and our implication in this remains potent.

The extent of the stage sequences included in *Benefit of the Doubt* became the focus of legal letters in 1967, when Peter Brook and the company decided to develop their own film adaptation from the show. When Brook invited Whitehead to make *Benefit of the Doubt*, there was apparently no hope of producing a feature version of *US*. But that changed when Brook's film of *Marat/Sade* opened in New York early in 1967 and, as the trade magazine *Variety* wrote in October 1967, 'it became possible to assemble a group of Yank investors for a film production' and to secure Walter Reade as a distributor.[107] The arrangement under which *Benefit of the Doubt* was made, as a letter to Whitehead written by Brook in September stressed, was that 'your film was to be primarily a documentary about the effects of *US* on its audience, in which stage sequences would be used purely as illustrations'.[108] Brook at this point had not seen the film, although had he done so it is highly unlikely he would have recognized it as respecting his stipulation. Now some seventy Americans had come together to fund a feature film version, but Bosley Crowther's review alerted these investors to the existence of *Benefit of the Doubt*. Legal letters passed between the parties, with Whitehead, who was never one to back away from a dispute, offering a robust defence. The American lawyers eventually withdrew and both films were distributed, with what was finally titled *Tell Me Lies* securing a wider showing and receiving a largely positive reception, albeit more as a intellectual provocation than as a satisfying fiction.

Script drafts preserved in the Peter Brook papers at the Victoria and Albert Museum (V&A) reveal that what became *Tell Me Lies* was at different stages during the scripting and production titled *Dreams Collide, Make and Break* and just *London*. What stays consistent is Brook's prologue:

This is neither a script, nor a treatment, it is a skeleton. The film will be a very complex mix of fiction that 'stimulates' [*sic*, presumably 'simulates'] a documentary – and cannot be scripted further. The actors who played *US* on the stage will improvise variants on their stage action in real life settings. Continually, however, they come across real individuals, who will present their own views and attitudes in genuinely un-rehearsed documentary conditions.

That *Tell Me Lies* was part-improvised throughout its shoot in the summer of 1967 is apparent from the rambling structure of the finished film. It begins as the story of a young couple, Mark and Pauline, played by Mark Jones and Pauline Munro from the cast of *US*, who are disturbed by photographs of the horrors of the war in Vietnam. Searching for ways to respond, they join protest marches and attend events organized for what is called Angry Arts Week. But it is clear that garden party displays of children's drawings, poetry readings and staged agit-prop are entirely ineffective. The brief scene of the theatre show contributes to a strongly self-reflexive strand throughout the film, which features frequent observations on its own operations, including two film editors offering a running commentary on events. Mao's Little Red Book makes several appearances, and one of the influences is very clearly Jean-Luc Godard's *La Chinoise* (1967).

At the core of *Tell Me Lies* is a long *verité* sequence in which Mark discusses Vietnam with a group of reactionary political commentators including Tom Driberg and Kingsley Amis. At the same party he is lectured by the black American civil rights activist Stokely Carmichael. Following this, the film works through sections of the original *US*, for which Brook and his collaborators endeavoured to find filmic equivalents. One of the most powerful sequences on stage was the story of the American Quaker Norman Morrison who set himself alight at the Pentagon as a protest against the war. This is acted out, as captions detail, by English actors in front of the American Embassy in Grosvenor Square. *Tell Me Lies* also includes, without a 'trigger' warning, still-shocking colour footage of Buddhist monks self-immolating in front of hundreds of other monks who simply watch and pray. But as with other archive film there is no explanation or context for the footage. At the end we return with Mark to his flat, where he challenges a friend about how long he can look at a photograph of a badly burned child before losing interest. As the camera pans to the open door of the room, Mark asks, 'If it came through the door, then what?' The frame settles on the open door in silence and stays there until the shot eventually fades to white. This is the cinematic parallel to the closing moments on stage, in which after one of the actors appeared to burn a live butterfly the cast sat and lay on the stage and stared at the audience in silence. The house lights came up, and the cast continued to stare – and to stare, until finally people began to leave.

Reactions to the film on its release in early 1968 ranged from the enthusiastic to the dismissive. 'On the stage', Dilys Powell wrote, 'it was exciting to see the methods of the cinema, the marriage of realistic and anti-realistic styles, boldly invading the theatre. On the screen there is no stylistic excitement since what is offered is a rag-bag of methods long familiar to anybody who goes to films.'[109] Perhaps the most negative response was written by *New York Times* critic Renata Adler: 'It is an extremely trivial exercise ... the direction is as unintelligent as the dialogue on which the picture rests ... The whole movie reflects the banal assumption that feeling is incompatible with reason.'[110] But another significant American critic, Hollis Alpert, wrote, 'What I like most about *Tell Me Lies* is its daring and impudence, its sense of outrage, its frankness.'[111] In the decades after its release, *Tell Me Lies* remained largely inaccessible, but it was restored in France in 2013 and released on DVD. Seen now, its constant shifts in style and tone are initially exhilarating but ultimately frustrating, as is the film's pessimism about the possibility of any kind of effective response to the exposed horrors. Offering answers, however, was never Brook's intention, and he was more concerned to question the polarization of the debate and to challenge the languages of absolute conviction.

Yet Brook himself was dissatisfied with the film, as he wrote in a letter to a friend after its completion:

> I haven't yet made a film I like ... I think making a film is excruciatingly difficult – and the very empirical nature of theatre is in a way a bad preparation because it makes me flexible towards detail and in a sense accommodating when one works, while proper shooting of a film requires every stroke to be right there and then. It is far, far more concentrated ... The film this year, *Tell Me Lies*, was very different, very free, very improvised. But I'm still searching for the form and the language.[112]

For many commentators, in his next film, which he would shoot early in 1969, Peter Brook would find a form and a filmic language that very precisely expressed his sense of the text with which he was working, Shakespeare's *King Lear*. But in the Peter Brook collection at the V&A there is a tantalizing trace of another Shakespeare film that he might have directed. On 18 January 1967, at just the moment when Peter Whitehead was invited to film *US* at the Aldwych, Michael Birkett wrote a letter to Brook detailing the ideas that the two had discussed for a film of *Measure for Measure*.[113] The proposed casting was ambitious: Paul Scofield as the Duke, Glenda Jackson as Isabella, Ian Richardson as Angelo, Michael Williams as Lucio and John Hurt as Claudio. Birkett suggested that they might also be able to tempt Michael Hordern to play Escalus and Leo McKern to take on Pompey. Brook appeared to link the new film to his 1950 staging, at least for the setting, which as Birkett noted must be 'as a first essential, composite and interconnected'. Rather than have a set built on a sound stage, 'we both agreed', Birkett wrote, 'that we should first think whether there is somewhere a natural location whose own character might give us something extra – something more than any designer could quite build for us'. The *Daily Mirror* building in London, an Italian renaissance or Austrian baroque palace, or perhaps a railway station were Birkett's immediate suggestions. But there is nothing further to indicate why the project did not proceed.

Changing gears in *King Lear*

'The problem in filming Shakespeare', Peter Brook said in a 1965 interview, 'is, how can you change gears, fluctuate between gears, styles and conventions as lightly and deftly as the mental processes inside a person, which can be reflected by blank verse but not by the consistency of each single image.'[114] Brook has directed only a single Shakespeare adaptation for the cinema, and it addresses very directly this challenge. His great feature film of *King Lear* attempts in its dizzying stylistic complexity to change gears constantly, and in doing so to fluctuate lightly and deftly between Godard and Antonioni, and between Artaud and Brecht. In 2016, I curated a season of RSC screen adaptations for London's Barbican cinema, and we were fortunate to project on a large screen an immaculate digital transfer of the film. I had watched a DVD of the film several times, but now the film's whites and greys and blacks were ravishing in a quite new way. The performances communicated with an extraordinary intensity, and the complexities and contradictions of Lear's vision, of Shakespeare's and of Brook's were almost overwhelming.

For the 1962 stage production Peter Brook put his cast through an extensive and unconventional rehearsal process.[115] Charles Marowitz, Brook's assistant director, wrote a journal of the process, in which he noted, as J.C. Trewin outlined, 'it was mainly about blindness and sight, sight that once acquired looks only into a void. The plot was Beckettian, the scene a metaphysical farce that ridiculed life, death, sanity and illusion.'[116] The result was a *King Lear* hailed by Kenneth Tynan as 'incomparable ... A great director ... has scanned the text with fresh eyes and discovered a new protagonist – not the booming, righteously indignant Titan of old, but an edgy, capricious old man, intensely difficult to live with' (Figure 6).[117] Several years before *Marat/Sade*, critics saw this *Lear* through the theatrical lenses of both Brecht and Artaud, and above all, of Samuel Beckett. As J.C. Trewin later wrote about an essay by the Polish activist and critic Jan Kott titled '*King Lear*; or, *Endgame*':

> This examined the tragedy in terms of Samuel Beckett's play: the theme of *Lear* was the decay and fall of the world, Man destroyed by a universe without reason or interest in human fate ... Brook had read the essay soon after the publication of the French version in 1962. When he directed *Lear* at Stratford that autumn, his basis was existential; he regarded the play as the 'epic unfolding of the nature of the absurdity of the human condition'.[118]

This was a *Lear* that did not seek sympathy from its audience, a production from which all sentiment had been leached and that was set in a bright, bleak, hostile world. Such too were the qualities that Brook and his collaborators brought to the screen version of the stage production, which was filmed

FIGURE 6 *Lear (Paul Scofield) asks his daughters who loves him best in Peter Brook's 1962 staging, which became the basis for the director's radical film* King Lear *(1971). Photograph by Angus McBean © RSC.*

far from Stratford-upon-Avon in the early months of 1969. As chronicled above, the film had been envisaged as one of the three that the RSC would produce under the Filmways deal. Despite Scofield's contentious withdrawal from *Macbeth, King Lear* was kept alive even after the souring of the actor's more general relationship with the RSC.

The main location for *King Lear* was a disused mink farm in the extreme north of Jutland, set amongst sand dunes, snow-bound for much of the time and with a freezing wind. Many of the knights and other attendants were local fishermen and farmers, who also contributed their distinctive shaggy ponies. To a visiting journalist Brook explained the link between the location and a key theme of the play: 'It is the comparison between closed and open spaces. And you can take that physically and metaphorically. The contrast between enclosed and free, protected and unprotected ... between blindness and sight.'[119] 'The two dangers that Brook and I wanted to avoid', Michael Birkett observed, 'were "authenticity" and "timelessness" ... One wants an audience to accept the world in which a story is happening as being plausible, real, something with which they can feel familiar from the moment the film starts.'[120] In this real landscape Brook opted for stark simplicity – of setting, costumes, music, as well as the purity of monochrome images. Henning Kristiansen's cinematography drew on the Scandinavian cinema of Carl Dreyer and Ingmar Bergman, working with brilliant whites and deep blacks to extend the drama's fundamental concern with sight and blindness.

Brook and Michael Birkett commissioned what the latter described as a 'translation' of the text from Ted Hughes before recognizing that it was essential to retain Shakespeare's poetry. Next, Brook wrote a narrative of the play, with no dialogue, and this was used to map out the script. Further significant changes were then made on location, and in the final film the play is significantly restructured and rearranged. Moreover, as Lillian Wilds has observed, 'Brook deliberately and systematically cuts all lines and scenes which supply motivation or act to mitigate what otherwise must be gratuitous cruelty.'[121] Beyond the text, Brook has written on his broader approach to the shoot, and to the overall style of the film:

> Shakespeare's plays ... are very complex, unique inventions, made up of an amazing variety of contradictory pieces cunningly strung together ... To capture this mosaic, we tried in the cinema to get away from any fixed style ... [and] we tried to evolve an impressionistic movie technique, cutting language and incident to the bone, so that the total effect of all the things heard and seen could capture in different terms Shakespeare's rough, uneven, jagged and disconcerting vision.[122]

The fragments Brook works with, sometimes cut at a frenetic pace, include abstract shapes and indistinct images, intimations of the void at the heart of the play in screens that are simply black, as well as characters speaking in profile or from behind, and extreme close-ups counterpointed by wide, almost empty landscapes. In his sympathetic biography of the director, his sometime collaborator Michael Kustow described one key sequence:

> As Lear builds up to his outburst on the final brink of madness, control seems to abandon the camera's gaze too ... we see Lear's face nestled

in thorns and briars, stung by pouring rain, illuminated by a sudden lightning flare, indistinguishable from microscopic close-ups of the worms and rodents among whom he has fallen. The cuts are so rapid that sometimes there is no time to recognise whether what you're looking at is animal, vegetable or human. It is the most radical vision of Shakespearean disintegration ever brought to the screen.[123]

On the film's release in the United States, Pauline Kael was dismissive of the film's style as well as of much else. 'Peter Brook's *King Lear* is gray and cold,' she judged, 'and the actors have dead eyes. I didn't just dislike the production – I hated it ... The cutting seems designed as an alienation device, but who wants to be alienated from Shakespeare's play and given the drear far side of the moon instead.'[124] Frank Kermode, was far more enthusiastic, hailing the film as 'the best of all Shakespeare movies'. Kermode was frustrated by many of the cuts and some of the detailed decisions of the film, but he concluded, 'the kind of truth this movie has in its last quarter of an hour can be got at in no other way'.[125] Later commentators have largely sided with Kermode, and the film has stimulated the most extensive critical literature associated with any RSC adaptation. Much of this has explored, with more legitimacy and substance than in the writing about Peter Hall's *Dream*, Brook's strategy of making, as Kenneth Rothwell has suggested, 'a movie about making movies'.[126] Rothwell has described exhaustively the techniques that Brook employed to this end: 'Like Jean-Luc Godard, Brook employs discontinuities, zoom-fades, accelerated motion, freeze frames, shock editing, complex reverse-angle and over-the-shoulder shots, montage, jump cuts, hand-held shots, silent-screen titles, eyes-only close-ups, and hand held as well as immobile cameras.'[127] Lillian Wilds linked this approach to Brook's relationship with Brecht's idea of alienation. 'Brook is utilizing the technical capabilities of cinema', Wilds wrote, 'to call the viewers' attention to the fact that they are watching a film, to block audience identification, to achieve – in fact – Brechtian alienation ... Brook explains alienation as "cutting, interrupting, holding something up to the light, making us look again".'[128] Far more intensely than in his other adaptations for the RSC, or in the films that he made both before and after *King Lear*, Peter Brook pushed the possibilities of the screen simultaneously to draw the viewer into a enveloping, entirely coherent world of cruelty and heartlessness, suffering and insanity, and at the same time, at every moment, to reveal the creative construction of this world so as to force the viewer to reflect and to take responsibility for their relationship to it. Just as for *Marat/Sade*, Artaud and Brecht were the guiding spirits in this most achieved and astonishing of all RSC adaptations. Unsurprisingly, perhaps, after more than a year filming in Jutland and then editing in Paris, Brook chose a contrasting project for his next encounter with Shakespeare. In the spring of 1970 he returned to Stratford to direct *A Midsummer Night's Dream*. 'I had a very strong wish', he said, 'to go as deeply as possible into a work of pure celebration.'[129]

Searching for the *Dream*

As I was writing this book, the one question I was asked time and again about the RSC's adaptation history, at least by those of a certain age, was whether a recording exists of Peter Brook's groundbreaking staging of *A Midsummer Night's Dream*. Premiered at Stratford on 27 August 1970, this remains the defining post-war production of a Shakespeare play in Britain.[130] Clive Barnes's review for *The New York Times* the next day captured the show's impact:

> Once in a while, once in a very rare while, a theatrical production arrives that is going to be talked about as long as there is a theatre, a production which, for good or ill, is going to exert a major influence on the contemporary stage ... If Peter Brook had done nothing else but this *Dream*, he would have deserved a place in theatre history.[131]

Brook had stripped away the historical traditions of staging and conjured into being a production that felt entirely contemporary, dazzlingly illuminating and totally joyous. As Sally Beauman registered, 'It became the most discussed, most written about, most analysed, and most imitated Shakespearean production of the century.'[132] It also became one of the most travelled productions, hailed by audiences in Stratford and London, and on tour in Britain, across Europe, in the United States, and in Japan and Australia. In 1971 my English teacher at school told our class about it, saying that if we went to London to see it we would remember it for the rest of our lives. My sixteen-year-old self caught a train to catch a matinee, and like so many others almost fifty years on I can indeed recall the occasion vividly.[133]

The conventional answer as to whether a screen version exists is, simply, 'No.' 'There is little record of Brook's *Dream* on film,' Peter Holland has asserted, '(unless a copy of the supposedly destroyed Japanese film of it surfaces one day).'[134] In a recent essay Brook recalled that there were many proposals to film the production but that he always refused, in part because of a fear that celluloid, especially once prints became scratched and dirty, could not adequately represent Sally Jacobs's white box set:

> Photography is essentially naturalistic and a film based only on whiteness, least of all a soiled and blotchy one, was unthinkable. Of course, a play can be filmed, but not literally. I've attempted this many times, and always a new form had to be found to correspond with a new medium. It can never be a literal recording of what the audience in the theatre once saw. Here I felt that nothing could reflect the zest and invention of the whole group. This truly was a live event.[135]

Notwithstanding this I have seen three screen versions of Peter Brook's *Dream*, and the suggestion that there may be at least one more adds to the

allure of this tale. Each of the extant versions is partial and imperfect, yet each is intriguing and invaluable. Moreover, Brook's recent reflections failed to acknowledge that he and Sally Jacobs began to plan a feature film version, and that Jacobs's sketches towards a storyboard are material witnesses to this.

On New Year's Day 1971 BBC Television broadcast a fifty-minute profile of the director titled *Review: Peter Brook*. The *Dream* was about to go on tour and an interview by the strand's editor James Mossman was illustrated with extracts filmed on stage in Stratford. These extracts have been extensively recycled in discussions and documentaries about theatre history and in other forms, including as a fine display in the 2016 British Library exhibition, 'Shakespeare in Ten Acts'.[136] The film opens with a fifty-eight-second continuous shot following Oberon (Alan Howard) and Puck (John Kane) descending on trapezes in Act 2, Scene 1 as they plot the humiliation of Titania. The most substantial sequence, which runs at just over three and a half minutes, begins with an abstracted detail of a whirling freekah and returns to the top of Act 2, Scene 1 and Puck's address to the fairies before cutting under a narration bridge to the middle of Act 2, Scene 2 and Hermia (Mary Rutherford) trapped in one of the forest's huge coils of wire. Voice-over thoughts from Brook come in over the performance, and motivate a cut to Oberon swinging wordlessly on his trapeze and another to Oberon and Puck bewitching Titania (Sara Kestelman): 'What thou seest when thou dost wake' (2.2.31). The other scenes preserved, in the order they appear in the film, are a moment of Theseus and Hippolyta (over which Brook speaks); a fragment of Act 3, Scene 1 from Bottom's 'I see their knavery' (3.1.116); the mechanicals meeting in Act 3, Scene 1 to discuss their performance; Oberon watching Helena (Frances de la Tour) pleading with Demetrius (Ben Kingsley) from Act 2, Scene 1; and the spectacular scene of Lysander (Christopher Gable) challenging Demetrius, 'Where art thou, proud Demetrius?' (3.2.401), with a taunting Puck on stilts, between which both lovers hurl themselves. Finally, there is a climactic montage comprising a moment with the mechanicals, Puck again with the fairies, and lastly Lysander rejecting Hermia, who is thrown upwards to grasp a trapeze, wriggling and shouting, 'O me, you juggler, you canker-blossom' (3.2.282).

Dismayingly partial as these extracts are, and obscured as a significant component are by voice-over, they still total a comparatively substantial thirteen minutes and two seconds, which represented perhaps one-tenth of the running time of the production. Shot on 16mm film, seemingly with a single camera, and combining master shots with occasional cutaways, they appeared in *Review* as disconnected moments with little regard for the narrative development of the play, with something of the quality of animated photographs. Barbara Hodgdon's characterization of publicity images suggests how apt is the comparison:

> the theatrical still is … a left-over, the visible remains of what is no longer visible, a fragment that steals theater … the theater photograph

undertakes a visual conversation with performance: silent, impoverished, partial, it seizes appearances, violently severs them from their original context; inseparable from and traversed by the lived experience of theater, it requires anecdote, narrative, to supplement it.[137]

The BBC's *Dream* extracts are indeed impoverished, serving but also needing the narrative of the television profile for which they were filmed. Here they illustrated a tale of Brook's intellectual development as a director that also embraced *Marat/Sade*. The *Dream* is constructed by the film as exclusively Brook's *Dream*, with no on-screen contributions from either cast (listed by name but not role in the credits) or any of the production's other creatives (who are not). Cut loose from this personal narrative, the extracts have a dominant role in the memorialization of the production, yet inevitably only in a radically reduced form. The supernatural world and, to a lesser extent, the mechanicals' plans for their play, are privileged over Athens, the lovers and the wedding celebrations. Nor is there any sense of, for example, Richard Peaslee's score (and its use of Mendelssohn's music) or of the cast's interaction with their audiences, both of which can be appreciated from the other recordings.

After the Aldwych opening in June 1971 a recording of the production (and perhaps also a second) was made with a portable videotape recorder (VTR). The known tape is held in the RSC archives at the Shakespeare Birthplace Trust (SBT) in Stratford-upon-Avon, where the only accompanying information is that it was recorded in 1971. Its origin is unclear, but it exists as three reels now transferred to DVD, the first two of which run for sixty-four minutes (which was then the standard length for a 1″ reel-to-reel videotape) and the third of which is only thirty-five minutes. The Academy ratio fixed frame takes in all but the edges of downstage and is bisected horizontally by the top of the white box set. Seemingly shot from the centre of the front row of the circle, the distanced, foreshortened image, which not infrequently jumps, rolls and flickers, is composed in tones of greys. Figures are clearly distinguishable, and with cues from the audio for the most part identifiable, but faces cannot be made out with any clarity. The audience is framed out but has a presence in the coughing and laughter caught in the single-channel sound. Speech is for the most part bright and distinct while the music and some of the shouted text suffers from distortion. There are breaks forced by reel changes, and as a consequence not quite all of the performance is recorded, with the end of Act 4 and the start of Act 5 missing between reels two and three. After the informal, apparently improvised calls, there are glimpses of the cast shaking hands with the front rows of the stalls. After which there is an additional mute scene, identified with the title 'previous rx [recording]', which may be the missing scene from the opening of Act 5.

As a supplement to the other traces of the production, including the promptbook, photographs and the BBC extracts, this recording can unquestionably assist in a reconstruction of the production. Patterns in the staging can be appreciated, and especially the counterpoint between the formality of Athens and the anarchy of the forest. Sequences of the audio are involving, but there is little sense that the tape is a satisfying viewing experience. Its primary value has to be regarded as archaeological, requiring careful excavation and interpretation for much to be made of it. Moreover, reproduction is forbidden and access to the original is restricted, requiring a pilgrimage to SBT's austerely functional viewing room. The production's brilliant designer Sally Jacobs is among those who have watched the tape, in part for her to determine whether it is the recording of the show that she remembers organizing at the Aldwych, which she says was sharper, clearer and in colour. In the Peter Brook collection at the V&A, however, there is a letter from her to the *Dream* touring manager Hal Rogers that suggests that there was just one recording. Enquiring about the best way to return the version that she had with her in Los Angeles, she wrote that, 'It consists of three reels of black and white 1″ tape, on spools enclosed in three separate plastic containers.'[138] Later correspondence indicates that Sally Jacobs left the tapes to be shipped back to Stratford, but there is no confirmation of their transit. More than twenty years later, Sally Jacobs tried to get the RSC to trace the tapes, but with no success (and I have had no more luck). She also mentioned in a letter to David Brierley that she had commissioned the tapes 'when I was story-boarding the projected film'.[139]

During the 1971 London run of the *Dream,* discussions about a possible film led to Sally Jacobs commissioning her videotape record, seemingly of the last performance at the Aldwych. 'As I was at the time living in Los Angeles,' she recalled recently, 'I thought I could be thinking about how to adapt it for the camera frame of cinema.' Preserved in the Theatre Collection of Harvard University's Houghton Library, her surviving sketches consist of sixteen pages of monochrome sketches and notes, together with six sheets of drawings in vivid colour, plus a black card in which is cut a hole with the shape of a widescreen frame (Figure 7). 'Before I had the chance to show [these drawings to] Peter,' Sally Jacobs recollected, 'I got news that there had been a change of plan, and that there was to be a world tour instead of the film.' Jacobs started to work with Brook on his plans to take a troupe of players to Africa to develop new work, and the film project was dropped.

'My [plan] was reimagining it completely as a piece of cinema,' Sally Jacobs said on seeing the sketches recently, and the pages detail her initial ideas for this process. They reveal thoughts for transforming the three-dimensional space of the stage to the two-dimensional plane of the screen, reshaping the patterning and choreography within the set to a pictorial frame. The drawing for Theseus's opening speech to Hippolyta has the lovers as close-up profiles on either side of the frame with a candle flickering between them. Puck's first appearance is envisaged as a descent from a black void into bright whiteness, while about the entrance of Titania and Oberon, Jacobs's notes ask, 'can they materialise – maybe also against black first – or the whole

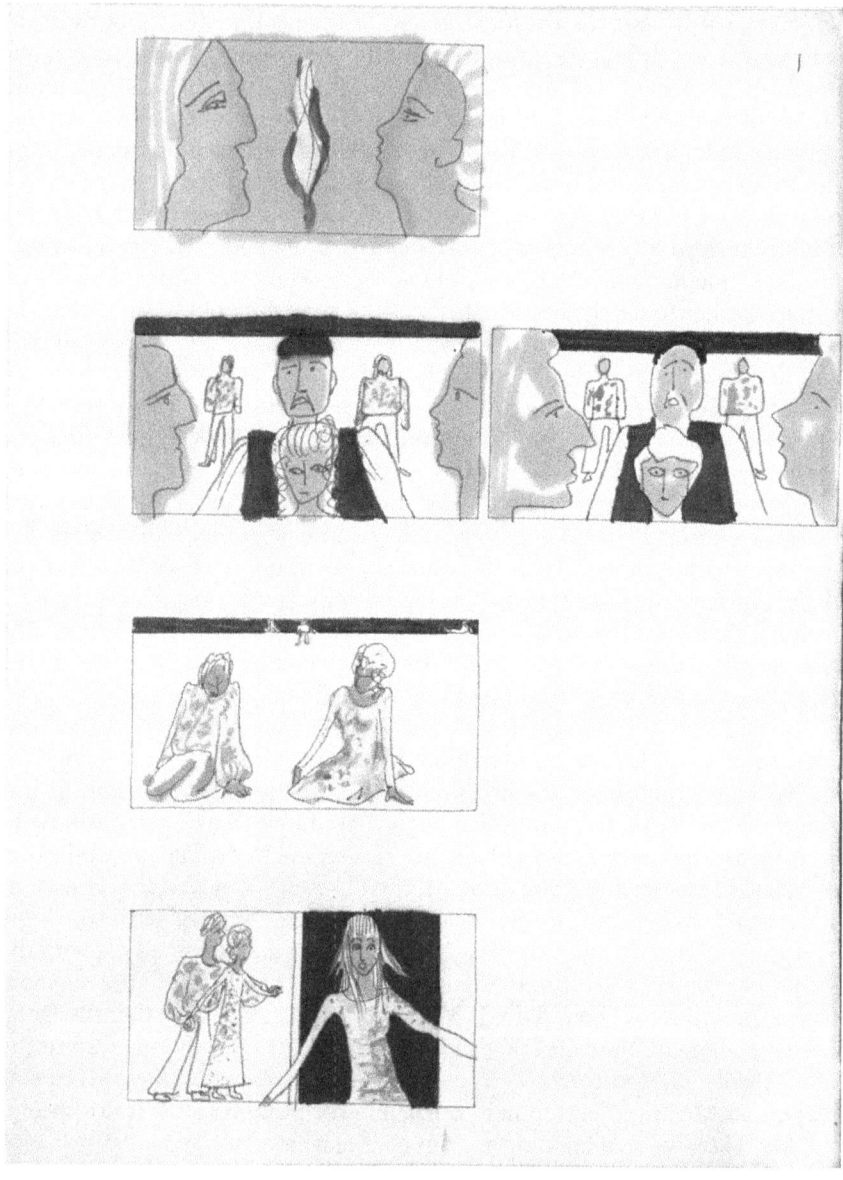

FIGURE 7 *A page from Sally Jacobs's designs for the opening of the unrealized film of Peter Brook's production of* A Midsummer Night's Dream *(1970). Image from MS Thr 878 (76), Houghton Library, Harvard University © Sally Jacobs.*

scene against black'. Several jottings record that she wanted entrances and exits to be achieved with camera effects and not through physical doorways. And on one page is the bracketed word 'chromakey', indicating that Jacobs was considering using the visual effects system of compositing images by 'keying' one on to the colour field of another. The final pages offer more elaborate versions of some of the earlier sketches, adding vibrant greens and purples and yellows for the costumes. These drawings were intended to be viewed through the hole in the card 'mask', which pointed up their contrast with the blackness surrounding the envisaged projection of the film. Nestled in an archival folder, these simple, beautiful sketches remain as further tantalizing traces of this *Dream* on screen. And there is yet one more screen version to consider.

An invitation in 1972 for the production to play in Japan was received enthusiastically in Stratford, but the available financing fell short of what was required. 'As the costs were so high', Peter Brook has written,

> could I agree to it being tele-recorded in performance so that it could be shown all over Japan and so contribute to their expenses? If we all agreed, they promised the recording would be destroyed in the presence of the British Consul. I discussed this with the cast, who had all been with me in refusing filming. This time it seemed impossible for us to say 'No.'[140]

The show was presented in Tokyo early the following year and was shown by the public broadcaster NHK.[141] Brook has recalled that a few weeks after the broadcast he received a parcel from one of the producers in Japan that contained what he has described as 'a set of large discs' (although this would have been before the availability of any format of laserdisc or similar). 'I found a player', Brook's remembered version of the tale continued, 'and discovered to my amazement that it looked very good. I sent a cable to Japan, telling them not to destroy the master. At once, a telegram returned. "This morning, in the presence of the British Consul, as you requested, the recording and the negative have been burned."'[142] Bill Wilkinson, however, who was working at the RSC at the time, has recalled the tale rather differently. He remembered a package of videotapes arriving in Stratford sometime after the broadcast. These were encoded in a Japanese format that meant they could not be viewed without being converted, which was a complex and expensive process only available in the United States. Some months later he and Peter Brook sat down to watch an initial section, and the director was so distressed by the recording's quality that they proceeded no further with the matter. Much as with Sally Jacobs's documentation, searches in Stratford nearly fifty years on have failed to find any of the discs or tapes.

The NHK archive confirmed during the writing of this book that they hold no material related to the broadcast of *A Midsummer Night's Dream* in 1973. But after I spoke on one occasion in Stratford about the destruction of the masters an academic from Japan mentioned that a friend owned an off-air recording. Months later, after I had also met with her distinguished colleague, a courier service brought a DVD on which was recorded what had presumably been taped with an early domestic U-matic system.[143] Exciting as this remarkable discovery was, this too is not the high-resolution screen version for which we might wish, even if it is fuller and with far more detail than the BBC fragments or the SBT recording. The images are in colour, and for the most part stable, while the audio is clear and is supplemented with prominent subtitles in Japanese. The broadcast from a theatre appears to have been made with either three or four cameras, and the visual style is functional and unadorned, with cutting that follows the dialogue and sparing use of zooms and dissolves. Shots embracing the width of the whole stage are combined with medium shots of small groups of characters and on occasions medium close-ups of couples. In the latter, facial expressions can be appreciated and enjoyed, although in the wides, with the white set occupying only the bottom third of the frame beneath the dark galleries above, the figures are ill-defined. On the first entrance of the mechanicals they leave the stage and walk amongst the audience, and the cameras follow them as the spectators laugh nervously, and the shots are reprised at the end as, after Puck closes with 'Give me your hands, if we be friends / And Robin shall restore amends' (5.1.427–28), the whole cast jumps from the stage to shake hands with those who have been watching. In the interval the recording cuts briefly to a caption card before stopping and jumping to the start of Part Two. And at the close, it finishes just as Alan Howard appears to be ready to address the audience from the stage.

This recording is by far the most complete way we have of experiencing the production now, and watching it on a laptop the image quality is tolerable. On a large-screen television the indistinctness is distressing and it is far outside the boundaries of that acceptable for projection. For forgiving individual consumption, however, the recording can be a rich and rewarding experience, even if the performances are enunciated and pitched for a large auditorium. There are moments at which this screen version is powerfully affective, especially as Titania and Bottom celebrate their nuptials with the fairies, one of whom, as Mendelssohn's wedding march crashes in and confetti and streamers rain down, has his raised arm and fist thrust between the weaver's legs in joyful priapism. I can recall the intensity of this moment as I watched in the Aldwych in the summer of 1971, but it is not simply nostalgia that thrills me once again as I see and hear it replayed.

'Only later', Peter Brook wrote of watching the tape sent to him from Japan and learning that the master had been destroyed,

> did I realise that this was a valuable reminder to stay with my own convictions. The life of a play begins and ends in the moment of performance. This is where author, actors and directors express all they

have to say. If the event has a future, this can only lie in the memories of those who were present and who retained a trace in their hearts. This is the only place for our *Dream*.[144]

Certainly, the afterlife of the production, and its extraordinary influence, may have been enhanced by the awareness that no recording was thought to exist. This has given every creator, whether on stage or on the page, the licence to imagine it in the form that they might have wished it to have taken. But as my search has uncovered, more concrete traces of Brook's *Dream* exist elsewhere than in the hearts of those who saw it on stage, and will continue to do so. Such traces may circulate as a network of fragments and relics, and further such shards may yet come to light. This web may be indistinct in parts, elements of it may be fragile, and for something to be made from it requires reconstruction and exegesis. Much as, of course, does a dream.

After the *Dream* Peter Brook began to travel through Africa with a troupe of actors and then he found a new theatrical home in Paris, in the atmospheric, effectively empty space of the Théâtre des Bouffes du Nord. He has continued his relentless experimentation and his unrivalled theatrical achievements, as well as his engagement with making richly distinctive screen versions of his stage productions, including *La Tragédie de Carmen* (1983), *The Mahabaratha* (1989) and *Hamlet* (2002). Although he has retained a relationship with the RSC, he returned only once to direct a new show in Stratford-upon-Avon, when in 1978 he staged – to mixed reviews – *Antony and Cleopatra* with Alan Howard and Glenda Jackson. The production was marked on screen in the documentary *After the Dream*, made for the BBC's *Omnibus* series. Scenes from the show were recorded both in rehearsal and on stage, played in full costume, and at the end of the film, after the production's opening, Brook contributed a reflection on the distance that had developed between him and the company for which he had done some of his finest work: 'the Royal Shakespeare Company to survive, and to survive brilliantly, has to expand, and the more it expands, the more technical and institutional it has to get in many respects. What we can do [in Paris] is a different sort of work because we're doing craftsman's work.' The RSC would continue to expand in subsequent years, although there are differing views on whether it did so brilliantly. The company would continue to contribute a number of productions for the small screen, but after the 1960s it would never again have either the close relationship with a broadcaster that it enjoyed with the BBC and nor would it attempt to forge a partnership with a film production company similar to that it largely failed to achieve with Filmways. Moreover, few other single figures have – at least to date – contributed to the company's screen history as significantly as, in their different ways, did Peter Hall and Peter Brook.

4

Intimate Spaces, 1972–82

Appointed as the RSC's second artistic director in February 1968, Trevor Nunn consolidated Peter Hall's achievements as he led the company throughout the next decade.[1] In 1978 Terry Hands was elevated as joint artistic director, and when Nunn stepped down in 1986 Hands took sole charge. Like his predecessor Nunn had to deal with a succession of funding crises as well as with the increasingly confident competition from the National Theatre.[2] Yet especially in the later 1970s Nunn oversaw consistently strong programmes of work at Stratford, where the company opened a third RSC auditorium as The Other Place, and in London, where The Warehouse became a fourth. Lean years of stringent austerity measures early in the decade were followed by a period after 1975 when there was widespread recognition of a new golden age for the RSC. There were triumphs with large-scale Shakespeare on the main Stratford stage, but central to the company's success in these years were its responses to a profound reshaping of British theatre. Smaller stages and auditoria, along with touring groups and their commitment to reaching new audiences, came increasingly to be seen as central.

Although there were no adaptations as radical as Peter Brook's film of *King Lear*, the RSC's screen history between 1972 and 1982 is arguably as rich as that of the previous decade. Key to this were new relationships with television, especially with the regional ITV companies ATV and Thames, and there were also a number of small-scale theatrical releases. Dominating this period were Trevor Nunn's own screen productions, including three significant Shakespeare adaptations co-directed for television with experienced multi-camera directors. Each of Nunn's recordings is close to the staging from which it originated, but collectively they showcase subtly distinct adaptation strategies. RSC films and broadcasts in this period also feature a gallery of compelling and complex performances from Helen Mirren, Glenda Jackson, Janet Suzman, Judi Dench, Ian McKellen and Roger Rees, among others. At the same time these broadcasts trace the RSC's embrace of the emerging theatrical imperatives of the moment, with shows adapted from the company's own smaller auditoria showcasing techniques that were developed for them. All of this culminated in two of the very finest RSC adaptations, both of which were Trevor Nunn initiatives: a claustrophobic and ritualistic *Macbeth* (Thames, 1979), developed from a staging at The Other Place, and the nine-hour *The Life and Adventures of Nicholas Nickleby* (Channel 4, 1982). The latter, a sweeping state-of-the-nineteenth-century-nation drama, was created for the Aldwych stage, but was forged by actors and creatives for whom the RSC's smaller stages and touring projects were foundational.

Screening the small stage

Emerging within and responding to the cultural and political debates of the late 1960s, the multiple movements corralled under such labels as small-scale, fringe or alternative theatre embraced a remarkable diversity of initiatives. There were groups committed to left-wing theatre, to women's theatre, black theatre, gay theatre and more, as well as those movements exploring new relationships between theatre makers and audiences, those seeking more progressive economic structures and those developing a strong social role for their practice.[3] Much of this work was created in new kinds of spaces, in halls and churches and basements, as well as in more conventional small-scale auditoria. For a large company like the RSC, smaller theatres had practical advantages, mitigating the risks of mounting new work and encouraging younger audiences with lower seat prices. Yet there was a more fundamental imperative, as Sally Beauman has described: 'small theatres became more than playing spaces, they became a cause: they were seen as classless and egalitarian: they were to banish rhetoric (*the* fashionable pejorative of the 1970s) and to promote close-range naturalistic truth (the most acceptable kind, perhaps, in a television age)'.[4]

Having taken over the 350-seat Arts Theatre for a season in 1962, mounted the Theatre of Cruelty season at LAMDA and the Donmar Theatre in 1964, and run the *Theatregoround* touring project since 1966, the RSC was practised at mounting productions in smaller spaces. Main stage work like *The Wars of the Roses* had been enriched by lessons from these projects, and in the case of Peter Brook's *Marat/Sade* and *US* had grown directly from them. In 1971, the RSC hired The Place, a contemporary dance venue close to Euston Station in London. A nine-week season in a 330-seat auditorium included a production of August Strindberg's *Miss Julie* from which a screen version would be made.[5] Directed by Robin Phillips, this featured a vivid central performance from Helen Mirren, who had first played with the RSC in the 1967 revival of Trevor Nunn's *The Revenger's Tragedy*. As early as 1970, at the age of twenty-five, Helen Mirren was the subject of *Doing Her Own Thing*, an ATV regional documentary artfully directed by John Goldschmidt. In thrall to its subject, the film, which carries a *naif* narration by the actor, reconstructs key scenes in her rise to RSC fame, including revered agent Al Parker restaging his first meeting with his future client. The second half of the thirty-five-minute film follows the actor preparing for an Aldwych performance of *Troilus and Cressida*, with just over six minutes of the show filmed on stage, featuring Mirren, David Waller as Pandarus and Michael Williams as Troilus. No other moving-image trace exists of John Barton's acclaimed 1968 production with Mirren's sensual and forcefully intelligent Cressida.

As a film project, *Miss Julie* is an outlier in the RSC's adaptation history. Shot on a sound stage at Pinewood with multiple cameras marshalled by the experienced television director John Glenister, it is an effective and intermittently powerful adaptation. Documentation about its production has to date proved elusive, but Marvin Liebman and Tony Tenser are credited as the film's executive producers. Liebman was an American activist who had run fundraising campaigns in the United States for anti-communist organizations. In the late 1960s he started a second career as a theatre producer in London. His partner on *Miss Julie*, Tony Tenser, had produced *Naked – as Nature Intended* (1961) and other nudist films as well as art house/exploitation cross-over features directed by Roman Polanski and Michael Reeves. Tenser also ran horror film specialists Tigon British Film Productions and it was Tigon's distribution operation that in 1972 released *Miss Julie* to modest returns.

A successful theatre and television actor, Robin Phillips directed what is recognized as the RSC's first modern-dress Shakespeare production, when in 1970 his *The Two Gentlemen of Verona* featured an on-stage swimming pool with Helen Mirren and Patrick Stewart in swimsuits and shades. But the company failed to embrace him, and according to one obituary 'he felt out of step with the Oxbridge mafia, notably Peter Hall and Trevor Nunn'.[6] After *Miss Julie* and other praised productions in London and Chichester, he became a highly successful artistic director of the Festival Theatre in Stratford, Ontario. In his theatre review of *Miss Julie* Harold Hobson praised Phillips's production as 'both intensely realistic and … powerfully symbolic [and] it inspires Helen Mirren to a definitive performance'.[7] For the film, the set by Phillips's regular collaborator Daphne Dare was transplanted to Pinewood with minimal changes, so that cameras often shoot off to the sides into a black void. The performances by Mirren, Donal McCann (Jean) and Heather Canning (Kristin), are precisely modulated for the camera, and their exemplary naturalism renders Strindberg's resonant, poetic text (in Michael Meyer's translation) entirely credible. Screen director Glenister subtly enhances the stage action with expressive framings, limited but telling camera moves, dissolves and occasional rapidly cut sequences. That this modest but meticulous adaptation is not more widely seen may be the result of its unconventional financing,[8] and it also deserves to be recognized as a significant precursor of NT Live and RSC Live from Stratford-upon-Avon cinema broadcasts. In the trailer for cinemas, over shots of the Royal

Shakespeare Theatre and the Aldwych, a stentorian voice-over promises, 'Now, all the excitement of a Royal Shakespeare Company first night comes to the screen of this theatre.'

In 1973 a second RSC season at The Place was less successful than the first, although there was praise for Athol Fugard's *Hello and Goodbye* directed by Peter Stevenson with Janet Suzman and Ben Kingsley. A screen version of this is another of the tantalizing 'ghost' adaptations that haunt this history, since the University of London contracted with the RSC to videotape this on stage. Enquiries suggest that if this screen version was indeed made, it may exist still within the London Metropolitan Archives, but the tape collection is not currently catalogued so as to allow it to be identified. The year 1973 was also when trial productions were first staged in a run-down hut owned by the company in Stratford. Trevor Nunn decided that this new space should be developed for at least one further year and he asked Buzz Goodbody to become its artistic director. She had joined the RSC in 1967, graduating from personal assistant to John Barton to directing shows for *Theatregoround* and at The Place, and working with Nunn as assistant director on the 1972 *Romans* season. In December 1973 she composed a manifesto for what she called The Other Place, grounding her plans in a concern to broaden the RSC's audience: 'The RSC is financed by the whole of society. We know why we play to an audience largely drawn from the upper and middle classes. We have to broaden that audience for artistic as well as social reasons. Unless we make the attempt – the classical theatre will become like Glyndebourne.'[9] Five decades on, Goodbody's anxieties remain a driving force for the RSC, and the memory of the remarkable success of the first The Other Place continues to inform debates and initiatives focused on broadening and enhancing the diversity of the company's audiences.[10]

The first season, which included productions of *The Tempest, Uncle Vanya* and a devised play by Mike Leigh, opened with Buzz Goodbody's stripped-back production of *King Lear*. She originally developed this for school audiences, although it later also played at The Place in London and toured to the United States. Performed by a cast of nine, with Tony Church (Lear) and Charles Dance (Edmund), together with a single musician, the production turned its back on the drama's epic qualities and played the text as a family tragedy.[11] But here too is another 'ghost' screen version that was definitely recorded but of which no trace can now be found.[12] A letter from the RSC's general manager David Brierley set out the simple conditions that permitted the University of Warwick's Audio-Visual Centre to make a video recording of *King Lear* on 11 July 1974.[13] The RSC was to receive a facilities fee of £25 and each actor, musician and member of RSC staff would get £17.75. The resulting recording could be used only within the University of Warwick for one year and any further use was dependent on additional fees being paid. Otherwise the recording had to be destroyed on 10 July 1975. Which, given that extensive enquiries have failed to bring a copy to light, seems likely to have happened, erasing forever the only moving images of any of Buzz Goodbody's work. The next year, four days after the press night of her widely praised The Other Place production of *Hamlet*, Buzz Goodbody took her own life.[14]

The remainder of the 1975 season was shepherded to the stage by director Barry Kyle, but the following year Trevor Nunn, in part out of regard for Buzz Goodbody and to develop her legacy, took over the running of The Other Place. During what he said was 'the most enjoyable year of my life at the RSC'[15] he staged a new production of *Macbeth*, which he had also recently directed on Stratford's main stage. Now he could bring Ian McKellen and Judi Dench to this 180-seat auditorium and, as is discussed below, to the television screen in one of the medium's most successful adaptations of Shakespeare. Also in 1976 at The Other Place, Ron Daniels directed a key new play of the decade, *Destiny* by David Edgar, and this too would be seen on television. Edgar's rigorously researched study of the developing far right political movement in Britain opened in September and transferred to the Aldwych the following May. It was received with exceptionally positive notices, with *The Observer's* Robert Cushman confidently stating that *Destiny* 'is, most importantly, the panoramic political play that writers of Mr Edgar's generation have been straining after for years'.[16] The political edge of BBC Television's *Play for Today* strand, which earlier in the decade had been the home for radical leftist dramas from Jim Allen, Ken Loach and Tony Garnett, was being reinvigorated under its new producer Margaret Matheson, and she determined to make a television version that was shown in November. As Tom May has exhaustively documented, Edgar made numerous changes to the script, and none of the television cast or production team had any connection with Ron Daniels's staging.[17] Nonetheless, there are inevitable intertextual links between the two presentations created little more than one year apart. May has also noted that, despite its clearly anti-fascist intent, '*Destiny* received very little criticism or obstruction from senior BBC management who were largely supportive and appreciative of it.' One factor in this institutional acceptance is likely to have been the cultural capital that the acclaimed RSC stage production had previously accrued.

Especially notable among later shows for The Other Place was Barry Kyle's 1983 promenade production of *The Dillen*, which was the focus of a half-hour BBC Midlands documentary directed by Mike Dornan.[18] The show used the small theatre as a base but spread out into the town's streets to explore the life of the working-class Stratford man George Hewins who was born in 1879. Adapted by Ron Hutchinson from a memoir compiled by Hewins's grand-daughter-in-law Angela Hewins, this was a rare RSC venture into community theatre and was intended by Kyle to fulfil Buzz Goodbody's vision for The Other Place by making 'something that got up and belonged to the town' and giving voice to 'another storyteller that wasn't Shakespeare ... to Stratford's proletarian Falstaff'.[19] With contributions from Kyle and from cast members Ron Cook and Peggy Mount, the film is a quietly involving testament to the commitment of the participating Stratford residents.

'Photographing a text' with Trevor Nunn

Perhaps because Peter Brook's production of *A Midsummer Night's Dream* dominated the start of the 1970s at the RSC, and also because a significant part of the company's new energy came to be focused at The Place and then The Other Place, a number of Shakespeare productions by the company in the early part of the decade were received without great enthusiasm. Elements of the workings of the theatre in the summer of 1970 were exposed in the hour-long film documentary *Shakespeare's Island*, written and directed by Lorna Pegram.[20] Co-produced by the BBC with veteran educational documentary maker George Buckland-Smith and his company Patria Pictures, this must surely have come across as old-fashioned even when it was first screened. Treating *The Tempest* as Shakespearean autobiography, the film parallels scenes from John Barton's 1970 staging, which featured Ian Richardson (Prospero), Ben Kingsley (Ariel) and Estelle Kohler (Miranda), with events in the playwright's life and their location at the traditional tourist spots of Stratford and its environs. By the end of both play and life, the leaden narration suggests that 'Shakespeare has captured the ultimate island – the imagination of man.' Not even Tony Church's reading can rescue such a line. Yet the film remains of interest, since it is the earliest extended portrait of the RSC at work, with sequences in the wings with stage manager Roger Howells and in the workshops with head of design Christopher Morley. Included along with a bland interview with Trevor Nunn is more than ten minutes of John Barton's production, filmed on stage and featuring Prospero's key exchanges with Miranda, Ariel and Caliban (Barry Stanton) located in a near-abstract setting.

Although there was little sense of change in *Shakespeare's Island*, as he established himself at the head of the company Trevor Nunn encouraged moves away from the austere naturalism that had been a keynote under Peter Hall, while at the same time stimulating the embrace of self-aware theatricality. Looking back, Colin Chambers, who was later to be the RSC's literary manager, wrote that 'the company under Nunn kept the social backdrop in sight but turned to a more private and personal scrutiny, a more romantic speaking style and a sharper, more intensive use of colour'.[21] Responding to these possibilities, a new generation of actors flourished, including Ian Richardson, Alan Howard, Norman Rodway and Patrick Stewart. But Sally Beauman's assessment of the company in the first half of the decade is ambivalent: 'Above all its confidence in its large-theatre Shakespeare work, the foundation for the entire edifice of the RSC, seemed fitful.'[22] The strengths and weaknesses were displayed during the 1972 *Romans* season, when for a Stratford stage newly equipped with hydraulic wonders, Nunn worked with associate directors Buzz Goodbody and Euan Smith to bring an opulent operaticism and notes of apocalyptic uncertainty to *Coriolanus, Julius Caesar, Antony and Cleopatra* and *Titus Andronicus*. In Stratford the critics were ambivalent, although the notices improved when the shows transferred to the Aldwych. Particular praise was lavished on Nunn's richly imagined *Antony and Cleopatra* with Janet Suzman as the Egyptian queen (Figure 8). Harold Hobson decreed that the production was 'much the best of the four' and wrote that 'Janet Suzman's Cleopatra sparkles in amorous variety.'[23]

Antony and Cleopatra must have appeared ripe for a deal within the cluster of conversations that the RSC continued to have with broadcasters. But at the same time the company had been endeavouring since 1969 to extricate itself from what were feared to be the restrictions of the Filmways contract. Direct funding from CBS was still a possibility, since the network had been delighted with the critical response to Peter Hall's *A Midsummer Night's Dream*. Ideas considered for a series of five projects

FIGURE 8 *Janet Suzman (Cleopatra) in the stage production by Trevor Nunn of* Antony and Cleopatra *(1972), later recorded by ATV. Photograph by Reg Wilson ©* RSC.

over seven years included a feature film about 'Shakespeare's women', and the proposed fee of £20,000 would have been welcome with the company facing a likely deficit in 1968/9 of £76,000.[24] There were also conversations, which also ultimately came to nothing, about the BBC broadcasting Terry Hands's acclaimed staging of *The Merry Wives of Windsor*. And members of the Executive Council were also taking advice about screen financing from Sir Lew Grade, managing director of ATV, the Midlands-based ITV company perhaps best known for its soap opera *Crossroads* and glossy mid-Atlantic film series including *The Saint* and *Danger Man*. A flamboyant showman whose companies represented talent, ran theatres and produced films, Grade was monitoring the emerging medium of videocassettes and sharing his knowledge with the RSC.[25] A pilot project for video distribution was proposed for early 1972, although the board was initially concerned that this might lead to legal action by Filmways, which had still not signed a termination agreement. A year later, however, the RSC had agreed a four-year production deal with ATV, including a fee of £25,000 for *Antony and Cleopatra*, and on 15 May 1973 Trevor Nunn had to offer his apologies for missing that day's board meeting because he was in the television studio directing the production.[26]

At the start of 1973, in addition to his interest in videocassettes, Lew Grade had a very specific reason for committing to a deal with the RSC. His ATV franchise had to be seen to be fulfilling the strictures, imposed by the regulatory Independent Broadcasting Authority (IBA), of providing a balanced and responsible output committed to 'programmes of merit'. But the IBA was concerned that Grade and those running the four other major ITV companies were offering schedules that were too aggressively commercial and neglectful of their public service responsibilities. Just before Christmas 1972 the IBA insisted on the inclusion in ITV's holiday programming of a Southern Television recording from Glyndebourne of Verdi's *Macbeth*. To head off further unwelcome interventions of this kind, early in 1973 Grade and his colleagues committed to six peak-time 'television events' each year. Among the first such productions from ATV were to be *Carmen* from the Royal Opera House and the RSC's *Antony and Cleopatra*.[27] The cultural capital of Shakespeare and of the company, having bolstered the public service mission of the BBC in the previous decade, was now recruited to serve the commercial imperatives of the corporation's rival.

Summing up his approach to small-screen adaptations of Shakespeare after *Othello* (1990), Trevor Nunn reflected that with each of his four productions, 'I was trying to use a very strict discipline for television – what I described as "shooting the text" rather than "shooting the action" – working a great deal in close-up, shooting the thought processes that made the complex, heightened language, accessible. Therefore, the television work was rather spare, monochromatic and stark.'[28] Working on his second adaptation, *The Comedy of Errors* (1978), he looked back to his first:

Antony and Cleopatra was a serious attempt to answer the question about the ideal of televising Shakespeare. I think it has to be done in a studio, with an element of artificiality – if the sky is blue and the trees are waving, everyone wonders why that actor is speaking in blank verse. The two main problems were, first, how to convey real people talking in a very heightened speech, and secondly, that the ratio was all wrong – there was much too much speech, and not enough pictures. That is why I wanted to strip everything out of the setting, to have everything suggested by texture and lighting – and not just that, but to concentrate on their faces. What we were doing was photographing a text.[29]

Although invariably referred to as television productions 'by Trevor Nunn', the question of authorship of these adaptations is complicated by his collaboration, mandated during the 1970s by union rules, with experienced multi-camera studio directors. On *Antony and Cleopatra*, Nunn received a 'Staged for television by ... ' credit, which was paired with 'Directed for television by Jon Scoffield.' In the years before *Antony and Cleopatra* Scoffield directed a string of variety spectaculars with singer Tom Jones and others. He would go on to be one of the directors on the first series of Thames Television's television musical *Rock Follies* (1977), which like *Antony and Cleopatra* made innovative, non-naturalistic use of studio recording techniques and video effects.

For *Antony and Cleopatra*, Nunn and Scoffield conjured into being an abstracted televisual space in which characters and objects are set against swathes of intense colour, canvases of brilliant white or voids of mysterious darkness. The public spaces of Rome have a transparent clarity whereas the early scenes in Egypt, bathed in reds and oranges, are layered and veiled, with gauzes, hazes and foregrounded elements. There is a modest employment of video effects too, as when Philo's delivery of his report of Antony dallying in Egypt is presented in black and white (or as close as video could then achieve), before a wall of subtly deforming soldiers' faces. Similarly exploiting advanced video technology of the time, the opening titles employ colour separation overlay (CSO) to create a decorative frieze of the figures in the drama.[30] Set within all of this are the faces of the cast, shot for much of the time in close-up and tightly composed groupings, and with almost no camera movement and few establishing shots. In this, and his claim to be 'shooting the text', Nunn's approach echoes that of Peter Hall on *A Midsummer Night's Dream*. Sharply edited sequences combine with shots held to observe an actor working through a speech. Yet the verse-speaking, and the finely calibrated performances, register assertively as if from the theatre, while the visual treatment as well as an elaborate audio mix of gulls, waves and the like, insist on the production's status as television. Watched and heard more than forty years later from a DVD of indifferent quality, the combination comes across as uncertain and uneasy, but this was not the perception of most critics at the time.[31] For *The Times* Leonard Buckley gushed, 'Shakespeare came to television last night. His genius found a whole new sphere in which to triumph. But you can say, too, that television came to Shakespeare. The electronic marvel took the Bard and made him its own .... Television lifted the production off the stage into its own ethereal element.'[32] In the broadsheets only Clive James, after praising the visuals, cautioned that 'Linguistically, however, it was an average production going on vile.' He felt that the production lacked pace, largely because the cast had been encouraged to act emotions around the lines rather than following Bernard Shaw's instruction that 'you must act Shakespeare on the lines and not in between'.[33]

In 1974 Trevor Nunn directed only one production for the main Stratford stage – an indifferently received *Macbeth* with Nicol Williamson – and only one large-scale show the following year. This was Henrik Ibsen's *Hedda Gabler* with Glenda Jackson and Patrick Stewart, which toured to Australia and North America before opening at the Aldwych. Much like *Miss Julie*, the almost accidental funding for the feature film version came from two American producers, both of whom had a connection to the production's female lead. George Barrie was the owner of the perfume and haircare company Fabergé Inc., and also a film executive who had financed the hit comedy *A Touch of Class* (1973) that starred Glenda Jackson. His partner on *Hedda*, Robert Enders, had moved to Britain in 1972 after a Hollywood career. In 1974 he also produced the actor in a film version for Ely Landau's American Film Theatre of Jean Genet's *The Maids*, derived from Christopher Miles's production at London's Greenwich Theatre. On that film the director of photography was Douglas Slocombe and the composer Laurie Johnson, and both reprised these roles for *Hedda*.[34] Although little-seen, this is a vibrant and distinguished screen adaptation, grounded in Nunn's own vernacular version of Ibsen's text and distinguished by fine performances circling around Jackson's haughty, flighty, fiercely intelligent Hedda. Although Peter Eyre as Tesman and Patrick Stewart as Lovborg are somewhat overshadowed, Timothy West as Block holds his own against Jackson's forcefulness. Indeed, in Act 1 a single shot held for more than five minutes celebrates the performances as Hedda coaxes from Mrs Elvsted (Jennie Linden) the tale of how she walked out on her husband. The gardens around the new Tesman home, together with a spacious conservatory (echoing John Napier's stage design), are used to open out the drama's claustrophobia, and the shifting relationships are delineated in the carefully judged compositions and movements of Slocombe's camera. The predominance of mid-shots, expertly employed framing in depth and the *mise en scene's* telling use of mirrors all distinguish this from Trevor Nunn's television Shakespeares. Even the moments of explicit melodrama, when an underscored shot lasts a beat longer than narratively necessary, land effectively. The film draws out Ibsen's comedy and serves well his tragedy, and *Hedda* deserves greater prominence in the director's filmography and that of the company for which he originally staged it.

A comedy, a tragedy and the Histories

In 1976 Trevor Nunn staged five new productions, including a sprawling musical version of *The Comedy of Errors* and a small-scale, ritualistic *Macbeth*, both of which he would bring to the screen. Premiered at Stratford in September 1976 before transferring to the Aldwych, *The Comedy of Errors* was an immediate gold-plated hit, winning the 1977 Olivier Award for Best New Musical. Nunn himself wrote the lyrics for the interpolated songs, and Guy Woolfenden's rock-inflected score adroitly complemented the setting of a modern-day, tourist-trap, T-shirt-bedecked Ephesus. Slapstick and dance, with choreography by Gillian Lynne, framed droll performances and fine verse-speaking from RSC regulars including Judi Dench, Richard Griffiths, Michael Williams, Mike Gwilym and Roger Rees. 'Gaiety rises from this production like a flock of brightly plumaged songbirds,' wrote J.W. Lambert.[35] The director recognized that translating the production to the screen was a quite different project from *Antony and Cleopatra*, as he confided to Peter Fiddick: 'It is also a play of no literary significance whatsoever, a mixture of bla[n]k verse, rhymed verse, and doggerel, that is largely unmemorable. Although it is exquisitely structured, it would be preposterous to be going on about "photographing the text."'[36] As a broad comedy, the production also demanded an audience's laughter. A decade earlier, the BBC screen version of Clifford Williams's staging enabled this by recording the production on stage before a full auditorium. The solution this time proved less satisfactory, although much of the stage production's pleasure is preserved on screen. The recording begins with a swan on the River Avon, an exterior shot of the Royal Shakespeare Theatre, and then audience members arriving in the rain, buying tickets and entering the auditorium. As they settle in their seats, music fades up and we see cast members waving and chatting from the stage. A cutaway reveals the official notice 'Cameras not allowed.' A latecomer dashing in is cut against closer, more brightly lit shots of pre-show action. Television promises a privileged surrogate visit to the theatre. The multiple electronic cameras now cross the line of the proscenium arch and enter the stage to present the actions and dialogue. The screen director for *The Comedy of Errors* was Philip Casson, a studio all-rounder who had recently worked on the prison drama *Within These Walls*, and there is no trace here of the distinctive visuals of *Antony and Cleopatra*.

The Comedy of Errors is conventionally shot as a studio drama, with only occasional close-ups for particular emphasis. Certain restrictions are obvious on what angles were possible because the cameras were shooting within the theatrical set. Hand-held cameras were also used as well as shots from the balconies. The price of such visual flexibility, however, was that almost all of the performance was recorded without an audience. Dimly lit, lower resolution images from the stalls of laughter and applause are cut in at appropriate moments, but for the most part the audience's response is provided by a crudely applied laugh track – and to ears forty years on this sounds unacceptably false.[37] The subtle exchange between performers and audience is missing, and the lack of authenticity blights the recording. Yet despite this error of comedy the strong moral sense that drives the production is retained. Of the recording, Kenneth Rothwell wrote, 'The most poignant moments come when Judi Dench as Adriana and Francesca Annis as Luciana exchange confidences about their "relationships" with men. Playing Barbara Shelley's Courtesan as a flagrant hussy underscores the womens' resentment. Nunn's probing treatment … shows again how the light-heartedness in Shakespearean drama may conceal monsters from the deep.'[38]

Remarkably, *The Comedy of Errors* opened on the main stage in Stratford just twenty days after Trevor Nunn's *Macbeth* had its press night down the road at The Other Place.[39] Ian McKellen had said that he wanted to act in the space in the 1976 season, and despite having only recently staged the play – unsatisfactorily as he felt – Nunn had offered him the Scottish king, with Judi Dench as Lady Macbeth. On the square stage of bare boards Nunn painted a circle to concentrate the action, and as Colin Chambers recalled,

> The actors sat inches away from the audience on upturned beer crates … Props were in full view at the side. The actors were all equal, and nothing happened until the audience had settled, and thereby signalled that they were ready to set off on the journey, as equals also. It was a journey of the imagination, exploring, appropriately, the power of Macbeth's mind to do what he fancied, and the discovery of its limitations, which were bound up with the individual's relationship to self, and of self to society.[40]

As Michael Mullin has elaborated, 'what Trevor Nunn had sought, his audience responded to: an enactment of a ritual, a performance that partook of exorcism and Satanism. The audience joined the actors as silent participants in this quasi-religious ceremony.'[41] Indeed, the sense of theatrical ritual is preserved in the full title used on screen of the Thames Television adaptation (even if the production is rarely referred to as such): *A Performance of Macbeth*.

With the four-year ATV deal coming to an end, another ITV company had spotted an opportunity to benefit from an association with Shakespeare and the RSC. Thames Television had held the London weekday franchise since 1968, and under director of programmes Jeremy Isaacs it had produced a string of award-winning programmes including *The World at War* (1973–74) and *The Naked Civil Servant* (1975). By 1978, when *Macbeth* was videotaped at Thames' Teddington Studios, the IBA was in the early stages of considering what changes might be made to the franchises in new contracts planned for 1980. A relationship with the RSC would enhance the company's proposed production schedule for the next decade, and, indeed, in the wake of the success of *Macbeth*, just such a three-year arrangement was announced in early December 1979. Three productions were planned, although once Thames' licence was secure, only the screen version of *Three Sisters*, discussed below, reached the screen. But in the spring of 1978, Thames paired Philip Casson again with Nunn, to reestablish their collaboration on *The Comedy of Errors* and to extend the approach that Nunn and Scoffield had explored on *Antony and Cleopatra*.[42]

The first shot is from directly above the circle, and the camera slowly descends as, with Guy Woolfenden's church organ score starting up, we are transported into this space of sacrament. The actors sit on the periphery and the camera at the circle's centre turns on itself as it moves from face to shadowed face. Throughout, the conventions of television realism are denied, even as the performances have a low-key, determinedly naturalistic intensity. Much of the drama is played in static two-shots or tight singles, with the lens on occasions seemingly only inches from a character's eyes or bloodied hand. But the camera is also at times restless and prowling, as when Macbeth first encounters the witches. As in *Antony and Cleopatra*, we see no backgrounds beyond the circle, but here (and lighting director Luigi Bottone deserves special credit) the void is simply black against which close-ups of the characters assert themselves. We are trapped in the circle with the actors – or rather with Macbeth and Lady Macbeth, both of whom at times address us directly. McKellen especially is mesmerizing as he confides his soliloquies. Then at the end there is a thrilling moment of action as Macbeth and Macduff (Bob Peck) flail at each other with their swords. We do not, however, see Macduff's triumphant killing and the resolutely downbeat close has Malcolm (Roger Rees) and his court stunned by the enormity of events.

In one of the most considered discussions of the adaptation to television of a theatre staging, Michael Mullin has analysed the banquet scene, noting that the studio shooting script includes dense instructions to the camera operators for agitated movements. Then the camera – and by extension the viewer – takes the position of Banquo's ghost, who is otherwise unseen. Macbeth's response 'allows us to see the scorpions that have filled his mind and that impel him to seek by any means to defy fate'.[43] As Kenneth Rothwell parsed this insight, 'Adroit camera angles and tight framing enhance the illusion that the screen is a mirror for ourselves rather than a frame for defining the actors.'[44] To draw his argument together, Mullin outlined five general principles that contributed to the success of the screen version, including the fact that the theatre production had been extensively played on stage, that the small stage created a close-up production style well-suited to the screen, and that the ritual elements on television were highly successful. In addition, he argued, 'the rhythm of the camerawork followed the emotional rhythms of the script' and 'the television medium was kept subordinate to the drama'. The principles, he concluded, suggest to television producers that Shakespeare plays produced in small studio theatres offer unusual opportunities for translation into television, and that TV Shakespeare works best when the emotional realities behind the poetry can be seen in close-up. In making this translation, and in revealing the emotional realities behind the play, this *Macbeth* on TV documents theatre history and at the same time makes it.[45]

In the later 1970s and early 1980s, although much of the attention from outside was focused on Trevor Nunn's leadership of the RSC, the company's artistic direction was also shaped in fundamental ways by Terry Hands. The two men were joint artistic directors after 1978, and Hands's work, especially with Shakespeare, was as admired as Nunn's. Terry Hands joined the RSC in 1966, brought in by Peter Hall from the Liverpool Everyman to run the *Theatregoround* project. His main stage debut was the much-admired production of *The Merry Wives of Windsor* in 1968, and the production was chosen for a tentative entry into an imagined market for educational videos. 'It was done by a man called Andrew Sinclair who clearly had no idea what he was doing,' Terry Hands recalled in interview, 'and this communicated itself to the company very quickly'.[46] A letter from David Brierley in response to a later approach proposing the production of educational videos echoed Terry Hands's dismissal. 'The lighting was bad,' he wrote, 'the sound appalling, and the artistic result deeply disappointing.'[47] Nothing of this exercise, which might have preserved at least a trace of the staging, can be found today.

In the early 1970s the company's artistic direction was set by Trevor Nunn and John Barton working closely with Hands, who concentrated on productions in Stratford, and David Jones, also an associate director after 1966, who was given responsibility for the Aldwych. David Jones shaped a new policy for London, bringing more transfers from Stratford and revivals of rarely performed classics including the plays of Maxim Gorky. At the same time, Jones was committed to film-making, having been one of the first producers on the BBC arts magazine series *Monitor*. In 1972 he directed a television biography of the nineteenth-century farm labourer and poet John Clare, with Patrick Stewart in the cast and narration by Tony Church, both stalwarts of the RSC.[48] Working with other RSC actors including Ben Kingsley, Brenda Bruce and Philip Locke, he also directed adaptations for television of tales by Thomas Hardy and Anton Chekhov.[49]

The 1975 season in Stratford saw Terry Hands triumph with new productions of *Henry IV, Part 1; Henry IV, Part 2;* and *Henry V,* with Alan Howard. The following year he produced the *Henry VI* trilogy, in the first professional performances of Shakespeare's full texts since Elizabethan times.[50] As with John Barton and Peter Hall's *The Wars of the Roses* a decade before, these three productions were especially acclaimed for the performances played throughout a single day. Unlike the earlier trilogy, however, this one attracted no interest from the national broadcaster. BBC

Television had decided that it was sufficiently confident to take on the whole canon as *The BBC Television Shakespeare*, without the involvement of the RSC or any other established theatre company. 'I wish them all luck,' Nunn told the journalist Peter Fiddick, 'but, of course, it's likely to swamp the market, especially if you're hoping for American help ... a new production is such a lottery, with no guarantees of success, and Shakespeare arouses such expectations that it's twice as difficult as anything else.' He had been hoping to set up a screen version of Terry Hands's *Henry V*, but he recognized the impact of the BBC venture. 'I just think it's such a shame,' he said, 'that we could be denied being able to record a production of a great play that really has worked.'[51]

Broadcast a year before the corporation's canon started, the BBC documentary *Arena Theatre: Hands off the Classics*[52] was a clunkily constructed exchange about the appropriate way to treat the texts of the great playwrights, including Ben Jonson and, most especially, Shakespeare. Bernard Levin took a traditionalist position, arguing initially that Peter Barnes's 1976 version for the Birmingham Rep of Jonson's *The Devil is an Ass* was an unacceptable travesty of the original. The attack broadened in the film to criticize directors who changed texts to suit idiosyncratic interpretations rather than presenting 'what Shakespeare wrote'. Foremost among those who offered ripostes were Terry Hands and John Barton, who both argued for the validity of different approaches at different historical moments. Hands, however, was dismissive of the extensive rewriting that Barton did for *The Wars of the Roses*.[53] Buried within the back and forth is a sequence from rehearsals for Hands's 1977 production of *Coriolanus*, together with brief performance extracts, with Alan Howard playing in costume to a single camera. Fragments of Coriolanus's speeches from Act 3, Scene 2 and Act 2, Scene 3 suggest why audiences responded so strongly to what is recalled elsewhere as Howard's complex, thrilling and disturbing characterization.[54] Subsequently, in one of the few direct links between a RSC staging and a production for *The BBC Television Shakespeare*, in 1984, almost at the end of the latter's cycle, Howard played Coriolanus in director Elijah Moshinsky's radically shortened version. Although Terry Hands was not involved in that, he recognized that for television 'Alan used where he could elements that we had explored more fully on the stage.'

While the BBC was preoccupied with its cycle of Shakespeare's plays and consequently demonstrating little concern for the RSC, the ITV regional companies had a very different attitude. Extending the interest demonstrated by the support for Trevor Nunn's Shakespeare adaptations with ATV and Thames, another of the commercial contractors, London Weekend Television (LWT), began what would prove to be a productive relationship with the company. In early 1978, recognizing the imminent franchise renewal round, the company started what would become its long-running arts series *The South Bank Show*, edited and presented by Melvyn Bragg. Its third programme included a half-hour profile of Alan Howard titled *The Player King*. The film is finely detailed and immediate, enhanced by the actor being happy to be interviewed backstage during performances. Vivid sequences from the current productions, shot close-up on stage, include Howard giving 'Once more unto the breach, dear friends' through to 'God for Harry, England and St George' (3.1.1–34) from *Henry V*, as well as, from *Henry VI, Part 3*, 'This battle fares like to the morning's war' to 'For what is in this world but grief and woe' (2.5.1–20), together with two scenes from *Coriolanus*, when the hero elects to face the people in the marketplace and when he is persuaded by his mother and son not to attack Rome. These slivers of Howard's performances are all the more precious for being the only surviving moving images (apart from restaged moments from *Coriolanus* noted above) from Terry Hands's revelatory productions.

Back at the BBC

In the fifteen years since the productions marking the 400th anniversary of Shakespeare's birth in 1964, the playwright's work had – apart from in the various RSC collaborations – rarely been well served by television. In the prime-time ITV schedule there had been only *The Merchant of Venice*, drawn from Jonathan Miller's 1970 National Theatre production with Laurence Olivier and Joan Plowright. In addition to a remarkable 1970 recording of the Prospect Theatre Company's *Richard II* with Ian McKellen, BBC Television had each year turned out, mostly for the *Play of the Month* strand, an unadventurous studio- or location-shot production. Producer Cedric Messina was refining his own small-screen 'heritage' template for the plays, assembling all-star casts but constraining creative ambitions by entrusting the productions to skilled but unimaginative directors such as Basil Coleman and James Cellan Jones. In 1978 Messina extended this approach as the first producer of *The BBC Television Shakespeare*, conceived as a cycle of thirty-seven productions across the next seven years.

In her detailed study of the series Susan Willis wrote of 'a latent rivalry' with the RSC adaptations of the 1970s and recognized that 'the BBC and RSC productions illuminate the issues surrounding studio-based drama'.[55] The first BBC recordings, shown in December 1978, were deeply traditionalist: *Romeo and Juliet* directed by Alvin Rakoff, described by one critic as 'the epitome of tasteful heritage Shakespeare';[56] David Giles's strongly cast, studio-shot production of *Richard II* with Derek Jacobi; and Helen Mirren in Basil Coleman's *As You Like It* filmed on location around Glamis Castle. Towards the end of the whole project James Bulman characterized the vision for the series established by Cedric Messina:

> Messina advised his directors to keep the audience unaware of theatrical conventions, omit as much artifice as possible, and dedicate themselves to the principle that Shakespeare, to be done right, must be done

naturalistically ... Messina was determined to satisfy popular taste. He depended on the use of 'realistic' film techniques to make Shakespeare palatable for a mass audience ... and by preserving the status quo, they apparently satisfied Messina's criteria for definitive productions.[57]

'All of the plays will be presented in a style true to the period in which they were set,' Messina told a journalist. 'There will be no modern dress versions, or eccentric interpretations.'[58] Responding to the first broadcast, television critic Clive James spun the conceit of a city called Messina to compare *Romeo and Juliet* with the RSC/ATV *Antony and Cleopatra*, which he claimed

> should have shown everybody that the way to get the effect of wealth with a television budget is to shoot tight on the actors; use a few good props; and keep the background darkly suggestive. But in Messina the lesson was never learned ... All the perspectives were evenly lit, as if specifically to reveal their poverty of detail. The eye went hungry, which made the ear ravenous. Unfortunately there was not much worth listening to.[59]

Such was the negative reaction to the early productions that Cedric Messina was replaced as the series producer after two years by Jonathan Miller, who also oversaw two years, with Shaun Sutton taking the role for the final three seasons. Both Miller and, more tentatively, Sutton moved away from screen naturalism, embracing in a number of notable productions by Miller himself, Elijah Moshinsky, Don Taylor and Jane Howell (whose *Henry VI* trilogy is the project's highpoint) both theatrical and at times self-consciously televisual techniques. The critical assessment of the series, however, as old-fashioned and irredeemably dull was determined during the first two years, and despite the variety and interest of later productions this remains the dominant view of the series.[60] Susan Willis contrasted Messina's aesthetic with what, on the basis of just *Antony and Cleopatra* and *Macbeth*, she identified as 'the RSC style':

> tragedy can be stripped down to essentials for television, radically by the RSC, which transfers a theatrical bareness almost directly to the camera, although these are not just taped stage plays ... Because the RSC productions appear to be state of the art, very modern, stylish, and up-to-date technical renditions of Shakespeare that play off of the latest theatrical conventions, they contrasted as fully as anything could to the early BBC productions.[61]

By becoming standard versions that are still in use in education four decades after its first transmissions, *The BBC Television Shakespeare* achieved significant commercial success. The series enjoyed wide dissemination first on VHS and later on DVD. Tapes were originally sold to schools and colleges along with licences for educational use at prices in excess of £300 for each production. But before the BBC productions were published both the RSC's *Antony and Cleopatra* and *The Comedy of Errors* were released as VHS tapes in 1983 by Precision Video, a subsidiary of Lew Grade's ACC conglomerate as was ATV (which in 1982 had become Central).[62] Retailing at £47.50 each, these titles at last fulfilled the dream of 'long-playing visual records' of Shakespeare that Peter Hall had outlined seventeen years before.

After *Macbeth* and *Three Sisters* three years later, which is discussed below, no ITV company worked again with the RSC on a screen adaptation. The stable duopoly of the BBC and IBA-regulated ITV that had sustained the public service offerings from the commercial contractors crumbled as new channels proliferated in the later 1980s and market forces reshaped the medium. In 1990, however, the RSC once again collaborated on an adaptation with the BBC, shooting on a sound stage Trevor Nunn's 1989 production of *Othello* with Willard White and Ian McKellen. Received with almost unanimous critical enthusiasm, this had been triumphantly staged in The Other Place, much as *Macbeth* had been a decade before, and was in fact the final production before the original tin hut was demolished.[63] With a setting and costumes that suggested the American Civil War, the drama was played domestically, intimately, naturalistically. Both the Othello of opera singer Willard White, taking on his first straight dramatic role, and Imogen Stubbs's Desdemona, were praised by the critics, but it was Ian McKellen's Iago that prompted the superlatives, with one critic writing that 'This is a devastating performance, precisely thought out in every detail, burning like molten steel, and controlled by a single-minded intelligence.'[64]

At the BBC the regular BBC One series of classic dramas *Play of the Month* had come to an end in 1983. In 1985, BBC Two took up the baton of burnishing stage plays for the box with its series *Theatre Night*, in which two RSC non-Shakespeare adaptations were presented in 1985 (see Chapter 5) and which was also the home for *Othello*. The series was then supplanted by *Performance*, which ran from 1991 to 1998, after which classic theatre essentially disappeared from the BBC for a decade. Indicative perhaps of the medium's deeply ambivalent attitude to the stage at this point is the bizarre choice for an interval feature during *Othello's* first transmission of a parodic 'masterclass' with Nigel Planer's spoof 'luvvie' character Nicholas Craig. The budget for *Othello*, which was partly provided by a co-production with the independent company Primetime, allowed for fifteen days on a sound stage at Elstree, with Nunn himself directing for the screen, as he had done on *Three Sisters*. In an on-set interview he again laid out his strategy for adapting Shakespeare to the small screen:

> What I've done ... is to give myself the exercise: how do you shoot the text? Well, the answer is you don't shoot spectacularly. You shoot the thought: you shoot everything you need to make the language work. You

don't describe what the language is already describing; you let it do its own work. You have to go against the visual grammar of film-making, because there is a rhythmic ingredient in the verse. If you cut just before, say, the end of a pentameter, then you've got two rhythms going – film rhythm and language rhythm. Even if an audience doesn't know why it is being irritated, it will seem abrasive.[65]

The frame for this approach to the text is a single courtyard set (by the masterful television designer David Myerscough-Jones, developing Bob Crowley's work for the stage), with sophisticated lighting conjuring up both night-time Venice and sun-soaked Cyprus. Nunn's cameras stand back from the action more than in *Macbeth*, with medium-shots predominating rather than the earlier production's near-obsessional reliance on close-ups. The result divided critics, with Sheridan Morley reflecting that, 'All television had to do here was show the original close up intensity of a chamber production which blazed with thoughtful reappraisal.'[66] For Patrick Stoddart, the production was 'as near to perfect a piece of television drama as you could get'.[67] James Saynor, by contrast, deplored the manner in which 'superb performances' had been combined with 'extreme compositional torpidity'.[68]

To date, Trevor Nunn has adapted one further RSC production for the screen, once again with Ian McKellen and in partnership with Primetime, albeit this time for Channel 4's digital channel More4. *King Lear* was a production created by the director in 2007 for the Courtyard Theatre, which had been built on the site of The Other Place as a replacement auditorium in Stratford while the Royal Shakespeare Theatre was being extensively remodelled. The production transferred to London, after which it was recorded at Pinewood, with Chris Hunt co-directing for the screen with Trevor Nunn. McKellen's performance is forcefully intelligent and he is supported by a strong ensemble, including Sylvester McCoy as the Fool and Romola Garai as Cordelia. But too often the staging, as one critic wrote responding to the theatre version, 'registers as a heightened costume melodrama, replete with black-hearted, sneering villains',[69] and the deployment of the multiple cameras in a dark, abstracted studio space is prosaic. There is little here of the invention or the visual expressivity that distinguished the screen adaptations of *Antony and Cleopatra* and *Macbeth*.

The Warehouse and a world elsewhere

By early 1977, with The Other Place producing work of exceptional quality that London audiences were demanding to see, there was a strong argument to open a space in the capital that was appropriate for small-stage transfers. Trevor Nunn asked Howard Davies to oversee the project, which would have a strong commitment to new writing as well as taking shows from TOP. A lengthy search eventually turned up the Donmar, which had been built in the nineteenth century as the vat room of a brewery, and had subsequently been a film studio, a fruit warehouse and latterly a rehearsal space and small auditorium. Peter Brook and Charles Marowitz had staged scenes from Genet's *The Screens* there as part of their 1964 Theatre of Cruelty experiments. The Warehouse opened in July 1977 and in its first seasons presented new plays by Howard Barker, Edward Bond, Barrie Keeffe, Peter Flannery, Stephen Poliakoff, Mary O'Malley and Pam Gems, among others.[70] Gems's *Piaf* with Jane Lapotaire as the French *chanteuse* was the only production presented at The Warehouse (after premiering at TOP) that was adapted directly for the screen. After Howard Davies's hugely successful production had also been seen at the Aldwych and in a West End transfer, a multi-camera recording was directed by Gary Halvorson before a live audience on Broadway, and this was first screened on the US cable service The Entertainment Network in June 1982. Two other significant plays by contemporary British writers that premiered at The Warehouse also, on the model of *Destiny*, eventually became television dramas or films, although with minimal cross-over of cast members or creative teams.

The television drama *No Excuses* began life as the play *Bastard Angel* by Barrie Keeffe staged at The Warehouse in January 1980. Central Television expanded the play into eight fifty-minute episodes that were screened with little fanfare and less critical enthusiasm in May and June 1983. On both stage and television Charlotte Cornwell played the late 1960s rock singer Shelly, once a star with her band Angels but now mired in creative doldrums.[71] In June 1980 The Warehouse presented Willy Russell's two-hander *Educating Rita*, focused on an Open University tutor and his Liverpudlian working-class student. Commissioned by the RSC, this was staged by Mike Ockrent with Mark Kingston and Julie Walters. A popular feature film adaptation followed in 1983, with Walters and Michael Caine working with director Lewis Gilbert. Another RSC show that became a popular feature film in 1983 was *Privates on Parade*, a farce with songs by Peter Nichols that played at the Aldwych in 1977. This concerned a fictional, and mostly gay, military song and dance troupe during the Malayan Emergency in 1948. Unusually for a feature film adapted from a stage play, the same director, Michael Blakemore, oversaw both, and Denis King's music also made the transfer. Denis Quilley, Joe Melia and Simon Jones reprised their stage roles in the HandMade Films production.

Perhaps the most significant play from these years to reach the screen, and also the one with the longest screen gestation, was Peter Flannery's *Our Friends in the North,* which was conceived when the writer was working with the RSC in Stratford in 1980. Observing rehearsals and performances of the small-scale touring productions of *Henry IV, Part 1* and *Henry IV, Part 2* as directed by Bill Alexander, Flannery decided to write an epic history play about post-war Britain, which was staged with a cast of eighteen by John Caird in 1982 at TOP, in Newcastle, and at the Barbican's small-scale theatre, The Pit. Fourteen years later, with a cast including Christopher

Eccleston, Gina McKee, Daniel Craig and Mark Strong, and a budget of £7.5 million, it emerged as a compelling nine-part drama on BBC Two. Flannery had rewritten his play in a myriad of ways, although he retained the original vision and, indeed, traces of the original catalyst of Shakespeare's Histories.[72] As Jeffrey Richards noted following the final episode, 'The serial captivated much of the country, sketching a panoramic view of life in Britain from the sixties to the nineties … At once sweeping and intimate, both moving and angry, simultaneously historical and contemporary.'[73] *Our Friends in the North* as a television series cannot be claimed as an adaptation of the RSC production, but the original commission and presentation associated the company to its credit with what became one of the defining small-screen dramas from the late twentieth century.

In the two decades between *All's Well That Ends Well* in 1968 and two shows in the autumn of 1985, to be discussed in Chapter 5, BBC Television produced only a single RSC adaptation. This was the offsite project *Every Good Boy Deserves Favour*, initially staged in early July 1977 at the Royal Festival Hall as a RSC collaboration with the London Symphony Orchestra. Scripted by Tom Stoppard with music by André Previn, the drama is set in a psychiatric hospital in Leningrad where a Russian dissident shares a cell with someone whose madness takes the form of believing he has his own eighty-piece orchestra. More than two years after its premiere, it reached BBC Two in November 1979 in a screen version co-directed by Nunn and Roger Bamford and recorded at Wembley Conference Centre. Documentation of its production has been impossible to track down, although *The Guardian* television previewer at the time wrote that it had 'been somewhat long, and, one gathers, a shade agonised in the making'.[74] Moreover, in the form that it eventually reached the screen the recording carries no acknowledgement or branding associating it with the RSC. A cast including Ian McKellen, Ben Kingsley, Frank Windsor and Barbara Leigh-Hunt play the text in abstracted spaces that initially appear to be in a studio but are then revealed as set within the orchestra and facing a watching audience. Visually the television version is distinguished by elements of electronic graphics that place the actors against fields of colour and that on occasions resize and reshape the frame.

In 1978 a group of actors including Ian McKellen persuaded the RSC to organize a tour of improvised venues in twenty-six towns across England and Scotland. The troupe travelled with productions of *Twelfth Night* and *Three Sisters*, which they played before minimal scenery in a style similar to that developed at The Other Place. They were also joined on the road by a crew for LWT's *The South Bank Show* under producer-director Andrew Snell (who had made the Alan Howard profile) and the result was the delightful 1979 documentary *The RSC on Tour*.[75] In contrast to *Shakespeare's Island* from eight years earlier, this is a close-up study shot behind flimsy stage flats and in makeshift dressing rooms. With only a slim narration from Melvyn Bragg, much of the film has a *verité* quality with frequent asides to the camera from McKellen. Scenes from *Three Sisters* shot on the travelling stage before John Bury's icon-inspired backcloth give a lucid sense of that production, but there is rather less of *Twelfth Night* in performance. The documentary also reveals that the RSC was approached to take *Three Sisters* into the West End but the actors turned this down 'since the majority felt to accept would be against the spirit of the tour'. Nonetheless the production travelled to the Edinburgh Festival, was seen at The Warehouse and was then recorded for television as the first – and as it turned out, the last – of a projected three-production deal with Thames. Ahead of the IBA awarding the next round of ITV franchises in late 1980, Thames contracted on 24 September 1979 to have for a fee of £150,000 the first option on RSC adaptations for the next three years, with the hope that *Piaf* and *Sherlock Holmes* in Frank Dunlop's 1974 production would be recorded along with *Three Sisters*.

Directed for the screen by Trevor Nunn, *Three Sisters* was broadcast between Christmas and New Year in 1981, occupying a slot that stretched from 9.00pm to half past midnight. John Bury's stage backcloth was retained only as the background for the title cards, and the drama plays out in near-abstract settings. Act 1 takes place in a spatially undefined bright white void, with Act 2 unfolding in near-darkness, initially lit only by candles. The third act has a moderately more specific setting and the final one takes place in woodland suggested by pale painted birches seen through mist. The characters are framed singly or in small groupings, and there are no conventional establishing shots, as Nunn brings his ideas of 'shooting the text' across from his earlier Shakespeare adaptations. But here the intimacy with which the vernacular of Richard Cottrell's translation is treated risks banality, and the complexities of the characters' relationships too often seem absent. It all makes for a distanced and demanding watch, as one critic wrote on the day after transmission: '*Three Sisters* was ultra-tasteful, ultra-sensitive, and for one viewer at least ultra-boring ... by swimming so tirelessly from mournful face to mournful face the camera neutralised the geometrical tensions which are always present on the stage.'[76] Whether because the broadcaster was disappointed with the production or with its critical reception, or whether once its franchise contract had been confirmed the association was no longer useful, Thames parted company with the RSC.

'Speak the speech ... '

On the evening of Sunday 9 December 1979 the second run of *The BBC Television Shakespeare* opened on BBC Two with the corporation's own production of *Henry IV, Part 1*. Less than half an hour after it finished, on the rival commercial channel, the RSC could be found running the first of two Shakespeare masterclasses. *Word of Mouth* was a pair of fifty-minute programmes mounted by LWT's arts strand *The South Bank Show* that brought together three RSC directors and six leading actors associated with the company. Whether intended to be such or not, the programmes were a riposte to the BBC monolith, in that they delighted in modesty and authenticity, were intellectual, rigorously focused on the text and concerned above all to discover meaning through analysis and performance. The programmes can also be seen as an idealized self-portrait of the company at the time, with a group of exceptional actors working intimately on textual analysis in an austere environment. Collegial, dressed casually and smoking occasionally are David Suchet, Patrick Stewart, Ian McKellen and Michael Pennington, together with the slightly marginalized Jane Lapotaire and Alan Howard. Prompting and guiding, cajoling and rewarding them are directors distinguished by their fearsome intelligence. The least prominent is a nervous Terry Hands, who makes only one short contribution to the first programme and is invisible in the second. Centre-stage, and the fount of wisdom, is the donnish John Barton. But the ringmaster is definitely Trevor Nunn, who directly addresses both the in-house audience and those sitting at home, and who also takes a writer credit. The setting is an unadorned television studio, with prominent pedestal cameras and mic booms contributing touches of Brechtian self-reflexivity while offering few distractions from the Word. Around a central playing area sit a studio audience in a configuration echoing the auditorium of The Other Place. The artists perch on folding chairs or on the floorcloth amidst the modest mess of a rehearsal room. Everyone is 'on book', reading Shakespeare's speeches from hand-held scripts. At times, basic electronic graphics subtitle lines of verse. Words, words, words.

At pains to stress that there is not one way to speak Shakespeare's verse, Trevor Nunn explores original pronunciation, onomatopoeia, the rhythm of blank verse and the use of counterstress for effect. The actors share the occasional anecdote, but the focus is firmly on the analysis of language. For the conclusion, Trevor Nunn appropriates the technique more often associated with John Barton of teaching with a Sonnet. He and David Suchet work through Sonnet 138 ('When my love swears that she is made of truth'), building together a character and dramatic situation for its affective expression. The second programme comprises three sections: John Barton working on the central section of Act 4, Scene 5 from *Troilus and Cressida*; a tour-de-force ten-minute monologue by Ian McKellen in which he speaks through and deconstructs Macbeth's 'Tomorrow and tomorrow and tomorrow' soliloquy (5.5.17–27), followed by his playing of this extracted from the Thames Television production; and Patrick Stewart reflecting on his playing of Enobarbus in two different productions. All of which, viewed today, remains stimulating, challenging and entirely accessible.

Press response to *Word of Mouth* was relatively low key, although Michael Billington praised the programmes as 'compulsive viewing ... revealing, funny, moving'.[77] A follow-up series was commissioned by Michael Kustow, an RSC employee in the 1960s and now arts commissioning editor at the new national broadcaster Channel 4. Recorded three years after *Word of*

Mouth, Playing Shakespeare was a more ambitious project in nine episodes written and presented by John Barton. All six actors from *Word of Mouth* return at points in the series, and they are joined by others including Norman Rodway, Lisa Harrow, Susan Fleetwood and Roger Rees as well as a handful of eminent figures as 'guest stars': Judi Dench, Donald Sinden and Peggy Ashcroft. Viewing the series nearly thirty-five years after transmission, the absence of any black or Asian actor is striking and shocking. Material from *Word of Mouth* is reprised but Nunn and Hands no longer appear, and the workshops are anchored under Barton's direction. The studio setting is now more consciously designed, referencing both rehearsal room and prop store, and with pale RSC branding on fabrics. Colour coordination also appears to have been introduced, with all the contributors now in beige, cream and variants of pastel shades. Cameras, mic booms and studio personnel appear frequently, signalling transparency, authenticity and the series' search for truth. The audience is both smaller and less present, which makes *Playing Shakespeare* more intimate and focused than *Word of Mouth*. At the same time it feels more structured and scripted. There are moments of humour and informality, but the tone for the most part is that of a tutorial. The programmes combine, not always comfortably, rigorous academic exchange, rehearsal give-and-take, masterclass didacticism and anthologized star-turn lollipops.

At the end of episode eight Barton offers something of a summing up, highlighting how textual clues for an actor are more numerous than might at first appear. He recognizes that there is no single, definitive way of playing Shakespeare, but he also believes that there are 'fruitful' ways and 'perverse' ones. The perverse ones can have value but only as 'an alternative to and not a realisation of Shakespeare'. Flouting any notion of the post-structuralist relativism that was beginning to take hold in the academy at the time, Barton is clear that there are inherent meanings in the texts and that these were intended by the author. 'Shakespeare *is* his text,' he stresses, continuing with an unthinking use of the masculine pronoun, 'so if you want to do him justice you have to look for and follow the clues he offers. If an actor does that he'll find that Shakespeare himself starts to direct him.' Such too was Peter Hall's belief, Trevor Nunn's and Terry Hands's, and it might be regarded as a vision statement for the company both then and, to a large extent, today.

The life and adaptations of *Nicholas Nickleby*

Having been recorded in 1982, *Playing Shakespeare* was eventually broadcast in the summer of 1984 on Channel 4. The very first programme commission for this new terrestrial television channel was the screen version of the RSC's epic adaptation of Charles Dickens's *The Life and Adventures of Nicholas Nickleby*. Initially broadcast in November 1982 as three two-hour programmes and a three-hour finale, this was the most substantial screen presentation of the company's work since *The Wars of the Roses* nearly two decades before.[78] The similarities with that earlier project included a production framework that involved an eight-week shoot with multiple electronic cameras on and around a stage, although in this case not the RSC's own but rather that of the fortuitously vacant Old Vic. Funding was provided not by BBC Television but via an international rights deal and a UK broadcaster that was not even on air when the deal was done. The production was also handled by one of the first significant independent producers in British television, Primetime Television. Channel 4 was established in a public service framework to cater for interests and concerns not otherwise represented on British television and, in the words of its founding statute, 'to encourage innovation and experiment in the form and content of programmes'.[79] To fulfil its objectives it was set up as a publisher of programmes made by others, including ITV contractors as well as independent producers, of which Primetime was one among several hundred newly founded enterprises. Carrying the cultural capital of the RSC and of an acclaimed stage show, *The Life and Adventures of Nicholas Nickleby* was a much-touted launch event for the new service that was targeting an upscale demographic. That the production was an adaptation of Dickens, and not Shakespeare, was also fruitful, for the playwright was too strongly associated at that point with the 'heritage' project of the BBC series. Dickens could be constructed, especially as channelled by writer David Edgar, as an alternative 'great writer' and a radical figure whose novels could be understood to critique the social agenda of the early years of Margaret Thatcher's Conservative government.

Conceived *in extremis* in early 1979 as a response to yet another financial crisis in the company, *Nicholas Nickleby* was Trevor Nunn's attempt to, in the words of assistant director Leon Rubin, 'harness in one work all the RSC's vast resources and demonstrate what that company could really achieve'.[80] With around fifty cast members contracted but with only a single production budget for a London season, Nunn gambled on what would become as significant a project for his RSC as *The Wars of the Roses* was for Peter Hall's. A lengthy rehearsal process began without either a script or the choice of which actors would take which roles. At the heart of this, and of the eventual production, was a significant number of those who had been on the 1978 tour of *Twelfth Night* and *Three Sisters*, including Roger Rees, Suzanne Bertish and Emily Richard. Four weeks into the process, Andrew Snell, who had made the earlier film about the tour, sought permission to make a feature-length film for *The South Bank Show*, and Leon Rubin has recorded the cast's concern about the presence of cameras. Filming access was debated and voted on and struck down and reconsidered and renegotiated.[81] One recalcitrant actor was eventually overruled, and Rubin has argued that the process of considering all this was a significant factor in the cast forging a sense of solidarity and collective enthusiasm. The resulting film, as a contemporary critic wrote, remains 'a moving, intelligent and informative record of the greatest piece of theatre seen in London for many years'.[82]

Nicholas Nickleby opened as two plays at the Aldwych in late June 1980 to an ambivalent press (Figure 9). There was praise for the cast, the script and the imaginative direction (John Caird shared the credit with Nunn), but some critics felt it was all too long and that it lacked dramatic tension and political bite. Audiences felt differently and adored the shows, as did I when I experienced them on the first Saturday when both parts were played. And Bernard Levin gave voice to our feelings:

> There is only one way to behave at the Aldwych; to surrender completely to the truth, which is that not for many years has London's theatre seen anything so richly joyous, so immoderately rife with pleasure, drama, colour and entertainment, so life-enhancing, yea-saying and fecund, so – in a word which embraces all these and more - so Dickensian ... we come out not merely delighted but strengthened, not just entertained but uplifted, not only affected but changed.[83]

The rest of the short six-week run sold out immediately and, after consideration of a commercial transfer that was ultimately deemed impossible, the show was revived at the Aldwych at the end of the year. By which point *Nicholas Nickleby* was a phenomenon, and several film proposals were

FIGURE 9 *David Threlfall (Smike) and Roger Rees (Nicholas) in the stage presentation of* The Life and Adventures of Nicholas Nickleby *(1980), which was later filmed for Channel 4. Photograph by Reg Wilson © RSC.*

received. Trevor Nunn insisted that any screen version must be of the full work. The rights and programme sales company Richard Price Television Associates (RPTA) accepted this stipulation and set up a partnership with the American oil company Mobil and the European distributor Reiner Moritz. 'We put together the financing', producer Colin Callender has recalled, 'and then went to Channel 4 and said, "We've got three-quarters of the financing in place, would you come on board as the UK broadcaster?"'[84] The channel issued contract number 00001 for four two-hour programmes, despite the UK rights costing £100,000 per hour, which was more than three times the new service's planned hourly spend. Nonetheless, the deal guaranteed the channel one of its headline commissions when it went on air in early November 1982.[85]

Nicholas Nickleby returned to the Aldwych for a third run in April to June, after which the production transferred to The Old Vic for an eight-week shoot. For three days the whole show was recorded with four cameras in an auditorium packed with an audience of paid extras. Material shot during this time is used for opening and closing sequences and as establishing shots for segments that were later filmed on the stage in a far more controlled and focused manner with just two, sometimes three, cameras. Although the whole production was recorded on 1" videotape, there is a marked difference in the image quality of the two approaches, and this is particularly notable when they are intercut, as when Nicholas's coach departs from the Saracen's Head for Yorkshire. The wide shots of the theatre appear flatly lit and are visually less defined, while the more intimate sections are expertly framed and lit specifically for the screen by television director Jim Goddard and director of photography Tony Imi.[86] As edited shot/reverse sequences more usually associated with a single-camera film style, and with far more controlled close mic-ing, they effectively implicate the viewer within the characters' exchanges and relationships. At the same time, since they were recorded without an audience, they carry no sense of a theatre's collective response, most especially the generous laughter prompted by the production's comedy.

A sequence from *The South Bank Show*,[87] filmed during the second run of Aldwych performances, illustrates how complex it would have been to add laughter. Fanny Squeers (Suzanne Bertish) has invited Nicholas (Roger Rees) to tea, fantasizing to herself and her friend Tilda Price (Cathryn Harrison) that despite having only encountered her casually on a couple of occasions, the young schoolteacher is in love with her. A bemused Nicholas endeavours to be polite, especially to Tilda, before the party is joined by Tilda's fiancé, the kindly but uncouth Yorkshireman John Browdie (Bob Peck). In *The South Bank Show* the scene is shot with two film cameras, using only stage lighting so that the setting fades away into black. Long and mid-shots keep the viewer at a distance, observing rather than becoming involved. But the attuned levels of laughter of the unseen audience productively enhance the comic effect. In the Primetime/Channel 4 adaptation, the scene is recorded frontally, as much of the drama is, as a three-camera electronic mix, in what is essentially the visual language of a sitcom. The relationship of the characters is clearer than in the documentary, as is the subtle intelligence of the performances, Roger Rees's especially. Without the laughter of an audience, however, the scene feels more poignant than comic. The production approach seeks to transform individual scenes such as this into prestige studio drama, aligning it with the classic serial tradition that had been offering multi-part Dickens adaptations to a television audience since BBC Television's seven-episode *The Pickwick Papers* (1952–53). Channel 4's chief executive Jeremy Isaacs was far from alone in his belief that 'a live theatre performance does not show up well on television', and so it had to be 'remade' for the medium.[88] But the screen version was unwilling to sacrifice the sense that *Nickleby* was a supreme *theatrical* triumph. So it begins with a shot of a chandelier that tilts down to reveal the almost empty Old Vic auditorium that gradually fills, through a progression of slow dissolves, with the theatre audience. Each part of the nine-episode version released on DVD closes with the same shot of stage calls and an applauding audience, over which the credits run. These conflicting demands shaped *Nickleby* as a screen hybrid that both parallels but is also distinct from *The Wars of the Roses*.

The complex and often uneasy medial status of the screen version is perhaps clearest in what was the closing sequence of the first of the two stage plays. Nicholas and Smike have joined the travelling troupe of the the Crummles and they participate in a ludicrous presentation of the final act of *Romeo and Juliet*. David Edgar inserts Shakespeare, who is only passingly referenced by Dickens, into the heart of the adaptation, and in the theatre the scene was an uproarious parody performance of bad acting, atrocious verse-speaking and a happy ending in which everyone but Tybalt is resurrected. (Edgar makes devastating use of this scene when he echoes it for the desperate death of Smike, which was wonderfully moving in the theatre and remains so after numerous viewings.) The burlesque is played for the cameras on a cramped truck against a cloth backdrop and is filmed with extensive use of a wide master-shot that, whether consciously or not, replicates the kind of fixed-camera frame of Frank Benson's 1911 *Richard III*. There are television-like cut-ins, but the sequence overall occupies a space that collides early cinema, stage and small screen. There is no laughter added for the absurd antics of the Crummles's players, but when they finish applause and appreciation breaks in. Whether the intended source of this is the imagined playhouse of the Crummles or the framing theatre of the Old Vic, is unclear. After which we have the (glorious) pastiche, also absent from Dickens, of an imagined late Victorian imperial anthem, 'See upon our smiling land'. As this comes to a close, first the Smike family join the stage-upon-a-stage and then all the other cast members, underlining the production's exposure of desperate inequality in the Englands of Queen Victoria and of Margaret Thatcher.[89]

The stage production of *Nicholas Nickleby* can be seen as a culmination of a central strand of the RSC's work that had begun a decade before with the first productions in The Other Place, exploring new acting styles, distinct audience relationships and collaborative techniques for rehearsals and staging. Trevor Nunn and John Caird drew these original approaches together with traditional RSC strengths, including the central importance of the ensemble, and also introduced the ambition that had made such a success of *The Wars of the Roses*. For the later stages of this journey, television was a significant partner, chronicling elements of it and adapting for the screen a number of major achievements, including *Nicholas Nickleby* itself. Over the next two decades, however, television, together with the cinema, were to be far less significant for the company and its self-presentation to the world. The first years of the RSC's existence had been precarious, but now the company was about to move into a purpose-built theatre as part of the Barbican arts complex. While this should have provided a greater element of stability, key decisions associated with the move eventually led to challenges to the RSC's very existence. The screen memories of these next years, and of their productions, are fewer and less vivid, at least as the fruits of conventional partnerships. But at the same time the collectivity of moving-image traces of the company was about to be radically expanded, even if the shifts were, as to a large extent they have remained, essentially invisible.

5

Toil and Troubles, 1982–2012

Three artistic directors saw the RSC through the decades between 1982, when the company moved into London's Barbican, and 2012, after the first full season in Stratford-upon-Avon's substantially remodelled Royal Shakespeare Theatre. In the years at the end of the century the company's finances remained precarious, and on occasions it struggled to defend its legitimacy. 'Although there were fitful splendours,' Michael Billington wrote of the RSC in the 1990s, 'one looked in vain for either the turbulent energy of the Nunn-Hands era or any hint of the radicalism that had informed the company's work in the past.'[1] Following two decades of seemingly existential crisis, it was only after Michael Boyd became artistic director in 2003 that a sense of stability returned. British theatre beyond the RSC changed profoundly during these years, with the dominance of Stratford and the National Theatre diminishing as other ensembles made their mark presenting classical texts, often in innovative and radical ways. Small companies such as Kick Theatre, founded by Deborah Warner in 1980, and Cheek By Jowl, brought into being by Declan Donnellan and Nick Ormerod the following year, staged groundbreaking interpretations of Shakespeare. The Citizens Theatre in Glasgow and Manchester Royal Exchange were only two of the regional theatres programming exciting productions of historical and contemporary texts. London spaces like the Almeida and the Donmar Warehouse, which the RSC vacated in 1981, also mounted innovative productions of Shakespeare alongside new plays, much as the RSC had pioneered in the 1960s. And in 1997 Shakespeare's Globe opened on London's South Bank, and was soon confounding sceptics by presenting critically acclaimed productions that attracted young and enthusiastic audiences.

In contrast to the 1960s and 1970s, adaptation of the RSC's work for the screen in subsequent decades was neither a corporate priority nor a personal one for the company's artistic directors. *Cyrano de Bergerac* (1985) with Derek Jacobi was the only one of the many productions directed by Terry Hands for Stratford and, after 1982, for the company's new Barbican

Theatre and The Pit shown *in toto* on television. Nor were any of Hands's – or indeed anyone else's – productions recorded in the Swan Theatre, which opened in Stratford in 1986. Gregory Doran, who would become RSC artistic director in 2012, has contrasted Trevor Nunn's productions with Hands's work in the 1980s, when he often collaborated with Alan Howard and the designer Abd'Elkader Farrah. Doran characterized these stagings as working with 'a more abstract, less literal, more European style'. 'This may account', Doran suggested, 'for their apparent lack of interest in committing their many great productions to film.'[2] Just as significant was the shift within British television away from drama drawn from the theatre. By the early 1980s ITV had largely abandoned the classics, and the productions that remained on the BBC were corralled into heritage strands including *Play of the Month* (1965–83) and *Performance* (1993–98), both of which frequently relied on period costumes and sets to conjure up cultural prestige. *Theatre Night* (1985–90) was another such series, and for this the BBC, drawing on external funding, partnered on adaptations of the RSC's *Molière* (1985) and *Tartuffe* (1985) as well as Trevor Nunn's *Othello* (1990). Adaptations were also infrequent under Terry Hands's successor, Adrian Noble, who was artistic director from 1991 to 2003. The only substantial screen versions of RSC productions during these years were Noble's own feature film version of *A Midsummer Night's Dream* (1996), a recording made at the Barbican of Gregory Doran's 1999 production of *The Winter's Tale* and Doran's television film of *Macbeth* (2001). Following on from Noble, Michael Boyd was wary of theatre adapted for the screen and was preoccupied with other concerns, but at the end of his tenure he committed to screen versions of two productions with Digital Theatre, although he remained sceptical about the process.

One consequence of the absence of screen versions is that the public memory of the company's work from the early 1980s to the mid-2000s is less vivid than that of the previous decades, and is reliant on the traditional fragile forms of written reviews and photographs, together with personal recollections. Terry Hands regrets that more was not recorded, mostly because of the loss of Alan Howard's performances. 'The RSC didn't even do archive filming until 1982,' he observed in a conversation for this book. 'Which is *terrible*. So all of Alan's great productions – *Coriolanus, Henry V* – all that work is in people's memories, not on the shelves.'[3] Nonetheless, as Hands's comment nods towards, the 1980s and 1990s saw the proliferation of numerous new forms of moving images linked to RSC productions, including internal archive recordings, extracts from shows for television, recordings with the National Video Archive of Performance (NVAP), electronic press kits (EPKs), trailers and videos from the education department. So while there may be only a few full-length television and film adaptations from the Hands, Noble and Boyd years, there is a profusion of archival fragments. I have endeavoured to identify and view every extant fragment of RSC performance footage from before 1981, and I am confident that I have seen almost all of these. After that, there was a rapid growth of recordings of performances, in whole or in part, and I have only been able to view certain highlights and other representative elements.

Into the Barbican theatres

Since the mid-1960s the RSC had been anticipating the move into a new London home in the theatres of the Barbican Centre. The company entered the 1980s, as Colin Chambers recorded, 'when the chill wind of monetarism was gathering speed, technically insolvent and having to borrow at increasingly high interest rates'.[4] The deal for occupancy at the Barbican, however, was a favourable one, and Trevor Nunn began to envisage more ambitious and technically complex productions. In the wake of the overwhelming success of *Nicholas Nickleby*, he wanted to see the company achieve the splendour of the best West End shows. His new policy, however, was far from universally popular, as Chambers wrote: 'It was an apparent reversal of the anti-decorative, actor-based approach associated with the RSC's best work as well as a response both to the minimalism of previous seasons and to the growing assertion by designers of their presence and contribution. They felt the company was too text-centred and had not kept up with continental scenography.'[5] Television captured this emphasis on the text in the *Word of Mouth* and *Playing Shakespeare* workshops. But the Barbican stage was now to be the home of RSC spectacles like the Peter Nichols and Monty Norman musical *Poppy* (1982), a lavish staging of Edmond Rostand's *Cyrano de Bergerac* (1983), a sprawling presentation of Brecht's *Mother Courage* (1984), and in 1985, alongside *Les Misérables*, David Edgar's political epic *Maydays*. BBC Television captured something of this time in the RSC's life in three documentaries: a preview of the new arts centre, titled simply *The Barbican*, on 2 March 1982, the day before it opened, and two documentaries for *Omnibus*, one filmed in Stratford as Howard Davies directed Bob Peck and Sara Kestelman in *Macbeth*,[6] and one that explored the background to *Poppy* and featured two of its musical numbers restaged in the television studio.[7] The twenty-minute report on the Stratford *Macbeth* is a close-up scrutiny of the rehearsal process and is followed by a lengthy studio exchange, with Michael Billington defending the production against the traditionalist strictures of host Barry Norman. The *Poppy* package, with cast members Geoffrey Hutchings and Jane Carr, survives as perhaps the lowest moment of the RSC on any screen anytime anyplace, with the restaged numbers from the political pantomime showcasing a dancing elephant, much dry ice and a chorus of Chinese 'coolies'. Any ironic distance that might have been achieved on stage is collapsed by the small-screen recording.

After *Nicholas Nickleby* Trevor Nunn and John Caird collaborated on two further large-scale shows for the RSC. The first was *Peter Pan*, which played in the Barbican theatre in the winter of 1982 to 1983 before being revived for the two following Christmas seasons. No screen version was made, but the BBC One *Omnibus* strand devoted a film to the production.[8] By that point Trevor Nunn was deep in discussions with producer Cameron Mackintosh about the French musical *Les Misérables* by Alain Boublil, Jean-Marc Natel and Claude-Michel Schönberg. His conditions for committing to the project included Caird as co-director and the RSC as a co-producer. 'I ... felt that it would be dishonest', Nunn said later, 'to use methods and approaches developed during the work on *Nicholas Nickleby* and to exclude John from this process.'[9] The RSC's involvement was controversial at the time but proved to be a sound commercial decision. Not only did the show make money for the RSC during its run at the Barbican, which by 1985 was proving to be exceptionally hard to programme profitably, but it also brought in significant royalties for many years to come.[10] In 2012 a lavish feature film of the musical was released that featured no elements of the original staging, and yet the RSC received a financial return from this too. Another BBC Television arts strand, *Saturday Review*, featured the stage production in a film report that included short extracts.[11]

The company's time at the Barbican began with problems including inadequate acoustics and temperamental stage technology; an unsatisfactory smaller space, The Pit, more or less improvised out of an underground rehearsal room; inadequate and subterranean backstage facilities; and the general inaccessibility of the whole Barbican complex. Over time improvements were made and the qualities of the main auditorium were increasingly acknowledged, but no one ever fell in love with the facilities. After just a year in its new home the RSC, along with the Royal Opera House, was put to the test with an imposed enquiry by the government's Efficiency Unit. The report by Clive Priestley was published in December 1983, and to the surprise of its commissioners acknowledged the strength of the theatre company's financial management and recommended that it should receive additional funding. The RSC's more aggressively commercial strategy had also been criticized by West End theatre managers concerned about public subsidy supporting a competitive organization. Yet the Priestley report rejected this censure also: 'It seems evident that there are the makings of a "mixed economy" between the subsidised and the commercial theatre, television and the cinema.'[12] The document acknowledged that the return to the RSC from fees and royalties from film, television and cassettes was relatively modest, although it recorded that just a year on from its Channel 4 broadcast the television adaptation of *Nicholas Nickleby* had made a net contribution of £150,000.[13] With echoes of the Filmways arrangement nearly two decades before, the Priestley report also included details of an apparently promising deal. For a basic fee of £300,000, with royalties on top, RKO-Nederlander had entered a three-year deal for worldwide distribution of recordings of RSC productions. It was envisaged that as many as four productions might be taped each year.

RKO-Nederlander was a joint venture of the RKO film and broadcasting organization, which ran radio and television stations, and the Nederlander theatre and production company, which owned or operated thirty auditoria in the United States as well as the RSC's former London home, the Aldwych. The Nederlander organization had presented a number of RSC hits on Broadway, including *Nicholas Nickleby, Sherlock Holmes* and *Cyrano de Bergerac*. The joint venture had already taped non-RSC productions including *Sweeney Todd* and *Lena Horne: The Lady and Her Music* for the developing cable television market. RSC shows envisioned for a similar treatment were announced as *Much Ado About Nothing, The Tempest, Peer Gynt* and *Cyrano de Bergerac*, all featuring Derek Jacobi, as well as *Poppy* and *A Doll's House*.[14] Priestley also noted, however, that 'Nederlander have since [signing the deal in January 1983] withdrawn from the agreement which now stands between RKO and the RSC.'[15] And of the possibilities floated, only *Cyrano de Bergerac* reached the screen, in Britain on Channel 4 in September 1985, under a version of this arrangement. The production credit on the transmission print reads 'A Stratford-Barbican Television Production', together with a note that the copyright of the production was 'RKO Pictures'.[16]

Cyrano de Bergerac on screen begins with a bravura three-minute shot from on high as the camera circles above a stage on which players and spectators are arriving. The production as a whole has, thanks to Ralph Koltai's sets, a sense of scale and spectacle. Another of its glories is Anthony Burgess's version of Rostand's 1897 original. Burgess had first translated the text in 1970 but for Terry Hands's heroic production he elaborated its poetry and puns in a scintillating celebration of language. Playing with pitch-perfect panache, Derek Jacobi as Cyrano wrenches heart-break from the words, and with a running time of almost three hours the recording is a remarkable television achievement. Shooting at the recently opened Limehouse Studios, Hands collaborated on the screen direction with Michael Simpson, a veteran of adaptations of classic plays for schools television. Seeking alternatives to conventional shot/reverse screen grammar, they made extensive use of a crane and played lengthy scenes on a single camera, which on occasions was hand-held. They also brought elements like candles (the fine studio lighting is by John Treays) and a vast chandelier into the foreground of frames. More than thirty years later, Terry Hands recalled the process:

> The problem was at that time, were you recording a production or rethinking it? Because the two media are completely different. Stage asks you questions, film gives you answers. So should [*Cyrano*] be a stage record or a re-think? And we tried to do both. For a start we tried to get rid of, or reduce to a minimum, the use of television's normal pedestal camera, with its terribly limited swing. With Ralph Koltai, the designer, we deliberately used floors that cameras could not run over, in order to stop the television people doing the normal television thing. And we had

a luxury thirteen days shooting, which was fantastic … So I was quite pleased with it.[17]

After a dearth of company adaptations, the autumn of 1985 saw something of a festival of RSC television. Just over a month after the transmission of *Cyrano de Bergerac*, BBC Television's *Theatre Night* broadcast two linked stage shows just a week apart. Both were also backed by RKO investment, although they were the last to be supported in this way. Dusty Hughes's adaptation of Mikhail Bulgakov's *Molière, or The Union of Hypocrites*, was first seen at The Other Place in August 1982.[18] Bill Alexander's production featured Antony Sher as the French playwright who becomes a slavish sycophant to the Sun King Louis XIV. The parallels with Bulgakov himself and Stalin were signalled on stage by a prologue set in Soviet Russia, which became framing sequences at the start and close of the television adaptation when Bulgakov takes a night-time phone call from the dictator. The show transferred to The Pit in the summer of 1983, when it was paired with Molière's own *Tartuffe*, with Sher again directed by Bill Alexander. Of Sher's personification of the crooked cleric, Michael Billington wrote, he 'is pure evil: Richard III with a rosary. With his long, black locks, daemonic eyes and pointy features … he exudes animal menace, creeping into a chair as if about to rape it.'[19] The pair of plays reached the screen after Sher's triumph in 1984 as Richard III himself, once more working with Bill Alexander for the RSC. *Molière* was broadcast first, in a studio production of great energy and flair, brilliantly imagined by designer Ralph Koltai and, like *Cyrano*, enhanced once more by the richly varied lighting of John Treays. *Tartuffe* followed a week later, with grand comic performances from Sher, Nigel Hawthorne and Alison Steadman, and a television studio style of clarity and elegance.[20] As Hugh Hebert wrote, 'What distinguished Bill Alexander's direction [of *Tartuffe*] was the ability to dispel the sense that we were just watching a stage production on film. And more important, he and his cast gave Molière's essentially two-dimensional characters a wonderful feel of solidity.'[21]

The television production took place towards the end of the plays's runs in London, and was enlivened by an element of subterfuge. *Tartuffe* was re-rehearsed for television first and recorded in a multi-camera studio at Television Centre. 'But then there was a BBC technicians' strike', Bill Alexander has recalled, 'and it was obvious that *Molière* was going to be completely scuppered, because everyone said it was going to be several weeks before the dispute was resolved.'[22] Instead of seeing the production go down, in the middle of one night the team smuggled the sets out of the BBC scenery workshop. They were taken to Limehouse Studios, where *Cyrano* had been recorded and where *Molière* was now rehearsed and recorded. Bill Alexander was engaged by the process of reworking the productions for television, but in common with his RSC colleagues, he saw screen adaptation as almost entirely peripheral to the central concern of creating productions for live audiences. 'As far as I was aware,' he recalled in a recent interview, 'generally speaking, there never seemed to be any interest at the RSC in filming their stuff in any way.'[23] In retrospect, *Tartuffe* and *Molière* can be seen as exemplars of the endgame for single plays made in television studios with multiple electronic cameras. Having been dominant since the 1930s, this production method and its aesthetic were being rapidly replaced by film-style shooting on location. Original scripts, invariably commissioned in series, were similarly favoured more frequently. Single dramas, and especially those with a theatrical heritage, were increasingly believed not to attract the broad viewerships that television drama now demanded. These factors became more significant as the stable audiences of the BBC/ITV duopoly were threatened by the offerings of cable, satellite and, soon, online services. Plays sat intransigently in the schedules for two hours and more and appealed largely to upscale, educated audiences. Such viewers were seen as 'super-served' in a way that, for a service funded by a universal licence fee, was now perceived to be inappropriate. Yet *Molière* and *Tartuffe* demonstrate the strengths and beauties of both stage adaptations for the small screen and of the studio production process at its most refined.

Although it was not preserved in a full-scale adaptation, Antony Sher's performance as Richard III was featured in a more peripheral engagement by television. On three occasions the BBC Two strand *Saturday Review* (1984–87), which brought together guests to discuss contemporary cultural events, turned its attention to RSC productions of Shakespeare. Each time key scenes were filmed from stagings that were otherwise not translated to a public screen. From Bill Alexander's *The Merry Wives of Windsor* six minutes were recorded of the start of Act 2, Scene 1, with Mistress Ford and Mistress Page discovering that Falstaff has sent each the same love letter. Janet Dale and Lindsay Duncan gossip beneath hair dryers – the production was set in the late 1950s – and the camera constructs the scene as if this were from a television soap.[24] The following year, embedded in a film essay with interviews with Sinéad Cusack (Lady Macbeth), Jonathan Pryce (Macbeth) and director Adrian Noble, were both part of the Act 2, Scene 2 'daggers' duologue (2.2.9–58) and Macbeth's soliloquy 'Is this a dagger I see before me?' (2.1.33–47).[25] As with all such illustrative extracts, there will have been pragmatic factors at play in their selection, including availability of the cast and the simplicity of staging. Almost all such extracts feature only a small number of actors, since each one would be due an Equity-determined fee, and review programmes operate on tight budgets. Similar considerations would have determined that neither music, which incurred fees to musicians, nor scene changes, requiring stage management to be paid, were featured.

The use in review shows and documentaries of scenes believed to be recognizable to a television audience aligns these fragments with the earliest Shakespeare adaptations. Writing about films based on literary sources from the years before 1907, Tom Gunning has identified productions that show just one or a short series of scenes from a play or a well-known novel.[26]

Relying on an audience's pre-existing knowledge of the source, these films, which might comprise just the duel from *Hamlet,* which Sarah Bernhardt filmed in 1900, or scenes from Herbert Beerbohm Tree's *King John* (1899), offer one or more 'peak moments'. The strategy paralleled the way in which famous scenes or speeches might be incorporated in vaudeville programmes, mounted as *tableaux vivants* and illustrated in magazines, and it drew on what the audience would be familiar with, not only from the text and previous productions but also from postcards and lantern slides. 'We might call this strongly intertextual practice,' Gunning wrote, 'which has little interest in the integrity of the text, a cinema of reference rather than adaptation, the goal being to recall a famous work or even a specific performance, rather than give a treatment of its narrative or dramatic content.'[27] Similarly, the practice of featuring scenes in documentaries or review programmes can be understood as television of reference. Other parallels with the early films discussed by Gunning include effacement of individual authorship and the use of the broadcast programme's host or narrator as a contemporary version of the live lecturer who often accompanied the earliest film shows. One of three 'peak moments' featured in the *Saturday Review* consideration of *Richard III* with Antony Sher is, inevitably, Gloucester's opening monologue, from 'Now is the winter of our discontent' (1.1.1–41). This is strikingly filmed, from a low angle and initially from a distance, and it jolts the viewer when at mid-point Sher leaps into the shot's foreground on his crutches. Recorded in perhaps two takes with a single camera, since the master-shot is complemented by close-ups, this two-minute forty-second 'film' is now a primary reference for our historical sense of the play and the production.[28]

Into the Swan Theatre

In October 1986, after a series of aggressively personal attacks in the press, Trevor Nunn stood down as RSC chief executive. Terry Hands, who had been deputy, took on the role, while the two men remained joint artistic directors. For several years there had been concerns inside and outside the RSC about Trevor Nunn's inaccessibility, during the sabbaticals that he took to direct *Cats* in 1981 and *Starlight Express* in 1984, but also when he was actually working with the RSC. He gradually withdrew from the company, leaving among other legacies the invaluable royalty stream from *Les Misérables* and, in Stratford, the third auditorium that in 1986 opened as the Swan Theatre. This transformed what had been the rehearsal space known as the Conference Hall, itself constructed on the footprint of the original Memorial Theatre that had burned down in 1926. It featured a thrust stage surrounded by three levels of wooden galleries that seated an audience of just over 400, and as Trevor Nunn explained on *Saturday Review,* the company hoped that the Swan Theatre would become a home for the works of Shakespeare's contemporaries, complemented by lesser-known classics from other cultures and periods as well as new plays.[29] This vision survives today and the house has seen numerous notable productions, including those in Gregory Doran's 'Jacobethan' season in 2002 and Maria Aberg's recent revelatory stagings of *King John* (2012), *Doctor Faustus* (2016) and *The Duchess of Malfi* (2018). But the only substantial television broadcast to have been made from the auditorium remains *The Richard Burton Drama Award Ceremony* and gala performance in January 1987.[30] The award, established by the RSC and *Radio Times* to celebrate new playwrights, was won by the then-unknown Lucy Gannon, but it appears to have lasted for only a single year. And to date the only production to have been recorded professionally by the company itself with the intention of a public presentation was Trevor Nunn's 2015 production with Henry Goodman of Ben Jonson's *Volpone*.

In 1987, following a particularly poor season at the Barbican box office there was talk of closing for a period the London theatres or even the Stratford auditoria. Sponsorships from Royal Insurance and Allied Lyons, later Allied Domecq, were crucial across this decade to make up the shortfall in public funding, as was the income from *Les Misérables*. Yet there was the perception that the relentless turnover of productions was unproductive, and while brilliant younger creatives including Deborah Warner, Nicholas Hytner and Katie Mitchell debuted stagings with the company, after a small number of shows they moved on to develop their careers elsewhere. Nor were any of the remarkable productions made by these directors transferred to television. Significant shows such as Deborah Warner's *Titus Andronicus* (1987) in the Swan Theatre and, in The Other Place, *King John* (1988),[31] were not recorded professionally, and nor were Nicholas Hytner's *The Tempest* (1988) and *King Lear* (1990), or Katie Mitchell's *A Woman Killed with Kindness* (1991), *Ghosts* (1993) and *The Mysteries* (1997). The only moving images of all of these are single-camera archival registrations. Looking back on the paucity of adaptations from the 1980s, Genista McIntosh, who was the RSC's planning controller from 1977 to 1984 and the company's senior administrator from 1986 to 1990, reflected that,

In those feverishly busy expansionist years, in the late 1970s and '80s, the effort to accommodate screen work within an already over-stretched programme often seemed disproportionate. Of course there were rewards for some, mainly the directors and actors, but not for others and not even that much for the RSC itself. The things that did get done over that period mainly happened as a result of determination on the part of individual directors, lobbying hard and bringing their own contacts to the table, and not as a deliberate policy choice, which is possibly why it looks so haphazard to the historian's eye.[32]

Towards the end of the 1980s increasingly fierce press criticism was focused on the company. In a wide-ranging analysis in the summer of 1987

Michael Ratcliffe wrote, 'There is every reason to be concerned that our greatest theatre company is bent on a suicidal course of expansive diffusion by which their passion, energies, commitment and whole purpose are being spread more and more thinly all the time.'[33] Much of the criticism cohered around the musical *Carrie* for which the RSC, weighed down at the start of 1988 by an accumulated deficit of £1.1 million, entered a US$7 million co-production with the German impresario Friedrich Kurz and other backers. Adapted from a Stephen King novel, with music by Michael Gore and sets by Ralph Koltai, this Terry Hands-directed show was dismissed as 'a resounding mistake' on its Stratford premiere and then went on to close on Broadway after sixteen previews and just five performances.[34] The reputational damage was significant, although as with all co-productions and collaborations, David Brierley had ensured that the company's finances were carefully protected. Channel 4's polemical strand *Opinions* gave theatre administrator Peter Stevens a soapbox from which to castigate the structures of arts funding in general and, in particular, the capitulation to the market of Terry Hands's RSC.[35] In response to the external pressure, Hands announced a formal power-sharing at the company with Bill Alexander and Adrian Noble. Surprisingly, Hands also gave an interview in which he envisioned the RSC becoming far more involved in film production:

> 'I'll get shot down for this, too,' [Hands] says, 'but I believe in the 1980s a major theatre company should be making films.' The model he has is the Royal Drottningholm Theatre in Stockholm with Ingmar Bergman where, he says, they do magnificent stage plays and every so often a movie. 'Most of Bergman's early film work was using his stage actors from his company and I wish we could do it here.'[36]

Nothing came of what was perhaps nothing, even if the article stressed that at least one film project was 'on the drawing board'. In April 1989 the RSC announced that Terry Hands would step down in 1991. There was further bad news early in 1990 when the company deficit was recognized at £2.9 million, and as a consequence several previously announced productions were cancelled and the closure was confirmed of the Barbican theatre and The Pit from early November 1990 to mid-March the following year. Months before, the journalist Nicholas de Jongh had asked, 'Must the company face up to true cut backs, surrendering its Barbican base? Can it, in the new electronic age, with video, satellite, and new television channels, find a new way of living by selling its productions to be seen on the screen?'[37] And de Jongh noted Terry Hands's aspiration to have a RSC producer who would be 'charged once more with the business of persuading companies to film RSC productions. This would accord with Arts Council and Government policy of giving the work of the four national companies an after-life on celluloid, thus making it accessible to audiences of hundreds of thousands or even millions.'[38] Revenue and reach had been the aspirations of the company for its screen adaptations for at least three decades since Peter Hall's 1959 *Dream*. They would remain so for the next thirty years, right through to today, even if reach has proved to be more achievable than revenue.

Memory

I click on a YouTube upload titled 'Carrie The Musical (Stratford Production) Full Show – 1988 OPENING NIGHT'.[39] After the appearance in 4:3 format of the familiar colour bars used to calibrate video images, ambient audio of an expectant audience can be heard over a black screen. Music kicks in, followed by what at first looks like an upwards horizontal wipe. The image resolves into a curtain rising, revealing a distanced, elevated shot of a performance area. Downstage, nearer to the camera, I can make out a group of female figures dancing. The bare box of a set has bright plain walls with a lighting grid above. Whites and greys and silvers flicker and flare in a picture that is largely drained of colour. The configurations and contortions of the dancers, seemingly in an aerobics class, are distinct. Individual faces, however, as well as the specifics of costumes, are beyond the limits of the playback. The show goes into a second number but there are still no opening credits of the kind customary on television. The camera remains immobile, and the frame does not zoom. The timeline indicates that there are still nearly two hours to come. What, I wonder, am I to make of this?

The upload is a video recording made by a camera fixed to the front of the RST circle during one of the first Stratford performances of Terry Hands's production of *Carrie*. From the associated comments and those on a *BroadwayWorld* discussion site, it appears not actually to be the opening night, when a potentially serious accident during a scene change was only narrowly avoided. Contributors have suggested that it is either the third or fourth show.[40] The video was illicitly obtained from the RSC archive at the Shakespeare Birthplace Trust (SBT), where it is one of more than 400 comparable performance recordings made by the company over nearly four decades. The first of these regular recorded inscriptions are from 1981 when Trevor Nunn's RST production of *All's Well That Ends Well* was videotaped, as were two The Other Place stagings, by John Caird of George Farquhar's *The Twin Rivals* and by Barry Kyle of *The Witch of Edmonton*. Many of the 1982 productions were similarly recorded and almost everything from 1983 onwards.

These recordings began as an extension of the audio-only taping that had been carried out, albeit not systematically, across the previous two decades. Technical systems manager at the time Simon Bowler has recalled that as visual recording technology became affordable it was logical to move to video.[41] The specific driver, however, was an agreement with, and financial support from, the Drama Department at the University of Warwick, which wanted access to videotapes for teaching purposes. This aligned with the company's own interest in having records to assist a production's restaging or transfer.[42] Initially those made in the RST were filmed on U-matic tape with a single camera (provided in a sponsorship deal with Sony), whereas those from The Other Place were captured on VHS from the show camera that relays a picture from the auditorium to the stage manager's desk. Agreements were negotiated with the technicians union NATTKE as well as with Equity and the Musicians Union, and to ensure that the recording could not be exploited commercially, it was agreed that only a distant fixed camera could be employed and that basic audio would be taken from a microphone above the stage. Control of the visuals was initially very basic, so that bright spots flared out and dark scenes were almost invisible. Technical improvements were made over the years, and once the company returned to the RST in 2010, a high-definition digital format was employed. Viewing copies are made available at SBT as DVDs, and the audio is archived separately and is accessible to scholars not only at SBT but also at the British Library.

Under the terms of the contracts with cast and creatives (who do not receive a fee for the recording), access to the tapes is restricted 'to bona fide scholars or theatre practitioners for private study' and has to take place at SBT. The associated legal framework further stipulates that 'under no circumstances shall such a recording be permitted to be played or exhibited in public or sold or used for any other than archive/understudy/transfer or re-rehearsal purposes'.[43] In theory, extensive rights clearance could release productions or extracts for public presentation, but the low resolution and distanced view renders them unsuitable. Even so, along with photographs, prompt books, reviews and written and oral reminiscences, these archive recordings constitute one key strand of the company's collective memory. They are alluring because they promise access to performances that have otherwise disappeared, yet their use by the company and by others is only occasional. It is almost as if the *idea* of the recordings offers the reassurance of permanence, while their reality respects what is believed by many to be the essential ephemerality of theatrical performance. Even the technical formats of U-matic and VHS, at least before transfer to digital files, carried both a promise of permanence and the awareness that each viewing or transfer contributed to the recording's degradation and ultimate disappearance. They could, and still can, be created without concern or interest only because their subsequent existence is so marginal. Were they to be technically more sophisticated, more widely seen and discussed, or made more easily available, they would almost certainly become a focus for discussions about, and perhaps resistance to, their value, their approach and aesthetics, and their legitimacy.

The experience of viewing these recordings is comparably contradictory. Decades of production and consumption of films, television programmes and other mainstream media forms, including conventional adaptations and translations of stage productions, have created for viewers today expectations about the screen grammar of dramatic performance. In a groundbreaking study of mainstream American cinema David Bordwell, Kristin Thompson and Janet Staiger identified the fundamentals of this grammar as the 'classical Hollywood style'.[44] Variants of this style, which embraces close-ups, continuity editing and shot/reverse dialogue sequences, are what we accept unthinkingly as the 'natural' or 'obvious' screen grammar for drama. Non-dominant forms of moving images, whether of early cinema from the years up to the mid-1900s or of avant-garde film from the 1960s and 1970s, offer alternatives, demanding that different ways of watching have to be learned. And indeed the RSC archival recordings share certain characteristics with these alternative histories, reproducing the fixed-shot convention of the earliest theatrical adaptations or the durational cinema of Andy Warhol's films such as *Sleep* (1963) and *Empire* (1964). As with early cinema or with Warhol, the act of viewing the archival documents is initially frustrating, and watching for any length of time is exceptionally demanding. Again, the *idea* of their style is seductive, because its apparent objectivity promises transparent and direct access. An awareness that they were cheap to produce and in a format that, once the viewer is at SBT, is convenient to play back, enhances this sense. 'Together these elements produce a narrative of immediacy,' Matthew Reason has suggested of similar performance documentation, 'with the production process being very close, direct and instant, which in turn favours an aesthetics, an ideology even, of immediacy.'[45] Yet the recordings are so hard to watch because almost all potential for affect is drained from them. The taped representations actively resist identification as well as emotional and intellectual involvement, keeping the viewer at a distance that is both literal and metaphorical, and rendering it impossible for her to develop an empathetic relationship with any character. Or almost, for while this is the case visually, the audio, while also of poor quality, is at least intelligible, communicating the verbal aspects of a performance, and as a consequence proffering the potential of involvement. Moreover, what these recordings also introduced in the early 1980s was a rupture with the linearity of viewing adaptations that to date had been the only option for cinema viewing and television broadcasts. The viewer who made the pilgrimage to SBT could begin fragmenting and authoring her individual viewing of an adaptation using the reverse, repeat and fast-forward capabilities of a videocassette player. Personal experience suggests that, more than thirty years on, archival recordings are frequently submitted to comparable dislocations, together with a sense of distraction that could not be more different from the heightened sense of attention that the original stage performance demanded.

Across thirty-five years, while many aspects of the machine vision that produced the archival recordings remained constant, there were both advances and variants. The image definition in the 2015 documentation of *Henry V*, shot in the RST, is significantly sharper than that of the 1982 Barbican taping of *The Winter's Tale*, and the colour is brighter. But even in the later tape, actors' faces are not clearly legible and costumes remain indistinct. The archival recording of *Henry V*, for which a RSC Live from Stratford-upon-Avon broadcast exists for comparison, also gives the lie to the supposed objectivity associated with this form. The automatic exposure setting of the camera, for example, means that the audience either side of the RST thrust stage appears on tape to be brightly lit, even after Chorus (played by Oliver Ford Davies) has left the stage and the house lights have come down. The upper galleries of Stephen Brimson Lewis's set are not included in the frame, nor the two 'voms' or walkways used to enter through the house to the front of the stage. The most notable variation in the form of the archival tapings came during a brief period of experimentation in the mid-1980s. Adrian Noble's staging of *Henry V* with Kenneth Branagh as the young king was documented with a fixed camera in the RST on 17 January 1985. Six days later an unnamed operator with a single camera recorded the production again, but this time panning and zooming to follow the action on stage. The frame is tighter than the unvarying wide shot, often observing figures just at full height, and this facilitates access to the features and expressions of faces. The camera also follows the person speaking as they move around the stage. At the end of the play, there is even an interpretative flourish as the image closes in slowly to a lone broadsword rammed into the stage amidst the corpses of Agincourt. This camera's engagement with the drama is basic and appears to be reactive rather than scripted, but its focus helps the viewer make sense of the drama and permits her to appreciate the performances to a far greater degree than the fixed wide shot. As a consequence, even as it abandons a supposed objectivity, the recording is easier and more pleasurable to watch.[46] As Simon Bowler has explained, frustration with the quality of the recordings on the part of both the RSC and the University of Warwick prompted these modest experiments with movement and minimal editing from a second camera, which were curtailed when an upgraded camera was introduced. 'Obviously the second manned camera was not in the agreement with the unions,' he admitted, 'but we were never found out.'[47]

A similar approach to the experimental RSC recordings was adopted for certain productions by the NVAP documentation project established by the Theatre Museum in 1992 and now operated by the Theatre Department of the V&A. An agreement with the Federation of Entertainment Unions permitted NVAP to record performances without paying artists' fees, and its first taping was the National Theatre production of *Richard III* with Ian McKellen. The public could view the results by appointment, without charge, and educational but not commercial use of the recordings was permitted. In 1997 director of the Theatre Museum and former television producer Margaret Benton, who established NVAP, defined the purpose of these archival recordings: 'to convey as faithful and as a [*sic*] detailed a record as possible of the original stage performance ... It should aim to be an eyewitness to the event taking place in the presence of a live audience, ideally from the point of view of a single spectator in the theatre, and should cover all the action.'[48] According to Jill Evans, later the project's video producer, NVAP explicitly rejected the distanced, fixed-camera model employed internally by the RSC because 'facial expressions and subtlety of performance would be lost as well as details of the set and costumes'.[49] The NVAP production model was closer to that of broadcast television, with shots from between two and four cameras live mixed by a director who had prepared a shooting script. This meant, however, as Evans noted, that 'the viewer would be told where to look rather than have the freedom to choose, as at a live performance'.[50] There were also differences from a conventional television translation of a staging: minimal deployment of close-ups, moderate use of camera movement and then only as motivated by the characters on stage, and fewer cuts, all of which were in the service of a presumed adoption of transparency and objectivity.[51]

NVAP has made more than forty recordings of RSC productions since *Hamlet* in 1993 with Kenneth Branagh directed by Adrian Noble. Notable recordings include Noble's acclaimed production of *The Cherry Orchard* in 1996, Gregory Doran's staging of *Antony and Cleopatra* with Harriet Walter and Patrick Stewart, and the RSC's popular hit *Matilda the Musical*, recorded after its West End transfer in 2012 and which rights restrictions otherwise prohibit being adapted for the screen. *The Cherry Orchard* was shot in the Swan Theatre with three frontally positioned cameras, the central one offering a master wide, with the other two positioned at a distance on either side so as to be able to shoot diagonally across the thrust stage. The audio, recorded on microphones positioned in the space (and not from radio mics), catches the expressiveness of the performances. The viewer is drawn into the drama, engaged and involved, even if the choice and sequencing of shots is not – as I would argue is done in the best RSC Live from Stratford-upon-Avon broadcasts – interpreting or enhancing the storytelling of the stage. A NVAP taping offers an aesthetic of neutrality appropriate to its intended audiences of theatre practitioners, educators and students. So here too are significant skeins of the RSC's memory, even if as with the company's own recordings, the recollections appear to be only occasionally called into service.

Adrian Noble's *Dream*

The RSC's succession solution announced on Terry Hands's departure in 1990 was a triumvirate headed by Adrian Noble, flanked by Genista McIntosh (soon to move to the National Theatre) and director Michael Attenborough. Among the policies to which they committed the company was a move away from the musicals of the previous decade, improvements at the Barbican during the self-imposed shutdown that ended in March 1991, and the re-opening in Stratford the same year of The Other Place. A new generation of directors were also welcomed, including Phyllida Lloyd, Steven Pimlott and Sam Mendes. But once again nothing of the work of these creatives was adapted for the screen. Interviewed for this book, Adrian Noble said:

> I always saw our principal brief, obviously, to bring live performance to as wide an audience as possible across the land. And I would judge the many requests that we had to broadcast our work with a fair degree of scepticism. People would quite literally come and say, I'm going to stick a camera in the front, and I was worried and I think quite rightly, that that would be more damaging to potential audiences than not having anything, because it struck me as just an easy way to make a buck.[52]

Snapshots of the company at the start of Adrian Noble's time as artistic director can be seen in the *Omnibus* documentary *Living Shakespeare – a Year with the RSC* broadcast in December 1991. This follows a small number of actors, including Sylvestra Le Touzel and Barry Lynch, through the season, and while it is a baggy portmanteau production it has little interest in the company's corporate travails. But it features key performance and rehearsal highlights including a scene from Phyllida Lloyd's Swan Theatre production of Thomas Shadwell's *The Virtuoso*, and both rehearsal and stage sequences from Sam Mendes's staging of Ben Jonson's *The Alchemist*. Both *Henry IV* plays directed by Adrian Noble also make an appearance, and there is a glorious hand-held shot that takes the viewer from the RST stage door through the behind-the-scenes areas and then out of the wings to peer into an empty auditorium. In the closing credits each member of that year's acting company is name-checked with an accompanying photograph, and there is just a single black actor, Josette Bushell-Mingo. Other television documentaries that engaged with the company in the decade focused on individual actors, including a 1994 *Omnibus* profile of Robert Stephens, *Every Inch a King*, with strikingly intimate footage of the actor preparing to play King Lear in Stratford; a 1997 film with Antony Sher playing Cyrano; and a film shown in 1999 about Nigel Hawthorne, also taking on Lear, in a RSC co-production with Yukio Ninagawa's company in Japan.[53] Tucked away in a BBC Two season devoted to stories of the Windrush generation was a delightful short presented by Rudolph Walker about Edric Connor, who arrived from Trinidad in 1944 and who was the first black actor to play in Stratford's Memorial Theatre.[54] He took the role of Gowar in the 1958 production of *Pericles*, and Rosemary Anne Sisson, who was the local newspaper critic at the time, is interviewed about Connor's performance.

In the early 1990s, buoyed by a three-year sponsorship deal with Allied Lyons while coping with standstill public funding, the company was able to set aside something of the turmoil of the previous decade. In a 1994 profile of Adrian Noble, however, the writer observed that, 'The RSC's exploratory, radical function has been lost in the battle for survival over the past ten years.'[55] There was a sense that the National Theatre under Richard Eyre had pulled ahead in the inevitable rivalry with the RSC, and from

1997 Shakespeare's Globe became another key focus for productions of the canon. In 1996 the company announced that it was to withdraw from the Barbican from May to October each year, and a disappointing stage adaptation of *Les Enfants du Paradis* had critics conjuring up the corpse of *Carrie*. It was becoming ever harder to bring major names to the Stratford stage, in part because being marooned in the Midlands made it difficult for actors to supplement theatrical wages with short television spots or voice-overs. As a consequence, as Michael Billington wrote, 'The RSC is increasingly a young company that gives new talent its first major exposure; but the National is where the talent goes to capitalise on its success.'[56] Yet Billington was among those who saw encouraging signs of a new boldness, identifying in 1998 that 'the most stimulating Stratford work in recent seasons has had a non-reverent, neo-Expressionist visual strangeness'.[57] His examples included productions by Tim Albery and Matthew Warchus, and *Measure for Measure* staged by Michael Boyd. Each of these suggested 'the possibility of a new aesthetic: one that may be less than textually pure but that draws on other traditions, including opera and cinema, as a key to the plays' eternal problems'.[58] Again, none of these productions were transferred to television or the cinema.

If almost nothing of this major stage work was adapted for the screen, the 1990s did bequeath two other comparatively substantial screen memories of the RSC's work. In the autumn of 1994 the RSC and the Barbican programmed the 'Everybody's Shakespeare' festival of productions, discussions and films. More or less aligned with this, BBC Television showcased one of its then-fashionable 'seasons' of broadcasts under the title 'Bard on the Box'. The RSC did not contribute a production, perhaps because of Adrian Noble's stated view that, 'To be absolutely hand on heart I've really enjoyed very little Shakespeare on television. Shakespeare was not a naturalistic writer and television tends to be a naturalistic medium.'[59] Instead David Thacker, a regular director at Stratford, mounted for the *Performance* strand a modern-dress studio production of *Measure for Measure*. Noble himself contributed an engrossing workshop, modelled on *Playing Shakespeare* and with Antony Sher, Joanne Pearce and Simon Russell Beale. This focused on scenes from the same play, including Isabella pleading with Angelo for the life of her brother Claudio.[60] Cautious as he was about Shakespeare on screen, Adrian Noble also collaborated with producer Paul Arnott on a collection of substantial excerpts from four recent productions together with contextual interviews: Noble's *King Lear* with Robert Stephens; Toby Stephens as *Coriolanus*, staged by David Thacker; Ian Judge's production of *Twelfth Night*, with Desmond Barrit; and Barrit as Bottom in Noble's *A Midsummer Night's Dream*.[61] Adorned with prominent Allied Domecq branding, these were released in 1995 on VHS and the short-lived videodisc format as *Royal Shakespeare Company Great Performances, Volume 1* (although there was to be no *Volume 2*): the performance extracts were filmed in costume and mostly in mid-shot, offering little sense of the stage settings, but as with similar scenes filmed at other moments in the company's history they now have considerable historical value.

Following on from these extracts, the *Dream* became the basis for the only substantial screen adaptation of a RSC staging during the 1990s, directed by Adrian Noble as a feature film, which was shot at the end of 1995 and released the following year. On its Stratford opening in August 1994, Michael Coveney was broadly positive about the stage production: 'Adrian Noble's humid, nagging revival on the main stage, set in a spartan square room with significant doors and a forest of pendant, naked lightbulbs, is full of fresh insight and intelligent playing. It just lacks ecstasy.'[62] But as was, and remains, almost inevitable with any production of the *Dream*, especially at the RSC, the critics drew on comparisons with Peter Brook's 1970 staging, which Coveney suggested Noble had set out 'both to evoke and subvert'. At the first night in Stratford was Paul Arnott, who had worked with Noble on the *Great Performances* recordings and who determined to translate the production into a feature film.

The mid-1990s were an optimal moment for filmed Shakespeare.[63] Kenneth Branagh's *Henry V* (1989), which followed his 1985 playing of the king at Stratford for director Adrian Noble, and especially his *Much Ado About Nothing* (1993), had demonstrated that there was an international market for modestly budgeted adaptations. By late 1995 at least six films were in production in Britain or the United States, one of which was Baz Luhrmann's game-changing *Romeo+Juliet* (1996). Another was the RSC *Dream*, which secured funding towards its £2.4 million budget from Channel 4 and the Arts Council's National Lottery fund. As had been the case with all adaptations since the Filmways fiasco, the RSC contributed rights, costumes and other elements but prudently did not participate in the funding. From the set at Bray Studios in late autumn 1995, Adrian Noble outlined his approach: 'I've tried to come at it ... [by] exploring the human imagination in all its different forms. Cinema as opposed to TV is an absolutely fantastic medium for fantasy. It seemed to me that the script could bear another layer of dreaming beyond those already in the stage production.'[64] The majority of the cast, including Alex Jennings (Theseus/Oberon), Barry Lynch (Puck) and Desmond Barrit (Bottom), remained from Stratford, and they were joined by Lindsay Duncan as Hippolyta/Titania, who had played the role for only the final fifteen performances of the Barbican transfer. Noble also wrote in a new character, an eight-year-old boy, in whose bedroom the film begins before it enters a far more elaborate world, which is styled as modestly baroque for the court and as realist for the mechanicals. As Noble acknowledged recently,

> I always thought that one of the things that cinema can do extremely well is fantasy. But we had nothing like the budget for a fantasy, that was the problem, and so the scenes that are most successful in my opinion are the scenes which we transformed into real locations, like the scout hut for Bottom.[65]

As a consequence of the limited funding, designer Anthony Ward's visuals failed to impress critic Eric Griffiths: 'Visual puns, light-bulbs and soap bubbles, umbrellas that serve as parachutes, the film has all the decorative good taste of [Channel 4's garish series] *The Big Breakfast*. Yet it often falls short of what can be easily achieved with video graphics.'[66] Another criticism of the film is that it remains too much in thrall to the theatre, signalled by a more or less ever-present floor of wooden stage boards.[67] Despite the compromises imposed by the budget, however, when the screen project was announced Adrian Noble joined the ranks of those who had previously had a vision that the RSC might have a future in films. 'Obviously our main aim will remain the theatre,' he was quoted as saying. 'But we believe passionately in proselytising the works of Shakespeare and our other work. It would be marvellous to make a film of *The Cherry Orchard* next.'[68] The director had just staged an admired version of Chekhov's play, but this dream was not to become a reality. Since then the RSC has not collaborated on a feature film adapted from any of its productions.

A plethora of paratexts

From the late 1990s onwards screen traces of RSC stagings, which already included feature films, broadcast television, newsreel items, extracts in documentaries and review programmes, and archival tapes made by the company and by NVAP, were further extended by an array of self-produced fragments that continues to proliferate today. In 1997 the communications team started to work with external video producers to create and issue electronic press kits (EPKs) featuring short scenes for editorial use by news media for major productions. Other video elements followed, from the education department and elsewhere within the company, initially for distribution via the RSC website and subsequently on YouTube. In 2009 the first video trailers were produced, again for online use to market individual productions. Several thousand of these screen elements have been created, most of them short and most related to a particular production. More recently, a number have been directly connected with screen adaptations of stagings. Many of the video trailers and EPK clips establish what can be understood as paratextual relationships with the stage productions, in that they prepare the viewer for an encounter with the theatrical experience to come. As Jonathan Gray has written, 'paratexts tell us what to expect, and in doing so they shape the reading strategies that we will take with us into the text, and they provide the all-important early frames through which we will examine, react to, and evaluate "textual" consumption.'[69] Yet paratexts are not only encountered by a viewer ahead of a production, since many are seen after attending a performance or without the viewer having experienced the actual staging. Many have also continued to circulate up to a decade after the run of a show, although rights limitations may limit the time they are available.

While paratextual trailers are specifically directed towards persuading the viewer to purchase a ticket for a particular show, the intended audiences across the range of screen snippets are more varied and, while they are often freely accessible, the reach of many of them is limited. No index is kept of their production or their survival, and while many are archived, there is no structured way to access them. Like the archival recordings of productions, and despite often extensive internal discussion ahead of their production about their approach and value, they have only marginal presences both within and beyond the company. They are understood to have an almost exclusively utilitarian function, whether this is to sell tickets or for classroom use, and they remain effectively invisible in journalistic or academic discourses around the RSC. Yet in however minimal a way each contributes to and shapes the available meanings of productions and screen adaptations, the company's own understandings of theatrical practice and education, and more generally the RSC's self-image. Many of these paratexts, in the manner of the earlier excerpts produced by broadcasters for documentaries and review programmes, also preserve the only moving-image traces of particular productions.

The first EPK was issued in late 1997 to showcase the coming season's forthcoming and touring productions. Documentation about the start of this initiative has proved impossible to track down, but it appears to have been prompted by an Arts Council England pilot study set up to support marketing for touring companies. 'The RSC will record a brief promotional video', *The Stage* reported in July 1997, 'for screening in the bars and foyers of venues to which it will be touring … Local television companies are also likely to be involved in the scheme, which would see television monitors installed at the participating theatres.'[70] The earliest EPKs videotaped for individual productions included ones for *The Merchant of Venice, Twelfth Night, Romeo and Juliet* and *Troilus and Cressida* (all 1998), and typically comprised a scene from the play that was shot on stage in multiple takes with a single camera and assembled during an edit. This was made available to broadcasters for use in magazine and review programmes, and much like the earlier sequences made by television companies themselves, these standalone scenes echoed the strategies of the early film and television productions of individual scenes. Indeed, just as those excerpts might be understood, following Tom Gunning's analysis of early film adaptations, as cinema and television of reference, these fragments of performance are media of reference. The first Shakespeare broadcasts by BBC Television in the late 1930s, for example, played one or two recognizable scenes as a discreet programme, as when on 3 February 1937 in the studio at Alexandra Palace, Margaretta Scott acted Rosalind to Ion Swinley's Orlando in a twelve-minute scene from Act 3, Scene 2 of *As You Like It*.[71] The RSC's EPK productions, some of which were later reused for educational purposes, echoed this approach, as with the six-minute extract from Act 3, Scene 2 of Maria Aberg's 2013 staging of *As You Like It*, with Pippa Nixon (Rosalind) and Alex Waldmann (Orlando), which continued to be available on the RSC Education YouTube channel five years later.[72]

In the years just after the millennium the RSC was able to take advantage, along with numerous other cultural organizations, of the fundamental shift away from a reliance on broadcaster partnerships for its moving-image collaborations. Falling costs of professional-quality cameras and desktop editing systems, increasing ease of use and more broadly based training, and – crucially – the emergence of alternative distribution structures meant that the company could begin not only to make its own small-scale productions but also to establish direct channels to audiences and, in some cases, to commercial markets. From 2009 onwards the company started to distribute videos on YouTube, where the extensive content can be broadly grouped as the EPK scenes considered above; didactic shorts conceived both for general audiences and for formal education; corporate and fundraising messages; and marketing contributions, including both audience interviews and trailers. Many of the videos also straddle two or more of these categories. At the time of writing the earliest RSC video on YouTube was an August 2009 peer-to-peer promotional tape, made for a trade conference, promoting the hardware-and-software gizmo, RSC Light Lock.[73]

The earliest formal trailer still available at the start of 2018 was one posted in December 2009 for *Arabian Nights*.[74] A second for the same production followed the next month, with a trailer for *King Lear* with Greg Hicks in February.[75] Effacing qualities traditionally identified as 'theatrical', such as verse-speaking and staging, the first *Arabian Nights* trailer in just over a minute foregrounds aural intensity and visual spectacle. Graphics identify the trailer as the RSC's and the production as playing in the Courtyard Theatre during a specified time period, but there is no indication of casting or of the production's director, writer or designer. Authorship of the trailer is restricted to a full-screen animated logo for Dusthouse, a production company that has worked regularly with the RSC for a decade. Many subsequent products follow this model, with the *King Lear* trailer, graced by Greg Hicks in full costume and make-up, emphasizing its 'cinematic' qualities by being shot on location and mastered in a widescreen format.[76] By the time of the 2016 *King Lear* directed by Gregory Doran and its revival in 2018, the range of available paratexts had developed to encompass trailers for the live cinema broadcast, for the DVD release and for the revival in New York, as well as witness statements from audience members and a spoken synopsis of the play by assistant director Anna Girvan. Many of the RSC's other productions over the past decade have accumulated a similar trail of paratextual elements, contributing to an unprecedented if largely unstructured and inchoate collective archive.

In a discussion of a comparable range of online paratexts for Cheek by Jowl's 2011 to 2014 production of John Ford's *'Tis Pity She's a Whore*, Pascale Aebischer suggested that these offer 'the user navigating between on-stage and online performances the opportunity to engage in a demanding cognitive performance in which each version of *'Tis Pity* is mentally held against the other versions'.[77] Moreover, she argued these clusters of online remediations

> fundamentally destabilise the authority of the live performance and the viewer's memory of that performance … As I repeatedly watch the clips, I recall moments of the production I had begun to forget. Other moments that are not included either recede in importance (they were not important enough, after all, to be selected) or become more important in my resistance to the choices made. Watching and re-watching the clips, I note my growing nostalgia for the liveness of theatre, my anxiety at the threat the immediacy of the living online performances pose to my memory of the live.[78]

Yet my sense is that for the viewer who has seen the stage production these short, modestly produced remediations, viewed mostly on small computer screens in a context of distraction without the focus of the theatre, seem unlikely to impart anything close to the intensity of the original or to prompt similar responses. While the trailers as threshold experiences may to a degree shape the user's engagement with a production seen subsequently, and while the traces that remain may contest the memories of the live experience, in my experience both remain subordinate, at least in the immediate aftermath, to the theatrical staging. Just as do other paratexts that are not moving images: photographs, reviews, the comments of friends. The actuality of the mediatized living does not at first significantly challenge or replace the memory of the live, although arguably it may do so increasingly as time passes. And as we have seen throughout this history, from Frank Benson's *Richard III* in 1911 onwards, these living traces increasingly constitute a hugely significant component of that memory for those who never saw the stage production as well as for those whose personal memories will inevitably fade.

Michael Boyd and the Histories

In May 2001 Adrian Noble announced significant changes to the company's organization. Dubbed internally as 'Project Fleet', this remodelling was received beyond the RSC with dismay. Actors were to be offered shorter and more flexible contracts. But this was interpreted as a dismantling of the ensemble principle and of commitments to continuity and growth, which were held to be at the heart of the company. The RSC was also to leave the Barbican the following year. Instead it would play in different London theatres depending on the show. Even more radically, the Royal Shakespeare Theatre was to be demolished and the site redeveloped. 'We are talking', Noble wrote, 'about the RSC becoming one of the first large companies to define itself through the work it does and the performances it gives rather than through the buildings it occupies.'[79] The first steps towards realizing this vision did not go well. By the autumn, John Peter could report excitedly that 'the RSC is in turmoil. Its reorganisation plans may be facing grave legal complications. What is happening is the most critical event in the history of the subsidised arts in this country.'[80] Then in April 2002, as the company began to present three shows at London's Roundhouse (with a residency that was to lose a significant sum), and just after Judi Dench wrote to *The Stage* about her concerns for the RSC's future, Adrian Noble resigned. The inevitable redundancies caused by the retreat from the Barbican had been hugely unpopular, as had the plan to replace the RST by a 'theatre village' that smacked of the worst aspects of heritage tourism. Expressing the feelings of many, Benedict Nightingale looked back with regret more than anger: 'It is not just nostalgia that convinces me that the company's artistic quality is not what it was 40, 30 or even ten years ago … after Noble's controversial tenure, someone must convince us not only that the RSC matters but that we need it at all.'[81] Three months later, in April 2002, Michael Billington responded cautiously but positively to the first press conference given by the new artistic director, Michael Boyd, writing that 'Only the work of flair and imagination, built around the company idea, will alter the current perception of the RSC as a flailing giant.'[82] Boyd had been much influenced by a period working in Moscow before founding Glasgow's Tron Theatre and starting to stage productions at Stratford in the early 1990s. Carefully and cautiously, he and general manager Vikki Heywood brought the RSC back from the brink, running down the deficit, encouraging exceptional work, developing the idea of ensemble playing, arranging for a London showing of significant productions like Gregory Doran's *All's Well That Ends Well* with Judi Dench, and in 2006 mounting *The Complete Works Festival* that saw all thirty-seven plays, together with Shakespeare's poems, performed in Stratford by the RSC and visiting companies.[83] In relation to screen versions of this work, Michael Boyd felt strongly that the company's priority had to be improving the work on stage. 'On one level', he said in an interview for this book, 'it felt a bit of a luxury to be thinking beyond that. Also, to be honest, at the beginning, hubristic.' He was similarly sceptical about plans for a new The Other Place to be developed for film production. 'I know you want to futureproof,' he recalled thinking, 'but it feels like you're going to jinx something if you're going to do that.'[84]

In September 2004 plans were announced for a full-scale redevelopment of the Royal Shakespeare Theatre, keeping the building's Art Deco facade and front of house features but rebuilding the auditorium around a thrust stage. Budgeted at £128 million, this development project was brought to a successful conclusion in November 2010 when the theatre reopened. And for the years from 2006 to 2010 the company moved to a new home, The Courtyard Theatre, which was built as a temporary structure on the site of The Other Place. Much later, planning permission for the redevelopment of this radical structure was granted, and in 2016 this opened once again as a complex of studio auditorium, café and rehearsal rooms proudly bearing the name of The Other Place. While the RST was dark, Michael Boyd extended the *This England: The Histories* project that had begun in 2000 to 2001 with Steven Pimlott, Michael Attenborough and Edward Hall. Boyd restaged his *Henry VI* trilogy and *Richard III* from the first presentation, and now himself directed *Richard II, Henry IV, Parts 1* and *2* and *Henry V*. 'Let me state unreservedly', Charles Spencer wrote, 'that [Michael] Boyd's history cycle offers some of the greatest acting, in some of the most imaginative and rigorous productions, that I have experienced in more than 30 years of professional theatre-going.'[85]

At which point this tale takes a personal turn. I had already worked with Gregory Doran, who was to succeed Michael Boyd as the RSC's artistic director in 2012, on television adaptations of his productions of *Macbeth* (2001) and *Hamlet* (2009), which are discussed in the next chapter. After the successful broadcast of *Hamlet* on Boxing Day 2009, BBC Television Director-General Mark Thompson asked me to explore a television adaptation of Michael Boyd's Histories cycle, which I worked on in the first months of 2010. I outlined two possible approaches to translating the eight stage productions into a media project for television and online. Envisaging shooting partly in the Courtyard Theatre and partly on location, the approaches were each budgeted at £6.7 million. I emailed my feasibility report on 7 May and within a couple of hours took a phone call from a BBC executive who thanked me for the document. Almost as an afterthought he added that I should know that the BBC was also now considering a proposal from Sam Mendes and Neal Street Productions to make a cycle of original films of Shakespeare's History plays. Such are the coincidences and contingencies of funding and producing adaptations. I doubt that anyone at the BBC even turned the title page of my report. Two years later, within the frame of the 2012 London Olympics, it was in the four films of *The Hollow Crown*, and not courtesy of the RSC, that Shakespeare's Histories again played out their engagements with ideas of national identity.[86]

What became apparent during my discussions with Michael Boyd was his ambivalence about the idea of translating theatre productions to the screen, which he also expressed at the RSC's autumn 2009 press conference. He was asked about NT Live's successful cinema broadcast of Racine's *Phèdre*, starring Helen Mirren, that had applied to theatre the approach of the Met Opera: Live in HD screenings. The screenings were 'a cool experience', he said, '[but] not in a million years better than being in the theatre … It will be a long time before cinema can capture anything more than a pale reflection of the art form … it is potentially exciting but I don't think anyone has cracked it yet'.[87] Michael Boyd elected not to have the RSC follow the NT Live model, but he did authorize a cautious collaboration with Digital Theatre, which resulted in two screen adaptations. One was of his own production of *As You Like It* and the other of a production of *The Comedy of Errors* developed for schools as a collaboration between the RSC and the touring group Told by an Idiot.

Digital Theatre was set up in late 2008 by the theatre director Robert Delamere and radio and television producer Thomas Shaw. This was a moment at which, in the wake of the success of Met Opera: Live in HD, a number of initiatives were exploring recording and distributing theatre productions. As the next chapter details, the RSC was examining the idea for a cinema broadcast of Gregory Doran's staging of *Hamlet* with David Tennant, Shakespeare's Globe put in place cinema screenings for recording of three productions from its 2009 season, Greenwich Theatre launched its Stage to Screen project of recordings for education, and NT Live's *Phèdre* was screened in June 2009. 'The year 2009 stands as a historical marker,' according to Leslie A. Wade, 'a time when new media technology confirmed its legitimacy and won full partnership in British theatre operations. At this juncture one can claim without question that British theatre had become mediatized.'[88] Backed by an initial investment of £1 million, Digital Theatre set out to create downloadable recordings with partners including the Almeida, the Young Vic and the Royal Court as well as the RSC. Marketed globally to individual consumers, and initially priced at £8.99 per download, Digital Theatre's catalogue soon featured a dozen or more productions. Recordings were made with between six and thirteen unobtrusively mounted cameras that were either fixed or with pans and zooms controlled by a remote operator. Two runs of each show were captured and a final edit made from the bundle of resulting recordings. What they were concerned to avoid, Delamere was quoted as saying, was 'a static, completely neutral filming, which is what people have seen for years and which doesn't accord with anyone's idea of film language'.[89] 'We want', he said, 'to create a mirror of living theatre ... to get away from this strange, two-dimensionality that you get if the cameras are boxed away.'[90]

The Comedy of Errors was a small-scale touring production developed as part of the Young People's Shakespeare project with Told by an Idiot, a company renowned for its playful and participatory stagings. With a text edited by Gary Owen to eighty fast-paced minutes, with inventive direction by Paul Hunter, and with much live music, it played in schools and community centres throughout 2009, as well as being accorded a short run in the Courtyard Theatre. While admiring its intent, warmth and obvious connection with young audiences, Lyn Gardner wrote, 'it is a little over-egged for adult tastes (though I did enjoy the cross-dressing cook with football bosoms), and there are times when the madcap invention threatens to suffocate the storytelling'.[91] Digital Theatre's cameras captured it in December at the Clapham Community Project, where the even lighting of the hall reveals an audience of schoolchildren seated on the ground around a bare platform. The judicious shot choices and fast cutting complement the boisterous comedy, resulting in an enjoyable, if modest, screen version. Oddly, its completion meant that, given the previous television versions of stagings by Clifford Williams and Trevor Nunn, *The Comedy of Errors* became the Shakespeare play of which the RSC had made the most full-length screen adaptations.

Michael Boyd's production of *As You Like It* with Katy Stephens (Rosalind) and Jonjo O'Neill (Orlando) was respectfully reviewed on its opening at the Courtyard Theatre in April 2009 (Figure 10). A sombre telling in dark tones, the production was visually cold and wintry, and to a degree emotionally so too. For Charles Spencer, however, it was 'a vision of the play that powerfully captures the dramatic movement from pain and fear to reconciliation and love'.[92] Digital Theatre took their cameras into the theatre on 1 and 2 September, and edited from the two runs a somewhat restless, rapidly cut adaptation. Movement between the multiple fixed cameras, with additional shots taken on stage, at times breaks with the sense of a coherent stage space. 'We gave Digital Theatre a go,' Michael Boyd said as he looked back at the recording, 'and we weren't blown away. There are things about the recording of *As You Like It* that were really well done. But it's not the show.'[93] For him, a crucial missing element from the screen version was the sense of the cast's complicity with the audience that is so central to live performance. As to whether he now regrets that more of the productions by himself and his peers in the first years of the century were not translated to the screen, he noted: 'Maybe I was a bit absolutist. I would almost rather

FIGURE 10 *Katy Stephens (Rosalind), Sandy Neilson (Duke Frederick) and Mariah Gale (Celia) in Michael Boyd's staging of* As You Like It *(2009), recorded by Digital Theatre. Photograph by Ellie Kurttz* © *RSC.*

have the honesty of a single or two-camera thing, that knew what it was, definitely a record, and you know it's not the show, than something that was still to some extent a pale reflection of the live experience.'[94]

As You Like It was shot in the Courtyard Theatre, which closed when the redeveloped RST reopened in November 2010. The redesigned theatre won plaudits from many, and feeling that to a degree his job was done, Michael Boyd announced that he would leave the company in late 2012. His tenure, for much of which he had collaborated closely with administrative head Vikki Heywood, was praised not only for the successful redevelopment of the RST but also for stabilizing the company's finances, strengthening the ensemble theatre-making process, while at the same time being sufficiently flexible to welcome in 'star' players such as Ian McKellen and David Tennant, and also significantly extending the company's education and outreach initiatives. Towards the end of Michael Boyd's reign, in December 2009, his core concerns were reflected in a further television documentary profiling the company. *The South Bank Show: The Royal Shakespeare Company* was the final film, after thirty-one years, in the venerable arts strand's life on ITV. 'The brave work is continuing,' editor and presenter Melvyn Bragg reflected in his closing voice-over, 'keeping this now well-established British institution full of new life as it moves into the future.' The parallels were clear between his vision of his own venture (which would have a further life on Sky Arts) and the one committed to making theatre in Stratford-upon-Avon and beyond. In the spring of 2012, rather than the fervid atmosphere that had accompanied previous handovers, there was a sense of calm recognition that the best person to succeed Boyd was a figure who had, amongst other qualities, a far greater enthusiasm for screening the stage. By this point Gregory Doran had already seen his production of *The Winter's Tale* recorded at the Barbican in 1999 and he had directed television films of his stagings of *Macbeth, Hamlet* and *Julius Caesar*. With these, the introduction at Doran's urging of the RSC Live from Stratford-upon-Avon cinema broadcasts in late 2013, and the significant growth of moving-image media from the Education department, in the early years of the twenty-first century the RSC was even more actively focused on screen adaptations than it had been during its first years under Peter Hall.

6

Now-ness: 2000–18

Having acted with the company for the first time in 1987, directing at Stratford from 1992, and chief associate director from 2003, Gregory Doran took over as RSC artistic director in September 2012. He inherited from Michael Boyd a stable, comparatively well-funded company (with a vital revenue stream from *Matilda the Musical*), as well as a richly renovated RST and the shell of what had been its temporary replacement, the Courtyard Theatre. In contrast to the previous two moments of succession, there was little sense of any threat to the company's future. In Siobhan Keenan's assessment at the time, 'few would dispute that the company is in a stronger position than it was when Boyd first took command of it'.[1] In the years since, commentators and audiences have been broadly positive about the quality of productions, albeit with the recognition that the company has lost the radical imperative of its earliest days. Doran's own stagings, including *Richard II* (2013), *King Lear* (2016) and *The Tempest* (2016), as well as the adaptation of Robert Harris's books, *Imperium* (2017), were critical and commercial successes, and on both the main stage and in the Swan Theatre he has encouraged bold younger directors, including Simon Godwin, Maria Aberg and Polly Findlay. In many ways, and not least because they were central to his own practice, Doran brought back into focus the company's traditional values, including close attention to the text and other craft skills associated with playing early modern drama. Challenges faced by the company included the revival of a commitment to new writing and the transformation of the Courtyard building into a new The Other Place, and these tasks have been led by Erica Whyman, who joined as deputy artistic director. A permanent London base was a further priority, and a partial solution to this was negotiated with an agreement to return annually to the Barbican theatre for a winter season from 2014 onwards.

In contrast to Michael Boyd's caution about NT Live and the like, Doran was certain that a comparable initiative was essential for the company. He coordinated the policy that the company would from 2013 onwards mount a single major staging, without repeats, of each of the thirty-six First

Folio plays plus *Pericles*. This vision was aligned with a live cinema strategy of broadcasting and recording each of these productions. At the time of writing there have been twenty-two RSC Live from Stratford-upon-Avon broadcasts, with *Twelfth Night* in early 2018 marking the halfway point in the completion of the canon. The majority of these recordings were also streamed without charge to schools across Britain, as one strand of the RSC's extensive and widely celebrated educational activities. In addition, the company's work for schools embraced original and substantial productions for the screen. Taking account also of broadcast co-productions including *Shakespeare Live! From the RSC* (2016), it was apparent that the company had by the mid-2010s become, albeit in a very different media environment, the moving-image production entity that Peter Hall envisaged back in the early 1960s. The imperative for Hall and his colleagues, in addition to personal ambition, was primarily financial, seeking market returns to sustain the aspirations of a fledgling company that had only minimal Arts Council support. Fifty years later, access, audience development, corporate profile and the mission to extend the experience of Shakespeare are all central to the company's strategy, but another driver for the RSC to be on multiple screens for many kinds of audiences is also financial. The key difference, however, is that the television profile, cinema broadcasts, screen-based educational activities and more now demonstrate the essential public value of the RSC, legitimating in a constrained financial climate Arts Council England support of approximately one-quarter of the company's operating costs. This chapter explores the extensive and diffuse screen manifestations of the RSC in the 2010s and grounds that story in Gregory Doran's developing involvement in moving-image adaptations from tentative experiments in the 1990s through to his three location-shot broadcast films. Before that story begins, however, it must be noted that I have been a central participant in much of this tale, and so the chapter has a more personal, implicated voice. Readers may wish to adopt an appropriately sceptical attitude to whatever criticality this tale carries and to the brief speculations about the future with which I close.

Taking to the screen

Gregory Doran's exploration of the transfer of stage productions to the screen began with *Titus Andronicus* in 1995 in which for Johannesburg's Market Theatre he directed his husband Antony Sher. This marked a notable return by the actor to the country of his birth just after the ending of apartheid. The South African Broadcasting Corporation recorded three performances with six cameras, together with a day of pick-up shots. Doran regards the compiled result as a respectable archival record. His next screen encounter came in 1999 at the Barbican when Heritage Theatre undertook a multi-camera recording of his production of *The Winter's Tale* with Sher as Leontes. Established by the former BBC producer Robert Marshall,

Heritage Theatre was a pioneering precursor of screened theatre beyond the traditional television context. A decade before NT Live's *Phèdre* in 2007, Marshall recognized that while the BBC and Channel 4 were continuing to broadcast opera and ballet, the small screen was ignoring theatre. Frustrated in his dealings with commissioners with little interest in such projects, he raised the capital to initiate independent recordings, releasing these on VHS, then DVD, and looking also for sales to television. Titles that followed *The Winter's Tale* included the Bristol Old Vic's production of Sheridan's *The Rivals* (2004), *Othello* (2007) from Shakespeare's Globe, and *The Mysteries* (2001) and *Primo* (2005), both made with the National Theatre.[2]

As Robert Marshall recalled about the early days of the project,

> Convincing theatre companies to allow cameras into their auditoriums wasn't easy. In fact it took years. Part of my strategy was to focus my efforts on one of the top companies; the RSC. My reasoning being that if we convinced them then other companies would likely be more amenable. So I became the proverbial squeaky gate until finally in 1999, the RSC relented and asked us to do *The Winter's Tale*.[3]

The shoot across two performances involved five cameras in frontal positions in the wide Barbican auditorium. The screen director was Robin Lough, who had trained and worked extensively with the BBC as a multi-camera director of drama and opera. He subsequently collaborated with Marshall on the majority of the Heritage Theatre titles, before going on to screen direct NT Live's *Phèdre*, and then *Richard II*, the first RSC Live from Stratford-upon-Avon production in 2013. He later directed for the screen numerous other NT Live broadcasts as well as the majority of the early live cinema productions from the RSC. 'The most challenging issue', Marshall reflected, 'was that the RSC had insisted on retaining the right to approve the recording before it was released – and in the event, the artistic director Adrian Noble did not approve it.' An educational package featuring only substantial extracts was released in 2000, and the DVD of the full production was only finally published in 2005. Two decades on, Gregory Doran recognized the archival value of the recording but felt that the experience was 'second hand'. As he said in an address to the 2016 World Shakespeare Congress,

> It somehow remains inert ... [and] failed to allow you to participate. You somehow felt outside looking in. And it did not solve the problem of scale. When the camera went in on a close up of Tony Sher as Leontes delivering one of his blistering rages, and projecting to the back row (Row T) of the Barbican Theatre, it felt uncannily like that dizzying dolly-zoom shot in *Jaws* where the camera zooms in on Roy Scheider seeing the shark for the first time. We wanted to capture the live-ness of the event, but somehow only caught its pastness.[4]

In 1999 Gregory Doran mounted a much-praised production of *Macbeth* in the Swan Theatre with Antony Sher and Harriet Walter. An international tour preceded a run the following spring at London's Young Vic. After seeing a performance Culture Secretary Chris Smith rang Channel 4's director of programmes Michael Jackson to urge him to commission a screen version. Channel 4 had during the 1980s demonstrated a strong commitment to performance, including broadcasts of Peter Hall's production of Aeschylus's *The Oresteia* (1983) from the National Theatre, and *The Mahabaratha* (1989), directed for both stage and screen by Peter Brook. Such work, however, had largely disappeared from the channel in the subsequent decade. The BBC's engagement with the theatre by the 1990s was similarly muted, although for the final series of the *Performance* strand in 1997 I produced (with my colleague Shaun Deeney) a version of Deborah Warner's National Theatre staging of *Richard II* with Fiona Shaw as Shakespeare's troubled monarch. This was made by my production company Illuminations, and we followed it with an innovative BBC Television version of Opera North's staging of Benjamin Britten's opera *Gloriana*. As on *Richard II*, *Gloriana* was directed for the screen by the stage production's director, in this case Phyllida Lloyd. Both Fiona Shaw, a friend of Phyllida Lloyd, and Antony Sher, were represented by the same agent, and from this came an invitation to Illuminations to produce *Macbeth* for Channel 4. Although there were many differences, the production model for both *Richard II* and *Gloriana* shared key elements, including a move off the stage to the studio, one space where most of the film could be shot, and the focus of predominantly single-camera filming. In both cases too the stage director was supported by an experienced director of photography and production team, so that even without an extensive track record in film she could become the screen director. My co-producer Sebastian Grant and I extended this approach to *Macbeth*, enhancing it at Gregory Doran's suggestion with an embrace of location filming rather than shooting in a studio.

As Doran has explained, he wanted to

> capture the excitement of watching that particular play in the theatre, the relentless hold it has upon you, the sense of being trapped in the same room with a couple planning murder. The spontaneity, the feeling you have that it is unfolding in real time before your eyes, and you could stop it if you wanted ... How can you begin to reproduce that sheer immediacy in a medium as fixed as film?[5]

It was also essential, Doran felt, that in contrast to most feature film adaptations of Shakespeare (including Roman Polanski's feted version), this *Macbeth* should preserve as much of the text as was feasible. In addition Doran wanted to strip away any irrelevant scenic details, and to present the action, which on stage unfolded in a non-specific contemporary world, in a setting that possessed 'a vivid neutrality'. Specific associations of places and times were to be avoided, and yet an identifiable sense of the real world had to be retained. In the summer of 2000 the Roundhouse in Camden, which in the 1960s had been converted from a locomotive shed into an arts centre, had just been renovated. Its spectacular central hall was empty, and there were staircases and corridors as well as an undercroft that offered claustrophobic spaces. The practised cast played their scenes as director of photography Ernie Vincze, who had worked around the world as a current affairs cameraman, sought to catch the action like a documentary filmmaker operating in a war zone. Shooting with a heavy Digibeta camera on his shoulder for long periods, he employed elements of *verité* film-making to achieve an edgy unpredictability, and the 'raw energy and dangerous intimacy' that Gregory Doran sought are apparent throughout.

The 125-minute television film of *Macbeth* was shot in just twelve days, and on what for television drama of the time was a modest budget of £400,000. The *Daily Mail*'s television critic described the production as 'the best television Shakespeare I have seen', and the critical reception overall was positive.[6] In a contrary later assessment, however, Susanne Greenhalgh questioned the efficacy of the film's deployment of specifically televisual codes. She acknowledged that the camerawork and editing achieved a sense of urgency and fear, but argued that the visual conventions trapped the characters in a labyrinth not unlike a game-show maze. For Greenhalgh,

> Doran's *Macbeth* is so saturated by the spectrum of media images and genres that flicker and hybridise across our screens worldwide, that there can be no 'collision', no distancing, finally no history. Instead the play is decontextualised, not in the 'real' of the contemporary political violence it claims to represent and seeks to make its audience witness, but rather in Baudrillard's realm of the simulacrum, where wars never really happened.[7]

Gregory Doran and I believed that *Macbeth* demonstrated a successful approach to the transfer of theatre to television in a dynamic, vivid and cost-effective manner. We had shown how a stage production could be adapted as television drama, retaining the now-ness of theatre and combining this with the close-up immediacy of the screen. We therefore endeavoured to interest both the BBC and Channel 4 in, among other projects, Doran's RSC productions of *Othello* (2004), with Sello Maake Ka-Ncube and Antony Sher, and *Antony and Cleopatra* (2006), with Patrick Stewart and Harriet Walter. Following the BBC's groundbreaking adaptation of Charles Dickens's *Bleak House* (2005), which was scheduled as mid-evening, mid-week half-hours, we pitched Shakespeare's tale of Egypt and Rome as a serial of half-hour episodes across five consecutive nights. The response was indifference. Despite tentative explorations of as-live in-theatre recording by the digital channel BBC Four in its first months in 2002, classic stage plays all but disappeared from the schedules in the twenty-first-century's first decade. Shakespeare nonetheless maintained a modest presence, with screen versions of Trevor Nunn's National Theatre *The Merchant of Venice* (2001) and his RSC *King Lear* (More4, 2008), and the BBC was a co-production partner with ARTE in Peter Brook's *The Tragedy of Hamlet* (2002). Channel 4 funded Tim Supple's film of *Twelfth Night* (2003) primarily for education audiences, and the opening of Shakespeare's Globe was marked by the BBC with live transmissions of *Richard II* (2003) and *Measure for Measure* (2004). And the BBC sustained in other ways its decades-long identification of the author at the centre of the nation's culture. *Shakespeare Re-told* (2006) adapted four of the plays with modern-day settings and language, and Michael Wood's four-part documentary series *In Search of Shakespeare* (2003) travelled the land exploring what was known of his biography. RSC actors along with Gregory Doran contributed scenes from a selection of plays. Yet we found it impossible to follow up what we believed had been *Macbeth's* key innovations.

'The play's the thing'

In early 2008 the RSC announced that Gregory Doran was to direct *Hamlet* with David Tennant, a casting coup guaranteed to attract exceptional attention. My interest as a producer now was to bypass (or perhaps complement) broadcast television and to apply to a classic play the model created by New York's Metropolitan Opera of live transmissions to cinemas. The first broadcast for the Met Opera: Live in HD series was of *The Magic Flute* in December 2006, and the presentation of *Eugene Onegin* in February 2007 impressed me enormously. I enthused to Gregory Doran that such broadcasts were

> at their best a thrilling experience. They are shot live in HD with at least a dozen cameras and excellent 5.1 sound … The advantages that the transmissions have over a television relay include the wonderful images in HD, the great sound and the live quality shared in a room with hundreds of other viewers. So people applaud and generally take part in a communal experience.[8]

Despite uncertainties about whether an aesthetic that demonstrably worked for opera transmission could be applied with creative success to the theatre, the RSC agreed to explore the idea, and they secured the backing of Picturehouse as distributors and a guarantee against loss from Arts Council England. We sought the participation of the BBC, Channel 4 or Sky Arts, but without success. Detailed negotiations followed, with the cast and creatives, with agents and with the actors' union Equity, and it was agreed that a final decision would be taken after the show opened. The production was revealed as set in a non-specific twentieth-century world with modern costumes (DJs and jeans) but avoiding datable anachronisms (no mobile phones). The reviews were exceptional, with Charles Spencer for *The Telegraph* later applauding a show with 'the hurtling intensity of a thriller … without doubt one of the finest productions of *Hamlet* I have ever seen, led by an actor of extraordinary courage and charisma who has made a persuasive claim to true greatness'.[9] The proposal for the live broadcast, however, had to be approved by each cast member and one felt strongly that it was inappropriate to present live theatre on the screen. By early September the plan had been abandoned.

In early December, on the press night of the production's London transfer, a back injury forced David Tennant to withdraw. Tennant's understudy Edward Bennett, who had been playing Laertes, took the title role for the next three weeks in a run that had sold out months before. Tennant returned to the production in the new year just a week before the show closed. All of which only heightened press and public fascination with the production. Recognizing the extraordinary levels of interest, the RSC began to explore ways of recording the production, even if only as a low-budget direct-to-DVD release. The demand for this was focused by an online petition for a DVD, which by mid-January had attracted more than 6,500 signatures. Gregory Doran now proposed that the RSC and Illuminations should develop a film version, which he believed would circumvent the concerns of the sceptical actor. Availability checks revealed that a summer shoot was possible, after David Tennant finished filming *Doctor Who* and while Patrick Stewart, who played Claudius, was performing *Waiting for Godot* in London. Co-producer Sebastian Grant and I adopted the one-location, single-camera filming model of *Macbeth* and calculated a likely budget of £900,000, eventually assembled from BBC Television, which now embraced the project with enthusiasm, WNET13 for PBS in the United States, and NHK in Japan, together with fee deferrals and a BBC Worldwide distribution advance against other sales. BBC Television contributed the largest element, recognizing now that *Hamlet* could be played at Christmas 2009 and capitalize on the interest of David Tennant's final appearance as Doctor Who. The BBC's only stipulation was that we not make a *movie*. They sought a contemporary, dynamic translation to the screen, but because they intended to market this as extending public access to this exceptional production, we had to retain distinguishable qualities of the stage production.

During the location search co-producer Sebastian Grant and Gregory Doran visited the former Catholic seminary of St Joseph's College in Mill Hill. At its heart we found a deconsecrated chapel that, like the rest of the site, was dilapidated but structurally sound. Parts of it had been used previously for filming, but there was no electricity, minimal water and toilet facilities, and extra security would be needed. Nonetheless we turned over for the first shot of three weeks of filming on 1 June. Much of the 'look' for the film was already set, and the production utilized the RSC props and costumes, although the latter needed enhancement for the demands of filming.[10] Production designer Robert Jones adapted his stage designs to the spaces of St Joseph's, with shiny black surfaces in the chapel that echoed the floor in the Courtyard Theatre. The main scenic element on stage had been a mirror across the rear of the playing area which, when Hamlet shot Polonius, cracked from side to side. Mirrors on this scale are hard to film with, and so Gregory Doran and director of photography Chris Seager threaded surveillance technology through the drama, replacing the theatrical metaphor with one more suited to the camera (Figure 11).

The schedule was demanding, but the chosen approach had advantages over the production of standard television drama. We were based at one location and the cast had a deep knowledge of their characters and their lines. Also, Doran and Seager developed a film language that was distinct from the usual master-shot and cut-in 'coverage' of conventional drama, and instead made extensive use of comparatively lengthy developing shots. This allowed the recording of more lines during a session than was usual in television drama. Throughout the shoot I wrote a daily blog, with the posts attracting a striking number of comments, and these were complemented by Twitter feeds from both Illuminations and the RSC. All of this contributed to the sense of an active and engaged conversation with future viewers, and the online conversation continued long after the filming itself.[11] Also new for a major theatre adaptation for television was the creation with BBC Learning of a complementary website that included extensive behind-the-scenes video sequences.[12] A thirty-five-minute *The Making of Hamlet* documentary was

FIGURE 11 *On the set of Gregory Doran's film of* Hamlet *(2009). Photograph by Ellie Kurttz © RSC/Illuminations.*

also edited to be included, together with a director's commentary throughout the film, on the DVD and Blu-ray. All of which exposed the production process of the adaptation in an unprecedented way, although each of the elements was approved by both the BBC and the RSC. Transmission was in the early evening on BBC Two on Boxing Day, 26 December.

BBC commissioning executive George Entwistle explained the BBC's thinking about *Hamlet* as a project extending beyond the film itself. 'We believe this version [of *Hamlet*],' he wrote, 'with this cast, has the potential to engage audiences who wouldn't normally turn up for Shakespeare.' He also stressed the importance of the BBC Learning website, which he hoped, 'will offer irresistible online journeys for anyone inspired by this superb TV version of the play, and provide an accessible, lasting record of the creativity and inspiration that went into the performance.'[13] Legitimation within the public service imperatives of the early twenty-first-century BBC was cast in terms of attracting a younger, less elitist audience for Shakespeare (which was also an overriding concern for the BBC for much of its output) as well as the film being the core of a broad educational initiative. Press response was almost unanimously positive with *Time Out* praising 'the rich texture of this stunning production ... a visually arresting style ... a mesmerising three hours'. Writing for *The Guardian*, Mark Lawson suggested that *Hamlet* 'should settle for some time the debate over whether it's possible to transfer theatre to TV: Gregory Doran's RSC production has been reimagined as an intimate, intense film'.[14] Approximately 900,000 viewers watched the film on transmission, which represented an audience share of 4.5 per cent across its full length. In the following twenty-four hours, more than 15,000 people downloaded or streamed the film on BBC iPlayer. A week after transmission, *The Observer* carried an article that began, 'Like many people, I had my love of Shakespeare reawakened by David Tennant's TV portrayal of Hamlet over Christmas.' The author of that piece was the British prime minister, Gordon Brown.[15]

In the wake of *Hamlet*, and as discussed above, I failed to secure the BBC's support for a screen version of Michael Boyd's Histories cycle, but another RSC screen opportunity opened up in late 2011. London was to host the Olympic Games the following summer, and the planning committee had undertaken, as Erin Sullivan has written, 'to reinvigorate and heavily showcase the cultural arm of the Olympic festivities by leveraging the UK's long-standing association with literary creativity and artistic heritage, from Shakespeare to Tolkien to Beatles to Britpop'.[16] A World Shakespeare Festival was to be coordinated by the RSC (in an ultimately uneasy partnership with Shakespeare's Globe) and complemented by a BBC season that came to be called 'Shakespeare Unlocked'. Erin Sullivan has identified the key concerns about the project:

Promotional materials for the World Shakespeare Festival took the label 'national poet' a step further, describing Shakespeare as 'the favourite playwright and artist of the whole world' – 'from national icon to global Olympic champion, if you will – and from a cynical point of view it would be easy to see the 2012 Year of Shakespeare as a continuation of Shakespeare's (and, by association, Britain's) cultural, national and global dominance.[17]

Yet as she also recognized the individual productions, and the totality that they made up, were complex, nuanced and richly diverse.

The RSC was once more turned to as the BBC's inevitable production partner, and the choice for a screen adaptation fell on Gregory Doran's staging of *Julius Caesar*. This was to be set in a contemporary but anonymous west African state and played with a cast of black actors. At one point the BBC suggested somewhat fancifully filming in and around the Palace of Westminster, but we eventually chose the more practicable location of an abandoned Chinese hypermarket in Colindale. Scheduling issues, however, forced the embrace of an unconventional hybrid approach to production. The BBC, which co-funded with The Open University, required the film to be shown ahead of the Olympics, but the production was still to be on stage at this point. As a consequence filming on location after the show had closed, as *Macbeth* and *Hamlet* had done, was ruled out. Recognizing that *Julius Caesar* is divided between public and private scenes, between backstage plotting and the episodes in the forum, Gregory Doran suggested that the former be shot on location and the latter in the theatre. Which is what, by bringing forward the stage rehearsals and inserting a break for the location shooting, we were able to do. We filmed in Colindale during a bitterly cold March, and then once the production had opened in the RST we brought in to the auditorium three fixed cameras and an on-stage crew to shoot two performances of the play's opening and the addresses to the mob by Brutus (Paterson Joseph) and Mark Antony (Ray Fearon).[18] Cast and costumes were common to both screen and stage, but the film utilized both the existing architecture of the shopping mall, including a broken escalator on which Caesar was assassinated, and several more conventional sets, such as for the courtyards of both Caesar's and Brutus's homes, to achieve a filmic *mise en scène*. The encounter of Brutus and Cassius with Casca at the end of Act 1, Scene 2 on film takes place in a urinal, whereas on the stage it was in an undefined area of Michael Vale's unitary setting. And the 'cinematic' is mobilized most obviously in the use of a low-fi mobile phone aesthetic to document, as if by one of the participants, the brutal street killing of Cinna the poet. In a challenging response to the stage production, which is equally applicable to the television film, Monika Smialkowska praised it as 'fresh and thought-provoking'. But she noted that Doran's decision to set the production in Africa was risky, perhaps especially when the World Shakespeare Festival was also hosting African companies. 'Representing another culture', she continued, 'can mean depicting it (from what position – equal or privileged?) or speaking for it (by what right?). In the postcolonial world, engaging in either of these activities is liable to arouse suspicions of cultural imperialism. By braving these suspicions, the RSC provided an arena where these important issues can be debated.'[19]

The television film of *Julius Caesar* can now be seen to comprise a loose trilogy with *Macbeth* and *Hamlet* in which the RSC and Illuminations developed a new screen form for the company, and for theatre on television more generally. But this approach has not been developed, despite television's return to a more sustained engagement with the stage in the 2010s. One strand of this revived interest has seen the production, with no involvement from the RSC, of more elaborate and more generously budgeted television films including the seven films in *The Hollow Crown* cycle (2012, 2016), adaptations of Ronald Harwood's *The Dresser* (2015) and Mike Bartlett's *King Charles III* (2017), a film of *King Lear* (2018), directed by Richard Eyre in contemporary settings, and a forthcoming Channel 4 series based on Lucy Kirkwood's *Chimerica,* originally presented at the Almeida Theatre. At the same time, BBC Television has embraced once again multiple-camera recordings made in theatres, including Ivo von Hove's production of *Antigone* (2017) from the Barbican theatre and the Almeida Theatre's *Hamlet* (2018) with Andrew Scott directed by Robert Icke. In part a direct consequence of Director-General Tony Hall's renewed commitment to the arts, these productions have also clearly been a response to the success of the non-broadcast initiatives, the emergence of which has been led by NT Live. The National Theatre began its highly successful series of cinema broadcasts in 2009 with *Phèdre*. High-definition cameras and 5.1 audio systems combined with satellite distribution and digital cinema projection meant that it was now feasible for cultural organizations to transmit stage performances directly to remote audiences, without the involvement of a television broadcaster. Within five years, not only the RSC but also the Royal Opera House, Glyndebourne Opera, English National Opera and Shakespeare's Globe had emulated this model with either live or recorded presentations in cinemas, and a number of smaller companies, including Hampstead Theatre, the Royal Court and Pilot Theatre had experimented with free streaming of productions online.[20]

'Live' from Stratford

In contrast to Michael Boyd's caution, when Gregory Doran took over as RSC artistic director in 2012 he made it a priority for the company to establish its own cinema broadcasts. In partnership (as had been planned on *Hamlet*) with distributors Picturehouse Entertainment (later Trafalgar Releasing), RSC Live from Stratford-upon-Avon began on 13 November 2013 with David Tennant as *Richard II*. This was also Doran's first production in his new role and the start of his initiative for the company to produce each of the First Folio plays without repeats on the main stage at Stratford across the following seven or eight years. *Henry IV, Part 1* and *Henry IV, Part 2*, both directed for the stage by Doran, and Simon Godwin's production of *The Two Gentlemen of Verona* followed as broadcasts in the 2014 summer season (Figure 12).[21] By the autumn of 2018, a further eighteen productions had been broadcast live, with the majority of these both streamed to schools, released on DVD and Blu-ray, and made available on online services both for education and general audiences. At a gathering of Shakespeare scholars in 2016, Gregory Doran enthused about the RSC Live from Stratford-upon-Avon broadcasts:

> They capture an immediacy. A danger if you like. But they also share the experience, by being a communal one ... You share the actual performance as you sit down in real time with the audience in Stratford to watch the production: you laugh with them, gasp, and cry with them, and applaud together at the end (a novel experience in the cinema!) and even if you are watching an encore screening the effect is curiously the same. You enjoy the now, now, very now-ness which is Shakespeare's appeal.[22]

The RSC's primary concern with the Live from ... broadcasts was to extend access to and develop audiences for its productions.[23] The company wanted to offer audiences across Britain and beyond experience of the company's

FIGURE 12 *Screen director Robin Lough preparing the RSC Live from Stratford-upon-Avon broadcast of* Henry IV, Part 1 *(2014). Photograph by Lucy Barriball © RSC.*

productions of Shakespeare without travelling to Stratford, to London or to the theatres visited on tour. It was also hoped that greater convenience and lower admission prices would attract audiences that might otherwise feel excluded from the theatre, although it is far from clear that this aspiration has been realized to any significant degree. Central to the project have been free schools screenings of Live from … recordings that are offered online with live introductions and Q&A sessions some weeks after each cinema broadcast. Extended access of these kinds was expected by Arts Council England (ACE) as a condition of its significant funding of the RSC (as it was of other organizations), and was enshrined in 2013 as a commitment in ACE's Strategic Plan: 'We will use digital technologies to engage and reach new audiences [and] extend the distribution of arts and culture through digital platforms.'[24] In addition to enhanced access there was a desire for the company to have high-quality archival recordings of its productions, for a range of uses including consultation by other practitioners and by scholars. And there was the belief that in the medium- to long-term RSC Live from Stratford-upon-Avon could contribute financially to the company, not least as the sole screen collection of First Folio plays to rival the *The BBC Television Shakespeare*, although to date, and despite profits from *Richard II* and *The Tempest*, the project's realization for the other broadcasts has required investment from the company's discretionary funds.

Cinema owners treat broadcasts of this kind, whether of theatre or opera, of comedy or sport, as 'event cinema', which is recognized as an expanding yet still marginal element of exhibition. As Martin Barker has detailed, 'Box office takings from these events are attractive in at least three ways. They are attracting back to cinemas audiences who had largely deserted them. They command a higher ticket price – with the bonus that many people book for whole seasons at one go. And they are, in the main, sell-out successes.'[25] He might have added also that the older, middle-class audiences that the broadcasts attract tend to spend freely on wine and other drinks in cinema bars. But the economics are more favourable to exhibitors than they are to the RSC acting as both producer and funder. When VAT, exhibitor and distributor fees are factored in, the producer may receive less than 25 per cent of the box office. NT Live have confirmed the production and rights costs of a standard live broadcast to be between £250,000 and £300,000, and the RSC costs are comparable. To achieve a meaningful return to the producer, a broadcast needs to take in excess of £800,000. And while subsequent revenue from discs, broadcast and streaming is welcome it is rarely substantial enough, at least in the short-term, to make up any losses. The RSC's comparatively late embrace of live broadcasts meant that the company benefited from NT Live having proved both that theatre on screen could be aesthetically successful, and also that there existed a committed and sizeable potential audience. NT Live had also done a great deal to reassure actors and other creatives, as well as their agents, that their stage work could be appropriately adapted to the screen and that responsible fee structures and rights packages could be agreed. The RSC's frameworks, which are subject to regular reviews, currently permit the company to exploit, in return for an initial fee and a later share of revenues, the Live from ... recordings in all media throughout the world in perpetuity.

From the start, Gregory Doran stipulated that the broadcasts would strive for the highest creative and technical standards, aspiring to adapt to the screen in a vivid and immediate form the theatrical experience of watching a performance in the Royal Shakespeare Theatre. The broadcast team aimed to construct with clarity the narrative of the performance for an attentive audience assumed to be viewing with others in a darkened auditorium. 'We are not making a movie,' remains a mantra that was repeated frequently by the broadcast team in explaining the process to prospective participants and others. With only the most minimal changes to the stage work, the productions have undergone a process of what might best be called 'translation'. This suggests both a strong degree of fidelity to a pre-existing original as well as a recognition of inevitable and intentional creative mediation. The broadcasts are dependent upon the precise positioning of cameras and microphones, the choice and sequencing of shots, the carefully planned adjustments throughout of audio levels, the pace of cutting and much more besides, all of which shape what reaches the screen. Six or seven cameras are deployed in the RST, three of which are on dollies facilitating movement along the full length of each side of the stage and across the front. A fourth camera is mounted on a substantial crane that can move around and within the playing space to achieve a great variety of shots as well as flowing movement along three axes. More than one hundred audio feeds come from radio mics on each of the actors, from the band room where live musicians play for each performance, and from the auditorium relaying laughs, the stillness of rapt attention and applause. Throughout the broadcast constant small adjustments by camera and crane operators, as well as the live audio mix, respond with sensitivity to the live encounter between a cast and an audience sharing the same space. All of which effects emphases and exclusions, contrasts and connections in a complex play of new meanings. The visual language of the broadcasts is clearly closely related to that of conventional cinema but at the same time, because it is achieved in real time and within a coherent space with its own fixed geometries, it is a specifically televisual language. Such hybridity can also be seen in the combination of elements conventionally understood as theatrical (origin, location, the playing) with the cinematic (visual spectacle, camera movement, social space of reception) and with the televisual (live-ness, the grammar of multiple cameras, a host).

The ways in which the numerous choices creating the hybrid language shape the meanings of the drama can be seen in an example of the broadcast of the deposition scene of Act 4, Scene 1 in *Richard II*. Richard (David Tennant) enters downstage right while Bolingbroke (Nigel Lindsay) and his court are gathered up-stage, and the high, angled wide-shot from the crane emphasizes the overthrown king's isolation from former friends and courtiers as well as the fact that his regal power has been stripped from him.[26] The broadcast choices reinforce the meanings suggested by the stage blocking and the white robes of Richard's costume, suggestive of Christ the martyr. On Richard's line 'Alack, why am I sent for to a king' (4.1.163) there is a cut to a closer shot with Richard centre frame and the court arrayed beyond him. His dominance of the scene is established, and his positioning begins to establish the audience's emotional connection with his plight. This shot, which remains almost static as Richard moves around the stage, is held for one minute and eighteen seconds, and the extended duration concentrates attention on Tennant's performance. At 'Give me the crown' (4.1.181) the broadcast returns to a high, wide shot but the camera now sits on the central axis; the sense of an impending confrontation is established, and the significance of Richard taking the crown from its cushion is emphasized by a cut at the precise moment that he touches it. Between 'Here, cousin' and 'Seize the crown' (4.1.182) there is a cut, again on an action as Richard's arm sweeps across, to a shot which has the crown centre-screen and Bolingbroke, who appears smaller than Richard, beyond. In the frame the crown is positioned almost above Bolingbroke's head – and yet still not established there. Bolingbroke comes slowly forward and the camera shot widens, but does not cut, until he and Richard are equal within the frame, positioned on either side of the crown still held by Richard. Cut to a big close-up of the crown with the hands of Bolingbroke and Richard holding it from each side. 'On this side my hand, and on that side thine' (4.1.183) says Richard out-of-frame, before a further cut to an angled two-shot of Bolingbroke screen-left and Richard screen-right, indicating, with the crown between them, that the next lines will, despite all of the power being now with the usurper, see the two of them sparring verbally for the throne. At each moment within this approximately three-minute sequence the cameras, scripted by screen director Robin Lough, are responding to the staging but also contributing actively to the meanings on offer. Yet there are also elements of the production that are missed or minimized by the broadcast. As Richard says, 'As Judas did to Christ' (4.1.171), in the staging he glares at Aumerle (Oliver Rix) in the group of courtiers, foreshadowing the profound betrayal that will occur in Act 5, Scene 5 of this production, when Aumerle (and not, as is more usually played, Sir Piers Exton) is revealed as Richard's murderer. But the camera shot is not sufficiently wide to catch Aumerle at just this point, and so the moment is lost. Had this been a film version, in which retakes were feasible, the shot could have been repeated to bring Aumerle into frame, but this is not possible in a continuous live broadcast. Echoing Sarah Bay-Cheng's characterization of the camera in filmed theatre being an active 'performer-observer',[27] Susanne Greenhalgh has suggested that successful mediations of the kind detailed here 'satisfy the often unconscious desires of an audience through a shifting gaze continually responding to the emotional dynamics of the performance unfolding on the screen'.[28] And Lily McLeish, assistant stage director on *The Two Gentlemen of Verona,* acknowledged this in a detailed response to the screen version:

> The camera/the edit directs the viewer's eye so the cinema audience is always watching an edited version of the play as opposed to being able to choose where to look at any given moment. So … I preferred the wider shots as I felt it allowed the audience to get a feeling for the production and the space. Of course I was also thrilled at how close the camera could get and enjoyed the detail immensely. Overall I think it is probably important to keep it wider as a constant reminder of the theatre and the live performance. But this is the thrill and freedom of this hybrid form: it enables us to swiftly move in between the intimacy of the close-ups and the openness of the wide-shots.[29]

'Lend my best attention'

Five years on from its debut with *Richard II*, RSC Live from Stratford-upon-Avon is a central element in an extensive international 'event cinema' industry that embraces not only theatre productions from NT and Shakespeare's Globe as well as from the Donmar Warehouse, Wyndham's Theatre and the Kenneth Branagh Theatre Company in London's West End, Manchester International Festival, the Comédie-Française and the Shakespeare Festival in Stratford, Ontario, but also opera and ballet, rock concerts, comedy gigs, author talks, the developing genre of e-sports and more.[30] In a manner similar to the ways Shakespeare has been used to launch and legitimate new media initiatives across the past two centuries,[31] productions from London's South Bank and from Stratford-upon-Avon have been central to establishing this hybrid form. In parallel there have been live and recorded Shakespeare productions presented online by, among other companies TR Warszawa, Cheek by Jowl, Forced Entertainment and Talawa Theatre.[32] The five RSC broadcasts in 2015 from Stratford were Christopher Luscombe's sumptuous pairing of *Love's Labour's Lost* and *Much Ado About Nothing* set just before and after the First World War, followed by Polly Findlay's staging of *The Merchant of Venice* and *Othello*, directed by Iqbal Khan with Hugh Quarshie and Lucian Msamati, and in the autumn Gregory Doran's vivid *Henry V*.[33] The productions in 2016 that marked the 400th anniversary of Shakespeare's death are noted below, while 2017 began with a broadcast of Doran's digital effects enriched production of *The Tempest* in collaboration with Intel and in association with The Imaginarium Studios. The brightness of the real-time avatar projections had to be enhanced to register effectively with the broadcast cameras, but otherwise this complex presentation played on screen in a way directly comparable to the other presentations. Four Rome plays followed that year: *Julius Caesar, Antony and Cleopatra, Titus Andronicus* and *Coriolanus*, and 2018's broadcasts were *Twelfth Night, Macbeth, Romeo and Juliet, The Merry Wives of Windsor* and *Troilus and Cressida*. The approach and aesthetic remained consistent throughout, and while the majority were directed for the screen by Robin Lough, others were directed by Dewi Humphreys, Matt Woodward and Bridget Caldwell.

The RSC broadcasts have attracted little journalistic attention. Neither cinema critics nor theatre critics see their brief as embracing event cinema broadcasts. This aligns with the popular perception that the broadcasts are effectively unmediated transpositions of a theatrical presentation.[34] External responses to the broadcasts were initially confined to a small number of blog posts, extensive Twitter reaction and emails, almost all of which have been strongly positive. The technical quality was consistently praised, and there has been enthusiasm both for the stage productions and for the enhanced possibility of access opened up by the broadcasts. Criticisms have been mostly confined to complaints about technical failings and about the paratexts that accompanied the productions in the form of introductions and interviews by Suzy Klein, and the short films screened before and during the intervals of the plays. A vocal minority would prefer the broadcasts to be plain and unaccompanied. The additional elements were intended to offer the cinema-goer privileged entry to aspects of the production process and interpretation of the staging that they might otherwise not be able to access (and that traditionally are included in theatre programmes). In addition, the paratexts distinguish the broadcast from a conventional film screening and are part of the justification of a ticket price that is higher than that for a feature film. The idea of a host is a televisual convention, developed for cultural events such as the Proms, and Klein was chosen in part because of her recognized cultural authority as a broadcaster. In the fifteen minutes before the start of each transmission, marketing and information slides (including the cast list) are interspersed with shots of the audience filling the Stratford auditorium. These reinforce the sense of the cinema audience being an extension of that in the RST, but like the other paratextual elements they contribute importantly to the RSC's shaping of its identity. Interval features about the costume workshop and the props department, for example, stress how the company sustains and develops vital craft skills for the theatre as well as providing employment in and around Stratford-upon-Avon. In addition, both paratexts and the performances, with the frequent inclusion of audience and auditorium elements, constantly return to the broadcast's theatrical origins. In doing so, they assert within and against the cinema, and by extension an ever more dominant screen culture, the fundamentals of theatre and the associated values of this older medium, including perhaps suggestions of an inherently greater authenticity.

In contrast to the relative lack of journalistic attention, broadcasts of Shakespeare, from the RSC and elsewhere, have been the focus of a rapidly developing degree of academic engagement. This interest has taken the form of conference papers and journal articles, the start of a number of doctorates, and in 2018 the publication of the first edited collection dedicated to the topic, *Shakespeare and the 'Live' Theatre Broadcast Experience*.[35] One key strand of these discussions has focused on the implications and contradictions of the 'live-ness' of these productions. In addition to their simultaneous presentation, the broadcasts are also accessed in delayed formats, whether these are 'encore' performances, in time-shifted presentations overseas, or in recorded media such as DVDs or online streams. Martin Barker and Erin Sullivan are among those who have explored ideas of 'live' that move beyond co-presence and simultaneity and focus instead on the 'a(s)-live' quality of the broadcasts.[36] Shared experience, including through the use of social media engagement, contributes to the productions being experienced as 'a-live'. Another set of questions circles around the authorship of the broadcasts, for which the screen director is responding 'faithfully' to the staging but inevitably shaping the screen version with her own interpretative choices.

Among the most astute responses to the new form is Pascale Aebischer's analysis of the dominant forms of the broadcasts from the two playhouses on London's South Bank, the National Theatre and Shakespeare's Globe. Aebischer argued that the dominant style of Shakespeare at the National has been a continuation of 'a nineteenth-century realist performance practice' and that NT Live's broadcasts from the Olivier auditorium have produced 'a predominantly illusionist Shakespeare' whereas 'broadcasts from Shakespeare's Globe between 2003 and 2016 reflected the company's predominantly presentational performance style'.[37] The illusionist style works to immerse the viewer in the space of, and action on, the stage, with depiction of and interaction with the theatre audience being largely elided from the performances (apart from aurally, especially as off-camera laughter). The culture, the productions and the space of Shakespeare's Globe have operated very differently and created a distinct on-screen sense, with the audience being very much present. Adopting the terms of this dichotomy, the RSC Live from Stratford-upon-Avon broadcasts might be seen to sit between these two approaches, at times moving into the stage world but frequently drawing back to reveal the theatre audience clearly visible on three sides of the thrust stage, and on occasions willing to be drawn into the action. Aebischer's exploration of these ideas helps us consider the connections between the spaces and places of these broadcasts, their aesthetics and the varied responses of audiences dispersed in locations and in time. Just a decade old in its contemporary form, although connected to and drawing upon media forms from more than a century, live theatre broadcasts remain compelling affectively and intellectually, and are central to key cultural changes. As Aebischer has also written, along with Susanne Greenhalgh,

> As theatres reinvent themselves as multimedia companies who distribute their work on multiple platforms, and as receiving venues add their

own cognitive prompts to stimulate (for their audiences) either the experience of being in the theatre or conversely frame broadcasts as part of film culture, what constitutes watching a production of Shakespeare undergoes a fundamental shift.[38]

Indeed. Yet at the same time fundamental shifts prompted by new media forms occurred when filmgoers watched Frank Benson's company play *Richard III* before the First World War and when television viewers saw on their screens at home the second part of *The Merry Wives of Windsor* from Stratford in the autumn of 1955. 'What constitutes watching a production of Shakespeare' has constantly evolved, both within the physical spaces shared by actors and audiences and throughout the virtual spaces opened up by screens of all kinds. Similarly changing constantly, and in ways comparably facilitated by media innovations, have been what constitutes teaching and learning about Shakespeare.

Education, education, education

Before the RSC began to make its own short videotapes for educational use in the mid-2000s the company had contributed on a number of occasions to BBC schools programmes. In the 1987 programmes *English File: Why Shakespeare?*, for example, RSC associate artists Estelle Kohler and Emrys James explored the characters of, first Olivia and Malvolio, and then the Macbeths.[39] Self-produced resources for schools, however, were restricted to print materials until early 2005 when the education department under Maria Evans began to create short videos that combined scenes from current productions with a focus on the interpretive choices made by creative teams. At this point, encouraged by Michael Boyd, the RSC was significantly extending its education and outreach work and making it central to the company's mission. Siobhan Keenan has identified the way in which 'ground-breaking projects such as the "Learning and Performance Network" (2006–16) [and] the "Stand Up For Shakespeare" campaign (2008–9) ... opened up the company to a much larger audience',[40] and this work has been substantially developed under Gregory Doran. As with the RSC's screen initiatives, education and outreach make the case for the public value of the company, helping to sustain the comparatively high level of Arts Council funding.

The early 'Exploring Shakespeare' videos focused on scenes from Michael Boyd's 2004 staging of *Macbeth* with Greg Hicks and *A Midsummer Night's Dream* directed by Gregory Doran the following year, and were intended for both generalist and learning-specific audiences. Frustratingly for the education department, these first short films were made under rights agreements lasting just five years, and so while they made an early appearance on the RSC's YouTube channel they had to be removed in 2010. They established a shortform model, however, that the department has continued to develop in subsequent videos for the online Shakespeare Learning Zone and in series like 'Text Detectives'.[41] As the current director of eduction, Jacqui O'Hanlon, has explained:

> Every director has to answer the same challenges for every production. Those key questions are the things that we surface with our educational resources, and then share how a creative team grapples with them, and then invite teachers and students to grapple with the same challenges ... Every single piece of [educational] content is about highlighting the actual interpretations that a group of actors and a director and designer and lighting deigner are all engaged in when they come together to make a play on one of our stages.[42]

By the autumn of 2018 the Shakespeare Learning Zone featured seven plays, with two additional ones being released each term. Video content from recent productions as well as newly shot material is embedded in resources that offer the user three different levels of information, depending on their previous knowledge.

Alongside this the RSC's website featured a range of other education-related material including introductions to the schools broadcasts with a British Sign Language (BSL) interpreter and the imaginative fifty-minute film *I, Cinna (the Poet)*, made in 2012 with one of the cast members, Jude Owusu, of that year's *Julius Caesar*.[43] Written by Tim Crouch as part of his series of dramas for young people focusing on some of Shakespeare's minor characters, and directed and shot by Robert McGroary, it is cast as a monologue addressed to the viewer. The production was realized with support from Ravensbourne College of Design and Communication, which then went on to collaborate on the schools screenings of RSC Live from Stratford-upon-Avon, and with the technology company Cisco. Aware that momentous historical events are taking place just outside his door, Cinna watches them on his television, which relays footage that is recognizably from the 2011 riots. The production was streamed to schools and was watched initially by around 15,000 students. As RSC education programme developer for the World Shakespeare Festival Tracy Irish has said, 'many young people have commented on how the production gave them a window on to a different world, but one not too far away'.[44] For Jacqui O'Hanlon, *I, Cinna* was a critical pilot that tested whether RSC Education could deliver a live stream 'that actively engaged its audience in responding in real time to what they were seeing ... What has felt critical to us is preserving the live theatre experience online and for students to feel part of a national audience of their peers who were all experiencing the same event.'[45] This concern also motivated the format of the live introductions and question and answer sessions accompanying the streams of the RSC Live from Stratford-upon-Avon recordings, as well as the company's most recent initiative, Live Lessons. The first of these in January

2018 employed three cameras to relay from a rehearsal room a staged version of the process of exploring a text and starting to develop movement with director Erica Whyman and actors Karen Fishwick and Bally Gill, who were playing the lovers in the forthcoming RSC production of *Romeo and Juliet*. A half-hour of process was followed by a discussion with the actors who also responded to tweets by watching students. Thirty years before such features were created with broadcasters for general audiences, as in the 1985 *Review* item discussed in Chapter 5 with Jonathan Pryce and Sinéad Cusack rehearsing a scene from *Macbeth*. Three decades on similar questions and concerns were being visualized, but now under the control of the RSC and shaped specifically for the audiences and demands of education.

2016 and all that

The 400th anniversary of Shakespeare's birth in 1964 was marked by the RSC in Stratford primarily by a revival of *The Wars of the Roses*, complemented by new productions of the other History plays. Fifty-two years on, for the 400th anniversary of the playwright's death, the company programmed a more varied Stratford offer, including new Shakespeare productions as well as Jonson's *The Alchemist*, Marlowe's *Doctor Faustus* and Aphra Behn's *The Rover* in the Swan Theatre. In 1964 the RSC was represented on television solely by the BBC's recording of *The Comedy of Errors*, with *The Wars of the Roses* being recorded for transmission the following Easter. On the Birthday itself, the RSC appears from the *TV Times* billing not to have taken a role, perhaps because of its BBC production deal, in a two-hour ITV outside broadcast. Instead, commentator Shaw Taylor and the regional company ATV showcased the traditional unfurling of the flags (much as the ceremony had been shown on screens since at least 1915), the Duke of Edinburgh visiting Shakespeare's Birthplace, and a tour of the anniversary exhibition. Far more expansively, in 2016 BBC Birmingham and BBC Arts drew together *Shakespeare Day Live*, an innovative sequence of online broadcasting with streams from around Stratford-upon-Avon leading up to *Shakespeare Live! From the RSC*. Also featured, for example, was President Obama's visit to Shakespeare's Globe and rehearsals for *The Winter's Tale* ballet at the Royal Opera House, as well as archive extracts and much more. This was the BBC's most ambitious web-only live presentation thus far and was yet one further conscription of Shakespeare to demonstrate the potential of a new media technology.[46]

At other moments in 2016 the RSC appeared on cinema screens in three of the Stratford presentations: Simon Godwin's production of *Hamlet* with Paapa Essiedu, *King Lear* with Antony Sher directed by Gregory Doran, and Melly Still's staging of *Cymbeline*. *A Midsummer Night's Dream*, directed by Erica Whyman for both Stratford and an extensive tour, was another of the RSC's Shakespeare stagings in 2016, and was especially distinctive because fourteen groups of amateur players took the roles of the mechanicals.[47] The amateurs, together with schoolchildren as the fairies, played both when the show toured to their local theatre and also for a small number of performances in Stratford. The *Dream,* however, to the title of which was officially appended A *Play for the Nation,* was not featured in the cinema broadcast series. Instead it was the focus of nine half-hour BBC One documentaries collectively titled as *The Best Bottoms in the Land.*[48] The tension between a central, professional show and dispersed contributions from across the country was captured by the nine films, each with a different tone and film-making team, made across the English regions. Erica Whyman worked with a strongly diverse professional cast and determined a setting of a dilapidated theatre in the late 1940s, resonant of national reconstruction and the moment of social progress just prior to the Festival of Britain. Around this, the stage and screen contributions of the amateurs, predominantly white and middle-aged, and hundreds of schoolchildren from right across the country, set in play a complex of ideas about nation and regions, about artistic practice and audiences, and in doing so reflected something of the BBC's own concerns with these concepts. Screens also took a central if technically temperamental role in the rehearsal process, as much of the project was coordinated and communicated online. And screens also spread the results alongside the documentaries, in extracts and associated features across radio and television schedules, including *BBC Breakfast, The One Show* and *Blue Peter,* in a BBC Academy training podcast, and in web content like the Birmingham actor playing Bottom, Chris Clarke, visiting a donkey sanctuary for inspiration.[49] Here was a paratextual excess of remarkable reach, combining accessibility and participation with achievement and cultural value.

The RSC's other central collaboration with television in 2016 was transmitted on Saturday 23 April, in keeping with the continuing alignment of author, birthdate, saint's day and nation, bound together now, as often before, by the pairing of the BBC and the RSC. *Shakespeare Live! From the RSC,* shown on BBC Two and simultaneously in cinemas, was a two-hour (plus twenty-four-minute overrun) celebration of Shakespeare's influence on the full range of performing art forms, including opera, ballet, jazz, musical theatre and rap. An elaborate variety show format, set beneath the Droeshout engraving of the author picked out in vivid neon, accommodated the opening of *West Side Story* and the closing of *A Midsummer Night's Dream,* as well as 'Brush Up Your Shakespeare' from *Kiss Me Kate,* an original composition from Akala, Duke Ellington's 'Such Sweet Thunder' and a *Romeo and Juliet* duet courtesy of Prokofiev and Kenneth MacMillan. Shakespeare from a world elsewhere was represented by brief video fragments of *uMabatha,* the Zulu version of *Macbeth,* and of Yukio Ninagawa's 'samurai' production of the same play. Saturated with references to the RSC's own history, with alumni including Judi Dench, Harriet Walter, Roger Allam and Paapa Essiedu; with cinematic references, such as Joseph Fiennes, who played the writer in *Shakespeare in Love*, presenting four short biographical films; and with televisual links too, most obviously to *Doctor Who*, via co-hosts David Tennant and Catherine Tate, this was a dense intertextual entertainment.[50]

One inspiration for *Shakespeare Live! From the RSC* was the acclaimed gala *50 Years on Stage*, mounted by the National Theatre as a celebration of its own history for a BBC Two transmission in November 2013. This broadcast combined televisual traces of NT shows with restagings of scenes from celebrated productions, some by Shakespeare but many not. The positive critical reception and comparatively large audience of nearly one million viewers eased the path to the screen of *Shakespeare Live! From the RSC*. This adopted a similar format, and like the National Theatre show situated itself strongly in the company's main auditorium. Yet it also drew on the familiar Stratford sights including Anne Hathaway's Cottage and, for Ian Bostridge singing 'Come away, death' from *Twelfth Night* with Antonio Pappano at the piano, Shakespeare's burial place in a candle-lit Holy Trinity Church. Writing for *The Stage,* Tim Bano reflected the enthusiasm with which the broadcast was generally received: 'as a sweeping selection of what Shakespeare is today, and what it can be, it's a stirring celebration of one man's achievements … *Shakespeare Live!* shows sprawlingly, messily and occasionally with breathtaking brilliance how a stage can be an entire world'.[51]

The production's most notable, and extensively noted, moment came at the close of a sketch, written by Gregory Doran, in which a line of Hamlets, including Rory Kinnear, Ian McKellen, Tim Minchin, Judi Dench ('Tis I, Hamlet the Dame') and Benedict Cumberbatch competed to instruct each other in the correct delivery of the line 'To be or not to be'. Earlier, Prince Charles, patron of the Royal Shakespeare Company, had been caught on camera sitting next to Doran in the front row of the circle. Now, unheralded, he strode on stage to top them all. Here was a potent moment (which quickly became a Twitter 'Moment') in which on the nation's screens the RSC forged together Shakespeare and Stratford, the British Broadcasting Corporation and the monarchy, leavening respect and reverence with wit, and then offering a contemporary inflection as the young actor Paapa Essiedu stepped forward to perform the full soliloquy flawlessly. Writing about the earlier NT broadcast Susanne Greenhalgh reflected that 'the interplay of theatrical and mediated performance disclosed the National Theatre's ambivalence concerning its own history of remediation'.[52] By contrast, for Greenhalgh *Shakespeare Live! From the RSC* 'celebrated a long-term partnership with the BBC in the service of a Shakespeare embodying the public and increasingly international value both institutions have sought to represent and disseminate'.[53] With Prince Charles's 'To be or not to be' widely circulated through social media channels, featured in the next day's newspapers, and subsequently seen across the USA when the show was acquired for PBS screening at Christmas 2016, and remaining on YouTube in a lengthy BBC-sanctioned extract, the RSC affirmed its public value on screen in an especially potent manner.[54]

'All the fair effects of future hopes'[55]

Over a century on from the filming of Frank Benson's *Richard III* in 1910, the RSC screen presences are manifold. At the company's core remain the rituals of actors and audiences sharing experiences in the same space at the same moment. But with almost all aspects of the company's productions on screens, whether as RSC Live from Stratford-upon-Avon broadcasts, in partnerships with broadcasters, in innovative educational content for schools and general audiences, in trailers and a plethora of other paratexts disseminated across social media, and in many different forms of archival preservation, stored and circulating, known and unknown, those rituals have been and are being mediated in an ever-expanding multitude of ways. Those rituals also have been and will be transposed and translated in emerging media forms, including participatory and networked projects like *Such Tweet Sorrow* (2010) and *A Midsummer Night's Dreaming* (2013).[56] The former was a contemporary adaptation of *Romeo and Juliet* played out on Twitter by six professional actors over five weeks. A collaboration with Mudlark, the project also operated across other platforms including Facebook and YouTube. Created with director Roxana Silbert and writers Bethan Marlowe and Tim Wright, it was met by a very mixed critical response from online users.[57] Nonetheless, in a nuanced discussion of the 'live' and 'mediatized' qualities of the experience, Geoffrey Way recognized that 'Through its recognition and incorporation of common user practices, *Such Tweet Sorrow* is an example of how social media can act as a stage for dramatic performance, shifting the dynamic between actor and audience.'[58] Three years later, the RSC collaborated with Google Creative Lab on a digital adaptation of *A Midsummer Night's Dream* that involved a real-time staging of the play across three midsummer days with actors, together with the unfolding of an online world peopled by thirty or so original characters related in some way to those in Shakespeare's text. In a thoughtful response written in the project's wake, co-creator Tom Uglow assessed it as 'a disruptive experiment and a hugely successful one if judged simply on what we learnt and where we now move forward from'.[59] Analysing the RSC projects, Erin Sullivan has also argued for the significance of such social media adaptations, proposing that they can

> reframe our understanding of critical appraisal and audience authority, provide new ways into dramatic characterisation, highlight the pleasures of shared emotion and experience, and encourage us to explore the possibilities of nonlinear storytelling. Perhaps most importantly, [they] can challenge us to think harder about theatre's ethical relationship to society and the audience's role in such matters, especially as the fictional looks more and more like the real.[60]

Alongside such dispersed, networked media, augmented reality (AR) and virtual reality (VR) are also likely to become significant for the company's work, developing in part from the remarkable collaborations with Intel and The Imaginarium Studios on *The Tempest* from 2016 to 2017.[61] The stages in Stratford and elsewhere remain at the centre of all these multiple mediations, but like many other contemporary cultural organizations, the RSC is continually and critically engaged in endeavouring to explore the impact of developing technologies on many aspects of practice and performance.

The immediate future for the RSC on screen is a commitment to continue with cinema broadcasts of the full cycle of the First Folio plays, to be completed in 2022. There is also active discussion about how to develop screen versions of the productions of early modern dramas played in the Swan Theatre. To date, and with notable exceptions discussed in previous chapters, the adaptation history of the company has been dominated by screen versions of Shakespeare's plays. Moreover, the relatively few exceptions amongst the mainstream adaptations have been of either late nineteenth-century dramas, like *The Cherry Orchard* (1962), *Miss Julie* (1972) and *Hedda* (1975), or of contemporary plays and productions, such as *Marat/Sade* (1967) and *Work is a Four Letter Word* (1968). In 2012 Peter Malin noted that in the previous twenty-five years the company had performed on stage only forty plays by Shakespeare's contemporaries, despite the company's professed commitment to this repertoire.[62] Yet to that point the only film or television adaptation of a RSC production by a writer who might, at a stretch, be classed as a contemporary is *Tartuffe* (1986) by Molière, born just four years before Shakespeare's death. No Marlowe on screen, no Webster, no Jonson. Under Gregory Doran the RSC has strengthened its focus on this work, with exceptional productions in the Swan Theatre of, among others, *Doctor Faustus, The Duchess of Malfi* and Aphra Behn's *The Rover*, but the only achieved screen version of any of this work is a multi-camera recording of Trevor Nunn's staging with Henry Goodman of Ben Jonson's *Volpone* (2015), which remains unreleased. Assessments of possible funding models for such recordings, especially in the face of a lack of interest from broadcast television, indicate how challenging is the production of high-quality recordings of non-Shakespearean early modern drama.

Even without the extension of the repertoire, the broad acceptance of the RSC Live from Stratford-upon-Avon screenings raises the question, as these presentations become increasingly significant to the RSC's relationships with its audiences, of whether and how they may impact on what is created for the stage. Despite a recognition that higher profile names on stage would boost box office returns, Gregory Doran is insistent that the company must continue to cast as directors wish for the stage productions only. Yet might directors begin, whether consciously or not, to shape their stagings with one eye at least towards how a production might appear on screen as well as in the RST? A parallel question was raised at an earlier media moment by the scholar Michèle Willems as she reflected on the possible impact on productions during the 1990s of the circulation of screen adaptations on videotape. 'Could we go as far as to say', she asked, 'that postmodern re-presentation of Shakespeare, with its self-referential system of echoes, allusions or even visual quotations, is in part at least the product of our new video culture?'[63] My sense is that a traditional theatrical culture is so strong within the RSC and amongst the directors with which the company has worked that the broadcasts are still regarded as only marginal by creative teams, welcomed by some as a trace of a production and merely tolerated by others. I believe a model could be developed in which a screen production has creative and commercial primacy, and a stage production is seen as largely a useful step towards that goal, but currently this is not in any way an aspiration for Stratford.

What may change, and what from my perspective most certainly should, is the place that the RSC's screen archive has in the creative life of the company. At present, as is the case in almost all arts organizations, in television and in media more generally, for recognizably responsible reasons, almost all the resource and time and energy is focused on the next show, the next programme, the next content drop. And then the one after that and the ones beyond. Yet, as this book has sought to explore, the RSC's past, as it remains available through the company's adaptation history, is one of extraordinary riches. And within three years, those within and beyond the company will have available a full canon of Shakespeare's plays on screen, created in less than a decade by a range of different directors and with distinct albeit overlapping casts, and unified by the theatrical space within which they were produced, by a consistent screen grammar, and by the standards of perhaps the finest classical theatre company in the world. Might this series, and the RSC screen archive more generally, which is being extended and enhanced every day, become an accessible, usable source for active, creative interpretations, drawing together the company's histories with its present practices and its future possibilities? May we dream that future practitioners in, to quote Cassius from *Julius Caesar*, 'states unborn and accents yet unknown' (3.1.126), will make use of the RSC on screen to imagine and create in wondrous new ways for both stages and for screens – and beyond?

NOTES

Introduction

1 Royal Shakespeare Company, 'Richard III Stage Footage/Act 1 Scene 1/2012/ Royal Shakespeare Company' [video], YouTube, 1 June 2012. Available online: https://www.youtube.com/watch?v=K9wzWYtYGBI (accessed 15 September 2018).

2 The First Folio contains thirty-six plays but the RSC has chosen, following much scholarship, to include *Pericles* in the canon.

3 Details of the RSC recordings can be found in the online archive catalogue of the Shakespeare Birthplace Trust, 'Discover Shakespeare'. Available online: http://collections.shakespeare.org.uk/?_ga=1.155166840.1142849762.148 2512864 (accessed 23 February 2017). For a list of National Video Archive of Performance (NVAP) recordings see Victoria and Albert Museum (V&A), 'Theatre & Performance Archives'. Available online: http://www.vam.ac.uk/ content/articles/t/nvap/ (accessed 23 February 2017).

4 Radio is not central to the concerns of this book, but a number of audio adaptations of RSC productions are considered in Chapter 1.

5 The literature on the processes and implications of transferring stagings to the screen is extensive. Key sources include Susan Sontag, 'Film and Theatre', *Tulane Drama Review*, 11 no. 1 (Fall 1966), 24–37; Robert L. Erenstein, ed., *Theatre and Television* (Amsterdam: International Theatre Bookshop, 1988), being proceedings of the 1987 International FIRT/NOS conference in Hilversum; Annabelle Melzer, '"Best Betrayal": The Documentation of Performance on Video and Film', 'Part 1' and 'Part 2', *New Theatre Quarterly*, 11 no. 42 (May 1995), 147–57, and 11 no. 43 (August 1995), 259–76; Matthew Reason, *Documentation, Disappearance and the Representation of Live Performance* (Houndmills: Palgrave Macmillan, 2006).

6 James Steichen, 'HD Opera: A Love/Hate Story', *The Opera Quarterly*, 27 no. 4 (2011), 446.

7 Barbara Hodgdon, 'The Visual Record: The Case of *Hamlet*', in David Wiles and Christine Dymkowski, eds, *The Cambridge Companion to Theatre History* (Cambridge: Cambridge University Press, 2014), 246.

8 Alan Sinfield, 'Royal Shakespeare: Theatre and the Making of Ideology', in Jonathan Dollimore and Alan Sinfield, eds, *Political Shakespeare: New Essays in Cultural Materialism* (Manchester: Manchester University Press, 1985), 158.

9 Irene Morra, 'History Play: People, Pageant and the New Shakespearean Age', in Irene Morra and Rob Gossedge, eds, *The New Elizabethan Age: Culture, Society and National Identity after World War II* (London: I.B.Tauris, 2016), 309.

10 Judith Buchanan, '"Look here, upon this picture": Theatrofilm, the Wooster Group *Hamlet* and the Film Industry', in Gordon McMullan and Zoe Wilcox, eds, *Shakespeare in Ten Acts* (London: The British Library, 2016), 213. Buchanan's article is an important discussion of how historical moving-image archive can be creatively reused and reinterpreted for new creative projects.

11 Sally Beauman, *The Royal Shakespeare Company: A History of Ten Decades* (Oxford: Oxford University Press, 1982).

12 Colin Chambers, *Inside the Royal Shakespeare Company: Creativity and the Institution* (London: Routledge, 2004), 175, 176.

13 See especially Susanne Greenhalgh, ed., 'Special Reviews Section: Live Cinema Relays of Shakespearean Performance', *Shakespeare Bulletin*, 32 no. 2 (2014), 255–78; Pascale Aebischer, Susanne Greenhalgh and Laurie Osborne, eds, *Shakespeare and the 'Live' Theatre Broadcast Experience* (London: Bloomsbury 2018).

14 Viewers affiliated with UK educational institutions can access pre-1990 BBC recordings of RSC productions via BBC, 'BBC Shakespeare Archive Resource'. Available online: http://shakespeare.ch.bbc.co.uk/ (accessed 15 September 2018).

15 Peter Brook, *The Quality of Mercy: Reflections on Shakespeare* (London: Nick Hern Books, 2013), 82.

16 Peter Brook, 'Discussion', *Cahiers théâtre Louvain* no. 46 (1981), 41.

17 Email from Yoshio Ueno, Chief Producer, NHK International, Inc., 18 January 2017.

Chapter 1

1 On the reassessment of early cinema in general see, inter alia, Thomas Elsaesser with Adam Barker, eds, *Early Cinema: Space, Frame, Narrative* (London: British Film Institute, 1990); Lee Grieveson and Peter Krämer, eds, *The Silent Cinema Reader* (London: Routledge, 2004); Simon Popple and Joe Kember, *Early Cinema: From Factory Gate to Dream Factory* (London: Wallflower, 2004).

2 Architects Dodgshun and Unsworth of Westminster combined Tudor, Elizabethan and Gothic elements; see Beauman, *Royal Shakespeare Company*, 12.

3 Beauman, *Royal Shakespeare Company*, 28–29. My discussion of Benson's work at Stratford, as well as the history of the Stratford companies and the RSC more generally, is greatly indebted to Beauman's book.

4 Drawing on Eleanor Elder's 1910 diary of the filming, J.C. Trewin lists only the first four productions; see *Shakespeare on the English Stage 1900–1964* (London: Barrie and Rockliff, 1964), 64. In her invaluable DVD commentary to *Richard III*, '*Richard III* DVD commentary' [audio commentary], *Play On: Shakespeare in Silent Film* (BFI Publishing, 2016), Judith Buchanan notes that the other two titles were announced by the production company but may or may not have been made.

5   Undated diary entry quoted in Trewin, *Shakespeare on the English Stage*, 64.

6   The extant print numbers thirteen scenes, but two sections (Hastings visiting the Princes in the Tower, which is identified as 'Scene 6a', and Hastings being led away to his execution) are sufficiently distinct to be regarded as separate scenes.

7   F.R. Benson Co Ltd. Ledger 1911. Shakespeare Birthplace Trust (SBT) RL1/1/23.

8   Judith Buchanan, *Shakespeare on Silent Film: An Excellent Dumb Discourse* (Cambridge: Cambridge University Press, 2009), 1–2. Buchanan suggests that only around forty silent Shakespeare films survive.

9   Buchanan, *Shakespeare on Silent Film*, 23–42, 74–75.

10   Rachel Low, *The History of the British Film 1906–1914* (London: George Allen & Unwin, [1948] 1973), 186–87.

11   Buchanan, '*Richard III* DVD commentary'.

12   Low, *History of the British Film 1906–1914*, 187. Low records that *Julius Caesar* was released on 25 March 1911, *Macbeth* on 9 April and *The Taming of the Shrew* on 22 April; the exact release date of *Richard III* is unknown.

13   Russell Jackson, 'Staging and Storytelling, Theatre and Film: *Richard III* at Stratford, 1910', *New Theatre Quarterly*, 16 no. 2 (2000), 120.The Benson company Ledger, noted above, contains details about production dates and payment that supplement Jackson's article.

14   Low, *History of the British Film 1906–1914*, 225. On the film's reputation and Benson's own, see also Judith Buchanan, 'Collaborating with the Dead: Revivifying Frank Benson's Richard III', 5–11. Available online: https://www.york.ac.uk/digital-editions/collaborating-with-the-dead/ (accessed 15 September 2018).

15   Buchanan, *Shakespeare on Silent Film*, 6.

16   Ibid., xix.

17   See Silents Now, 'Silents Now'. Available online: http://silents-now.co.uk/ (accessed 8 January 2018). Details of the Middleham Castle screenings are at Silents Now, '*Richard III* at Middleham Castle'. Available online: http://silents-now.co.uk/home/shows/richard-iii-2/richard-iii-middleham/ (accessed 8 January 2018). On the Middleham screenings, see Buchanan, 'Collaborating with the Dead', 18–20.

18   *Stars in their Courses* (BBC National Programme, 29 April 1933).

19   Shakespeare's baptism is documented as having taken place on 26 April 1564, but his birth three days earlier, while fitting with custom at the time, is only speculation.

20   See Johanne M. Stockholm, *Garrick's Folly: The Shakespeare Jubilee of 1769 at Stratford and Drury Lane* (London: Methuen, 1964).

21   See Susan Brock and Sylvia Morris, '"Enchanted ground": Celebrating Shakespeare's Birthday in Stratford-upon-Avon', in Christa Jansohn and Dieter Mehl, eds, *Shakespeare's Jubilees, 1769–2014* (Zurich: Lit Verlag, 2015), 31–50.

22   Ibid., 42.

23 Ibid., 47.

24 On Ben Iden Payne, see Robert Speaight, *William Poel and the Elizabethan Revival* (Cambridge, MA: Harvard University Press, 1954); Marion O'Connor, *William Poel and the Elizabethan Stage Society* (Cambridge: Chadwyck-Healey, 1987).

25 Broadcast, 4 July 1937.

26 John Bayliss, 'As We Still Like It', *Radio Times*, 2 July 1937, 7.

27 Susanne Greenhalgh, 'Shakespeare and Radio', in Mark Thornton Burnett, Adrian Streete and Ramona Wray, eds, *The Edinburgh Companion to Shakespeare and the Arts* (Edinburgh: Edinburgh University Press, 2011), 544.

28 Beauman, *Royal Shakespeare Company*, 165.

29 See British Library, 'Help: Listening and Viewing Service'. Available online: https://www.bl.uk/reshelp/inrrooms/stp/sound/listening.html (accessed 29 January 2017).

30 J.C. Trewin, *Peter Brook: A Biography* (London: Macdonald, 1971), 54.

31 See T.C. Kemp, 'Moralising and Romancing', *Radio Times*, 3 April 1953, 21.

32 *Radio Times*, 23 October 1953; the Third Programme broadcast was on Sunday afternoon 25 October.

33 In addition to *Measure for Measure* (1950), recordings are extant of *The Merchant of Venice* and *King Lear* (both 1953), *Antony and Cleopatra* (1954) and *Cymbeline* (1957); these can be accessed via the British Library's Listening and Viewing Service.

34 On 29 April 1950; according to the *Radio Times* billing he discussed his topic 'from the standpoint of a producer', 21 April 1950, 41.

35 Broadcast weekly, 10–31 January 1990.

36 See Michael Quinn, 'Remastered: The Legendary Argo Shakespeare Recordings', *The Stage*, 27 January 2017. Available online: https://www.thestage.co.uk/features/2017/remastered-the-legendary-argo-shakespeare-recordings/ (accessed 29 January 2017).The recordings were initially issued as the Argo Shakespeare between 1957 and 1964. Digitally remastered they were re-released in 2016 as a 100-CD set by Decca; see Decca Records, 'Shakespeare the Complete Works'. Available online: http://decca.com/shakespeare/ (accessed 29 January 2017).

37 These recordings are preserved in the British Library Sound Archive and are accessible via the Listening and Viewing Service. Two CD compilations, selected by Gregory Doran, have been released by the British Library: *The Essential Shakespeare Live* (2005) and *The Essential Shakespeare Live Encore* (2009).

38 Greenhalgh, 'Shakespeare and Radio', 544.

39 BFI Player, 'Shakespeare's Country', [Video] 1926. Available online: https://player.bfi.org.uk/free/film/watch-shakespeares-country-1926-online (accessed 17 October 2018).

40 One example is BFI Player, 'Shakespeare Memorial Theatre', [Video] 1926. Available online: https://player.bfi.org.uk/free/film/watch-shakespeare-memorial-theatre-1926-online (accessed 17 October 2018).

41 BFI Player, 'British and Best', [Video] 1928. Available online: https://player.bfi.
    org.uk/free/film/watch-british-and-best-1928-online (accessed 17 October 2018).

42 British Pathé, 'For New Shakespeare Memorial Theatre 1928' [Video].
    Available online: https://www.britishpathe.com/video/for-new-shakespeare-
    memorial-theatre (accessed 17 October 2018).

43 British Pathé, '"Sweetest Shakespeare – Fancy's Child" 1932' [Video]. Available
    online: https://www.britishpathe.com/video/sweetest-shakespeare-fancys-child/
    (accessed 17 October 2018).

44 British Pathé, 'Shakespeare's Birthday 1938' [Video]. Available online: https://
    www.britishpathe.com/video/shakespeares-birthday-2 (accessed 17 October 2018).

45 BFI Player, 'Shakespeare Land', [Video] 1910. Available online: https://player.
    bfi.org.uk/free/film/watch-shakespeare-land-1910-online (accessed 17 October
    2018).

46 BFI Player, 'Stratford-on-Avon', [Video] 1925. Available online: https://player.
    bfi.org.uk/free/film/watch-stratford-on-avon-1925-online (accessed 17 October
    2018).

47 Nicola J. Watson, 'Shakespeare on the Tourist Trail', in Robert Shaughnessy,
    ed., *The Cambridge Companion to Shakespeare and Popular Culture*
    (Cambridge: Cambridge University Press, 2007), 200.

48 Douglas Lanier, *Shakespeare and Modern Popular Culture* (Oxford: Oxford
    University Press, 2002), 150.

49 Watson, 'Shakespeare on the Tourist Trail', 210.

50 BFI Player, 'Around the Town, No. 110', [Video] 1922. Available online:
    https://player.bfi.org.uk/free/film/watch-around-the-town-no110-1922-online
    (accessed 17 October 2018).

51 BFI Player, 'England's Shakespeare', [Video] 1939. Available online: https://
    player.bfi.org.uk/free/film/watch-englands-shakespeare-1939-online (accessed
    17 October 2018).

52 Roberta E. Pearson, 'Shakespeare's Country: The National Poet, English
    Identity and British Silent Cinema', in Andrew Higson, ed., *Young and
    Innocent?: The Cinema in Britain, 1896–1930* (Exeter: University of Exeter
    Press, 2002), 179.

53 Stanley Baldwin, *On England, and Other Addresses* (London: Philip Allan,
    1926), 7.

54 Both Ayrton and Holloway had appeared at Stratford with Frank Benson's
    company before the First World War.

55 British Pathé, 'Shakespeare's Birthday – A Royal Occasion 1950' [Video].
    Available online: https://www.britishpathe.com/video/shakespeares-birthday-a-
    royal-occasion (accessed 17 October 2018).

56 *Down Your Way* [Radio Programme] (Light Programme, 19 December 1948);
    About Britain [TV Programme] (BBC TV, 23 April 1954).

57 BBC Archive, '1951: Newsreel: Stratford Festival Season', [Video] Facebook,
    29 March 2018. Available online: https://www.facebook.com/BBCArchive/
    videos/vb.100865096953196/547463355626699/?type=2&theater (accessed
    17 October 2018).

58 On interwar television Shakespeare, see John Wyver, 'An Intimate and Intermedial Form: Early Television Shakespeare from the BBC, 1937–1939', in Peter Holland and Emma Smith, eds, *Shakespeare Survey 69: Shakespeare and Rome* (Cambridge: Cambridge University Press, 2016), 347–60.

59 Details of this and other Shakespeare adaptations can be accessed via the invaluable Learning on Screen *Shakespeare* online database, BUFVC (British Universities and Colleges Film and Video Council), 'Shakespeare' [Database]. Available online: http://bufvc.ac.uk/shakespeare/ (accessed 15 December 2016).

60 Beauman, *Royal Shakespeare Company*, 170.

61 Anthony Quayle, 'Foreword', in John Dover Wilson and T.C. Worsley, eds, *Shakespeare's Histories at Stratford 1951* (London: Max Reinhardt, 1952), vii.

62 See Michael Brooke, '*Henry IV* On Screen', *BFI screenonline*. Available online: http://www.screenonline.org.uk/tv/id/1048622/ (accessed 23 January 2017).

63 *Radio Times*, 17 August 1951, 38, 41.

64 In addition to *Macbeth* on 3 December 1937 companies from The Old Vic performed scenes from *Measure for Measure* on 25 October 1937; the Birmingham Rep visited on 2 October 1938 to give Adelaide Eden Philpotts's comedy *Laugh with Me*, and to perform the theatre's adaptation of *The Swiss Family Robinson* on 29 January 1939. The company returned to the studios on 28 July 1946 to play James Bridie's *Mr Bolfry*.

65 Broadcast on 16 July 1952; see BUFVC, 'The Two Gentlemen of Verona', Shakespeare Database. Available online: http://bufvc.ac.uk/shakespeare/index. php/title/av37272 (accessed 12 September 2018).

66 A directly comparable concern was expressed by regional theatres and touring companies sixty years later as live relays to cinemas grew in popularity in the early 2010s.

67 Agreement between BBC and TNC, 3 July 1952, BBC WAC T16/35/2.

68 Cecil Madden to Programme Organiser, Television [memo], 31 August 1953, BBC WAC T16/35/3.

69 Michael Barry to W.L. Streeton [memo], 10 September 1953, BBC WAC W16/35/3.

70 W.L. Streeton to Michael Barry [memo], 15 September 1953, BBC WAC W16/35/3.

71 The ceremony on 31 July 1951 was broadcast live on television with Dame Sybil Thorndike reading an ode composed for the occasion by Poet Laureate John Masefield.

72 Beauman, *Royal Shakespeare Company*, 212.

73 W.L. Streeton to Joanna Spicer [memo], 3 February 1955, BBC WAC T16/35/4.

74 Cecil Madden [memo], 4 March 1955, BBC WAC T16/35/4.

75 Joanna Spicer to W.L. Streeton [memo], 17 March 1955, BBC WAC T16/35/4.

76 Joanna Spicer [memo], 14 July 1955, BBC WAC T16/35/4.

77 Philip Hope-Wallace, '*The Merry Wives of Windsor* Stratford Production', *The Manchester Guardian*, 13 July 1955, 5.

78 'It Took Only an Hour, but Oh! the Work Involved', *Birmingham Gazette*, 4 October 1955.

79 Ibid.

80 Camera plan included in *The Merry Wives of Windsor* prompt book [with television script], SBT RSC/SM/1/MEW/1.

81 'Peeps behind the Scenes', *Stratford-upon-Avon Herald*, 17 October 1955.

82 ARR, *The Merry Wives of Windsor,* 25 October 1955, BBC WAC VR/55/492.

83 'Was the Stratford Trip Worth It?', *Birmingham Mail*, 3 October 1955.

84 Philip Hope-Wallace, 'Drama: In the Basket', *The Listener*, 6 October 1955, 569.

85 R.A.S. (Rosemary Anne Sisson), 'Gratifying, if a little lunatic!', *Stratford-upon-Avon Herald*, 17 October 1955.

86 Hope-Wallace, 'Drama: In the Basket', 569.

87 For *An Age of Kings*, see Emma Smith, 'Shakespeare Serialised: *An Age of Kings*' in Robert Shaughnessy, ed., *The Cambridge Companion to Shakespeare and Popular Culture* (Cambridge: Cambridge University Press, 2007), 134–49; for television's productions of the History plays in these years, see John Wyver, '"A Profound Commentary on Kingship": The Monarchy and Shakespeare's Histories on Television, 1957–65', in Irene Morra and Rob Gossedge, eds, *The New Elizabethan Age: Culture, Society and National Identity after World War II* (London: I.B.Tauris, 2016), 267–88.

88 Minute Book 3, RSC Executive Council, 29 January 1948. SBT RSC/AA/1/3.

89 Minute Book 3, RSC Executive Council, 13 October 1953, 22 April 1954. SBT RSC/AA/1/3.

90 Minute Book 4, RSC Executive Council, 9 July 1958, SBT RSC/AA/1/4.

91 J.W. Barnes, Encyclopaedia Britannica, to Sir Fordham Flower [letter], 4 July 1958, text included in Minute Book 4, RSC Executive Council, 9 July 1958, SBT RSC/AA/1/4.

92 Paul Prescott, 'Sam Wanamaker', in Cary M. Mazer, ed., *Great Shakespeareans: Volume 15* (London: Continuum, 2013), 166–67.

93 Peter Hall, *Making an Exhibition of Myself* (London: Oberon Books, 2000), 139.

94 Trewin, *Shakespeare on the English Stage*, 240.

95 Philip Hope-Wallace, 'Less Romance – and Less Poetry – In *A Midsummer Night's Dream*', *The Manchester Guardian*, 3 June 1959, 5.

96 Paul Robeson, together with Mary Ure, who played Desdemona, was interviewed by Independent Television News (ITN), on 6 April 1959, and the following weekend he appeared in conversation with Al Alvarez on the BBC arts magazine *Monitor* (12 April); see BUFVC, '*Monitor* (12/04/1959)', Shakespeare Database. Available online: http://bufvc.ac.uk/shakespeare/index.php/title/av36829 (accessed 11 February 2017).

97 The Museum of Broadcast Communication, 'Encyclopedia of Television – Hubbell Robinson'. Available online: http://www.museum.tv/eotv/robinsonhub.htm (accessed 11 February 2017).

98   Ibid.

99   See Dennis McDougal, *The Last Mogul: Lew Wasserman, MCA and the Hidden History of Hollywood* (Boston, MA: De Capo Press, 2001).

100 William Boddy, *Fifties Television: The Industry and its Critics* (Urbana: University of Illinois Press, 1993), 206.

101 For titles and credits of the full series, see '*Startime* (TV series)', Wikipedia (last modified 29 June 2018). Available online: https://en.wikipedia.org/wiki/Startime_(TV_series)#cite_note-LM-2 (accessed 1 January 2019).

102 Fletcher Markle to Peter Hall [letter], 2 October 1959, SBT, box of 16mm film print, *A Midsummer Night's Dream* (1959).

103 'Agreement between The Shakespeare Memorial Theatre and Hubbell Robinson Productions Inc.' [contract], 2 November 1959, SBT, box of 16mm film print, *A Midsummer Night's Dream* (1959).

104 Keith Gascoigne, 'Stratford Plays to 40m. TV Audience', *Birmingham Post*, 1 December 1959.

105 The kit comprised three RCA TK-12 Image Orthicon cameras (standard for outside broadcast use since 1954), two of which were equipped with zoom lenses, and an Ampex VR 1000 Quad machine that recorded black-and-white electronic images on 2-inch videotape. For information about Intercontinental Television I am indebted to one of the production team, George Anderson; personal email, 12 February 2017.

106 This initial section of the introduction was selected to open the first RSC Live from Stratford-upon-Avon cinema broadcast in November 2013.

107 Simon Callow, *Charles Laughton: A Difficult Actor* (London: Vintage, 2012), 261.

108 The print was first presented and discussed by Russell Jackson in 2012; a digital transfer was made in 2013.

Chapter 2

1   Holland Bennett to Patrick Russell [letter], 23 April 1964, BBC WAC T3/693/1.

2   See Beauman, *The Royal Shakespeare Company*, 233–46. Peggy Ashcroft, Eric Porter and Dorothy Tutin were among the first artists to be signed to the new deals, as was Peter O'Toole, although he was to break his contract within a year.

3   In addition to the account in Beauman, *The Royal Shakespeare Company*, 246–65, the public and private battles of these years are recounted in Chambers, *Inside the Royal Shakespeare Company*, 6–30.

4   A decade later Ken Russell's spectacular film *The Devils* (1971) drew on both Whiting's drama and the play's own source, Aldous Huxley's non-fiction novel *The Devils of Loudun* (1952). The RSC had no relationship with the feature film, although Max Adrian who played Father Pierre Barre on stage appeared on screen as the chemist Ibert.

5   Douglas Marlborough, 'Stratford Theatre Plumps for BBC Television', *Daily Mail*, 6 April 1961.

6   The television audience was also familiar with Giraudoux's work, since *Amphitryon 38* was shown by BBC TV in 1958, and the ITV company Granada broadcast a translation of *Tiger at the Gates* in 1960.

7   Jack W. Lambert, 'The Lady of the Lake', *Sunday Times*, 15 January 1961, 33.

8   Peter Jackson, '*Ondine* Excerpt Was a Sheer Delight', *Yorkshire Post*, 13 April 1961.

9   Broadcast extracts on *Monitor* [TV Programme] (BBC TV, 23 April 1961); the programme is not extant.

10 *Monitor* [TV Programme] (BBC TV, 7 May 1961); nothing of this programme exists in the archives.

11 *Monitor* [TV Programme] (BBC TV, 5 November 1961).

12 Agreement between BBC and Governors of the Royal Shakespeare Theatre, 5 October 1962, RSC administrative records.

13 'Television Project: The Royal Shakespeare Company and the BBC', WAC T3/693/1; the undated memo is preserved along with contract drafts dated April 1962 and must therefore pre-date this.

14 Ibid.

15 Asa Briggs, *The History of Broadcasting in the United Kingdom*, Volume 5: *Competition* (Oxford: Oxford University Press, 1995), 396; quotations from *Daily Sketch*, 5 May 1969.

16 Tom Cornford, 'The English Theatre Studios of Michael Chekhov and Michel Saint-Denis, 1935–1965', PhD thesis, University of Warwick, 2012, 234.

17 Quoted in Gordon McVay, 'Peggy Ashcroft and Chekhov', in Patrick Miles, ed., *Chekhov on the British Stage* (Cambridge: Cambridge University Press, 1993), 91.

18 Michel Saint-Denis, 'Chekhov and the Modern Stage', *Drama Survey*, 3 (Spring–Summer 1963), 80.

19 Michael Billington, *Peggy Ashcroft* (London: John Murray, 1988), 194.

20 See Chambers, *Inside the Royal Shakespeare Company*, 145–51.

21 See Anon., 'On TV Tonight', *Oxford Mail*, 13 April 1962, which is typical of the extensive preview coverage.

22 Billy Smart, 'Three Different *Cherry Orchards*, Three Different Worlds: Chekhov at the BBC, 1962–81', *Critical Studies in Television*, 9 no. 3 (Autumn 2014), 69. Smart's article offers a comparative reading of scenes from the 1962 production together with later BBC presentations in 1971 and 1981.

23 ARR, 'The Royal Shakespeare Company in *The Cherry Orchard*', 9 May 1962, BBC WAC VR/62/210.

24 Anon., 'The Cherry Orchard', *The Stage & Television Today*, 19 April 1962, 11.

25 Anon., 'Coin-in-slot TV Company', *The Times*, 8 October 1960, 4.

26 At the time of writing, although BHE had stopped making new productions in 1967, the company's work has remained available on DVD, with details at

BHE, 'Welcome to British Home Entertainment'. Available online: http://www.britishhomeentertainment.co.uk/ (accessed 22 April 2017).

27 Home Service broadcasts on 12 September and 26 December 1961.

28 Public trials of pay-TV in 1966 and 1967 failed to convince the government that the initial experiments should be developed further, and BHE stopped making new productions, leaving its backers with a loss estimated at £350,000.

29 The story of BHE and the National is explored in detail by Daniel Rosenthal, *The National Theatre Story* (London: Oberon Books, 2013), 110–13, 116. The first BBC television adaptations of National Theatre productions, *Much Ado About Nothing* and *A Flea in her Ear*, were screened in 1967.

30 When *The Hollow Crown* premiered on stage at the Aldwych the cast featured Max Adrian, Barton himself, Richard Johnson and Dorothy Tutin, but for the film Paul Hardwick replaced Johnson.

31 Although he is not credited on screen, David Jones was the film's co-director, according to Montague Haltrecht, 'From *Monitor* to the Aldwych', *The Scotsman*, 8 January 1966.

32 Minute Book 4, RSC Executive Council, 24 February 1967, SBT RSC/AA/1/4.

33 David Jones to Planning Committee [memo], 13 October 1967, SBT.

34 Beauman, *The Royal Shakespeare Company*, 247.

35 'Found at Last – Enchantment in the Forest', *Daily Express*, 5 July 1961.

36 Michael Billington, 'Great Performances: Vanessa Redgrave in *As You Like It*', *The Guardian*, 27 April 2015. Available online: https://www.theguardian.com/stage/2015/apr/27/vanessa-redgrave-rosalind-as-you-like-it (accessed 12 August 2018).

37 Ronald Eyre, '*As You Like It*', *Radio Times*, 14 March 1963, 45.

38 Robert Shaughnessy, *Shakespeare in Performance*: As You Like It (Manchester: Manchester University Press, 2018), 58.

39 ARR, '*As You Like It*', 17 April 1963, BBC WAC VR/63/177.

40 Mary Crozier, 'Review: *As You Like It*', *The Guardian*, 23 March 1963, 5.

41 Beauman, *The Royal Shakespeare Company*, 248–49.

42 Kenneth Tynan, 'Brecht through the Mincer', *The Observer*, 16 September 1962, 20.

43 John Russell Taylor, 'Drama: Seventy-five Minutes', *The Listener*, 9 January 1964, 91.

44 Mary Crozier, '*The Comedy of Errors* on BBC TV', *The Guardian*, 2 January 1964, 7.

45 ARR, '*The Comedy of Errors*', 24 January 1964, BBC WAC VR/64/12.

46 See Billy Smart, 'Old Wine in New Bottles: Adaptation of Classic Theatrical Plays on BBC Television 1957–1985', PhD Thesis, Royal Holloway College, 2010, 84–98.

47 Michael Bakewell, 'The Television Production', in John Barton in collaboration with Peter Hall, *The Wars of the Roses* (London: British Broadcasting Corporation, 1970), 231.

48 Beauman, *The Royal Shakespeare Company*, 270–71.

49 Peter Hall, 'Introduction', in Barton with Hall, *Wars of the Roses*, vii.

50 Ibid., x.

51 See Dominic Sandbrook, *Never Had It So Good: A History of Britain from Suez to The Beatles* (London: Little, Brown, 2005), 602–26, 640–68.

52 See Smith, 'Shakespeare Serialized', 134–49.

53 Bakewell, 'The Television Production', 231.

54 Ibid.

55 Interviewed in Michael Williams, 'The Wars of the Roses', *Radio Times*, 1 April 1965, 43.

56 See memo by John Henderson, 4 February 1964, BBC WAC T5/693/1.

57 Numerous memos in BBC WAC T5/693/1 attest to the problems of editing the series into episodes of roughly equal length so that they could be marketed internationally.

58 Eveline Peacock, 'Technical Equipment Wars of the Roses' [memo], 23 September 1964, BBC WAC T5/693/1.

59 Bakewell, 'The Television Production', 232.

60 John Caughie, *Television Drama: Realism, Modernism, and British Culture* (Oxford: Oxford University Press, 2000), 77.

61 Bakewell, 'The Television Production', 233.

62 '*Edward IV* Scene 36', in Barton with Hall, *Wars of the Roses*, 109–10.

63 '*Edward IV* Scene 39', in Barton with Hall, *Wars of the Roses*, 116–17.

64 See Jeremy Butler, *Television Style* (London: Routledge, 2010), 26–48.

65 Bakewell, 'The Television Production', 235.

66 Ibid., 234.

67 Sydney Newman to Michael Barry [letter], 26 April 1965, WAC T5/693/1.

68 *Sunday Night: How to Stop Worrying and Love the Theatre* [TV Programme] (BBC One, 20 February 1966); *The Impresarios: Peter Hall* [TV Programme] (BBC Two, 9 October 1967).

69 Broadcast BBC Two, 22 November 1966.

70 Broadcast BBC Two, 14 September 1968.

71 Broadcast BBC Two, 13 April 1968.

72 Beauman, *The Royal Shakespeare Company*, 281.

73 Chambers, *Inside the Royal Shakespeare Company*, 41; Chambers also includes more detailed background about the setting up of *Theatregoround*.

74 Quoted in Stephen R. Lawson, 'The Old Vic to Vincennes: Interviews with Michael Kustow and Peter Brook', *Theatre*, 7 no. 1 (1975), 81.

75 Beauman, *The Royal Shakespeare Company*, 285.

76 Production file is BBC WAC T5/1068/1–2; Bernard Adams, '*Days in the Trees*', *Radio Times*, 16 February 1967, 39.

77 ARR, '*Days in the Trees*', 14 March 1967, BBC WAC VR/67/123.

78 Stanley Reynolds, 'Television', *The Guardian*, 4 June 1968, 6.

79 B.A. Young, 'Aldwych: *All's Well That Ends Well*', *Financial Times*, 18 January 1968.

80 Helen Wheatley, *Spectacular Television: Exploring Televisual Pleasure* (London: I.B.Tauris, 2016), 57.

81 Twenty-three issues of *Flourish* were published during these years, with the newsletter successively adopting three distinct formats. A complete run is preserved in the British Library. In early 1974 *Flourish* was replaced by a more professional publication, *The RSC Newspaper*, which came out quarterly until 1990.

82 Anonymous, untitled editorial, *Flourish*, 2 (Autumn-Winter 1964–65), unpaginated.

83 Terence Hawkes, 'Drama in Camera', *The Listener*, 8 June 1967, 744.

84 Anonymous, 'Live Theatre Dead?', *Flourish*, 9 (Summer 1967), 2–3; the subsequent issue devoted a further three pages to readers' responses to Hawkes. Terence Hawkes's full article appeared as 'Drama in Camera', *The Listener*, 8 June 1967, 743; emphases in the original.

Chapter 3

1 Minute Book 4, RSC Executive Council, 25 September 1963, SBT RSC/AA/1/4.

2 Christopher Mann Ltd was a well-established company with strong connections in the British film industry and known for grand offices overlooking Hyde Park.

3 Minute Book 4, 1 January 1965.

4 Minute Book 4, 6 May 1966.

5 Dick Patterson to Peter Hall [letter], 21 June 1966, Filmways file, SBT.

6 Ibid.

7 Ibid.

8 Robert Murphy, *Sixties British Cinema* (London: BFI Publishing, 1992), 257–58. See also Alexander Walker's detailed study *Hollywood, England: The British Film Industry in the Sixties* (London: Michael Joseph, 1974).

9 Deborah Willis, 'Marlowe our Contemporary: *Edward II* on Stage and Screen', *Criticism*, 40 no. 4 (Fall 1998), 602. See also Pascale Aebischer, 'Marlowe in the Movies', in Emily C. Bartels and Emma Smith, eds, *Christopher Marlowe in Context* (Cambridge: Cambridge University Press, 2013), 317.

10 Hall, *Making an Exhibition of Myself*, 196.

11 Piri Halsz, 'London: The Swinging City', *Time*, 15 April 1966.

12 Quoted in Hunter Davies, 'All the World's a Screen', *The Sunday Times*, 26 June 1966, 9.

13 Minute Book 4, 9 September 1966.

14 The text is published in Henry Livings, *Plays One* (London: Oberon Books, 2001).

15 A further link was that the music was composed by Guy Woolfenden who Peter Hall had installed as the RSC's Head of Music at the RSC in 1961. The electronic music pioneer Delia Derbyshire also contributed to the soundtrack.

16 Murphy, *Sixties British Cinema*, 273.

17 Hall, 'Wednesday 30 January [1974]', in John Goodwin, ed., *Peter Hall's Diaries: The Story of a Dramatic Battle* (London: Hamish Hamilton, 1983), 79; ellipsis in the original.

18 Quoted in Davies, 'All the World's a Screen'.

19 Michael Birkett to Peter Hall [letter], 9 August 1966, SBT 'Filmways' file. In the letter Birkett disparages the approach of veteran film director Paul Czinner's 'boring old methods of half a dozen cameras firing away simultaneously from the proscenium' which he says 'are diametrically opposite to the way we are thinking'.

20 George Farmer to Peter Hall [letter], 3 November 1966, SBT 'Filmways' file.

21 'Shakespeare to be Filmed in Colour', *Sheffield Telegraph*, 3 November 1966.

22 Daily Telegraph Theatre Correspondent, 'Shakespeare Company to be Built Up Again', *Daily Telegraph*, 10 November 1966.

23 Minute Book 4, 19 April 1967.

24 David Nathan, 'Shakespeare, with Important Readings from the Met Office', *The Sun*, 2 October 1967.

25 *Daily Cinema*, 1 November 1967.

26 John Russell Taylor, 'Peter Hall on the Challenge of Films', *The Times*, 15 April 1967, 7.

27 Quoted in T.S. Ferguson, 'What's Happening: Midsummer in Autumn', *The Sunday Telegraph*, 5 November 1967.

28 Minute Book 4, 3 November 1967.

29 Michael Birkett to Derek Hornby [letter], 12 December 1967, SBT 'Filmways' file.

30 'Hall's Film on TV', *Evening Standard*, 20 January 1969.

31 John Russell Taylor, 'A Pleasurable Western', *The Times*, 30 January 1969, 7.

32 Richard Roud, 'Midwinter's Drag', *The Guardian*, 31 January 1969, 8.

33 Peter Hall, 'Why the Fairies Have Dirty Faces', *The Sunday Times*, 26 January 1969, 55. Hall continued to justify his approach in two extended and informative interviews later that year: with Gordon Gow, 'In Search of a Revolution', *Films and Filming*, September 1969, 40–46, and with Roger Manvell, 'On the Dank and Dirty Ground', *Journal of the Society of Film and Television Arts*, no. 37 (Autumn 1969), 11–15.

34 Michael Mullin, 'Peter Hall's *Midsummer Night's Dream* on Film', *Educational Theatre Journal*, 27 no. 4 (December 1975), 522, 534.

35 Jack Jorgens, *Shakespeare on Film* (Bloomington: Indiana University Press, 1977), 52. See also Frank Occhiogrosso, 'Cinematic Oxymoron in Peter Hall's *A Midsummer Night's Dream*', *Literature/Film Quarterly*, 11 no. 3 (1983), 175.

36 Graham Holderness, 'Radical Potentiality and Institutional Closure: Shakespeare in Film and Television', in Jonathan Dollimore and Alan Sinfield,

eds, *Political Shakespeare: New Essays in Cultural Materialism* (Manchester: Manchester University Press, 1985), 187.

37 Ibid., 188.

38 Peter S. Donaldson, '"Two of Both Kinds": Modernism and Patriarchy in Peter Hall's *A Midsummer Night's Dream*', in Lisa S. Starks and Courtney Lehmann, eds, *The Reel Shakespeare: Alternative Cinema and Theory* (Madison, NJ: Fairleigh Dickinson University Press, 2002), 44.

39 Substantial sections of Ian Hogg's diary are reproduced in Garry O'Connor, *Paul Scofield: The Biography* (London: Sidgwick & Jackson, 2002), 214–15.

40 D.A.N. Jones, 'Strange Abuse', *The Listener*, 24 August 1967, 251.

41 Michael Birkett to Marty Ransohoff [letter], 13 February 1968, SBT 'Filmways' file.

42 Riou Benson to George Farmer [letter], 8 February 1968, SBT 'Filmways' file.

43 Derek Hornby to George Farmer [letter], 5 September 1968, SBT 'Filmways' file.

44 Minute book 6, 1 November 1968, SBT RSC/AA/1/6.

45 Walker, *Hollywood England*, 441.

46 Ibid., 444.

47 Manvell, 'On the Dank and Dirty Ground', 11.

48 Minute book 6, 30 November 1969.

49 Steven H. Gale, *Encyclopaedia of British Humorists: From Geoffrey Chaucer to John Cleese* (London: Taylor & Francis, 1996), 849.

50 Produced by Guy Vaesen, broadcast 25 April 1968.

51 See Michael Billington, *Harold Pinter*, rev. edn (London: Faber and Faber, 2007), 196–202.

52 A short-lived experimental format, Multivista was associated with the production company LMG Film Services, which also used it, along with Alan Hume, for the sex comedy *Not Now Darling* (1973). The credit on the National Film Archive print of *Landscape* is 'A Royal Shakespeare Company filmed by Angle Films Ltd [which was Peter Hall's company, that later made *Akenfield*] in association with LMG Film Services Ltd.'

53 Billington, *Harold Pinter*, 162; for a detailed discussion of the play and of the London production, see 162–78.

54 Broadcast on the ITV network, 3 October 1965.

55 As 'Jim' Goddard more than fifteen years later he would oversee the television translation of the RSC's *Nicholas Nickleby*.

56 For additional details, including reviews of each of the productions, see Raymond Benson, 'Remember … the American Film Theatre', *CinemaRetro*, 16 April 2009. Available online: http://www.cinemaretro.com/index.php?/ archives/3150-REMEMBER...THE-AMERICAN-FILM-THEATRE!.html (accessed 28 January 2018).

57 Rights problems meant that the series largely disappeared after the first showings, and it was only in 2004 that the productions began to be seen again and released in handsome DVD restorations with informative extras.

58 Peter Hall, 'Interview about *The Homecoming*', *The American Film Theatre Collection: The Homecoming* [DVD] (Ind-DVD, 2004).

59 Ibid. See also the careful script analysis, comparing the film with the London and New York productions, by Bernard F. Dukore, 'Pinter's Revised *Homecoming*', *Educational Theatre Journal*, 30 no. 2 (May 1978), 151–56.

60 Brook's largely undocumented encounters with television began in 1949, with a live BBC studio production of his original script *Box for One,* set in a Soho telephone kiosk. This was broadcast 10 June 1949, with Marius Goring; lost. Brook wrote another television play, *The Birthday Present,* which was directed in 1953 by Tony Richardson. I have been unable to trace a script of *The Birthday Present,* but the Peter Brook collection at the V&A includes a draft television script for *A House of Cards,* a historical drama suggested by E.T.A. Hoffmann's tale *Gambler's Luck* and credited to Brook and Thomas Browne. This appears not to have been produced.

61 Additional discussions of and responses to *The Beggar's Opera* include Trewin, *Peter Brook,* 68–70; Michael Kustow, *Peter Brook: A Biography* (London: Bloomsbury, 2005), 74–76; Edward Trostle Jones, *Following Directions: A Study of Peter Brook* (New York: Peter Lang, 1985), 127–30. Raymond Durgnat eviscerates the film and Brook's direction in *A Mirror for England* (London: Faber & Faber, 1970), 112–13; Pauline Kael's positive 1961 review is reprinted in *I Lost It at the Movies: Film Writings, 1954–65* (London: Jonathan Cape, 1966), 105.

62 This was made in New York for the prestigious television series *Omnibus* (1952–61), which the TV-Radio Workshop of the Ford Foundation produced for the CBS network. Broadcast live on 18 October 1953, the production is a seventy-three-minute condensation stringing together shortened versions of only the scenes to which Lear is central.

63 Broadcast on 6 September 1954 with television presentation by Alan Chivers; no recording is known to exist.

64 Kenneth Tynan, 'Chamber of Horrors', *The Observer*, 21 August 1955, 11.

65 Peter Brook, 'Baked in That Pie', in *The Quality of Mercy: Reflections on Shakespeare* (London: Nick Hern Books, 2013), 42–43.

66 Ibid.

67 Jennifer Barnes, '"Posterity is Dispossessed: Laurence Olivier's *Macbeth* Manuscripts in 1958 and 2012', *Shakespeare Bulletin*, 30 no. 3 (Fall 2012), 268.

68 Ibid., 269.

69 Anon., '*Hamlet* Televised in Moscow', *The Manchester Guardian*, 2 December 1955, 12. On the new ITV channel's magazine show *Christmas Afternoon,* broadcast 25 December, Brook introduced film of the recent visit to the Soviet Union, although nothing of this nor any Russian recording has to date come to light.

70 Broadcast 27 February 1956; see Olwen Terris, 'The Forgotten Hamlet', *Shakespeare Bulletin*, 25 no. 2 (Summer 2007), 35–39; also Shakespeare, '*Hamlet*'. Available online: http://bufvc.ac.uk/shakespeare/index.php/title/av66532 (accessed 28 December 2017).

71 Directed and co-written by Brook with Denis Cannan (who would later co-script *US*), this was based on a variant of the Jonah myth.

72   Introduced and edited by Huw Wheldon, this was broadcast on 2 February 1958, BBC TV.

73   For the production of *Lord of the Flies*, see Kustow, *Peter Brook*, 117–23; other accounts and assessments include Trewin, *Peter Brook*, 117–22; Trostle Jones, *Following Directions*, 136–42. Brook's own thoughts are in the essay 'Lord of the Flies', in *The Shifting Point: Forty Years of Theatrical Exploration, 1946–87* (London: Methuen Drama, 1989), 193–98. In 1996 Brook, along with several of his cast, returned to the island where *Lord of the Flies* was shot for the arts documentary *Time Flies* (BBC Two, 23 November 1996), directed by Richard Dale, which I produced for Illuminations and BBC Television.

74   Beauman, *The Royal Shakespeare Company*, 249.

75   The production was broadcast by the Third Programme on 17 October 1963.

76   Quoted in Albert Hunt and Geoffrey Reeves, *Peter Brook* (Cambridge: Cambridge University Press, 1995), 68.

77   Ibid., 71; more generally on the production, 65–83.

78   Filmed by the BBC as a challenging, experimental recording for *Late-Night Line-Up* and broadcast on 30 December 1969, the drama by then known as *The Marowitz Hamlet* has a radically reworked and fractured text, startlingly stylized playing, a white box for a set and the small cast in modern dress with heavy make-up. The fifty-nine-minute film that exists in the archives appears to have been shot at the Open Space Theatre on 16mm, but has no titles or credits.

79   The English version was prepared by Geoffrey Skelton with verse adaptation by Adrian Mitchell. Some commentators shorten the title to *The Marat/Sade* but the version without the definite article is preferred here, not least as it is the one usually employed by Brook.

80   The rehearsals and production are explored in depth in Hunt and Reeves, *Peter Brook*, 84–95. See also Kustow, *Peter Brook*, 137–43, and for the film, 151–53. *Monitor*, which also featured an interview between editor Jonathan Miller and Brook, was broadcast on BBC One on 1 December 1964.

81   Hunt and Reeves, *Peter Brook*, 89.

82   Peter Brook, 'Introduction', in Peter Weiss, ed., *The Persecution and Assassination of Marat as Performed by the Inmates of the Asylum of Charenton under the Direction of the Marquis de Sade* (London: Calder and Boyars, 1965), 5.

83   Ibid., 6.

84   Bernard Levin, 'One of the Most Amazing Plays I've Ever Seen', *Daily Mail*, 21 August 1964.

85   Before the transfer of *Marat/Sade*, on 19 October 1965, Brook and David Jones co-directed a late-night RSC reading of Peter Weiss's 'oratorio-stage-documentary' about the Holocaust, *The Investigation*, which was also being presented on that date in thirteen theatres in East and West Germany. The reading was audio recorded for the BBC by producer Hallam Tennyson and extracts were broadcast by the Third Programme on 23 November.

86   Peter Brook, 'Filming a Play', in *The Shifting Point: Forty Years of Theatrical Exploration, 1946–1987* (London: Methuen, 1988), 189.

87   Ibid., 189.

88   Michael Birkett's letter to cast [draft letter], 15 March 1966, SBT 4/83 B6.

89   Brook can be glimpsed at work on the film in Don Levy's documentary *Opus* (1967). A two-minute sequence appears to combine footage filmed by Levy with sequences from *Marat/Sade*.

90   Ian Wright, 'Bloodletting in the bath house', *The Guardian*, 28 June 1966, 7.

91   Brook, 'Filming a Play', 189–90.

92   Philip Oakes, 'Causing a Necessary Pain', *The Sunday Times*, 24 July 1966, 8[S]-9[S].

93   See Dilys Powell, 'Beyond the Bars', *The Sunday Times*, 12 March 1967, 23.

94   Ernest Callenbach, '*Marat/Sade* by Peter Brook', *Film Quarterly*, 20 no. 4 (Summer 1967), 56–57; for a recent assessment see Amy Simmons, '*Marat/Sade* (Peter Brook, 1967)', *Senses of Cinema*, 82, March 2017. Available online: http://sensesofcinema.com/2017/1967/marat-sade/ (accessed 28 December 2017).

95   Evan M. Torner, 'The Cinematic Defeat of Brecht by Artaud in Peter Brook's *Marat/Sade*', *EDGE: A Graduate Journal for German and Scandinavian Studies*, 1 no. 1 (2009), 2. Available online: http://scholarworks.umass.edu/edge/vol1/iss1/1 (accessed 12 May 2018).

96   Ibid., 3.

97   Quoted in Oakes, 'Causing a Necessary Pain', 8[S].

98   In the original Aldwych programme, *US* was ascribed to Peter Brook (director), Sally Jacobs (designer), Richard Peaslee (music), Adrian Mitchell (lyrics), Denis Cannan (original text), Geoffrey Reeves and Albert Hunt (associate directors), Michael Kustow and Michael Stott (adaptors of documentary material).

99   Quoted in Trewin, *Peter Brook*, 155.

100 Peter Brook, 'Introduction', in Peter Brook and others, *The Book of US* (London: Calder and Boyars, 1968), 10.

101 Reeves, Hunt and Kustow all participated in the production of *US*, and they have written detailed accounts of the rehearsal process and the production itself, in Hunt and Reeves, *Peter Brook*, 96–120, and Kustow, *Peter Brook*, 159–71.

102 Brook, *Threads of Time* (London: Methuen, 1998), 140–41.

103 This speech is omitted from *Tell Me Lies*.

104 Bosley Crowther, 'Film Festival: Peter Whitehead's Impressions of "London Scene"', *The New York Times*, 27 September 1967.

105 Nicole Zand, '*Benefit of the Doubt*, Review, 1965' [sic], *Nouvelles Littéraires*, 16 May 1968, reprinted in *Framework*, 52 no. 1 (Spring 2011), 339.

106 Robert Chilcott, 'The Films of Peter Whitehead', *Vertigo*, 8 (March 2007). Available online: https://www.closeupfilmcentre.com/vertigo_magazine/issue-8-march-2007/the-films-of-peter-whitehead/ (accessed 12 May 2018).

107 Anon., 'Documentaries Click, Whitehead Foresees Capital for Features', *Variety*, 4 October 1967, 20.

108 Peter Brook to Peter Whitehead [letter], 18 September 1967, Peter Brook Collection, V&A Theatre and Performance Collections GB71 THM/452/8/60, File 3.

109 Dilys Powell, 'Time Out of War', *The Sunday Times*, 18 February 1968, 49.

110 Renata Adler, 'Screen: *Tell Me Lies*', *The New York Times*, 13 February 1968, 46.

111 Hollis Alpert, 'Race and Outrage', *Saturday Review*, 3 February 1968, 46.

112 Peter Brook to Robert Facey [letter], 1968, quoted in Kustow, *Peter Brook*, 180.

113 Michael Birkett to Peter Brook [letter], 18 January 1967. Peter Brook Collection, V&A Theatre and Performance Collections GB71 THM/452/4/28. I have found no mention of this project in any of the Brook literature and it makes no appearance in the extensive Filmways correspondence, so it is not clear if the feature was envisaged as part of that.

114 Quoted in Geoffrey Reeves, 'Shakespeare on Three Screens: Peter Brook Interviewed by Geoffrey Reeves', *Sight & Sound*, Spring 1965, 23.

115 The rehearsals are chronicled in detail by Brook's assistant director Charles Marowitz, whose '*Lear* Log' was printed first in *Encore* in 1963, and then in David Williams, ed., *Peter Brook: A Theatrical Casebook* (London: Methuen, 1988), 6–22. Other accounts of the production are in Trewin, *Peter Brook*, 126–30; Kustow, *Peter Brook*, 176–78; and Hunt and Reeves, *Peter Brook*, 44–56.

116 Trewin, *Peter Brook*, 125.

117 Kenneth Tynan, 'The Triumph of Stratford's *Lear*', *The Observer*, 11 November 1962, 26.

118 Trewin, *Peter Brook*, 125; see also Jorgens, *Shakespeare on Film*, 235–51.

119 Quoted in Kenneth Pearson, '*Lear* in a Cold Country', *The Sunday Times*, 25 May 1969, 55.

120 Michael Birkett and Roger Manvell, '*King Lear*: From Page to Screen', *Journal of the Society of Film and Television Arts*, 37 (Autumn 1969), 18.

121 Lillian Wilds, 'One *King Lear* for Our Time: A Bleak Film Vision by Peter Brook', *Literature/Film Quarterly*, 4 no. 2 (Spring 1976), 160.

122 Peter Brook, 'Filming *King Lear*', in *The Shifting Point: Forty Years of Theatrical Exploration, 1946–87* (London: Methuen Drama, 1989), 206.

123 Kustow, *Peter Brook*, 177.

124 Pauline Kael, 'Peter Brook's "Night of the Living Dead"', *The New Yorker*, 11 December 1971, 135.

125 Frank Kermode, 'Shakespeare in the Movies', *The New York Review of Books*, 4 May 1972.

126 Kenneth Rothwell, *A History of Shakespeare on Screen: A Century of Film and Television* (Cambridge: Cambridge University Press, 2004), 143.

127 Ibid., 143–44.

128 Lillian Wilds, 'One *King Lear* for Our Time', 162.

129 Quoted in Trewin, *Peter Brook*, 172.

130 Accounts include Beauman, *The Royal Shakespeare Company*, 303–08; Kustow, *Peter Brook*, 187–94.

131 Clive Barnes, 'Theater: Historic Staging of *Dream*', *The New York Times*, 28 August 1970, 15.

132 Beauman, *The Royal Shakespeare Company*, 304.

133 Amongst the most charming accounts of seeing the production is Peter Holland's in his invaluable essay about the production, '"The revolution of the times": Peter Brook's *A Midsummer Night's Dream*, 1970', in Gordon McMullan and Zoe Wilcox, eds, *Shakespeare in Ten Acts* (London: The British Library, 2016), 161–80.

134 Holland, '"The revolution of the times"', 164.

135 Peter Brook, 'A Cook and a Concept', in *The Quality of Mercy: Reflections on Shakespeare* (London: Nick Hern Books, 2013), 80–81.

136 15 April – 6 September 2016, accompanied by the catalogue, McMullan and Wilcox, *Shakespeare in Ten Acts*.

137 Barbara Hodgdon, 'Photography, Theater, Mnemonics; or, Thirteen Ways of Looking at a Still', in W.B. Worthen with Peter Holland, eds, *Theorizing Practice: Redefining Theatre History* (Basingstoke: Palgrave Macmillan, 2003), 89.

138 Sally Jacobs to Hal Rogers [letter], 15 May 1972, Peter Brook Collection, V&A Theatre and Performance Collections, GB71 THM/452/3/30.

139 Sally Jacobs to David Brierly [letter], 28 July 1995, Peter Brook Collection, V&A Theatre and Performance Collections, GB71 THM/452/3/30.

140 Brook, 'A Cook and a Concept', 81.

141 See Akihiko Senda, 'The Rebirth of Shakespeare in Japan: From the 1960s to the 1990s', trans. Ryuta Minami, in Takashi Sasayama, J.R. Mulryne and Margaret Shewring, eds, *Shakespeare and the Japanese Stage* (Cambridge: Cambridge University Press, 1999), 20–21.

142 Brook, 'A Cook and a Concept', 81–2.

143 U-matic recorders using 3/4″ tape were available for the domestic market in Japan from 1971 onwards, although their cost was such that most machines were used in business contexts. Betamax systems were first released in 1975 and VHS recorders were marketed in 1976. I am deeply grateful to Kazuko Matsuoka for sharing her precious recording of the NHK *Dream*, and to Michiko Suematsu for making this possible.

144 Brook, 'A Cook and a Concept', 82.

Chapter 4

1 Broadcast during the week of his appointment on 3 February 1968, BBC Television arts strand *Review* included a seven-minute interview with a moustachioed Trevor Nunn, who comes across as earnest and nervous. 'I'm more and more convinced', he says, 'that the focus of our work should be on the actor and really only on the actor.'

2 The National Theatre mounted productions at The Old Vic until 1976 when its building on the South Bank opened.

3 See Sandy Craig, ed., *Dreams and Deconstructions: Alternative Theatre in Britain* (Ambergate: Amber Lane Press, 1980), and specifically in relation to the RSC, Colin Chambers, *Other Spaces: New Theatre and the RSC* (London: Eyre Methuen/TQ Publications, 1980).

4 Beauman, *The Royal Shakespeare Company*, 311–12.

5 The season also featured Buzz Goodbody's production of Trevor Griffiths's study of revolutionary ideology *Occupations*, first staged in Manchester in 1970. Granada TV broadcast a production by Michael Lindsay-Hogg in 1973, with a different cast. See Mike Poole and John Wyver, *Powerplays: Trevor Griffiths in Television* (London: BFI Publishing, 1984), 30–42.

6 Michael Coveney, 'Robin Phillips Obituary', *The Guardian*, 30 July 2015. Available online: https://www.theguardian.com/stage/2015/jul/30/robin-phillips (accessed 30 June 2018).

7 Harold Hobson, 'Definitive *Miss Julie*', *The Sunday Times*, 31 October 1971, 38.

8 The film was broadcast on BBC Two on 21 May 1974 and was later released in the UK on DVD.

9 Quoted in Chambers, *Other Spaces*, 34; chapter 4 of the book provides a detailed chronicle of the first season at The Other Place. See also Alycia Smith-Howard, *Studio Shakespeare: The Royal Shakespeare Company at The Other Place* (Aldershot: Ashgate, 2006), especially 26–29.

10 The Other Place was closed as a theatre by the RSC in 1989 and the building was used for administration storage until it was largely demolished to make space for the Courthouse Theatre. This was the RSC's main Stratford auditorium while the RST was rebuilt between 2006 and 2010. Further substantial conversion work led to the building's re-opening in 2016 as The Other Place, with the Studio Theatre, rehearsal rooms and other facilities. The spirit and ideas of Buzz Goodbody deeply informed this most recent conversion.

11 For a detailed discussion of the production see Chambers, *Other Spaces*, 61–63; see also Smith-Howard, *Studio Shakespeare*, 35–42.

12 During my fruitless search for the tape, Professor Anthony Howard provided significant assistance and recalled having seen the recording. In an email (11 November 2017) he remembered 'a key scene when Tony Church speaks as a homeless man before becoming Lear, and scary shots of Edgar and Edmund's huge swords thrashing the air just over the audience's heads – no-one was used to studio Shakespeare yet!'.

13 David Brierley to Peter Bowen [letter], undated [July 1974?]. File 'Video Recordings 1969–1975', SBT.

14 On *Hamlet* and Buzz Goodbody's suicide, see Smith-Howard, *Studio Shakespeare*, 69–82.

15 Quoted in Chambers, *Other Spaces*, 43.

16 Robert Cushman, 'Further Thoughts on the RSC's Fascists', *The Observer*, 22 May 1977, 30.

17 Tom May, 'An Ideology in Red, White and Blue in Tooth and Claw: David Edgar's *Destiny* (1978) – Part 1 of 3', *British Television Drama*, 31 March 2017. Available online: http://www.britishtelevisiondrama.org.uk/?p=7040 (accessed 20 June 2018).

18 Broadcast in the BBC One Midlands region 'opt-out' slot 13 January 1984.

19 Quoted in Catherine Prentice and Helena Leongamornlert, 'The RSC Goes Walkabout: *The Dillen* in Stratford, 1983', *New Theatre Quarterly*, 69 (February 2002), 51; the article is a rich account of the production of *The Dillen* and the social and political context it which it was created.

20 Broadcast on Shakespeare's Birthday, *Omnibus: Shakespeare's Island* (BBC One, 23 April 1971).

21 Chambers, *Inside the Royal Shakespeare Company*, 61.

22 Beauman, *The Royal Shakespeare Company*, 322.

23 Harold Hobson, 'Rough-hewn Roman', *The Sunday Times*, 28 October 1973, 37.

24 Minute book 6, 24 February 1969, SBT RSC/AA/1/6.

25 Minute book 6, 11 May 1971.

26 Minute book 6, 15 May 1973.

27 For the background to and details of these negotiations see Jeremy Potter, *Independent Television in Britain*: Volume 3: *Politics and Control, 1968–80* (London: Macmillan, 1989), 103–07.

28 Quoted in François Laroque, 'Interview Given by Trevor Nunn, Director of the Film *Twelfth Night*', *Cahiers Elisabéthains*, 52 (October 1997), 89.

29 Quoted in Peter Fiddick, 'Shakespeare in 625 Lines', *The Guardian*, 18 April 1978, 8.

30 On the development of CSO and its use at this time in BBC studio dramas, see Leah Panos, 'Stylised Worlds: Colour Separation Overlay in BBC Television Plays of the 1970s', *Critical Studies in Television*, 8 no. 3 (Autumn 2013), 1–17.

31 For discussions of the ATV adaptation, see Rothwell, *A History of Shakespeare on Screen*, 105–06; Samuel Crowl, 'A World Elsewhere: The Roman Plays on Film and Television', in Anthony Davies and Stanley Wells, eds, *Shakespeare and the Moving Image: The Plays on Film and Television* (Cambridge: Cambridge University Press, 1994), 153–55.

32 Leonard Buckley, 'Television Makes the Bard its Own', *The Times*, 29 July 1974, 7.

33 Clive James, 'Sir Lew and the Serpent of Old Nile', *The Observer*, 4 August 1974, 26.

34 The film followed a BBC Television adaptation with Janet Suzman and Ian McKellen, directed by Waris Hussein (BBC One, 20 October 1972).

35 J.W. Lambert, 'High Comedy and Low Spirits', *The Sunday Times*, 3 October 1976, 37.

36 Fiddick, 'Shakespeare in 625 lines'.

37 Fiddick, 'Shakespeare in 625 lines', describes Nunn adding the laughter 'at the centre of an array of knobs, dials, and electronic craftsmen'.

38 Rothwell, *Shakespeare on Screen*, 104.

39 *Macbeth* press night, 9 September 1976; *The Comedy of Errors*, 29 September 1976.

40 *Chambers, Other Spaces*, 68.

41 Michael Mullin, 'Stage and Screen: The Trevor Nunn *Macbeth*', *Shakespeare Quarterly*, 38 no. 3 (Autumn 1987), 355.

42 On *Macbeth*, Trevor Nunn's credit is 'Produced and conceived for television by' and Casson's is 'Directed for television by'.

43 Mullin, 'Stage and Screen', 358.

44 Rothwell, *Shakespeare on Screen*, 106.

45 Mullin, 'Stage and Screen', 359.

46 Sinclair was a writer who had not previously made a film, although he was later to direct an eccentric adaptation of Dylan Thomas's *Under Milk Wood* with Elizabeth Taylor and Richard Burton.

47 David Brierley to Jo Durden-Smith [letter], 1 January 1970. File 'Video Recordings 1969–1975', SBT.

48 *Omnibus: John Clare – 'I am...'* (BBC One, 8 February 1970).

49 *Wessex Tales: Barbara of the House of Grebe* (BBC Two, 12 December 1973); *2nd House: An Artist's Story* (BBC Two, 2 February 1974). Jones presented BBC Two's *Review* series in 1971 to 1972, and in 1977 he became producer of the BBC's *Play of the Month* strand for which he oversaw distinguished productions by Jane Howell, Peter Wood and Alan Clarke. In 1979 he left for New York to set up, on principles derived from the RSC, a resident theatre company for Brooklyn Academy of Music.

50 See Beauman, *The Royal Shakespeare Company*, 325–29, 338–43.

51 Fiddick, 'Shakespeare in 625 Lines'.

52 Broadcast 9 November 1977; producers Dennis Marks, Alan Yentob. A full transcript of the programme was published in *The Listener*, 5 January 1978, 17–19.

53 The topic was returned to on television in a 1985 programme for schools, *Daytime on Two: General Studies – Updating Shakespeare* (broadcast 11 March), which brought together in discussion John Barton, Michael Bogdanov and Michael Pennington.

54 Irving Wardle, 'Strong, Stupendous Mr Howard', *The Times*, 22 October 1977, 7; Bernard Levin, 'Shakespeare Wins Hands Down', *The Sunday Times*, 23 October 1977, 39; Nicholas de Jongh, '*Coriolanus*', *The Guardian*, 5 June 1978, 8.

55 Susan Willis, *The BBC Shakespeare Plays: Making the Televised Canon* (Chapel Hill: University of North Carolina Press, 1991), 94. See also Maurice Hindle, *Shakespeare on Film*, 2nd edn (London: Palgrave, 2017), 251–57.

56 Michael Brooke, '*Romeo and Juliet* (1978)', BFI screenonline. Available online: http://www.screenonline.org.uk/tv/id/526875/index.html (accessed 22 January 2018).

57 James C. Bulman, 'The BBC Shakespeare and "house style"', *Shakespeare Quarterly*, 35 no. 5 (1984), 572–73.

58 Peter Fiddick, 'The Avon Catalogue', *The Guardian*, 1 December 1978, 8.

59 Clive James, 'The Fantastic Voyage', *The Observer*, 10 December 1978, 20.

60 See Michael Brooke, '*BBC Television Shakespeare, The* (1978–85)', *BFI screenonline*. Available online: http://www.screenonline.org.uk/tv/id/459382/index.html (accessed 12 June 2018; Jack Jorgens, 'The BBC-TV Shakespeare Series', *Shakespeare Quarterly*, 30 no. 3 (Summer 1979), 411–15.

61 Willis, *The BBC Shakespeare Plays*, 99–100.

62 See Peter Waymark, 'If Shakespeare Be Your Cup of Tea, Play On...', *The Times*, 15 October 1983, 5.

63 The Other Place was resurrected for the first time in 1990 as a new building on the same site.

64 John Peter, 'How to Give a Blind Moor New Vision', *The Sunday Times*, 27 August 1989, 9[S1].

65 Robert Gore-Langton, 'A Round, Unvarnish'd Tale', *The Listener*, 1 February 1990, 36.

66 Sheridan Morley, 'For this Relief...', *The Times*, 25 June 1990, 21.

67 Patrick Stoddart, 'Close-ups of Claustrophobia', *The Sunday Times*, 1 July 1990, 16[S3].

68 James Saynor, 'Presence and Sensibility', *The Listener*, 28 June 1990, 38.

69 Ben Brantley, '*Lear* Stripped Bare', *The New York Times*, 14 September 2007.

70 For a detailed, critical consideration of The Warehouse and plays presented there in 1977–80, see Chambers, *Other Spaces*, especially 47–60, 71–79.

71 For an appraisal of *No Excuses* see 'Telly Viewer', '*No Excuses*', *Curious British Telly*, 20 April 2013. Available online: http://www.curiousbritishtelly.co.uk/2013/04/no-excuses.html (accessed 21 December 2017).

72 See Michael Eaton, *Our Friends in the North* (London: BFI Publishing, 2005); this is an exemplary study of the series.

73 Jeffrey Richards, 'The BBC's Voice of Two Nations', *Independent*, 13 March 1996. Available online: https://www.independent.co.uk/voices/the-bbcs-voice-of-two-nations-1341796.html (accessed 22 January 2019).

74 Anonymous, 'Preview: Wednesday', *The Guardian*, 10 November 1979, 18.

75 A BBC regional documentary made a decade later, *Northern Arts: The RSC Tour* (BBC, 30 August 1988), presents the the company on tour in Cumbria with *Happy End*.

76 Michael Church, 'A Bewildering Sort of Poetry', *The Times*, 30 December 1981, 9.

77 Michael Billington, 'How to Suit the Word to the Action', *The Guardian*, 15 December 1979, 11.

78 The production was also shown in nine one-hour episodes in television markets beyond the UK and USA. For a discussion of the broadcast and video formats, see Galen Fott, 'The RSC's *Nicholas Nickleby*, from Stage to Screen',

[Blog] *Blogfott*. Available online: http://blogfott.blogspot.co.uk/2016/01/the-rscs-nicholas-nickleby-from-stage.html (accessed 11 January 2018).

79 11 (1) c, Broadcasting Act 1981, chapter 68 (London: Her Majesty's Stationery Office, 1981).

80 Leon Rubin, *The Nicholas Nickleby Story: The Making of the the Historic Royal Shakespeare Company Production* (London: Heinemann, 1981), 14. Rubin's book is a fascinating insider's account packed with illuminating details, including that Nunn had been discussing a film adaptation for the Stratford company of George Eliot's *Felix Holt* with David Edgar before approaching him to adapt *Nickleby*.

81 Rubin, *The Nicholas Nickleby Story*, 68.

82 Michael Ratcliffe, 'The Novel Birth of a Great Drama', *The Times*, 3 August 1981, 9.

83 Bernard Levin, 'The Truth about Dickens in Nine Joyous Hours', *The Times*, 8 July 1980, 14.

84 Dalya Alberge, 'Producer Colin Callender: Power behind the Scenes', *Financial Times*, 1 December 2017.

85 See Paul Bonner with Lesley Aston, *Independent Television in Britain: New Developments in Independent Television 1981–92: Channel 4, TV-am, Cable and Satellite* (Basingstoke: Palgrave Macmillan, 2003), 52.

86 The main camera operators were Dave Swann and Barry Dodd, and I am grateful to Barry Dodd for a discussion about the production process.

87 *The South Bank Show: Nickleby & Co.* (LWT for ITV Network, 2 August 1981).

88 Jeremy Isaacs, *Storm Over 4: A Personal Account* (London: Weidenfeld and Nicolson, 1989), 169.

89 The song is sung by a Shakespeare company in *The West Wing: Posse Comitatus*, broadcast by NBC in the USA on 22 May 2002, where it is an ironic counterpoint to President Bartlet deciding whether or not to assassinate the Qumari Defence Minister.

Chapter 5

1 Michael Billington, *State of the Nation: British Theatre from 1945* (London: Faber & Faber, 2009), 341.

2 Gregory Doran, 'Think When We Talk of Horses…', in Peter Holland, ed., *Shakespeare Survey no. 70* (Cambridge: Cambridge University Press, 2017), 4.

3 Telephone interview, 20 November 2017.

4 Chambers, *Inside the Royal Shakespeare Company*, 76.

5 Ibid.

6 Broadcast on BBC One, 4 April 1982.

7 Broadcast on BBC One, 17 October 1982.

8 Broadcast on BBC One, 16 January 1983.

9 Quoted in Edward Behr, *The Complete Book of Les Misérables* (New York: Arcade Publishing, 1993), 66.

10 In July 1986 Nicholas de Jongh reported that the RSC made £650,000 at the Barbican and would receive one-third of the profits from the West End; 'Back Stage Blues', *The Guardian*, 1 July 1986, 9.

11 Broadcast on BBC Two, 12 October 1985.

12 Clive Priestley, *Financial Scrutiny of the Royal Shakespeare Company: Report to the Earl of Gowrie, Minister for the Arts* (London: Her Majesty's Stationery Office, 1983), 163. The report is available at https://archive.org/details/op1278121-1001 (accessed 12 September 2018).

13 Ibid., 123.

14 Frank J. Prial, 'US Cable TV to Get Royal Shakespeare Shows', *The New York Times*, 13 January 1983, 15.

15 Priestley, *Financial Scrutiny*, 486.

16 In contrast to my exploration of earlier financing arrangements for RSC productions, I was unable to locate documentation about either the RKO-Nederlander deal or Stratford-Barbican Television.

17 Telephone interview, 20 November 2017.

18 Broadcast on BBC Two, 27 October 1985.

19 Michael Billington, 'Tartuffe', *The Guardian*, 29 July 1983, 15.

20 Broadcast on BBC Two, 3 November 1985.

21 Hugh Hebert, 'Shelf Shock', *The Guardian*, 4 November 1985, 11.

22 Telephone interview, 11 February 2018.

23 Ibid.

24 Broadcast on BBC Two, 20 July 1985.

25 Broadcast on BBC Two, 15 November 1986. The series adopted a similar strategy, combining extracts with reviews, with The Other Place production of *Les Liaisons Dangereuses,* with *Les Misérables* and with Adrian Noble's Stratford production of *Kiss Me Kate* (BBC Two, 28 September 1985, 12 October 1985, and 14 February 1987, respectively).

26 See Tom Gunning, *D.W. Griffith and the Origins of American Narrative Film* (Champaign: University of Illinois Press, 1994), 39.

27 Tom Gunning, 'The Intertexuality of Early Cinema', in Robert Stam and Alessandra Raengo, eds, *A Companion to Literature and Film* (Oxford: Blackwell, 2004), 129.

28 Broadcast on BBC Two, 14 July 1984. The series returned to the production on 15 June 1985, when co-host Minette Marin interviewed Antony Sher about his book, *The Year of the King.*

29 Broadcast on BBC Two, 22 March 1986.

30 Broadcast as a daytime programme on BBC One, 23 January 1987.

31 On *King John*, see Smith-Howard, *Studio Shakespeare*, 117–23.

32 Email to the author, 1 February 2018.

33 Michael Ratcliffe, 'How to Stop the RSC Falling on its Sword', *The Observer*, 21 June 1987, 8.

34 Nicholas de Jongh, 'Carrie on', *The Guardian*, 20 February 1988, 16. On the show's finances and its disastrous opening in New York, see Insight, 'How Poor Carrie Ignored a Lesson', *The Sunday Times*, 22 May 1988, 10,.

35 Broadcast on Channel 4, 26 May 1988.

36 John Vidal, 'The Selection of the Fittest', *The Guardian*, 7 April 1988, 33.

37 Nicholas de Jongh, 'Uneasy Lies the Head', *The Guardian*, 9 November 1989, 21.

38 Ibid.

39 Carrie White, 'Carrie The Musical (Stratford Production) Full Show – 1988 OPENING NIGHT', [Video] YouTube, 6 September 2012. Available online: https://www.youtube.com/watch?v=iOTxiLYFF-Y (accessed 3 January 2018).

40 See Sweeedboy, '*Carrie* Revival?'. *Broadway World*, 31 October 2003. Available online: https://www.broadwayworld.com/board/readmessage. php?thread=895768&page=1 (accessed 3 January 2018).

41 Telephone interview, 4 June 2018.

42 There were occasional additional uses, as when insurers viewed a tape of *Peter Pan* to understand the context of an accident that had occurred.

43 Thanks to Michelle Morton, image manager, RSC, for this information; email 24 January 2018.

44 See David Bordwell, Kristin Thompson and Janet Staiger, *The Classical Hollywood Cinema: Film Style and Mode of Production to 1960* (London: Routledge, 1988). The profoundly influential work of this volume has been much debated over the years since.

45 Reason, *Documentation, Disappearance and the Representation of Live Performance*, 77.

46 Other productions were documented in this manner, including *Peter Pan* in the 1984 Barbican revival, but the SBT index for access copies at present fails to differentiate between versions or to indicate whether a moving variant was made.

47 Telephone interview, 4 June 2018.

48 Margaret Benton, 'Capturing Performance at London's Theatre Museum', *Museum International*, 49 no. 2 (1977), 27–28.

49 Jill Evans, 'Recording Theatre for Education', *Viewfinder*, no. 70 (March 2008), 18.

50 Ibid.

51 Several of the early NVAP recordings, were shot with just a single camera, including at least two with the RSC, of David Edgar's *Pentecost*, recorded at the Young Vic in September 1995, and of *The Herbal Bed* in The Pit in January 1997. For each of these the camera deployed degrees of reframing and tightening to follow the on-stage action.

52 Telephone interview, 15 March 2018.

53 Broadcast respectively 24 May 1994, 5 October 1997, and 15 October 1999.

54 Broadcast on BBC Two, 16 August 1998.

55 Michael Coveney, 'Noble Pursuit of Spreading the Bard', *The Observer*, 13 February 1994, C5.

56 Michael Billington, 'What's Wrong with the RSC?', *The Guardian*, 21 February 1996, A10. His answer was 'absolutely nothing'.

57 Michael Billington, 'A Very British Coup', *The Guardian*, 2 May 1998, 13.

58 Ibid.

59 Quoted in David Nathan, 'Putting the Bard in Focus', *The Times*, 15 October 1994, 6[S1].

60 Broadcast on BBC Two, 17 October 1994.

61 For the list of excerpts, see the Films Media Group catalogue entry, 'Royal Shakespeare Company: Great Performances', Films Media Group. Available online: https://www.films.com/id/8214 (accessed 17 May 2018).

62 Michael Coveney, 'Theatre: Filth Well Worth Revelling In', *The Observer*, 7 August 1994, C11.

63 See Rupert Widdicombe, 'Shakespeare on Film', *The Sunday Times*, 19 November 1995, 5[S8].

64 Quoted in Matt Wolf, 'From Stratford to the Screen', *The Times*, 19 December 1995, 37.

65 Telephone interview, 15 March 2018.

66 Eric Griffiths, 'Sorry, Loves', *Times Literary Supplement*, 27 December 1996, 19.

67 For further discussion of the film, see Rothwell, *A History of Shakespeare on Screen*, 232–34; Judith Buchanan, *Shakespeare on Film* (Harlow: Pearson Education, 2005), 133–38.

68 Alexandra Frean, 'RSC Transfers the Shakespearean Dream to Celluloid', *The Times*, 22 September 1995, 6.

69 Jonathan Gray, *Show Sold Separately: Promos, Spoilers and Other Media Paratexts* (New York: NYU Press, 2010), 26.

70 Phil Gibby, 'ACE Pilot Scheme Backed by RSC', *The Stage*, 10 July 1997, 4.

71 See Wyver, 'An Intimate and Intermedial Form', 349–50.

72 RSC Shakespeare Learning Zone, 'Act 3, Scene 2 | *As You Like It* | Royal Shakespeare Company', [Video] YouTube, 8 June 2015. Available online: https://youtu.be/Yc90Uhv8hFM (accessed 23 February 2018).

73 Royal Shakespeare Company, 'The RSC Light Lock is Launched at PLASA 192008', [Video] YouTube, 18 August 2009. Available online: https://youtu.be/o3WUTekzqmo (accessed 18 September 2018).

74 Royal Shakespeare Company, 'TRAILER: *Arabian Nights*', [Video] YouTube, 11 December 2009. Available online: https://youtu.be/5TKcAUC9K8g (accessed 18 February 2018).

75 Royal Shakespeare Company, 'FEATURE TRAILER: *King Lear* – Royal Shakespeare Company (RSC)', [Video] YouTube, 12 February 2010. Available online: https://youtu.be/uvA_gUDGKik (accessed 18 February 2018).

76 Also online in early 2018 were three standalone extracts recorded on stage of the production itself.

77 Pascale Aebischer, *Screening Early Modern Drama: Beyond Shakespeare* (Cambridge: Cambridge University Press, 2013), 151.

78 Ibid., 152.

79 Adrian Noble, 'Opinion', *The Times*, 1 June 2001, 2.

80 John Peter, 'Bloodbath at the RSC', *The Sunday Times*, 18 November 2001, 16[S9].

81 Benedict Nightingale, 'Departure is a Tragedy of His Own Making', *The Times*, 25 April 2002, 3. Television caught up with these events in a BBC Four programme presented by *The Sunday Times* arts editor Richard Brooks, *Trouble at the RSC*, broadcast 3 September 2002.

82 Michael Billington, 'Man with a Vision and Mountain of Problems', *The Guardian*, 26 July 2002, 4.

83 The internal debates and processes of these years are chronicled in Robert Hewison, John Holden and Samuel Jones, *All Together: A Creative Approach to Organisational Change* (London: Demos, 2016). Available online: http://creative-blueprint.co.uk/library/item/all-together-a-creative-approach-to-organisational-change (accessed 18 August 2018).

84 Interview, 13 April 2018.

85 Charles Spencer, 'Shakespeare's Histories – The Best I Have Seen in Thirty Years', *The Telegraph*, 18 April 2008. Available online: https://www.telegraph.co.uk/culture/theatre/drama/3672706/Shakespeares-Histories-the-best-I-have-seen-in-thirty-years.html (accessed 15 September 2018).

86 See Peter Kirwan, '*The Hollow Crown* – An Introductory Essay', *Drama Online*, 2017. doi:10.5040/9781474208659.

87 Quoted in Charlotte Higgins, 'Cinema vs Theatre: No Contest Says RSC Chief', *The Guardian*, 30 September 2009. Available online: https://www.theguardian.com/stage/2009/sep/30/rsc-theatre-better-than-cinema (accessed 15 September 2018).

88 Leslie A. Wade, 'The London Theatre Goes Digital: Divergent Responses to a New Media', in J.K. Curry, ed., *Theatre Symposium, Volume 19: Theatre and Film* (Tuscaloosa: University of Alabama Press, 2011), 55.

89 Quoted in Josh Spero, 'Digital Theatre: From Page to Stage to Screen', *theartsdesk.com*, 24 February 2010. Available online: http://www.theartsdesk.com/theatre/digital-theatre-page-stage-screen (accessed 4 February 2018).

90 Quoted in Stephen Adams, '"iTunes for Theatre" Will Offer Plays for £8.99', *The Telegraph*, 26 October 2009.

91 Lyn Gardner, '*The Comedy of Errors*', *The Guardian*, 20 May 2009. Available online: https://www.theguardian.com/stage/2009/may/20/review-comedy-of-errors (accessed 12 May 2018).

92 Charles Spencer, '*As You Like It*, Review', *The Telegraph*, 29 April 2009. Available online: https://www.telegraph.co.uk/journalists/charles-spencer/5245542/As-You-Like-It-review.html (accessed 2 February 2018).

93 Interview, 13 April 2018.

94 Ibid.

Chapter 6

1 Siobhan Keenan, 'The Royal Shakespeare Company at 50', *Shakespeare*, 8 no. 2 (June 2012), 198.

2 Personal email from Robert Marshall, 20 May 2018, which also included his account of the later years of Heritage Theatre: 'It all went south when, around 2008–9, both the NT and The Globe decided to produce these recordings in-house and the team of crafts-people around the likes of Robin [Lough] began working directly for the theatre companies themselves. There was no doubt they had taken the production model that we had established and obviously they had far more capital to draw on then we could raise – so we gradually stopped doing recordings.'

3 Email from Robert Marshall, 20 May 2018.

4 Doran, 'Think When We Talk of Horses... ', 6.

5 Ibid., 7.

6 Peter Paterson, 'Macbeth', *Daily Mail*, 2 January 2001.

7 Susanne Greenhalgh, '"Alas poor country!" Documenting the Politics of Performance in Two British Television *Macbeths* Since the 1980s', in Pascale Aebischer, Edward J. Esche and Nigel Wheale, eds, *Remaking Shakespeare: Performance across Media, Genres and Cultures* (Basingstoke: Palgrave Macmillan, 2003), 108.

8 John Wyver to Gregory Doran [email], 16 March 2008.

9 Charles Spencer, 'David Tennant as Hamlet at the Novello Theatre, Review', *The Telegraph*, 8 January 2009. Available online: https://www.telegraph.co.uk/journalists/charles-spencer/4174524/David-Tennant-as-Hamlet-at-the-Novello-Theatre-review.html (accessed 1 September 2018).

10 The props included the celebrated skull of former concert pianist André Tchaikowsky, who had donated it to be used in a production, as it had been on the Courtyard Theatre stage.

11 One further unlooked outcome might also be noted. Director Rupert Goold, who at that point was planning a television film of his staging of *Macbeth* from Chichester Festival Theatre, began following our posts. A few days later he contacted Illuminations to discuss Sebastian Grant and me producing his film, and in the following months we filmed *Macbeth* with support from PBS and the BBC. This television version was shown in Britain and the United States in late 2010.

12 Archived at BBC, 'Hamlet'. Available online: http://www.bbc.co.uk/hamlet/archive.shtml (accessed 18 October 2018).

13 George Entwistle, '*Hamlet* for the Cross-platform Age', [Blog] *About the BBC*, 16 December 2009. Available online: http://www.bbc.co.uk/blogs/aboutthebbc/2009/12/hamlet-for-the-crossplatform-a.shtml (accessed 11 August 2018). 'Lasting' is, inevitably, a somewhat fluid idea in a context such as this. In August 2018, the website remains online but is 'archived' and no longer updated; http://www.bbc.co.uk/hamlet/archive.shtml; some links are broken, http://www.bbc.co.uk/hamlet/making_of/ (accessed 11 August 2018).

14 Mark Lawson, 'The Play's the Thing', *The Guardian*, 12 December 2008. Available online: https://www.theguardian.com/commentisfree/2008/dec/12/david-tennant-hamlet-theatre (accessed 12 July 2018).

15 Gordon Brown, 'An Age of Aspiration Can Benefit Everyone', *The Guardian*, 3 January 2010. Available online: https://www.theguardian.com/politics/2010/jan/03/gordon-brown-education-aspiration (accessed 18 August 2018).

16 Erin Sullivan, 'Olympic Performance in the Year of Shakespeare', in Paul Edmondson, Paul Prescott and Erin Sullivan, eds, *A Year of Shakespeare: Re-living the World Shakespeare Festival* (London: Bloomsbury, 2013), 5. The volume includes reviews of each of the productions in the festival.

17 Sullivan, 'Olympic Performance', 9.

18 Paterson Joseph has written a fascinating study of the stage production and his role within it; *Julius Caesar and Me* (London: Bloomsbury Methuen Drama, 2018).

19 Monika Smialkowska, 'Julius Caesar', in Paul Edmondson, Paul Prescott and Erin Sullivan, eds, *A Year of Shakespeare: Re-living the World Shakespeare Festival* (London: Bloomsbury, 2013), 93–94.

20 For the historical background, see Susanne Greenhalgh, 'Guest Editor's Introduction, Special Performance Reviews Section: Live Cinema Relays of Shakespearean Performance', *Shakespeare Bulletin*, 32 no. 2 (Summer 2014), 255. This introduction, together with the reviews, was the first substantial critical engagement with the hybrid form of live theatre in cinemas.

21 The production process for the 2014 broadcasts is detailed in John Wyver, 'Screening the RSC Stage: The 2014 Live from Stratford-upon-Avon Cinema Broadcasts', *Shakespeare*, 11 no. 3 (2015), 286–302.

22 Doran, 'Think When We Talk of Horses…', 9.

23 See Gregory Doran: 'We want to bring the work we make in Stratford-upon-Avon to the widest possible audience. Taking our productions live into cinemas and direct into schools is the next logical step.' Quoted in Royal Shakespeare Company, 'Productions to Be Broadcast Live from Stratford-upon-Avon' [Press Release], 28 May 2013. Available online: http://www.rsc.org.uk/about-us/press/releases/live-broadcast-from-stratford-upon-avon.aspx (accessed 21 December 2014).

24 Arts Council England, *Great Art and Culture for Everyone: 10-Year Strategic Framework, 2010–2020* (Manchester: Arts Council England, 2013), 29.

25 Martin Barker, *Live to Your Local Cinema: The Remarkable Rise of Livecasting* (Basingstoke: Palgrave Macmillan, 2013), 2.

26 Royal Shakespeare Company, '*Richard II* Stage Footage | Act IV, Scene 1 – The Deposition Scene | 2013 | Royal Shakespeare Company', [Video] YouTube, 21 November 2013. Available online: https://youtu.be/6UHaMJEE0MM (accessed 20 November 2017).

27 Sarah Bay-Cheng, 'Theatre Squared: Theatre History in the Age of Media', *Theatre Topics*, 17 no. 1 (March 2007), 40.

28 Greenhalgh, 'Guest Editor's Introduction', 259.

29 Email to the author, quoted with permission, 30 September 2014.

30 See Timothy King, 'Streaming from Stage to Screen: Its Place in the Cultural Marketplace and the Implication for UK Arts Policy', *International Journal of Cultural Policy*, 24 no. 2 (2018), 220–35.

31 See Alan Galey, *The Shakespearean Archive: Experiments in New Media from the Renaissance to Postmodernity* (Cambridge: Cambridge University Press, 2014).

32 An invaluable filmography of digital theatre broadcasts of Shakespeare, 2003 to 2017, compiled by Rachael Nicholas, is in Pascale Aebischer, Susanne Greenhalgh and Laurie E. Osborne, eds, *Shakespeare and the 'Live' Theatre Broadcast Experience* (London: Bloomsbury, 2018), 227–42.

33 This production of *Much Ado About Nothing* was initially presented in Stratford as *Love's Labour's Won*, and the title was retained for the Live from ... broadcast as well as a subtitle on the DVD release.

34 For a rare exception see Michael Billington, 'Let's Stop Pretending that Theatre Can't be Captured on Screen', *The Guardian*, 18 June 2014. Available online: http://www.theguardian.com/stage/2014/jun/18/ghosts-digital-theatre-richard-eyre-almeida (accessed 19 December 2017). In a discussion of the Digital Theatre recording of *Ghosts*, Billington wrote, 'while I remain an evangelist for live theatre, I think it's time we stopped pretending that it offers an unreproducible event. A theatre performance can now be disseminated worldwide with astonishing fidelity.'

35 Aebischer, Greenhalgh and Osborne, *Shakespeare and the 'Live' Theatre Broadcast Experience*.

36 See Barker, *Live to Your Local Cinema*; Erin Sullivan, '"The Forms of Things Unknown": Shakespeare and the Rise of the Live Broadcast', *Shakespeare Bulletin*, 35 no. 4 (Winter 2017), 627–62.

37 Pascale Aebischer, 'South Bank Shakespeare Goes Global: Broadcasting from Shakespeare's Globe and the National Theatre', in Pascale Aebischer, Susanne Greenhalgh and Laurie E. Osborne, eds, *Shakespeare and the 'Live' Theatre Broadcast Experience* (London: Bloomsbury, 2018), 114, 115.

38 Pascale Aebischer and Susanne Greenhalgh, 'Introduction', in Pascale Aebischer, Susanne Greenhalgh and Laurie E. Osborne, eds, *Shakespeare and the 'Live' Theatre Broadcast Experience* (London: Bloomsbury, 2018), 13.

39 First broadcast on BBC Two, 27 November, 4 December 1987.

40 Keenan, 'The Royal Shakespeare Company at 50', 197.

41 Royal Shakespeare Company, 'Shakespeare Learning Zone'. Available online: https://www.rsc.org.uk/shakespeare-learning-zone (accessed 12 September 2018).

42 Telephone interview, 12 June 2018.

43 Royal Shakespeare Company, '*I, Cinna (The Poet)* Full-length Film | 2012 | Royal Shakespeare Company', [Video] YouTube, 11 April 2013. Available online: https://www.youtube.com/watch?v=6xQAr5le0UU (accessed 20 September 2018).

44 Quoted in Tracy Irish, with Paul Prescott and Erin Sullivan, 'Performing Shakespeare in the Olympic Year: Interviews with Three Practitioners', in Paul Prescott and Erin Sullivan, eds, *Shakespeare on the Global Stage: Performance and Festivity in the Olympic Year* (London: Bloomsbury, 2015), 70.

45 Telephone interview, 12 June 2018.

46 Shakespeare Day Live remains online, with the majority of its links still active, see BBC, 'Shakespeare 2016 Lives'. Available online: https://www.bbc.co.uk/events/ehw2mb/live/c96v4f (accessed 11 August 2018).

47 See Royal Shakespeare Company, 'Meet the Bottoms | A Midsummer Night's Dream: A Play for the Nation | Royal Shakespeare Company', [Video] YouTube, 24 June 2015. Available online: https://youtu.be/FLioHikLF3M (accessed 23 April 2018).

48 Broadcast in regional opt-out slots on 20 May 2016.

49 See Ed Barlow, 'The Best Bottoms in the Land', [Blog] *About the BBC*, 20 May 2016. Available online: http://www.bbc.co.uk/blogs/aboutthebbc/entries/4b941a2a-44ac-4994-a9ee-d59773737ee0; Barlow was the series producer. For the Chris Clarke clip, see 'Method Acting', [Video] BBC One, 18 May 2016. Available online: https://www.bbc.co.uk/programmes/p03vjpff (both accessed 11 August 2018).

50 The programme was conceived and assembled by Gregory Doran; the designer was Robert Jones; Bridget Caldwell was the screen director; Phil Dolling was the BBC executive producer, and Catherine Stirk producer for the BBC; I was the RSC producer.

51 Tim Bano, 'Shakespeare Live! Review – "a stirring celebration"', *The Stage*, 24 April 2016. Available online: https://www.thestage.co.uk/reviews/2016/shakespeare-live/ (accessed 11 August 2018).

52 Susanne Greenhalgh, 'The Remains of the Stage', in Pascale Aebischer, Susanne Greenhalgh and Laurie E. Osborne, eds, *Shakespeare and the 'Live' Theatre Broadcast Experience* (London: Bloomsbury, 2018), 34.

53 Ibid., 35.

54 BBC, '"To be or not to be?" with Benedict Cumberbatch & Prince Charles – Shakespeare Live! From the RSC', [Video] YouTube, 23 April 2016. Available online: https://www.youtube.com/watch?v=kEs8rK5Cqt8 (accessed 11 August 2018).

55 Valentine in *The Two Gentlemen of Verona*, 1.1.50.

56 See Erin Sullivan, 'Shakespeare, Social Media, and the Digital Public Sphere: *Such Tweet Sorrow* and *A Midsummer Night's Dreaming*', *Shakespeare*, 14 no. 1 (2018), 64–79.

57 See Jake Orr, 'Such Tweet Sorrows: Such a Let Down', *A Younger Theatre*, 6 May 2010. Available online: https://www.ayoungertheatre.com/such-tweet-sorrows-such-a-let-down/ (accessed 8 August 2018).

58 Geoffrey Way, 'Social Shakespeare: *Romeo and Juliet*, Social Media and Performance', *Journal of Narrative Theory*, 41 no. 3 (Fall 2011), 418.

59 Tom Uglow, 'An Epilogue: 21 Things I Learnt from *Midsummer Night's Dreaming* with the RSC', *BBH Labs*, 24 October 2013. Available online: http://bbh-labs.com/an-epilogue-21-things-i-learnt-from-midsummer-nights-dreaming-with-the-rsc/ (accessed 8 August 2018).

60 Sullivan, 'Shakespeare, Social Media, and the Digital Public Sphere', 65.

61 See Intel, '400 years in the Making – Intel x The RSC | Experience Amazing', [Video] YouTube, 28 November 2016. Available online: https://youtu. be/1GH1KNNvv4w (accessed 18 October 2018). Discussion of the RSC's networked media projects and its explorations with AR and VR are beyond the scope of this volume.

62 Peter Malin, '"Entertaining strangers": 50 Years of Shakespeare's Contemporaries at the Royal Shakespeare Company', *Shakespeare*, 8 no. 2 (2012), 219–41.

63 Michèle Willems, 'Video and its Paradoxes', in Russell Jackson, ed., *The Cambridge Companion to Shakespeare on Film* (Cambridge: Cambridge University Press, 2007), 45.

FILMOGRAPHY

Titles with no listed writer are by William Shakespeare. Stage and broadcast dates are for the respective premieres. Availability is as at autumn 2018 in the United Kingdom.

Access to the online BBC Shakespeare Archive Resource is restricted to education users: http://shakespeare.ch.bbc.co.uk (accessed 8 November 2018).

The BFI Viewing Service offers access to BBC productions; details at https://www.bfi.org.uk/archive-collections/searching-access-collections/research-viewing-services (accessed 8 November 2018).

Ald: Aldwych Theatre, London
Bar: Barbican Theatre, London
RST: Royal Shakespeare Theatre, Stratford-upon-Avon
SMT: Shakespeare Memorial Theatre, Stratford-upon-Avon
TOP: The Other Place, Stratford-upon-Avon

Feature films

Hedda

Low-budget adaptation of *Hedda Gabler*, filmed on location and on a sound stage.

prod co: Bowden Productions Ltd
stg: 15 July 1975, TOP; *USA release*: December 1975; *UK release*: February 1977
wr: Henrik Ibsen; *stg dir*: Trevor Nunn; *scn dir*: Trevor Nunn
w: Glenda Jackson (Hedda Gabler), Peter Eyre (Tesman), Patrick Stewart (Lovborg), Timothy West (Block)
Not currently available.

The Homecoming

Studio-shot, with location scenes, film version produced for American Film Theatre.

prod co: Cinévision/American Film Theatre
stg: 26 March 1965, Ald; *US cinema release*: 29 October 1973
wr: Harold Pinter; *stg dir*: Peter Hall; *scn dir*: Peter Hall

w: Paul Rogers (Max), Ian Holm (Lenny), Cyril Cusack (Sam), Terence Rigby (Joey), Michael Jayston (Teddy), Vivien Merchant (Ruth)
Available on DVD from Ind-DVD.

King Lear

Film version, shot in Jutland, based on 1962 stage production with Paul Scofield.

prod co: Athéna Films/Filmways/Laterna Films
stg: 6 November 1962, RST; *UK release*: 23 July 1971
stg dir: Peter Brook; *scn dir*: Peter Brook
w: Paul Scofield (Lear), Irene Worth (Goneril), Susan Engel (Regan), Cyril Cusack (Albany)
Available on DVD from UCA.

Landscape

Thirty-five-minute film shot on a sound stage using innovative Multivista filming process.

prod co: Angle Films/LMG Film Services
stg: 2 July 1969, Ald; *UK release*: 1976
wr: Harold Pinter; *stg dir*: Peter Hall; *scn dir*: Peter Hall
w: Peggy Ashcroft (Beth), David Waller (Duff)
Accessible via BFI Viewing Service.

A Midsummer Night's Dream

Feature film adaptation of Peter Hall's frequently revived production, shot on location at Compton Verney.

prod co: Filmways Pictures / Royal Shakespeare Enterprises Ltd
stg: 17 April 1962, RST; UK *release*: 30 January 1969
stg dir: Peter Hall; *scn dir*: Peter Hall
w: Ian Richardson (Oberon), Judi Dench (Titania), Paul Rogers (Bottom), Helen Mirren (Hermia), Diana Rigg (Helena), Michael Jayston (Demetrius), David Warner (Lysander)
Currently unavailable in the UK, although previously released on DVD.

A Midsummer Night's Dream

Adaptation filmed on a sound stage.

prod co: Arts Council England/Capitol Films/Channel Four Films/Edenwood/
Miramax
stg: 3 August 1994, RST; *UK release*: 29 November 1996
stg dir: Adrian Noble; *scn dir*: Adrian Noble

w: Lindsay Duncan (Hippolyta/Titania), Alex Jennings (Theseus/Oberon), Desmond Barrit (Bottom)
Available on DVD from Channel 4.

Miss Julie

Low-budget adaptation filmed with multiple cameras on a studio sound stage.

prod co: Tigon
stg: 27 October 1971, The Place; *UK release*: 10 November 1972
wr: August Strindberg; *stg dir*: Robin Phillips; *scn dir*: John Glenister
w: Helen Mirren (Julie), Donal McCann (Jean), Heather Canning (Kristin)
Available on DVD from SlamDunk Media.

The Persecution and Assassination of Marat as Performed by the Inmates of the Asylum of Charenton under the Direction of the Marquis de Sade (aka Marat/Sade)

Adaptation filmed on a studio sound stage.

prod co: Marat/Sade Productions
stg: 20 August 1964, Ald; *UK release*: 8 March 1967
wr: Peter Weiss; stg dir: Peter Brook; *scn dir*: Peter Brook
w: Patrick Magee (Sade), Ian Richardson (Marat), Glenda Jackson (Charlotte Corday)
Not currently available.

Richard III

Condensed stage production filmed on Shakespeare Memorial Theatre stage.

prod co: Co-operative Cinematograph Company
stg: 29 April 1886, SMT; *UK release*: 1911
stg dir: Frank Benson; *scn dir*: unknown
w: Frank Benson (Richard III), Constance Benson (Lady Anne)
Included on DVD/Blu-ray *Play On! Shakespeare in Silent Film* from BFI (2016).

Tell Me Lies

Film developed from the stage show *US*, shot on location in London.

prod co: Ronorus
stg: 13 October 1966, Ald; *UK release*: February 1968
wr: Dennis Cannan, Michael Kustow, Michael Scott, Peter Brook
stg dir: Peter Brook; *scn dir*: Peter Brook

w: Mark Jones (Mark), Pauline Munro (Pauline)
Available in restored version on DVD from French distributor Blaq Out.

Work is a Four Letter Word

Film developed from Henry Livings's play *Eh?*, shot on location in Birmingham and on a studio sound stage.

prod co: Cavalcade Films
stg: 29 October 1964, Ald; *UK release*: 7 June 1968
wr: Henry Livings, Jeremy Brooks; *stg dir*: Peter Hall; *scn dir*: Peter Hall
w: David Warner (Valentine), Cilla Black (Betty), Alan Howard (Reverend Mort)
Not currently available.

Selected television and 'event cinema' performances

All's Well That Ends Well

Multi-camera studio recording, and the first British television production of Shakespeare in colour.

stg 1 June 1967, RST; *bcst*: 3 June 1968, BBC Two
stg dir: John Barton; *scn dir*: Claude Whatham
w: Catherine Lacey (Countess of Roussillon), Sebastian Shaw (King of France), Ian Richardson (Bertram), Lynn Farleigh (Helena)
First half accessible via BBC Shakespeare Archive Resource; second half currently lost.

Antony and Cleopatra

Multi-camera studio recording.

stg: 15 August 1972, RST; *bcst*: 28 July 1974, ATV for ITV
stg dir: Trevor Nunn; *scn dir*: Jon Scoffield
w: Richard Johnson (Mark Antony), Janet Suzman (Cleopatra), Corin Redgrave (Octavius Caesar), Patrick Stewart (Enobarbus)
Available on DVD from Network.

As You Like It

Multi-camera studio recording.

stg: 4 July 1961, RST; *bcst*: 22 March 1963, BBC
stg dir: Michael Elliott; *scn dir*: Ronald Eyre
w: Vanessa Redgrave (Rosalind), Rosalind Knight (Celia), Patrick Allen (Orlando)
Accessible via BBC Shakespeare Archive Resource.

As You Like It

Multi-camera recording by Digital Theatre, made on the Courtyard Theatre stage.

stg: 28 April 2009, Courtyard; *UK release*: 2011
stg dir: Michael Boyd; *scn dir*: Robert Delamere
w: Katy Stephens (Rosalind), Mariah Gale (Celia), Jonjo O'Neill (Orlando)
Available online via Digital Theatre.

The Cherry Orchard

Studio recording of production of Chekhov's drama, premiered in Stratford and then transferred to Aldwych.

stg: 5 December 1961, RST; *bcst*: 13 April 1962, BBC
stg dir: Michel Saint-Denis; *scn dir*: Michael Elliott
w: Peggy Ashcroft (Madame Ranevsky), John Gielgud (Gaev), Judi Dench (Anya),
Dorothy Tutin (Varya), Ian Holm (Trofimov)
Accessible via BFI Viewing Service.

The Comedy of Errors

Multi-camera recording made at the Aldwych Theatre with an invited audience.

stg: 19 December 1962, Ald; *bcst*: 1 January 1964, BBC
stg dir: Clifford Williams; *scn dir*: Peter Duguid
w: Ian Richardson (Antipholus of Ephesus), Alec McCowen (Antipholus of
Syracuse), Diana Rigg (Adriana), Janet Suzman (Luciana), Donald Sinden (Solinus)
Accessible via BBC Shakespeare Archive Resource.

The Comedy of Errors

Recorded on the RST stage with multiple cameras.

stg: 29 September 1976, RST; *bcst*: 18 April 1978, ATV for ITV
stg dir: Trevor Nunn; *scn dir*: Philip Casson
w: Mike Gwilym (Antipholus of Ephesus), Roger Rees (Antipholus of Syracuse),
Judi Dench (Adriana), Francesca Annis (Luciana)
Available on DVD from Network.

The Comedy of Errors

Digital Theatre's multi-camera recording shot in a school of the RSC Young
People's production in association with Told by an Idiot.

stg: 7 August 2010, Courtyard; *UK release:* 2011
stg dir: Paul Hunter; *scn dir*: Robert Delamere

w: Richard Katz (Antipholus of Syracuse), Dyfan Dwyfor (Dromio of Ephesus), Jonjo O'Neill (Dromio of Syracuse)
Available online via Digital Theatre.

Cyrano de Bergerac

Multi-camera recording made at Limehouse Studios, produced by Stratford-Barbican Productions with Channel 4 and RKO.

stg: 27 July 1983, Bar; *bcst*: 15 September 1985, Channel 4
wr: Edmond Rostand, Anthony Burgess: *stg dir*: Terry Hands; *scn dir*: Michael Simpson
w: Derek Jacobi (Cyrano), Sinéad Cusack (Roxane)
Not currently available.

Days in the Trees

Multi-camera studio recording with location-shot inserts.

stg: 9 June 1966, Ald; *bcst*: 22 February 1967, BBC One
wr: Marguerite Duras; *stg dir*: John Schlesinger; *scn dir*: Waris Hussein
w: Peggy Ashcroft (The Mother), George Baker (The Son), Frances Cuka (Marcelle)
No known copy.

Every Good Boy Deserves Favour

Multi-camera recording made at Wembley Conference Centre.

stg: 1 July 1977, Royal Festival Hall; *bcst*: 9 May 1979, BBC Two
wr: Tom Stoppard, André Previn; *stg dir*: Trevor Nunn; *scn dir*: Roger Bamford, Trevor Nunn
w: Ian McKellen (Alexander), Ben Kingsley (Ivanov), Barbara Leigh-Hunt (Teacher)
Accessible via BFI Viewing Service.

Hamlet

A RSC/Illuminations co-production for BBC, WNET 13 and NHK, filmed on location.

stg: 5 August 2008, Courtyard; *bcst*: 26 December 2009, BBC Two
stg dir: Gregory Doran; *scn dir*: Gregory Doran
w: David Tennant (Hamlet), Patrick Stewart (Claudius), Penny Downie (Gertrude), Mariah Gale (Ophelia)
Available on DVD from BBC.

Henry IV, Part 1

Live studio broadcast of extracts in the *For the Children* strand.

stg: 3 April 1951, SMT; *bcst*: 19 August 1951, BBC
stg dir: Anthony Quayle; *scn dir*: Naomi Capon
w. Anthony Quayle (Falstaff), Richard Burton (Prince Hal), Alan Badel (Poins),
Robert Hardy (Traveller)
No known recording.

The Hollow Crown

Filmed version of John Barton's miscellany about English kings and queens,
produced by BHE for pay-TV distribution.

stg: 19 March 1961, Ald; *UK release:* 1965
stg dir: John Barton; *scn dir*: Charles Dubin
w: Max Adrian, John Barton, Paul Hardwick, Dorothy Tutin
Accessible via BFI Viewing Service.

I, Cinna (the Poet)

Film version of stage monologue developed for RSC Education and released online.

stg: 20 June 2012; *UK release:* 2 July 2012
wr: Tim Crouch; *stg dir*: Tim Crouch; *scn dir*: Robert McGroary
w: Jude Owusu (Cinna)
Available online via YouTube, https://youtu.be/6xQAr5le0UU (accessed
5 November 2018).

Julius Caesar

A RSC/Illuminations co-production for BBC and The Open University, filmed on
location and on stage in the RST.

stg: 28 May 2012, RST; *bcst*: 24 June 2012, BBC Four
stg dir: Gregory Doran; *scn dir*: Gregory Doran
w: Paterson Joseph (Brutus), Cyril Nri (Cassius), Jeffery Kissoon (Julius Caesar),
Adjoa Andoh (Portia)
Available on DVD from Illuminations.

King Lear

A RSC/Primetime co-production for More4, filmed with multiple cameras on a
sound stage.

stg: 31 May 2007, Courtyard; *bcst*: 25 December 2008, More4
stg dir: Trevor Nunn; *scn dir*: Trevor Nunn with Chris Hunt
w: Ian McKellen (Lear), Romola Garai (Cordelia), Frances Barber (Goneril),
Monica Dolan (Regan)
Available on DVD from Metrodome.

The Life and Adventures of Nicholas Nickleby

Nine-hour television version, filmed at The Old Vic as a Primetime production for Channel 4.

stg: 21 June 1980; *bcst*: 7–28 November 1982, Channel 4
wr: David Edgar after Charles Dickens; *stg dir*: Trevor Nunn, John Caird; *scn dir*: Jim Goddard
w: Roger Rees (Nicholas), David Threlfall (Smike), John Woodvine (Ralph), Bob Peck (Sir Mulberry Hawk)
Not currently unavailable, although previously released on DVD by Metrodome.

Macbeth

Multi-camera recording made at Teddington Studios.

stg: 9 September 1976, TOP; *bcst*: 4 January 1979, Thames for ITV
stg dir: Trevor Nunn; *scn dir*: Philip Casson
w: Ian McKellen (Macbeth), Judi Dench (Lady Macbeth)
Available on DVD from Fremantle.

Macbeth

Film version shoot on location at the Roundhouse, London.

stg: 16 November 1999, Swan; *bcst*: 1 January 2001, Channel 4
stg dir: Gregory Doran; *scn dir*: Gregory Doran
w: Antony Sher (Macbeth), Harriet Walter (Lady Macbeth)
Available on DVD from Illuminations.

The Merry Wives of Windsor

Live broadcast of the second of three acts from the Shakespeare Memorial Theatre.

stg: 12 July 1955, SMT; *bcst*: 2 October 1955, BBC
stg dir: Glen Byam Shaw; *scn dir*: Stephen Harrison
w: Anthony Quayle (Falstaff), Angela Baddeley (Mistress Page), Joyce Redman (Mistress Ford)
Accessible via BBC Shakespeare Archive Resource.

A Midsummer Night's Dream

Recording made for US television by Hubbell Robinson Productions of shortened version, with an introduction by Charles Laughton.

stg: 2 June 1959, SMT; *bcst*: Not broadcast
stg dir: Peter Hall; *scn dir*: Fletcher Markle

w: Charles Laughton (Bottom), Robert Hardy (Oberon), Mary Ure (Titania)
Available for viewing at Shakespeare Birthplace Trust, Stratford-upon-Avon.

Molière

Studio-shot version of Bulgakov's drama in an adaptation by Dusty Hughes, paired with the production of Molière's *Tartuffe*.

stg: 12 August, 1982, TOP; *bcst*: 27 October 1985, BBC Two
wr: Mikhail Bulgakov, Dusty Hughes; *stg dir*: Bill Alexander; *scn dir*: Richard Bramall
w: Antony Sher (Bulgakov/Molière), Derek Godfrey (King Louis XIV)
Accessible via BFI Viewing Service.

Ondine

As-live broadcast from Aldwych Theatre of the second of three acts with introduction by Peter Hall.

stg: 12 January 1961, Ald; *bcst*: 11 April 1961, BBC
wr: Jean Giraudoux; *stg dir*: Peter Hall; *scn dir*: John Vernon
w: Leslie Caron (Ondine), Richard Johnson (Hans), Gwen Ffrangcon-Davies (Queen Isolde)
No known recording.

Othello

Studio-shot version, produced with Primetime for BBC.

stg: 24 August 1989, TOP; *bcst*: 23 June 1990, BBC Two
stg dir: Trevor Nunn; *scn dir*: Trevor Nunn
w: Willard White (Othello), Ian McKellen (Iago), Imogen Stubbs (Desdemona), Zoë Wanamaker (Emilia)
Available on DVD from Metrodome.

Piaf

As-live recording of Pam Gems's musical drama, made at the Plymouth Theatre on Broadway.

stg: 11 October 1978, TOP; *USA bcst*: 9 June 1982
stg dir: Howard Davies; *scn dir*: Gary Halvorson
w: Jane Lapotaire (Edith Piaf), Zoë Wanamaker (Toine), David Leary (Manager, Emcee), Robert Christian (Marcel)
Not currently available.

RSC Live from Stratford-upon-Avon

Live cinema broadcasts of Shakespeare productions from RST, intended to result in a full cycle of all the First Folio plays by 2022.

cinema broadcasts: from 13 November 2013, continuing
stg dir: Gregory Doran, Simon Godwin, Christopher Luscombe, Iqbal Khan, Polly Findlay, Melly Still, Angus Jackson, Blanche McIntyre, Erica Whyman, Fiona Laird (to end 2018)
scn dir: Robin Lough, Dewi Humphreys, Matt Woodward, Bridget Caldwell (to end 2018)
Available on DVD from Opus Arte and online via Digital Theatre.

Shakespeare Live! From the RSC

Two-hour live broadcast from RST for BBC Two and event cinema presentation, co-produced by RSC and BBC.

stg and first broadcast: 23 April 2016, RST
wr: Gregory Doran and others; *stg dir*: Gregory Doran; *scn dir*: Bridget Caldwell
w: Judi Dench, Paapa Essiedu, Ian McKellen, Roger Allam, Harriet Walter and others
Available on DVD from BBC.

Tartuffe

Studio-shot version of Molière's drama, paired with the production of Bulgakov's *Molière*.

stg: 28 July 1983, The Pit; *bcst*: 3 November 1985, BBC Two
stg dir: Bill Alexander; *scn dir*: Tom Kingdon
w: Antony Sher (Tartuffe), Alison Steadman (Elmire)
Accessible via BFI Viewing Service.

Three Sisters

Studio recording of touring production of Anton Chekhov's drama.

stg: 28 July 1978, tour; *bcst*: 29 December 1981, Thames for ITV
stg dir: Trevor Nunn; *scn dir*: Trevor Nunn
w: Susanne Bertish (Masha), Janet Dale (Olga), Emily Richard (Irina)
Not currently available.

Volpone

Multi-camera as-live recording of Ben Jonson's comedy made in the Swan Theatre.

stg: 3 July 2015, Swan; *bcst*: unreleased
stg dir: Trevor Nunn; *scn dir*: Richard Lynn
w: Henry Goodman (Volpone), Matthew Kelly (Corvino)
Not currently available.

The Wars of the Roses: Henry VI, Edward IV, Richard III

Three recordings of the trilogy created by Peter Hall and John Barton made by BBC
Television on the stage of the RST.

stg: 20 August 1963, RST; *bcst*: 8, 15, 22 April 1965, BBC One
stg dir: Peter Hall, John Barton; *scn dir*: Michael Hayes, Robin Midgley
w: David Warner (Henry VI), Peggy Ashcroft (Queen Margaret), William Squire (Suffolk), Ian Holm (Gloucester), Janet Suzman (Joan la Pucelle, Lady Anne)
Available on DVD from Illuminations.

The Winter's Tale

As-live recording made by Heritage Theatre in the Barbican Theatre.

stg: 25 March 1999, Bar; *UK DVD release:* 2005
stg dir: Gregory Doran; *scn dir*: Robin Lough
w: Antony Sher (Leontes), Alexandra Gilbreath (Hermione), Estelle Kohler (Perdita)
Available on DVD from Heritage Theatre.

Selected documentaries

Arena Theatre: Hands Off the Classics

A film essay about the legitimacy (or not) of radical contemporary interpretations of classic plays, with contributions from, among others, John Barton and Terry Hands and RSC performance extracts featuring Alan Howard.

bcst: 9 November 1977 *scn dir*: Dennis Marks
Accessible via BBC Shakespeare Archive Resource.

Benefit of the Doubt

Documentary about the RSC's collectively authored engagement with the Vietnam War, mounted at the Aldwych Theatre in the summer of 1966 by director Peter Brook. Includes extensive performance footage shot on stage.

UK release: 1967 *scn dir*: Peter Whitehead
Available on DVD *Peter Whitehead and the Sixties* from BFI Publishing.

The Best Bottoms in the Land

Nine regional half-hour documentaries about the amateur companies involved in Erica Whyman's production of *A Midsummer Night's Dream: A Play for the Nation* in the summer of 2016.

bcst: 20 May 2016, regional opt-outs, BBC One *scn dir*: various
Accessible via BFI Viewing Service.

The Dillen

Half-hour documentary about Barry Kyle's 1983 promenade production about George Hewins, a working man born in Stratford-upon-Avon 1879, centred on The Other Place but also taking place in the town's streets.

bcst: 13 January 1984, BBC Midlands regional opt-out slot *scn dir*: Mike Dornan
Accessible via BFI Viewing Service.

England's Shakespeare

Travelogue produced by the London, Midland and Scottish Railway encouraging tourists to visit Stratford-upon-Avon and the surrounding area, with brief appearances by actors from the Shakespeare Memorial Theatre together with a visit to the theatre itself.

UK release: 1939 *scn dir*: unknown
Available online via BFI Player, https://player.bfi.org.uk/free/film/watch-englands-shakespeare-1939-online (accessed 8 November 2018).

Monitor: The Devils of Loudun

Film report for *Monitor*, shot in Loudun, France, with an extended interview with playwright John Whiting and brief studio performance extracts.

bcst: 26 February 1961, BBC *scn dir*: Nancy Thomas
Accessible via BFI Viewing Service.

Omnibus: Shakespeare's Island

Profile of the company as a new production of *The Tempest* is being mounted, with contributions, among others, from John Barton and Trevor Nunn.

bcst: 23 April 1971, BBC Two *scn dir*: Lorna Pegram
Accessible via BBC Shakespeare Archive Resource.

Omnibus: After the Dream

Profile of Peter Brook after the opening of his Aldwych production of *Antony and Cleopatra* and as he began to develop the Centre for Theatre Research in Paris.

bcst: 30 November 1978, BBC Two *scn dir*: Dennis Marks
Accessible via BFI Viewing Service.

Omnibus: Living Shakespeare – a Year with the RSC

Study of the company in its thirtieth season, as Adrian Noble was taking over as artistic director.

bcst: 6 December 1991, BBC One *scn dir*: David Evans
Accessible via BFI Viewing Service.

Playing Shakespeare

Nine-episode studio-shot masterclass about Shakespeare's language, written and presented by John Barton, with numerous actors including David Suchet, Lisa Harrow, Alan Howard, Judi Dench, Patrick Stewart, Ian McKellen and Peggy Ashcroft.

bcst: from 29 July 1984, Channel 4 *scn dir*: John Carlaw
Available on DVD from Acorn Media.

Review: Peter Brook

Interview with Brook by James Mossman tied to the director's radical staging of *A Midsummer Night's Dream*, with thirteen minutes of filmed extracts from the production.

bcst: 1 January 1971, BBC Two *scn dir*: David Heycock
Accessible as *Throwing Out the Cobwebs* via BBC Shakespeare Archive Resource.

The South Bank Show: The Player King

Half-hour profile of Alan Howard, shot during the 1977 season at Stratford, including performance extracts from the History plays and *Coriolanus*.

bcst: 28 January 1978, LWT for ITV *scn dir*: Andrew Snell
Not currently available.

The South Bank Show: The RSC on Tour

Documentary following the company's 1978 tour of *Twelfth Night* and *Three Sisters* to regional venues.

bcst: 4 February 1979, LWT for ITV *scn dir*: Peter Walker
Not currently available.

The South Bank Show: Word of Mouth

Two-part masterclass about performing Shakespeare's language, recorded with multiple cameras in LWT's studio.

bcst: 9 and 16 December 1979, LWT for ITV *scn dir*: Peter Walker
Not currently available.

The South Bank Show: Nickleby & Co.

Feature-length filmed documentary following the making of the production, with substantial performance extracts filmed at the Aldwych.

bcst: 2 August 1981, LWT for ITV *scn dir*: Andrew Snell
Not currently available.

The South Bank Show: The Royal Shakespeare Company

The final edition of the flagship arts strand on ITV explores the company's programme of work inspired by Russia and the former Soviet Union under artistic director Michael Boyd.

bcst: 27 December 2009, LWT for ITV *scn dir*: Naomi Wright
Not currently available.

Sunday Night: How to Stop Worrying and Love the Theatre

Documentary feature about *Theatregoround*, recorded on location as an outside broadcast, with extensive performance extracts.

bcst: 20 February 1966, BBC One *scn dir*: Peter Montagnon
Accessible via BBC Shakespeare Archive Resource.

Tempo Profile: Harold Pinter

Extracts from original Aldwych production of *The Homecoming*, in a multi-camera studio recording, are included in a film profile of Harold Pinter.

bcst: 3 October 1965, ABC for ITV *scn dir*: James Goddard
Available on DVD *Tempo – Volume 1* from Network.

BIBLIOGRAPHY

Aebischer, Pascale. 'Marlowe in the Movies'. In *Christopher Marlowe in Context*, edited by Emily C. Bartels and Emma Smith, 316–24. Cambridge: Cambridge University Press, 2013.

Aebischer, Pascale. *Screening Early Modern Drama: Beyond Shakespeare*. Cambridge: Cambridge University Press, 2013.

Aebischer, Pascale. 'South Bank Shakespeare Goes Global: Broadcasting from Shakespeare's Globe and the National Theatre'. In *Shakespeare and the 'Live' Theatre Broadcast Experience*, edited by Pascale Aebischer, Susanne Greenhalgh and Laurie E. Osborne, 113–32. London: Bloomsbury, 2018.

Aebischer, Pascale and Susanne Greenhalgh. 'Introduction'. In *Shakespeare and the 'Live' Theatre Broadcast Experience*, edited by Pascale Aebischer, Susanne Greenhalgh and Laurie E. Osborne, 1–18. London: Bloomsbury, 2018.

Aebischer, Pascale, Susanne Greenhalgh and Laurie E. Osborne, eds. *Shakespeare and the 'Live' Theatre Broadcast Experience*. London: Bloomsbury, 2018.

Arts Council England. *Great Art and Culture for Everyone: 10-Year Strategic Framework, 2010–2020*. Manchester: Arts Council England, 2013.

Baldwin, Stanley. *On England, and Other Addresses*. London: Philip Allan, 1926.

Barker, Martin. *Live to Your Local Cinema: The Remarkable Rise of Livecasting*. Basingstoke: Palgrave Macmillan, 2013.

Barlow, Ed. 'The Best Bottoms in the Land'. [Blog] *About the BBC*, 20 May 2016. Available online: http://www.bbc.co.uk/blogs/aboutthebbc/entries/4b941a2a-44ac-4994-a9ee-d59773737ee0 (accessed 11 August 2018).

Barnes, Jennifer. '"Posterity is dispossessed": Laurence Olivier's *Macbeth* Manuscripts in 1958 and 2012'. *Shakespeare Bulletin*, 30 no. 3 (Fall 2012), 263–98.

Barton, John in collaboration with Peter Hall. *The Wars of the Roses*. London: British Broadcasting Corporation, 1970.

Bay-Cheng, Sarah. 'Theatre Squared: Theatre History in the Age of Media'. *Theatre Topics*, 17 no. 1 (March 2007), 37–50.

BBC. 'BBC Shakespeare Archive Resource'. Available online: http://shakespeare.ch.bbc.co.uk/ (accessed 15 September 2018).

BBC. 'Hamlet'. Available online: http://www.bbc.co.uk/hamlet/archive.shtml (accessed 18 October 2018).

BBC. 'Shakespeare 2016 Lives'. Available online: https://www.bbc.co.uk/events/ehw2mb/live/c96v4f (accessed 11 August 2018).

BBC. '"To be or not to be?" with Benedict Cumberbatch & Prince Charles – Shakespeare Live! From the RSC'. [Video] YouTube, 23 April 2016. Available online: https://www.youtube.com/watch?v=kEs8rK5Cqt8 (accessed 11 August 2018).

BBC Archive. '1951: Newsreel: Stratford Festival Season'. [Video] Facebook, 29
    March 2018. Available online: https://www.facebook.com/BBCArchive/videos/
    vb.100865096953196/547463355626699/?type=2&theater (accessed 17
    October 2018).
Beauman, Sally. *The Royal Shakespeare Company: A History of Ten Decades*.
    Oxford: Oxford University Press, 1982.
Behr, Edward. *The Complete Book of Les Misérables*. New York: Arcade
    Publishing, 1993.
Benson, Raymond. 'Remember ... the American Film Theatre'. *CinemaRetro*,
    16 April 2009. Available online: http://www.cinemaretro.com/index.php?/
    archives/3150-REMEMBER...THE-AMERICAN-FILM-THEATRE!.html
    (accessed 28 January 2018).
Benton, Margaret. 'Capturing Performance at London's Theatre Museum'. *Museum
    International*, 49 no. 2 (1977), 25–31.
BFI Player. 'Around the Town, No.110', [Video] 1922. Available online: https://
    player.bfi.org.uk/free/film/watch-around-the-town-no110-1922-online (accessed
    17 October 2018).
BFI Player. 'British and Best', [Video] 1928. Available online: https://player.bfi.org.
    uk/free/film/watch-british-and-best-1928-online (accessed 17 October 2018).
BFI Player. 'England's Shakespeare', [Video] 1939. Available online: https://player.
    bfi.org.uk/free/film/watch-englands-shakespeare-1939-online (accessed 17
    October 2018).
BFI Player. 'Shakespeare Land', [Video] 1910. Available online: https://player.bfi.
    org.uk/free/film/watch-shakespeare-land-1910-online (accessed 17 October
    2018).
BFI Player. 'Shakespeare Memorial Theatre', [Video] 1926. Available online: https://
    player.bfi.org.uk/free/film/watch-shakespeare-memorial-theatre-1926-online
    (accessed 17 October 2018).
BFI Player. 'Shakespeare's Country', [Video] 1926. Available online: https://player.
    bfi.org.uk/free/film/watch-shakespeares-country-1926-online (accessed 17
    October 2018).
BFI Player. 'Stratford-on-Avon', [Video] 1925. Available online: https://player.bfi.
    org.uk/free/film/watch-stratford-on-avon-1925-online (accessed 17 October
    2018).
BHE (British Home Entertainment). 'Welcome to British Home Entertainment'.
    Available online: http://www.britishhomeentertainment.co.uk/ (accessed 22
    April 2017).
Billington, Michael. *Harold Pinter*, rev edn. London: Faber & Faber, 2007.
Billington, Michael. *Peggy Ashcroft*. London: John Murray, 1988.
Billington, Michael. *State of the Nation: British Theatre from 1945*. London: Faber
    & Faber, 2009.
Birkett, Michael and Roger Manvell. '*King Lear*: From Page to Screen'. *Journal of
    the Society of Film and Television Arts*, 37 (Autumn 1969), 15–21.
Boddy, William. *Fifties Television: The Industry and its Critics*. Urbana: University
    of Illinois Press, 1993.
Bonner, Paul with Lesley Aston. *Independent Television in Britain: New
    Developments in Independent Television 1981–92: Channel 4, TV-am, Cable
    and Satellite*. Basingstoke: Palgrave Macmillan, 2003.

Bordwell, David, Kristin Thompson and Janet Staiger. *The Classical Hollywood Cinema: Film Style and Mode of Production to 1960*. London: Routledge, 1988.

Briggs, Asa. *The History of Broadcasting in the United Kingdom,* Volume 5: *Competition*. Oxford: Oxford University Press, 1995.

British Pathé. 'For New Shakespeare Memorial Theatre 1928' [Video]. Available online: https://www.britishpathe.com/video/for-new-shakespeare-memorialtheatre (accessed 17 October 2018).

British Library. 'Help: Listening and Viewing Service'. Available online: https://www.bl.uk/reshelp/inrrooms/stp/sound/listening.html (accessed 29 January 2017).

British Pathé. 'Shakespeare's Birthday 1938' [Video]. Available online: https://www.britishpathe.com/video/shakespeares-birthday-2 (accessed 17 October 2018).

British Pathé. '"Sweetest Shakespeare – Fancy's Child" 1932' [Video]. Available online: https://www.britishpathe.com/video/sweetest-shakespeare-fancys-child/ (accessed 17 October 2018).

Broadcasting Act 1981. London: Her Majesty's Stationery Office, 1981.

Brock, Susan and Sylvia Morris. '"Enchanted ground": Celebrating Shakespeare's Birthday in Stratford-upon-Avon'. In *Shakespeare's Jubilees, 1769–2014*, edited by Christa Jansohn and Dieter Mehl, 31–56. Zurich: Lit Verlag, 2015.

Brook, Peter. 'Discussion'. *Cahiers théâtre Louvain*, no. 46 (1981), 41–6.

Brook, Peter. *The Quality of Mercy: Reflections on Shakespeare*. London: Nick Hern Books, 2013.

Brook, Peter. *The Shifting Point: Forty Years of Theatrical Exploration, 1946–87*. London: Methuen Drama, 1989.

Brook, Peter. *Threads of Time*. London: Methuen, 1998.

Brook, Peter, and Others. *The Book of US*. London: Calder and Boyars, 1968.

Brooke, Michael. '*BBC Television Shakespeare, The* (1978–85)'. *BFI screenonline*. Available online: http://www.screenonline.org.uk/tv/id/459382/index.html (accessed 12 June 2018).

Brooke, Michael. '*Henry IV* On Screen'. *BFI screenonline*. Available online: http://www.screenonline.org.uk/tv/id/1048622 (accessed 27 January 2017).

Brooke, Michael. '*Romeo and Juliet* (1978)'. *BFI screenonline*. Available online: http://www.screenonline.org.uk/tv/id/526875/index.html (accessed 22 January 2018).

Buchanan, Judith. 'Collaborating with the Dead: Revivifying Frank Benson's *Richard III*'. Available online: https://www.york.ac.uk/digital-editions/collaborating-with-the-dead/ (accessed 15 September 2018).

Buchanan, Judith. '"Look here, upon this picture": Theatrofilm, the Wooster Group *Hamlet* and the film industry'. In *Shakespeare in Ten Acts*, edited by Gordon McMullan and Zoe Wilcox, 197–214. London: British Library, 2016.

Buchanan, Judith. '*Richard III* DVD commentary', [Audio commentary] *Play On: Shakespeare in Silent Film* [DVD]. London: BFI Publishing, 2016.

Buchanan, Judith. *Shakespeare on Film*. Harlow: Pearson Education, 2005.

Buchanan, Judith. *Shakespeare on Silent Film: An Excellent Dumb Discourse*. Cambridge: Cambridge University Press, 2009.

BUFVC (British Universities and Colleges Film and Video Council). '*Monitor* (12/04/1959)', Shakespeare Database. Available online: http://bufvc.ac.uk/shakespeare/index.php/title/av36829 (accessed 11 February 2017).

BUFVC (British Universities and Colleges Film and Video Council). 'Shakespeare', [Database]. Available online: http://bufvc.ac.uk/shakespeare/ (accessed 15 December 2016).

BUFVC (British Universities and Colleges Film and Video Council). 'The Two Gentlemen of Verona', Shakespeare Database. Available online: http://bufvc. ac.uk/shakespeare/index.php/title/av37272 (accessed 12 September 2018).

Bulman, James C. 'The BBC Shakespeare and "house style"'. *Shakespeare Quarterly*, 35 no. 5 (1984), 571–81.

Butler, Jeremy. *Television Style*. London: Routledge, 2010.

Callenbach, Ernest. '*Marat/Sade* by Peter Brook'. *Film Quarterly*, 20 no. 4 (Summer 1967), 54–57.

Callow, Simon. *Charles Laughton: A Difficult Actor*. London: Vintage, 2012.

Caughie, John. *Television Drama: Realism, Modernism, and British Culture*. Oxford: Oxford University Press, 2000.

Chambers, Colin. *Inside the Royal Shakespeare Company: Creativity and the Institution*. London: Routledge, 2004.

Chambers, Colin. *Other Spaces: New Theatre and the RSC*. London: Eyre Methuen/TQ Publications, 1980.

Chilcott, Robert. 'The Films of Peter Whitehead'. *Vertigo*, 8 (March 2007). Available online: https://www.closeupfilmcentre.com/vertigo_magazine/issue-8-march-2007/the-films-of-peter-whitehead/ (accessed 12 May 2018).

Clarke, Chris. 'Method Acting'. [Video] BBC One, 18 May 2016. Available online: https://www.bbc.co.uk/programmes/p03vjpff (accessed 11 August 2018).

Cornford, Tom. 'The English Theatre Studios of Michael Chekhov and Michel Saint-Denis, 1935–1965'. PhD thesis, University of Warwick, 2012.

Craig, Sandy, ed. *Dreams and Deconstructions: Alternative Theatre in Britain*. Ambergate: Amber Lane Press, 1980.

Crowl, Samuel. 'A World Elsewhere: The Roman Plays on Film and Television'. In *Shakespeare and the Moving Image: The Plays on Film and Television*, edited by Anthony Davies and Stanley Wells. Cambridge: Cambridge University Press, 1994.

Decca Records, 'Shakespeare the Complete Works'. Available online: http://decca. com/shakespeare/ (accessed 29 January 2017).

Donaldson, Peter S. '"Two of Both Kinds": Modernism and Patriarchy in Peter Hall's *A Midsummer Night's Dream*'. In *The Reel Shakespeare: Alternative Cinema and Theory*, edited by Lisa S. Starks and Courtney Lehmann, 43–58. Madison, NJ: Fairleigh Dickinson University Press, 2002.

Doran, Gregory. 'Think When We Talk of Horses … '. In *Shakespeare Survey no. 70*, edited by Peter Holland, 1–9. Cambridge: Cambridge University Press, 2017.

Dukore, Bernard F. 'Pinter's Revised *Homecoming*', *Educational Theatre Journal*, 30 no. 2 (May 1978), 151–56.

Durgnat, Raymond. *A Mirror for England*. London: Faber & Faber, 1970.

Eaton, Michael. *Our Friends in the North*. London: BFI Publishing, 2005.

Elsaesser, Thomas with Adam Barker, eds. *Early Cinema: Space, Frame, Narrative*. London: British Film Institute, 1990.

Entwistle, George. '*Hamlet* for the Cross-platform Age'. [Blog] *About the BBC*, 16 December 2009. Available online: http://www.bbc.co.uk/blogs/aboutthebbc/2009/12/hamlet-for-the-crossplatform-a.shtml (accessed 11 August 2018).

Erenstein, Robert L., ed. *Theatre and Television*. Amsterdam: International Theatre Bookshop, 1988.

Evans, Jill. 'Recording Theatre for Education'. *Viewfinder*, no. 70 (March 2008), 17–19.

Films Media Group. 'Royal Shakespeare Company: Great Performances'. Available online: https://www.films.com/id/8214 (accessed 17 May 2018).

Fott, Galen. 'The RSC's *Nicholas Nickleby*, from Stage to Screen'. [Blog] *Blogfott*. Available online: http://blogfott.blogspot.co.uk/2016/01/the-rscs-nicholas-nickleby-from-stage.html (accessed 11 January 2018).

Gale, Steven H. *Encyclopaedia of British Humorists: From Geoffrey Chaucer to John Cleese*. London: Taylor & Francis, 1996.

Galey, Alan. *The Shakespearean Archive: Experiments in New Media from the Renaissance to Postmodernity*. Cambridge: Cambridge University Press, 2014.

Goodwin, John, ed. *Peter Hall's Diaries: The Story of a Dramatic Battle*. London: Hamish Hamilton, 1983.

Gow, Gordon. 'In Search of a Revolution'. *Films and Filming*, September 1969, 40–46.

Gray, Jonathan. *Show Sold Separately: Promos, Spoilers and Other Media Paratexts*. New York: NYU Press, 2010.

Greenhalgh, Susanne. '"Alas poor country!" Documenting the Politics of Performance in Two British Television *Macbeths* since the 1980s'. In *Remaking Shakespeare: Performance across Media, Genres and Cultures*, edited by Pascale Aebischer, Edward J. Esche and Nigel Wheale, 93–114. Basingstoke: Palgrave Macmillan, 2003.

Greenhalgh, Susanne, ed. 'Guest Editor's Introduction, Special Performance Reviews Section: Live Cinema Relays of Shakespearean Performance'. *Shakespeare Bulletin*, 32 no. 2 (2014), 255–78.

Greenhalgh, Susanne. 'The Remains of the Stage'. In *Shakespeare and the 'Live' Theatre Broadcast Experience*, edited by Pascale Aebischer, Susanne Greenhalgh and Laurie E. Osborne, 19–40. London: Bloomsbury, 2018.

Greenhalgh, Susanne. 'Shakespeare and Radio'. In *The Edinburgh Companion to Shakespeare and the Arts*, edited by Mark Thornton Burnett, Adrian Streete and Ramona Wray, 541–47. Edinburgh: Edinburgh University Press, 2011.

Grieveson, Lee and Peter Krämer, eds. *The Silent Cinema Reader*. London: Routledge, 2004.

Gunning, Tom. *D. W. Griffith and the Origins of American Narrative Film*. Champaign: University of Illinois Press, 1994.

Gunning, Tom. 'The Intertexuality of Early Cinema'. In *A Companion to Literature and Film*, edited by Robert Stam and Alessandra Raengo, 127–43. Oxford: Blackwell, 2004.

Hall, Peter. 'Interview about *The Homecoming*', [Film] *The American Film Theatre Collection: The Homecoming* [DVD]. Ind-DVD, 2004.

Hall, Peter. *Making an Exhibition of Myself*, 2nd edition. London: Oberon Books, 2000.

Hewison, Robert, John Holden and Samuel Jones. *All Together: A Creative Approach to Organisational Change*. London: Demos, 2016. Available online: http://creative-blueprint.co.uk/library/item/all-together-a-creative-approach-to-organisational-change (accessed 18 August 2018).

Hindle, Maurice. *Shakespeare on Film*, 2nd edition. London: Palgrave, 2017.

Hodgdon, Barbara. 'Photography, Theater, Mnemonics; or, Thirteen Ways of Looking at a Still'. In *Theorizing Practice: Redefining Theatre History*, edited by W.B. Worthen with Peter Holland, 88–119. Basingstoke: Palgrave Macmillan, 2003.

Hodgdon, Barbara. 'The Visual Record: The Case of *Hamlet*'. In *The Cambridge Companion to Theatre History*, edited by David Wiles and Christine Dymkowski, 246–66. Cambridge: Cambridge University Press, 2014.

Holderness, Graham. 'Radical Potentiality and Institutional Closure: Shakespeare in Film and Television'. In *Political Shakespeare: New Essays in Cultural Materialism*, edited by Jonathan Dollimore and Alan Sinfield, 182–201. Manchester: Manchester University Press, 1985.

Holland, Peter. '"The revolution of the times": Peter Brook's *A Midsummer Night's Dream*, 1970'. In *Shakespeare in Ten Acts*, edited by Gordon McMullan and Zoe Wilcox, 161–79. London: British Library, 2016.

Hunt, Albert and Geoffrey Reeves. *Peter Brook*. Cambridge: Cambridge University Press, 1995.

Intel. '400 years in the Making – Intel x The RSC | Experience Amazing'. [Video] YouTube, 28 November 2016. Available online: https://youtu.be/1GH1KNNvv4w (accessed 18 October 2018).

Irish, Tracy with Paul Prescott and Erin Sullivan. 'Performing Shakespeare in the Olympic Year: Interviews with Three Practitioners'. In *Shakespeare on the Global Stage: Performance and Festivity in the Olympic Year*, edited by Paul Prescott and Erin Sullivan, 43–78. London: Bloomsbury, 2015.

Isaacs, Jeremy. *Storm Over 4: A Personal Account*. London: Weidenfeld and Nicolson, 1989.

Jackson, Russell. 'Staging and Storytelling, Theatre and Film: *Richard III* at Stratford, 1910'. *New Theatre Quarterly*, 16 no. 2 (2000), 107–21.

Jorgens, Jack. 'The BBC-TV Shakespeare Series'. *Shakespeare Quarterly*, 30 no. 3 (Summer 1979), 411–15.

Jorgens, Jack. *Shakespeare on Film*. Bloomington: Indiana University Press, 1977.

Joseph, Paterson. *Julius Caesar and Me*. London: Bloomsbury Methuen Drama, 2018.

Kael, Pauline. *I Lost It at the Movies: Film Writings, 1954–65*. London: Jonathan Cape, 1966.

Keenan, Siobhan. 'The Royal Shakespeare Company at 50'. *Shakespeare*, 8 no. 2 (June 2012), 195–201.

King, Timothy. 'Streaming from Stage to Screen: Its Place in the Cultural Marketplace and the Implication for UK Arts Policy'. *International Journal of Cultural Policy*, 24 no. 2 (2018), 220–35.

Kirwan, Peter. '*The Hollow Crown*: An Introductory Essay'. *Drama Online*, 2017. doi:10.5040/9781474208659.

Kustow, Michael. *Peter Brook: A Biography*. London: Bloomsbury, 2005.

Lanier, Douglas. *Shakespeare and Modern Popular Culture*. Oxford: Oxford University Press, 2002.

Laroque, François. 'Interview Given by Trevor Nunn, Director of the Film *Twelfth Night*'. *Cahiers Elisabéthains*, 52 (October 1997), 89–96.

Lawson, Stephen R. 'The Old Vic to Vincennes: Interviews with Michael Kustow and Peter Brook'. *Theatre*, 7 no. 1 (1975), 81.

Livings, Henry. *Plays One*. London: Oberon Books, 2001.

Low, Rachel. *The History of the British Film 1906–1914*. London: George Allen & Unwin, [1948] 1973.

McDougal, Dennis. *The Last Mogul: Lew Wasserman, MCA and the Hidden History of Hollywood*. Boston, MA: De Capo Press, 2001.

McVay, Gordon. 'Peggy Ashcroft and Chekhov'. In *Chekhov on the British Stage*, edited by Patrick Miles, 78–100. Cambridge: Cambridge University Press, 1993.

Malin, Peter. '"Entertaining strangers": 50 Years of Shakespeare's Contemporaries at the Royal Shakespeare Company'. *Shakespeare*, 8 no. 2 (2012), 219–41.

Manvell, Roger. 'On the Dank and Dirty Ground'. *Journal of the Society of Film and Television Arts*, no. 35 (Autumn 1969), 11–15.

May, Tom. 'An Ideology in Red, White and Blue in Tooth and Claw: David Edgar's *Destiny* (1978) – Part 1 of 3'. *British Television Drama*, 31 May 2017. Available online: http://www.britishtelevisiondrama.org.uk/?p=7040 (accessed 20 June 2018).

Melzer, Annabelle. '"Best Betrayal": The Documentation of Performance on Video and Film – Part 1'. *New Theatre Quarterly*, 11 no. 42 (May 1995), 147–57.

Melzer, Annabelle. '"Best Betrayal": The Documentation of Performance on Video and Film – Part 2'. *New Theatre Quarterly*, 11 no. 43 (August 1995), 259–76.

Morra, Irene. 'History Play: People, Pageant and the New Shakespearean Age'. In *The New Elizabethan Age: Culture, Society and National Identity after World War II*, edited by Irene Morra and Rob Gossedge, 308–36. London: I.B.Tauris, 2016.

Mullin, Michael. 'Peter Hall's *Midsummer Night's Dream* on Film'. *Educational Theatre Journal*, 27 no. 4 (December 1975), 529–34.

Mullin, Michael. 'Stage and Screen: The Trevor Nunn *Macbeth*'. *Shakespeare Quarterly*, 38 no. 3 (Autumn 1987), 350–59.

Murphy, Robert. *Sixties British Cinema*. London: BFI Publishing, 1992.

Museum of Broadcast Communication, The. 'Encyclopedia of Television – Hubbell Robinson'. Available online: http://www.museum.tv/eotv/robinsonhub.htm (accessed 11 February 2017).

Ochiogrosso, Frank. 'Cinematic Oxymoron in Peter Hall's *A Midsummer Night's Dream*'. *Literature/Film Quarterly*, 11 no. 3 (1983), 174–78.

O'Connor, Garry. *Paul Scofield: The Biography*. London: Sidgwick & Jackson, 2002.

O'Connor, Marion. *William Poel and the Elizabethan Stage Society*. Cambridge: Chadwyck-Healey, 1987.

Panos, Leah. 'Stylised Worlds: Colour Separation Overlay in BBC Television Plays of the 1970s'. *Critical Studies in Television*, 8 no. 3 (Autumn 2013), 1–17.

Pearson, Roberta E. 'Shakespeare's Country: The National Poet, English Identity and British Silent Cinema'. In *Young and Innocent?: The Cinema in Britain, 1896–1930*, edited by Andrew Higson, 176–90. Exeter: University of Exeter Press, 2002.

Poole, Mike and John Wyver. *Powerplays: Trevor Griffiths in Television*. London: BFI Publishing, 1984.

Popple, Simon and Joe Kember. *Early Cinema: From Factory Gate to Dream Factory*. London: Wallflower, 2004.

Potter, Jeremy. *Independent Television in Britain*, Volume 3: *Politics and Control, 1968–80*. London: Macmillan, 1989.

Prentice, Catherine and Helena Leongamornlert. 'The RSC Goes Walkabout: *The Dillen* in Stratford, 1983'. *New Theatre Quarterly*, 69 (February 2002), 47–58.

Prescott, Paul. 'Sam Wanamaker'. In *Great Shakespeareans, Volume 15*, edited by Cary M. Mazer, 151–210. London: Continuum, 2013.

Priestley, Clive. *Financial Scrutiny of the Royal Shakespeare Company: Report to the Earl of Gowrie, Minister for the Arts.* London: Her Majesty's Stationery Office, 1983. Available online: https://archive.org/details/op1278121-1001 (accessed 12 September 2018).

Quayle, Anthony. 'Foreword'. In *Shakespeare's Histories at Stratford 1951*, edited by John Dover Wilson and Thomas C. Worsley, vii–x. London: Max Reinhardt, 1952.

Quinn, Michael. 'Remastered: The Legendary Argo Shakespeare Recordings', *The Stage*, 27 January 2017. Available online: https://www.thestage.co.uk/features/2017/remastered-the-legendary-argo-shakespeare-recordings/ (accessed 27 January 2017).

Reason, Matthew. *Documentation, Disappearance and the Representation of Live Performance.* Basingstoke: Palgrave Macmillan, 2006.

Rosenthal, Daniel. *The National Theatre Story.* London: Oberon Books, 2013.

Royal Shakespeare Company. 'FEATURE TRAILER: *King Lear* – Royal Shakespeare Company (RSC)'. [Video] YouTube, 12 February 2010. Available online: https://youtu.be/uvA_gUDGKik (accessed 18 February 2018).

Royal Shakespeare Company, '*I, Cinna (The Poet)* Full-length Film | 2012 | Royal Shakespeare Company'. [Video] YouTube, 11 April 2013. Available online: https://www.youtube.com/watch?v=6xQAr5le0UU (accessed 20 September 2018).

Royal Shakespeare Company. 'Meet the Bottoms | A Midsummer Night's Dream: A Play for the Nation | Royal Shakespeare Company'. [Video] YouTube, 24 June 2015. Available online: https://youtube/FLioHikLF3M (accessed 23 April 2018).

Royal Shakespeare Company. 'Productions to Be Broadcast Live from Stratford-upon-Avon'. [Press Release] 28 May 2013. Available online: http://www.rsc.org.uk/about-us/press/releases/live-broadcast-from-stratford-upon-avon.aspx (accessed 21 December 2014).

Royal Shakespeare Company, '*Richard II* Stage Footage | Act IV, Scene 1 – The Deposition Scene | 2013 | Royal Shakespeare Company'. [Video], Youtube, 21 November 2013. Available online: https://youTube/6UHaMJEE0MM (accessed 20 November 2017).

Royal Shakespeare Company. '*Richard III* Stage Footage/Act 1 Scene 1/2012/Royal Shakespeare Company'. [Video] YouTube, 1 June 2012. Available online: https://www.youtube.com/watch?v=K9wzWYtYGBI (accessed 15 September 2018).

Royal Shakespeare Company. 'The RSC Light Lock is Launched at PLASA 192008'. [Video] YouTube, 18 August 2009. Available online: https://youtu.be/o3WUTekzqmo (accessed 18 September 2018).

Royal Shakespeare Company. 'Shakespeare Learning Zone'. Available online: https://www.rsc.org.uk/shakespeare-learning-zone (accessed 12 September 2018).

Royal Shakespeare Company. 'TRAILER: *Arabian Nights*'. [Video] YouTube, 11 December 2009. Available online: https://youtu.be/5TKcAUC9K8g (accessed 18 February 2018).

Rothwell, Kenneth. *A History of Shakespeare on Screen: A Century of Film and Television*. Cambridge: Cambridge University Press, 2004.

RSC Shakespeare Learning Zone. 'Act 3, Scene 2 | *As You Like It* | Royal Shakespeare Company'. [Video] YouTube, 8 June 2015. Available online: https://youtu.be/Yc90Uhv8hFM (accessed 23 February 2018).

Rubin, Leon. *The Nicholas Nickleby Story: The Making of the the Historic Royal Shakespeare Company Production*. London: Heinemann, 1981.

Sandbrook, Dominic. *Never Had It So Good: A History of Britain from Suez to The Beatles*. London: Little, Brown, 2005.

Senda, Akihiko. 'The Rebirth of Shakespeare in Japan: From the 1960s to the 1990s'. Translated by Ryuta Minami. In *Shakespeare and the Japanese Stage*, edited by Takashi Sasayama, J. R. Mulryne and Margaret Shewring, 15–37. Cambridge: Cambridge University Press, 1999.

Shakespeare Birthplace Trust. 'Discover Shakespeare'. Available online: http://collections.shakespeare.org.uk/?_ga=1.155166840.1142849762.1482512864 (accessed 23 February 2017).

Shaughnessy, Robert. *Shakespeare in Performance*: As You Like It. Manchester: Manchester University Press, 2018.

Silents Now. '*Richard III* at Middleham Castle'. Available online: http://silents-now.co.uk/home/shows/richard-iii-2/richard-iii-middleham/ (accessed 8 January 2017).

Silents Now. 'Silents Now'. Available online: http://silents-now.co.uk/ (accessed 8 January 2017).

Simmons, Amy. '*Marat/Sade* (Peter Brook, 1967)'. *Senses of Cinema* 82, March 2017. Available online: http://sensesofcinema.com/2017/1967/marat-sade/ (accessed 28 December 2017).

Sinfield, Alan. 'Royal Shakespeare: Theatre and the Making of Ideology'. In *Political Shakespeare: New Essays in Cultural Materialism*, edited by Jonathan Dollimore and Alan Sinfield, 182–205. Manchester: Manchester University Press, 1985.

Smart, Billy. 'Old Wine in New Bottles: Adaptation of Classic Theatrical Plays on BBC Television 1957–1985'. PhD Thesis, Royal Holloway College, 2010.

Smart, Billy. 'Three Different *Cherry Orchards*, Three Different Worlds: Chekhov at the BBC, 1962–81'. *Critical Studies in Television*, 9 no. 3 (Autumn 2014), 65–76.

Smialkowska, Monica. 'Julius Caesar'. In *A Year of Shakespeare: Re-living the World Shakespeare Festival*, edited by Paul Edmondson, Paul Prescott and Erin Sullivan, 91–4. London: Bloomsbury, 2013.

Smith, Emma. 'Shakespeare Serialised: *An Age of Kings*'. In *The Cambridge Companion to Shakespeare and Popular Culture*, edited by Robert Shaughnessy, 134–49. Cambridge: Cambridge University Press, 2007.

Smith-Howard, Alycia. *Studio Shakespeare: The Royal Shakespeare Company at The Other Place*. Aldershot: Ashgate, 2006.

Sontag, Susan. 'Film and Theatre'. *Tulane Drama Review*, 11 no. 1 (Fall 1966), 24–37.

Speaight, Robert. *William Poel and the Elizabethan Revival*. Cambridge, MA: Harvard University Press, 1954.

'*Startime* (TV series)', Wikipedia (last modified 29 June 2018). Available online: https://en.wikipedia.org/wiki/Startime_(TV_series)#cite_note-LM-2 (accessed 1 January 2019).

Steichen, James. 'HD Opera: A Love/Hate Story'. *The Opera Quarterly*, 27 no. 4 (2011), 443–59.

Stockholm, Johanne M. *Garrick's Folly: The Shakespeare Jubilee of 1769 at Stratford and Drury Lane*. London: Methuen, 1964.

Sullivan, Erin. '"The Forms of Things Unknown": Shakespeare and the Rise of the Live Broadcast'. *Shakespeare Bulletin*, 35 no. 4 (Winter 2017), 627–62.

Sullivan, Erin. 'Olympic Performance in the Year of Shakespeare'. In *A Year of Shakespeare: Re-living the World Shakespeare Festival*, edited by Paul Edmondson, Paul Prescott and Erin Sullivan, 3–11. London: Bloomsbury, 2013.

Sullivan, Erin. 'Shakespeare, Social Media, and the Digital Public Sphere: *Such Tweet Sorrow* and *A Midsummer Night's Dreaming*'. *Shakespeare*, 14 no. 1 (2018), 64–79.

Sweeedboy. '*Carrie* Revival?'. *Broadway World*, 31 October 2003. Available online: https://www.broadwayworld.com/board/readmessage. php?thread=895768&page=1 (accessed 3 January 2018).

'Telly Viewer'. '*No Excuses*', *Curious British Telly*, 20 April 2013. Available online: http://www.curiousbritishtelly.co.uk/2013/04/no-excuses.html (accessed 21 December 2017).

Terris, Olwen. 'The Forgotten *Hamlet*'. *Shakespeare Bulletin*, 25 no. 2 (Summer 2007), 35–39.

Torner, Evan M. 'The Cinematic Defeat of Brecht by Artaud in Peter Brook's *Marat/ Sade*'. *EDGE: A Graduate Journal for German and Scandinavian Studies*, 1 no. 1 (2009): article 1. Available online: http://scholarworks.umass.edu/edge/vol1/iss1/1 (accessed).

Trewin, J.C. *Peter Brook: A Biography*. London: Macdonald, 1971.

Trewin, J.C. *Shakespeare on the English Stage 1900–1964*. London: Barrie and Rockliff, 1964.

Trostle Jones, Edward. *Following Directions: A Study of Peter Brook*. New York: Peter Lang, 1985.

V&A (Victoria and Albert Museum). 'Theatre & Performance Archives'. Available online: http://www.vam.ac.uk/content/articles/t/nvap/ (accessed 23 February 2017).

Wade, Leslie A. 'The London Theatre Goes Digital: Divergent Responses to the New Media'. In *Theatre Symposium*, Volume 19: *Theatre and Film*, edited by J.K. Curry, 54–68. Tuscaloosa: University of Alabama Press, 2011.

Walker, Alexander. *Hollywood, England: The British Film Industry in the Sixties*. London: Michael Joseph, 1974.

Watson, Nicola J. 'Shakespeare on the Tourist Trail'. In *The Cambridge Companion to Shakespeare and Popular Culture*, edited by Robert Shaughnessy, 199–226. Cambridge: Cambridge University Press, 2007.

Way, Geoffrey. 'Social Shakespeare: *Romeo and Juliet*, Social Media and Performance'. *Journal of Narrative Theory*, 41 no. 3 (Fall 2011), 401–20.

Weiss, Peter. *The Persecution and Assassination of Marat as Performed by the Inmates of the Asylum of Charenton under the Direction of the Marquis de Sade*. London: Calder and Boyars, 1965.

Wheatley, Helen. *Spectacular Television: Exploring Televisual Pleasure*. London: I.B.Tauris, 2016.

White, Carrie. 'Carrie The Musical (Stratford Production) Full Show – 1988 OPENING NIGHT'. [Video] YouTube, 6 September 2012. Available online: https://www.youtube.com/watch?v=iOTxiLYFF-Y (accessed 3 January 2018).

Wilds, Lillian. 'One *King Lear* for Our Time: A Bleak Film Vision by Peter Brook'. *Literature/Film Quarterly*, 4 no. 2 (Spring 1976), 159–64.

Willems, Michèle. 'Video and its Paradoxes'. In *The Cambridge Companion to Shakespeare on Film*, edited by Russell Jackson, 35–46. Cambridge: Cambridge University Press, 2007.

Williams, David, ed. *Peter Brook: A Theatrical Casebook*. London: Methuen, 1988.

Willis, Deborah. 'Marlowe Our Contemporary: *Edward II* on Stage and Screen'. *Criticism*, 40 no. 4 (Fall 1998), 599–622.

Willis, Susan. *The BBC Shakespeare Plays: Making the Televised Canon*. Chapel Hill: University of North Carolina Press, 1991.

Wyver, John. 'An Intimate and Intermedial Form: Early Television Shakespeare from the BBC, 1937–1939'. In *Shakespeare Survey 69: Shakespeare and Rome*, edited by Peter Holland and Emma Smith, 347–60. Cambridge: Cambridge University Press, 2016.

Wyver, John. '"A Profound Commentary on Kingship": The Monarchy and Shakespeare's Histories on Television, 1957–65'. In *The New Elizabethan Age: Culture, Society and National Identity after World War II*, edited by Irene Morra and Rob Gossedge, 267–88. London: I.B.Tauris, 2016.

Wyver, John. 'Screening the RSC Stage: The 2014 Live from Stratford-upon-Avon Cinema Broadcasts'. *Shakespeare*, 11 no. 3 (2015), 286–302.

Zand, Nicole. '*Benefit of the Doubt*, Review, 1965', *Nouvelles Littéraires*, 16 May 1968, reprinted in *Framework*, 52 no. 1 (Spring 2011), 339–40.

INDEX